W9-AHE-672

"Edward Blum and Paul Harvey's masterful book is a breath of fresh air in our toxic religious culture of learned ignorance and unlearned bigotry."
—CORNEL WEST

"In starkly poetic prose, this book takes a seemingly simple idea—examine evolving depictions of Jesus in America—and delivers punch after punch. Blum and Harvey provide a new, paradigm-changing window into the issues of race, religion, and power. Anyone wanting to grasp the depth of religion and race in the United States needs this book. It will transform what you thought you knew."—MICHAEL O. EMERSON, Rice University, author of *Divided by Faith: Evangelical Religion and the Problem of Race in America*

"An original, impressive, and eye-opening work—as compelling in its vivid detail as it is astonishing in its immense historical sweep. *The Color of Christ* sets a new standard and establishes a new starting point for anyone interested in the intersection of race and religiosity in the United States. An illuminating study, for which we will long be indebted."—MATTHEW FRYE JACOBSON, author of *Whiteness of a Different Color: European Immigrants and the Alchemy of Race*

"Blum and Harvey are two of the most talented scholars of race and religion in the United States, and this pathbreaking book integrates important historical analysis with beautiful and compelling narrative. *The Color of Christ* brilliantly draws on original research, the latest scholarship, and popular culture to transform the ways that we see Jesus past and present."—MATTHEW AVERY SUTTON, author of *Aimee Semple McPherson and the Resurrection of Christian America*

"The refreshing and engaging story of how the concept of white Jesus was appropriated and used by Americans of all ethnicities to support their cultural, social, and religious intentions. Blum and Harvey's solid historical writing and deft use of material culture and media bring a fresh viewpoint to the subject of race and religion in America."—ANTHEA BUTLER, author of *Women in the Church of God in Christ: Making a Sanctified World*

THE COLOR OF CHRIST

EDWARD J. BLUM   PAUL HARVEY

THE **COLOR** OF **CHRIST**

THE SON OF GOD & THE SAGA OF
RACE IN AMERICA

The University of North Carolina Press   *Chapel Hill*

All rights reserved. Manufactured in the United States of America.
Designed by Sally Fry and set in Charter and The Sans by Rebecca Evans.
The paper in this book meets the guidelines for permanence and durability
of the Committee on Production Guidelines for Book Longevity of the
Council on Library Resources. The University of North Carolina Press
has been a member of the Green Press Initiative since 2003.

Library of Congress Cataloging-in-Publication Data
Blum, Edward J.
The color of Christ : the Son of God and the saga of race in America /
Edward J. Blum and Paul Harvey.
p. cm.
Includes bibliographical references (p.   ) and index.
ISBN 978-0-8078-3572-2
1. Jesus Christ. 2. United States—Church history. 3. Racism—Religious
aspects—Christianity. 4. Racism—United States. 5. African Americans—
Religion. 6. Indians of North America—Religion. I. Harvey, Paul,
1961– II. Title.
BR515.B59 2012
232—dc23   2012004088

16 15 14 13 12   5 4 3 2 1

In memory of **ELIJAH JAMES BLUM,**

December 12, 2010–August 31, 2011

Mom, Dad, and Uncle Paul miss you

CONTENTS

ILLUSTRATIONS

In a world filled with images of Jesus, this one made headlines. He stood in a stained-glass window wearing a simple white robe and a dark tunic. He held a staff in his left hand and with the knuckles of his right tapped gently on a large brown door. Wavy auburn hair fell to his shoulders, while his feet were bare. When sunlight struck the glass just so, kindness radiated from his white face and warmth from his brown eyes. This was a comforting Jesus who forgave sinners, blessed bread for the hungry, and promised peace to the anxious. For decades he had been with this black congregation in Birmingham, Alabama. But on one Sunday morning in September 1963, terror struck. Dynamite set by white supremacists outside of Sixteenth Street Baptist Church just after 10:20 A.M. exploded, and the face of Jesus shattered into a thousand shards of glass. In the blink of an eye, the prince of peace was made a casualty of race war.

At Sixteenth Street Baptist Church that morning, the children had heard a Sunday school lesson on "the love that forgives." Four little girls were then in the basement lounge to freshen up. Denise McNair was the youngest. She was eleven years old and had thick straight hair that fell below her shoulders. Addie Mae Collins was fourteen, wore glasses most of the time, and kept her hair short. Carol Robertson and Cynthia Wesley were fourteen too. Carol's hair was longer, like Denise's; Cynthia had a smile that beamed with joy.

But on that day, they died. Their lives were cut short because segregationists despised the aspirations of African Americans to vote, purchase homes, protect themselves, and receive fair treatment in the courts. They died, too, because they were at church that morning to worship Jesus.

Jesus had lived in the window for decades. He had listened as the congregation sang about his love, his sacrifice, and his triumph. He had been

Jesus in the stained-glass window at Sixteenth Street Baptist Church in Birmingham, Alabama, after the bombing on September 15, 1963. Photograph courtesy of the Birmingham, Alabama, Public Library Archives, File 85.1.16.

their good shepherd who heard their stories and shared their sufferings. He had been a white sacred figure who inspired his black followers to rally against white supremacy in the early civil rights crusade, but now his face was gone. The place where it had shone was reduced to a gaping scar.[1]

The holy face had become a hole in the wall; four little girls were dead; and throughout the United States and the world people had to make sense of what seemed so senseless. What did it all mean, and where was Jesus?

The bomb struck on Anne Moody's twenty-third birthday. She was in Mississippi eating breakfast with her family when the radio broadcast carried the news. Anne rushed out of her home in fury. "Now talk to me, God," she demanded. "Come on down and talk to me." She was tired of the Lord Almighty, and her spiritual disgust was stoked by a sense of similarity with the deceased. "You know, I used to go to Sunday school when I was a little girl . . . and I believed in you. I bet you those girls in Sunday school were being taught the same as I was when I was their age. . . . Are you going to forgive their killers? You not gonna answer me, God, hmm? Well, if you don't want to talk, then listen to me." It was the end of Moody's faith in nonviolence and the end of her faith in the Lord too. She kept praying, though, to the God she no longer believed in. The color of God would determine her level of rage. "I know you must be white," she fumed. "And if I ever find out you are white, then I'm through with you. And if I find out you are black, I'll try my best to kill you when I get to heaven."[2]

Jesus had his face blown out just three weeks after the epic March on Washington, when Martin Luther King Jr. had shared his "dream" of a day when "little black boys and black girls will be able to join hands with little white boys and white girls as sisters and brothers." Now in Birmingham for the funerals, King had to explain why these little girls would never hold hands with anyone again. He had to explain why they were martyrs not for the content of their character but for the color of their skin. He told a crowd of thousands that these "children—unoffending, innocent, and beautiful—were the victims of one of the most vicious and tragic crimes ever perpetrated against humanity." They died "nobly" as "martyred heroines." "They did not die in vain," King proclaimed. He encouraged the congregants to take heart that God could make good from evil: "If one will hold on, he will discover that God walks with him, and that God is able to lift you from the fatigue of despair to the buoyancy of hope, and transform dark and desolate valleys into sunlit paths of inner peace."[3]

As always, King was eloquent and affirming. He loved and believed in the power of Jesus, as did those little girls. Yet King was impotent. He could not bring them back.

In mourning, the poets cried and the singers wailed. Langston Hughes lamented:

Four little girls
Who went to Sunday School that day
And never came back home at all—
But left instead
Their blood upon the wall.

Joan Baez, the emerging star of folk music, sang about the limits of song:

On Birmingham Sunday a noise shook the ground.
And people all over the earth turned around.
For no one recalled a more cowardly sound.
. . . .
The Sunday has come and the Sunday has gone.
And I can't do much more than to sing you a song.

John Coltrane had no words, but his melodically piercing tune "Alabama" rhythmically moved in time with King's eulogy. The rumble of the drums mixed with a turbulently unsettled piano line as the tenor saxophonist's blowing summoned listeners to depths they could never vocalize.[4]

The fate of these girls was tragic; the meaning of what happened to Jesus was complicated. He could be resurrected to fill the hole in the sanctuary and somehow the holes in many hearts. But what was the meaning of his destruction, and how should he be replaced? In New York City, two of America's best-known thinkers debated what it meant for the white Jesus of a black church to have his face blown out. Theologian Reinhold Niebuhr and novelist and essayist James Baldwin addressed this question: "Does the missing face on this stained-glass window which survived the bombing suggest a meaning?" Through a visual representation of Christ's body and what happened to it, they explored the deepest questions of American society, God's justice, and the workings of evil.

The inability of whites to respect human rights left Niebuhr frustrated. He had spent his career as a pastor, writer, and professor grappling with the ethical dilemmas of modern society. He had become one of the nation's most popular theologians, providing guidance to Americans high and low. Powerful politicians sought his insights, while recovering alcoholics prayed his prayers as they took their twelve steps. But Niebuhr had little to offer now. The faceless white Christ meant that the white church had lost face. "As far as the church is concerned, it represents a failure," Niebuhr sighed. He found light a scarce resource in those dark days, and neither the serenity prayer nor the ethical understanding of moral men living in an immoral society seemed to bring him comfort.

By contrast, Baldwin was more positive. The author of *The Fire Next Time*, whose anger toward white supremacy burned so hot that he had invoked God's words to Noah that the flood was merely a prelude and that the next judgment would be with fire, found a spark of hope in the tragedy. "The absence of the face is something of an achievement," Baldwin suggested, "since we have been victimized so long by an alabaster Christ." Where others saw meaninglessness, Baldwin found possibility. It was another chance to make life where death had reigned. "If Christ has no face," then we must give "him a new face. Give him a new consciousness. And make the whole ideal, the whole hope, of Christian love a reality. As far as I can tell, that has never really been a reality in the two thousand years since his assassination." Baldwin then called for a boycott of Christmas.

True believers could avoid the material celebration of Christ's birth and use economic might to make moral right.[5]

When Americans looked at the faceless Jesus, they had more questions than answers. Racial and religious complexity ran rampant. Here was a white Jesus at a black church. Here was a center of civil rights activism targeted by white supremacists who destroyed a white icon. Perhaps the "alabaster Christ" of Sixteenth Street Baptist Church could no longer stand to watch the bloodshed and the hate of white supremacy. Perhaps this translucent-but-stained Jesus needed the white terrorists to free him from their tyranny. Or perhaps the bomb revealed Christ's nature in the realm of American race relations: blind and feeble. He may have saved the souls of those little girls, but he did not protect their bodies. His shattered image held symbolic significance, but no one agreed precisely on what it meant.

When the blast shattered Jesus in Birmingham, it was not only his biblical words, actions, or ethics that mattered; Christ's body mattered too. His image, what it signified, where it was placed, what happened to it, and how it would be replaced shaped the dialogue in fundamental ways. His form provided an entrée for Americans to evaluate and debate their most deeply held ideas about race, religion, the nation, the sacred, and the workings of power.

Like most representations of Jesus in America, this one could not utter a word. But it had stories to tell. How he got into a black church was one story; how he sanctified white supremacy for some and opposition to racial injustice for others was another; what his iconic destruction meant to Americans stood as another tale; how he would be remade—as he always seemed to be after attack—was another; and how he inspired millions of Americans to tell their own stories and to walk their own journeys was yet another burden placed upon Christ's body. This book is about those many stories and how the supposed Son of God played a leading role in the saga of race in America.

THE HOLY FACE OF RACE

How is it that a Jewish prophet from the Roman era ran so explosively into the American obsession with race that his image has been used to justify the worst atrocities of white supremacy as well as inspire the most heroic of civil rights crusades? *The Color of Christ* explores the ways Americans gave physical forms to Jesus, where they placed them, and how they remade the Son of God visually time and again into a sacred symbol of their greatest aspirations, deepest terrors, lowest actions, highest expressions, and mightiest strivings for racial power and justice. *The Color of Christ* chronicles a multiplicity of American dreams and visions and, by showing how Americans imagined and depicted Jesus Christ's body, skin tone, eye color, brow shape, and hairstyle, reveals a new face of the power and malleability of race in our history.

At the center of this book is the story of white Jesus figures made, embraced, challenged, and reformed over the last five centuries; how he rose to become a conflicted icon of white supremacy; how he changed appearances subtly with shifting perceptions of who was considered genuinely white; and how he was able to endure all types of challenges to remain the dominant image of God's human form in the nation and throughout the world.

Jesus changed shape as a white figure in the United States because who was considered white and what being white meant have mutated over time. The parameters of who was deemed white, what their whiteness meant, and how it was connected to citizenship rights have shifted, sometimes dramatically, sometimes delicately, throughout American history. Whiteness as a category of identity and as a marker for privilege has been created, tested, and transformed repeatedly, and white Jesus figures have been reworked to fit the varied circumstances. *The Color of Christ* uses white Jesus imagery to explore the varying contours of whiteness, to show how fluid it has been, to reveal how its potency enveloped the sacred, and to delineate how his holy whiteness has been used to sanctify racial hierarchies.[1]

By wrapping itself with the alleged form of Jesus, whiteness gave itself a holy face. But he was a shape-shifting totem of white supremacy. The differing and evolving physical renderings of white Jesus figures not only bore witness to the flexibility of racial constructions but also helped create the perception that whiteness was sacred and everlasting. With Jesus as white, Americans could feel that sacred whiteness stretched back in time thousands of years and forward in sacred space to heaven and the second coming.[2]

The white Jesus, however, was never a stable or completely unifying symbol of white power. The white Jesus at Sixteenth Street Baptist Church, for instance, clearly meant something different to his followers there than the Jesus figures worshiped by the white terrorists who bombed the building. The Bible lacks a definitive description of Christ's body, so anyone taking the Good Book seriously could wonder about the pictures made of him and craft his or her own visual displays. Drawing Christ as white, moreover, could undermine the very authority of whiteness. Christ's words of justice and mercy and his sacrificial crucifixion ran counter to white power and privilege. *The Color of Christ* thus highlights alternative tales in which the white Christ and other nonwhite images of Jesus challenged the authority of white supremacy. This book charts the places where Christ's whiteness was secretively transformed to undermine white power or to create experiences that mediated and challenged racial discrimination. It also follows the flow of nonwhite Jesus figures that questioned assumptions of his holy whiteness.

The racial odyssey of Jesus in America is a long one. It begins with Christ coming to North and South America in the age of exploration. Confusion seemed then to reign far more than did Christ. Cross-cultural interactions and complexities left the sacred terrain unsteady, and no group had the power to determine which images of Jesus would be dominant, if any. While Catholic Europeans brought Jesus across the ocean in various guises, English Puritans destroyed visual depictions of him. They censored them in the New World and abandoned the field of sacred sight. In the colonial America that became the United States, Jesus had no authoritative physical presence. Puritans and their children struggled to make sense of the geographical and visual distance they felt from Christ. They expe-

rienced spiritual confusion most acutely when relating to native popula-
tions around them, who questioned Christ and claimed sacred visions of
their own. Jesus seemed distant in this dangerous world, a realm especially
frightening for West African captives and Native Americans. Before they
encountered Jesus as white, they experienced him in terms of bloody conflict, mystifying interactions, and, most often, extreme subjugation.

During the eighteenth and nineteenth centuries, Christ came alive as a
physical presence. British colonial America became a land of visions and
visionaries. Up and down the East Coast, white, black, and red Americans
longed to see the sacred. When some did, they either beheld him radiat-
ing light so brightly that they could not see his face or as so bloodied that
their imaginations were drawn to his wounds. Before Jesus was known for
being white in this America, he was venerated for being bloody red. When
the United States formed, moreover, the Son of God was anything but a
dominant hero or national symbol. Jesus as a physical symbol was not to be
found in the revolutionary republic. Despite the public dominance of white
Protestantism, the America of the founding era was anything but a Jesus
nation.

The white American Jesus first rose to power and prominence in the
early nineteenth century. This was an era of the expansion of slavery and
the often fraudulent and violent grabbing of Native American lands. It was
also a moment of nation building and defining. Whiteness became a crucial
symbol of national identity and citizenship. A new band of Protestants tried
to win the young nation for Jesus by mass-producing and mass-distributing
him. His racial affiliation, however, was soon embroiled in controversy. Unjust treatment of Native Americans and the enlargement of the cotton kingdom made Jesus a troubled symbol of American freedom and growth. Native Americans variously denounced whites for being so foolish that their
ancestors crucified their own god or tried to bring Christ to North America
as an Indian guide. One even directly called the new white visual Jesus a
sacred fraud and claimed that Jesus and his disciples were "colored." At
the time, hardly anyone listened. Two hundred years later, these claims
provoked a media firestorm.

Southern whites before the Civil War tried to sanctify slavery and Christianize slaves by presenting Jesus as a servant. The plan backfired, though,
as a group of African Americans took this savior, found in him a personal
friend to those who suffered (like they did), and heard him whispering
freedom in their ears. Many transformed the white and servant Jesus into
a trickster of the Trinity. He was a white man who destabilized white su-

premacy. Just as amazing, a host of northern whites felt similarly. They joined these slaves in viewing Christ as either a southern slave in spirit or a white man who aligned with black Americans. Proslavery forces may have won the battle for the Bible, but they lost the joust for Jesus. By the time of the Civil War, Christ had become symbolically affiliated with southern slaves, leaving slaveholders with their blood up for a fight.

The middle of the nineteenth century witnessed the United States expand, splinter, and reconstruct. Beliefs about Christ's skin tone, eye color, and beard and his connection to racial troubles of the day grew in importance. In the midst of Christ's first physical renderings in the United States and the nation's expansions and conflicts, new religions—most famously Mormonism—were born that focused on his holy whiteness. Union soldiers in the Civil War marched to a new hymn that taught that since a faraway savior had "died to make men holy" they should now "die to make men free." Confederates considered Christ to be on their side, but when they lost national independence and their slaves, they thought themselves buried with Jesus. They arose from the ashes of physical and spiritual chaos with a new savior, one who shared their sufferings during Reconstruction. Now they, not enslaved blacks, were crucified under an imperial regime, just as Jesus had been. The most belligerent sons of former Confederates clothed the Son of God as they did their horses—in white. He became not just a member of the Ku Klux Klan but its original founder.

The Civil War, emancipation, and radical Reconstruction fractured white national unity and cut the direct ties between whiteness and citizenship. This opened the door for challenges to the association of Jesus with whiteness. But as the United States was rebuilt during Reconstruction, as it grew through industrialization, immigration, and imperialism, and as it took greater steps into world affairs, the white American Jesus was refashioned. His whiteness morphed at the same time it was elevated to the symbol of white national unity and power.

In response to emancipation, new immigration, and adventures in global imperialism, the parameters of American whiteness were severely shrunk. Whiteness became a more exclusive category, and even Congress joined in with severe immigration restrictions against southern and eastern Europeans in the 1920s. In the mix, the white Jesus was given a new face. White Americans sanctified their disdain for Jewish and Catholic immigrants by crafting and globally distributing a blond-haired, blue-eyed, non-Semitic Jesus. Faith in and depictions of this new "Nordic" Christ symbolized white Americans' righteousness—and self-righteousness—as they took control of foreign peoples, lynched black men, and barred or discriminated against immigrants. White supremacists linked new bodies of Jesus to his moral qualities of love, mercy, and grace. They presented their racial ideology as sacred, and therefore as above human creation and beyond human control.

These were also the years of the first concerted efforts against the white Jesus and his links to white authority. Several white reformers, including Mark Twain, mocked the idea of Christ's whiteness as emblematic of American morality. Native Americans battled to create new messiahs in the face of dispossession and reservations, finding them sometimes in Christ figures who prophesied the return of the buffalo. It was a bewildering and contradictory time for many Native Americans. At boarding schools, white schoolteachers taught them to become "civilized" by cutting their hair short but also by putting their faith in the long-haired Jesus seen in paintings on school walls. Most black Americans of the age used white images of Jesus in their churches and homes, but a growing number now had the resources, space, and autonomy to picture the savior beyond whiteness. Some even had the production capabilities to create new images of Jesus. These were the first expressions of what would later be called "black liberation theology."

In the 1920s and 1930s, the faces of Jesus came under assault. A host of white, black, and red Americans viewed the sacred images of their childhoods alternatively as too feminine, too white, or too rural. Businessmen and workers thought the old Jesus was too weak but then disagreed over what his manly body would look like. From Harlem, an ensemble of poets, novelists, playwrights, and artists rejected the white Jesus images around them. They blackened him for the first time with paintings that portrayed him as a lynch victim and by telling new tales of the Son of God born in the American South, teaching racial harmony and economic justice, and then crucified for such southern heresies.

From southern California, film directors presented Jesus as a white-skinned "King of Kings" whose ideas of liberty and justice rose above all other religious and political systems. Somehow, too, this Jesus blessed the objectives of the Ku Klux Klan. Over time, as markets and mentalities changed what was fashionable and trendy, the Hollywood Jesus emerged as younger, tanner, tougher, and shorn of his overt racism. Whether through the use of Technicolor or advanced computer imaging, he remained a white man witnessed by billions throughout the world. As the United States rose to superpower status in the twentieth century, it also became the world's most active exporter of white Jesus imagery. Through film and art, American businessmen, moviemakers, and missionaries offered the world white Christ figures to consume and worship.

During the mid-twentieth century, the white Jesus encountered both his greatest challenge and his most enduring new face. The test came not from Hollywood or from Harlem but from the sons of preacher men and the lessons of the "least of these." Grievances against Christ and new Jesus figures animated the era of the civil rights movements and they captured the spirit of the 1960s. Whether it was civil rights activists conceiving of Christ as the architect of nonviolent resistance, or Native American peyote journeyers locating Jesus among the stars with their ancestors, or new liberation theologians denouncing the "honky Christ," or college students seeing Jesus as a rebellious hippie, Americans played with the body of Jesus. His holy face was once again symbolic of a changing America.

Underneath the turbulence, however, emerged a new popular consensus about Christ's body. It came from a surprising source too—a midwestern painter who crafted his work first for Fundamentalist Christians. Warner Sallman painted what became the most widely reproduced piece of artwork in world history. His *Head of Christ* (1941) adorned living rooms, bedrooms, Sunday schools, and films. It became a shared resource among Protestants and Catholics, who had fought with each other for so long. Its ubiquity soon inspired countless imitations and parodies, which spoke to but never lessened its power. It was so iconic that to combat "card-carrying members of the Communist Party," one American minister wanted every Christian to carry a small print of Sallman's Christ in their wallets. Reproductions of this *Head of Christ* multiplied at an epic rate. Even as white Americans of the civil rights era were compelled to open their schools, neighborhoods, restaurants, borders, and ballot boxes to nonwhites, they held fast to this white vision of Jesus. No matter how many critics denounced its stereotypical white features or his apparent passivity or femininity, this *Head of Christ* became the literal face of Jesus to millions.

The rise of the digital age at the end of the twentieth century made it possible not just to remake Jesus but to locate any number of revisions. By the twenty-first century, all one had to do was type "black Jesus" or "Chicano Jesus" or "Asian Jesus" or "Yogi Jesus" into an internet search engine and all sorts of holy faces pop up. Black and red Americans had fought to make and imagine Jesus beyond whiteness. New immigrant groups, especially those from Latin America and from Asia after immigration reform in 1965, could present Jesus in racial guises without defamation. Conflict came only when Christ was made black and tied to radical politics. In 2008, the race of Jesus helped produce a political firestorm and almost cost the son of an African immigrant his bid for the White House.

The long history of Jesus and race left sacred whiteness challengeable and even changeable. But for the most part it was still assumable and marketable. As part of the *Da Vinci Code* craze, millions of readers stared intently at European artwork to see if Mary Magdalene was really at the Last Supper with the white Jesus (as if novelist Dan Brown or painter Leonardo da Vinci would have known what Christ or the other characters looked like, let alone how they gestured or whom they slept with). The paintings supposedly held secrets of sexual power, Brown fantasized, but no one wondered about the racial hierarchy hidden in plain sight. Dan Brown never wondered if the whiteness of the painted figures had any meaning at all. Only a few years earlier, hundreds of millions sat spellbound as they watched a white, brown-eyed Jesus (even though the actor portraying him had blue eyes) beaten to a bloody pulp. No one in Mel Gibson's *The Passion of the Christ* (2004) spoke English, but it did not matter. Watching Jesus and his body mattered.

Created, worshiped, scorned, and debated for 400 years, Jesus and his complexion took a new turn after the civil rights era. They became, for the first time, objects of humor. *The Passion* produced tears, while *South Park*, Alanis Morissette, Will Ferrell, Jon Stewart, and Stephen Colbert drew out sardonic laughter. From comedy routines to nightly sitcoms, from cartoon books to movies, Jesus jokes and barbs about his body became a way for Americans to laugh out their racial and religious uncertainties. As a coping mechanism for all that they had endured and all they had failed to accomplish in terms of racial justice, laughing at the Lord let Americans vent their political, social, and religious frustrations. Behind the laughter lay centuries of unresolved historical struggles over what it meant to place a racial face onto a divine-yet-human figure.

A Body of Power

This book focuses on the creation and exercise of racial and religious power through images of Jesus and how that power has been experienced by everyday people. *The Color of Christ* keys on when and how certain Jesus figures achieved social notoriety, how they influenced and were influenced by political, racial, economic, and cultural transformations, and how various groups have lived with these images, transformed them, and attempted to dethrone the prevailing figures. Since power is the ability to put into effect one's goals and to maintain status despite opposition, this book centers primarily on white Protestants, who held significant authority from the seventeenth to the nineteenth centuries. It secondarily examines Catholics and Mormons, who grew in strength and number in the late nineteenth century and throughout the twentieth century, and then briefly explores how Jews, Hindus, Buddhists, Seventh-Day Adventists, Muslims, rationalists, and some others experienced the impact of Christ's supposed race but never had the strength to impose on society an image that would become dominant. We trace as well how the largest groups of people of color have interacted with prevailing Jesus images over the longest amount of time, especially African Americans and Native Americans, to show how racial images influenced their lives. Jesus figures played a role in how everyday people both practiced their faiths and experienced their racial issues.

This book does not delve deeply into every group's interactions with or representations of Jesus. It does not examine in detail how Muslims, Buddhists, Jews, or Hindus have related to him, nor does it focus intently on the amazing diversity within Protestantism and Catholicism. This book, moreover, does not account for every physical manifestation of Jesus. In the realms of material culture, multicultural diversity, and religious distinctions, there is simply too much. There are too many physical renderings of Christ, and the particularities of group difference are such that to discuss each one would overwhelm the overall points of this book.

But the sheer variety of people living in the United States, the almost limitless number of Jesus images now created, and the massive diversity within broader faith traditions testify to several important aspects of this study. They give further evidence to the importance of how a land that was settled, in part, by Puritan iconoclasts from England became one of the most abundant producers and consumers of diverse Jesus imagery. They also show how white versions of Jesus became so culturally dominant that virtually all groups had to contend with them, even if the images did not look like them, come from their tradition, or directly bear on their faith.

To focus on the holy face of Jesus in America is to reckon with the making and power of race. By honing in on Christ's body and how Americans encountered it through artwork, dreams, visions, descriptions, and assumptions, this book reveals a great deal about the people of the United States: their passions, creativities, dilemmas, and problems. The body of Christ ascended from being largely unknown and inconsequential among the colonial people who would create the United States in the seventeenth and eighteenth centuries to becoming an object of obsession, adoration, confusion, conflict, and comedy by the twenty-first century. The stories here reveal how through this course the sacred has been racialized and how the spiritualization of race has given notions of human difference not only a life beyond scientific studies or anthropological insights but also a sense of eternal worth.[3]

Jesus became such an important visual presence linked to racial categories that even those who wanted to avoid discussions of his race have found it impossible. Although millions of Americans have considered Christ's race irrelevant to their faith in him or thoughts about his life, they cannot avoid displays of him or questions about his racial affiliation. Martin Luther King Jr., for instance, wanted Americans to look beyond the color of Christ's skin and at the content of his character. King and the civil rights movement he championed, however, could not escape debates and assumptions about the race of Christ. The power of Jesus imagery and its racial connections became so widespread that even those who desired to sidestep it could not.

In part, racial assumptions about Jesus were unavoidable because the images were often presented to children at very young ages. Whether through tracts, Sunday school cards, or church art or on television and in movies, visual depictions of Christ lodged the idea of his whiteness deep within cultural conventions and individual psyches. Before many children could consider other lessons of faith or morality, they had seen images of white Christs and experienced adults seeming to regard the pictures as authentic. The goal of the pictures was to teach Christianity, but an unintended consequence was to create an often unspoken belief that Jesus was white. This made Christ's whiteness a psychological certainty. It could be felt without thought and presumed without proof. To imagine Jesus as other-than-white would demand a conscious process of unlearning.[4]

Several critical elements have fundamentally shaped which images gained power at particular moments. First has been the combustible combination of race and religion.[5] In the form of Jesus, these two forces became deeply intertwined. At times, religion created and reinforced racial hierarchies. By spiritualizing social concerns, such as slavery, land expropriation, tribal removals, segregation, or interracial marriage, Americans imbued racial issues with cosmic significance. Novelist Richard Wright claimed in 1945 that the "apex of white racial ideology was reached when it was assumed that white domination was a God-given right."[6] Linking Christ to whiteness helped make this happen. It allowed for racial ideas to offer themselves as beyond time and space. It allowed for modern conceptions to be translated back to biblical ages and forward in time to anticipations of Christ's return. The white Jesus promised a white past, a white present, and a future of white glory.

At other times, religious ideas and images challenged racism, whether in the form of novelist Harriet Beecher Stowe imagining a whipped slave as she took communion and then writing *Uncle Tom's Cabin* or of artists painting new black, red, or brown portraits of Jesus to inspire pride in peoples rendered nonwhite. At times wicked, at other times wondrous, the combination of race and religion continues to impact Americans—whether discussing pressing political concerns, such as terrorism and presidential politics, or making personal decisions, such as where to attend church or whom to marry.

Gender and sex were significant in representations of Jesus as well, and they heightened the importance of determining and displaying Christ's race. By giving Jesus particular body forms, clothing styles, and physical postures, Americans drew the Son of God into discussions not only of manliness and femininity but also of various approaches to sexuality. His long straight hair, a staple of legends, lies, and art that was used to make him white in American visual culture, has at times marked his effeminacy and at other times his manliness. Ideas of his skin tone and the look of his eyes have been rendered masculine or feminine depending on the historical situations. His closeness to children in art, for instance, has been on occasion seen as domestic (and hence deemed feminine) or has been considered as patriarchal (and hence deemed masculine).[7]

Christ's appearance has been brought to bear on sexual matters too. His supposed whiteness was used in the nineteenth and early twentieth centuries to condemn and render illegal interracial sexuality; and then in the twentieth and twenty-first centuries, Christ's body became a sexual object as part of America's growing obsessions with beauty and body image. Mormon painters presented Jesus as white with brawny pectoral muscles to show off the manliness (and whiteness) of Mormonism, while comedians of the twenty-first century joke about fantasies of Jesus in tight blue jeans and about marrying this "sexy savior." The course of Christ's body throughout American history shows that his racial presentations were inseparable from gender assumptions and sexual perspectives.[8]

Material forces too have influenced which depictions of Jesus gained dominance and when they did. Manufacturing power, technological developments, infrastructure improvements, social space, and capital have all played a role. The histories of objects and the powers they obtain are linked to developments in production, marketing, and distribution. For theological reasons, for instance, Puritans in the colonial period did not want images of Jesus. If they did, they could have purchased them from Catholics or put them on their church walls. But they did not have the capacity to mass-produce or distribute them widely. They did not have the machinery or the capital to create images and push them into the lives and minds of others around them or throughout the world. When in the nineteenth century Americans created and distributed images of Jesus, they were able to do so because of new printing technologies, marketing strategies, roads, canals, and railroads.[9]

Making Jesus visually and marketing him throughout the land took time, capital, and freedom. Access to technology and social resources has never been equal, and these inequalities have been a factor in what images of Jesus have been created and how they have obtained cultural authority. In the first decades of the twentieth century, for instance, a sociologist asked a young African American what Jesus looked like. He responded, "Pictures I've seen of Him are all white so I just took for granted He was a white man."[10]

Even as the technological developments of the contemporary digital age have made it possible for anyone with access to a computer to create and distribute images, videos, and even news, the power of the past continues to exert remarkable influence on the present. Past power helps explain why white Jesus figures have continued to be produced and disseminated at such incredible rates and why they have defeated any and all rivals for mass appeal. Even after the civil rights crusades and liberation theologies of the mid-twentieth century devastated the notion of Christ's whiteness, white faces of Jesus continue to be created at an astonishing rate and dominate the field of holy representation.

Those historically with less money, power, time, and autonomy may have had the desire and the creativity to make these objects, but they often lacked the opportunities and resources to put into material form their religious or racial convictions. To account for their approaches to and experiences with the race and color of Christ, *The Color of Christ* often turns to music, poetry, sermons, and visions. Through these media, Americans of the past and present have demonstrated remarkable creativity. Some forged subversive saviors amid sinister situations, while others found through spirituality the capacity to live with material disadvantage.

Just as material culture, technological developments, and social power have played a role in how Jesus has been rendered and the meanings attached to those images, geography and place have factored in critically as well. Place matters for presentation. Slavery developed and expanded in the American South, in part because of geographical and agricultural particularities, and it was there that Jesus experienced many of his sharpest racial contrasts, conflicts, and complications. New York City was a main importer and exporter of goods (including visual imagery of Jesus) because of its deep harbor, its link to western New York via the Erie Canal system, and its emergence as a center of capital accumulation. Southern California became the hub of America's film industry and cinematic portrayals of Christ, in part because of the number of days that one could film outside. This influenced not only the backdrop for Christ's life but also the casting of who played him. And Native Americans who rallied to prophets like Wovoka—who in the early twentieth century declared himself "the only living Jesus there is"—did so in part because they proclaimed the return of the buffalo to the prairie-grass frontier. These geographical experiences of North, South, East, and West affected how Jesus was considered, depicted, and distributed within the United States and then the world.

Imagined geographies mattered too. What Americans thought about Israel of biblical times affected what they imagined Jesus to look like. Before the mid-nineteenth century, Americans thought they knew a lot about biblical Palestine, but few had been there. Few had seen the place or the people. But in their Bibles, sermons, imaginations, visions, and Sunday schools, Americans thought long and hard about the geography of the biblical era. And that was not all. Dynamic journeys of spirit and mind transported some Americans away from the brutality of slavery to the Middle East so they could be with Jesus as he suffered. Others resurrected Christ in the American past, present, or future to handle such dilemmas, seeking Christ's spirit in a land marred by discriminations of race, class, gender, and sexuality. Sacred journeys brought Americans to Jesus and Jesus to Americans in interactive and imaginative ways.[11] In short, place, technology, and material culture were crucial to the physical representations of Jesus and to which images rose to social and cultural dominance.

Myths of Race and Religion in America

The Color of Christ confronts several myths about religion in America and offers readers historical tools to interpret the Christ images they encounter around them. Whether seen in a bedroom picture or on a cartoon television show, whether beheld during a dream or on the silver screen, the bodies of

Jesus and how we interact with them are tethered to the histories discussed here.

The first myth is that racial and ethnic groups necessarily create God or gods in their own image.[12] This myth renders material, social, and cultural power meaningless; it transforms the resourcefulness of everyday people into little more than ethnic chauvinism; and it fails to take particulars of faith and society into account.

When Christianity's premise of a divine incarnation in the particular bodily form of Jesus collided with the American obsession with race, representations of the holy became critical for the nation's identity and struggles. Moreover, individuals have worshipped Christ figures that looked little like them. Jesus at Sixteenth Street Baptist was white, but the congregation was predominantly African American and rallied against white supremacy. That was and is the norm, and not just for black congregations. Outspoken African Americans from the late nineteenth century to the present have complained vigorously about the presence and power of the "honky" Jesus in their communities, while some Native American novelists and theologians have depicted American history as part of a "whole Jesus scheme" according to which whites poured poison into their communities through a white-skinned Jesus.[13]

This myth fails to address so many questions. How and why has he been embraced by people deemed nonwhite? How has a land colonized by Puritan iconoclasts become one of his greatest image producers? What shall we make of whites who reject his white image, and how do we account for the moments he as a white man was put to the service of dismantling white privilege?

The myth does historical damage too. It pretends that American history can be told from unique, segregated racial perspectives and that each group has its own distinct relationship with Jesus. This is not so. American history has been defined by continuous interracial contact and conflict. Racial groups in the United States have never been separated enough to make Jesus firmly in their own images. They have always encountered Christ in conversation with one another. The myth suggests that racial and ethnic identities are permanent and inflexible. What does one do with white artists who joined the Harlem Renaissance and painted Christ as a lynch victim, or with Indian spirit journeyers who saw Jesus in red and white skin? How does one address debates and differences within ethnic communities over how Jesus should be represented?

The Color of Christ uncovers what this myth hides. It showcases intense and widespread cultural interaction between and among groups and reveals that the religious experiences of particular racial or religious groups cannot be told separately or divorced from material forces or dynamics of power. White Americans were not simply reinforcing white supremacy with white Jesus imagery, and African Americans and Native Americans were not simply brainwashed fools for putting faith in a white savior. There was so much more at stake, and there were many more meanings and ways to make meaning than appear at a quick glance.

Another myth is that Americans inherited iconography through European artwork and merely replicated it. This myth portrays Americans as simple players in a broad Eurocentric Western chauvinism. This is untrue as well. It undervalues the crucial place of the United States in Jesus production and distribution. It downplays the tremendously different roads Jesus took in Europe and the United States as an influential persona and how Americans' obsessions with Christ's body have continued to drive the world's interest, even as Europe has secularized in many ways. The myth also fails to see how particular political, social, and legal issues within the United States have come to influence Jesus imagery for the world. It ignores how the United States became one of the greatest producers of images of Jesus, universalist notions of freedom, and particular privileges of whiteness all at the same time.

This myth also conceals one of the most fascinating stories in American history, in which a medieval falsehood was recounted as a fact in the nineteenth century and then forgotten during the twentieth. When white Americans developed their own artwork to display Jesus as white, they joined European artistic traditions to a fraudulent letter known only by a handful of scholars today as the "Publius Lentulus letter." Written sometime between the tenth and the fourteenth centuries, it falsely claimed to come from a governor of Judea during Christ's lifetime. Publius Lentulus, who probably never existed, purportedly wrote to a Roman official of "a man of great power, called Jesus Christ." The letter contained a vivid description that linked physical appearance with moral qualities.

> He is a man of medium size; . . . he has a venerable aspect, and his beholders can both fear and love him. His hair is of the color of the ripe hazel nut, straight down to the ears, but below the ears wavy and curled, with a bluish and bright reflection flowing over his shoulders. It is parted in two on the top of the head, after the pattern of the

Nazarenes. His brow is smooth and very cheerful, with a face without a wrinkle or spot, embellished by a slightly ruddy complexion. His nose and mouth are faultless. His beard is abundant, of the color of his hair, not long, but divided at the chin. His aspect is simple and mature, his eyes are changeable and bright. He is terrible in his reprimands, sweet and amiable in his admonitions, cheerful without loss of gravity. He was never known to laugh, but often to weep. His stature is straight, his hands and arms beautiful to behold. His conversation is grave, infrequent and modest. He is the most beautiful among the children of men.[14]

Puritans knew it was a fraud and so did Americans for much of the nineteenth century. But over the course of that century, as slavery expanded and whiteness became a symbol of civic status, the reputation of the letter ascended. By the early twentieth century, a group of white supremacists were so dedicated to making Jesus an emblem of their racial power that they consciously transformed it from a tall tale to an established truth. When the civil rights era demolished the idea that Jesus was white and showed the Publius Lentulus letter to be a lie, the legend died. The images it inspired did not. Americans who embraced the letter gave the whiteness of Christ a fabricated history of authenticity. The letter has had a lasting impact not because it has been consciously remembered but because it has been embedded in artwork that did not have to justify itself.

A third myth is that black liberation theology was born in the 1960s. This myth emerged recently when American media outlets set out to explain the preaching of the Reverend Jeremiah Wright. This Chicago minister's claim that Jesus was black and that whites crucified him, and the fact that presidential aspirant Barack Obama was a member of this congregation, led reporters to the theological works of James Cone. A son of the South but doing theological work in the North, Cone became the most famous writer of the 1960s and 1970s to tie Jesus to African American experiences.[15]

The origins myth, which was in part generated by Cone and his colleagues, placed too much of a burden on his work. It also hid much. The myth obscured the centuries-long struggle of marginalized peoples to present Jesus beyond whiteness; it separated black theology from Native American and Mexican American encounters with Christ; it diminished the important role black women, Latino Americans, Native Americans, and white authors, writers, and artists played in undermining assumptions of Christ's whiteness; and it failed to show how the longer history of challenges to white Christ images made it possible for other groups to present Jesus in various guises without widespread opposition.

The most recent myth, gobbled up by the general public, is that the United States was, is, and may always be a "Jesus nation." This idea skirts the politically charged problem of whether the United States is a "Christian nation" and turns instead to how Jesus was made time and again to fit "American norms." Richard Wightman Fox offered a rich history of Jesus in America and how he has been alternatively viewed as a personal savior, cultural hero, and national obsession, while religious scholar Stephen Prothero put it this way: "In the book of Genesis, God creates humans in His own image; in the United States, Americans have created Jesus, over and over again, in theirs."[16]

The racially charged nature of the making and unmaking of Jesus as a white man remains elusive in the rich works of Prothero and Fox. This is a contentious history that has Jesus ignored, downgraded, transformed, blown up, spit on, mocked, denied, and, at times, hated.

The Color of Christ highlights more centrally than such previous works that there was never a universal American culture for Jesus to uphold. Racial categories and hierarchies made sure of this. But there were dominant conceptions of Christ that were used and challenged as part of struggles for independence, authority, and freedom. When slaves told stories of Jesus helping them escape the South, for instance, their Christ was not only breaking federal law but also acting quite differently than the master class would have accepted from their savior. To say that masters and slaves were engaged in the same historical process is to misunderstand the nature of their conflict and to devalue the role Jesus played in racial dissension, conflict, and frustration.

The Color of Christ pushes against these myths. It shows how the body of Jesus rose from irrelevant to critical in American history, how the white Jesus became a dominant and unstable symbol of white American supremacy, how he was refashioned with changes to whiteness, and how millions of women and men of color put their faith in him while transforming him in subtle ways. It demonstrates how liberation theologies emerged first among everyday peoples and then among theologians. And it explains how white Christ imagery has had the power to last and shape-shift even after massive assaults from civil rights crusades, scientific discoveries, and demographic transformations.

As Americans created and beheld Jesus visually, they made a sacred window through which they could see their hopes, fears, dreams, and conflicts in racial and religious forms. At Birmingham in 1963, his face became a literal window. How it was filled told yet another story about the power, place, and holy face of Jesus in America.

When Jesus Returned to Sixteenth Street Baptist Church

It did not take long for Jesus to come back to the windows of Sixteenth Street Baptist. Once again his body and the process by which it was made revealed so much. From across the Atlantic Ocean, children in Cardiff, Wales, heard of the horrible blast on that September Sunday. They started a "penny campaign" to replace the shattered glass. Business leaders followed the little children and commissioned local artist John Petts to design a new window. *The Wales Window for Alabama* has Jesus with short black hair and a dark face. His arms are outstretched as if on a cross. His right hand is extended upward to show strength. The raised fist became a symbol of defiance in 1966 when television cameras captured Stokely Carmichael—a young, brash leader of the Student Non-Violent Coordinating Committee—proudly raising his hand in a fist and proclaiming "black power." It was easy thereafter to interpret the Christ of Birmingham as a messiah of defiance. His other hand, though, is open wide to offer acceptance and love. A stream of water from a fire hose makes the horizontal line of the cross, while bullet holes on the top beam symbolize gunfire against children in South Africa. Christ's words "You Do It to Me"—the words meant to be preached before the bombing of September 15, 1963—are under his feet.

Race, religion, material culture, technology, art, space, and gender collided to make and place the new Jesus at the church. Instead of a white Jesus, Sixteenth Street Baptist now had a black Son of God. The children of Wales did not hear the news in weeks or months; it took only hours for new media technologies to inform them of the terrible deeds of September 15. The glass took only a few months to create, transport, and install at the church. It cost significant cash, though. Sixteenth Street Baptist Church spent more than $200,000 to repair its sanctuary and auditorium. Multiple geographies intersected there too. The glass came from across the Atlantic Ocean, just as British and Africans had come centuries earlier, and the artist linked racial violence in the American South with that in South Africa. Racial discrimination in two distinct continents was merged into and mapped onto the body of Christ. And through the representation of a violated black man, the church mourned the deaths of four young girls.

The holy face of Christ was so vital that even when it was blown to pieces, it had to be replaced and it had to have a race.[17]

The saga of Jesus at Sixteenth Street Baptist Church was but one of the fascinating tales of Jesus as the holy face of race in America. Other moments, people, and Christ figures have more stories to tell. White Christ images have sanctified white supremacy as well as troubled it. Black and red Christ representations have disturbed whites, while tapping into communal debates and divisions among peoples of color. These images came from conflict and they made it possible for immigrant communities to create their own images of Jesus without severe provocation. By turning to bodies of Jesus, red, white, and black Americans have sought to make sacred sense of their worlds. In the process, they have taken and given life; they have justified injustice and battled against it; and they have cried out in agony while bending their knees in gratitude.

PART ONE

BORN ACROSS THE SEA

CHAPTER ONE

WHEN CHRIST
CROSSED THE ATLANTIC

Tituba had seen more than most. An enslaved woman purchased in Barbados and perhaps originally from South America, she found herself in the middle of an uproar in the small colonial village of Salem, Massachusetts. Her owner, Samuel Parris, was born in England and ventured to the New World as a boy. After Harvard, he became a cantankerous Puritan minister who complained as much about his lack of firewood as he did about the sins of the world. In the early 1690s, he seemed obsessed with the devil. "There are devils as well as saints in Christ's church," Parris exclaimed in one sermon. Then he located evil in the heart of their community: "If ever there were witches, men & women in covenant with the devil, here are multitudes in New England. . . . Now hundreds . . . are discovered in one shire."[1]

Tituba was terrified when the devil first appeared to her, or at least that is what she told the court in 1692 when summoned to speak. He demanded that she worship him and instructed her to hurt the children of the village. After pinching her skin and pulling her hair, he tempted her with "pretty things." When the court asked her who the devil was now using to harm Salem's children, the Indian slave who possessed so much spiritual sight cried out, "I am blind now, I cannot see."[2]

There was nothing out of the ordinary for Tituba—or for any Native American, slave, or Puritan—to claim to perceive sacred forces working around them. Colonists lived in an enchanted world where lightning, rainbows, and bumps in the night could be rendered as acts of God or designs of the devil. What was strange in Salem was that authorities looked to Tituba for help. Salem had been bedeviled, and their outpost community was spinning out of control. Children accused elders; women accused men; slaves claimed spiritual vision; and political, religious, and judicial leaders asked them for supernatural guidance. Sacred fears reverberated so widely and so intensely that by the end of the season more than twenty colonists had been executed or had died in prison. Tituba, however, was not one of them.[3]

The devil was everywhere in Salem, and he could take any number of physical forms. One witnessed him as a "little black bearded man." Another saw him as "a black thing of a considerable bigness," and yet another beheld a black dog to be Satan. The devil came as a Jew and as a Native American as well. But we need not be fooled—the devil did not always come in blackness or redness. Sarah Bibber saw "a little man like a minister with a black coat on and he pinched me by the arm and bid me to go along with him." The devil could corrupt, seduce, and use the bodies and souls of British colonists, their children, and many others.[4]

Jesus seemed absent amid the madness. Ann Putnam narrated a frightful tale in which the forces of evil were hell-bent on her destruction. She went before the court to denounce Martha Corey and Rebecca Nurse for being in league with the devil. Putnam remembered lying down one day in March when suddenly the spirit of Martha Corey tortured her. Corey's apparition demanded that Putnam sign her name in a little red book—the devil's book of death. According to Putnam, "No tongue can express" the "Hellish temptations" she endured. Then, and even worse, Rebecca Nurse's spirit came and spewed hate against God and "blasphemously denied . . . the power of the Lord Jesus Christ to save my soul."[5]

Where was the savior in all this? Court proceedings never mentioned Tituba seeing him; Ann Putnam said nothing of him swooping in to save her from torment. Of all the dozens examined, only one claimed to encounter Christ. Sarah Bridges met a man who said his name was Jesus. Perhaps the Son of God had come to battle the devil, and Salem's faithful would witness the final showdown of Armageddon prophesied in the Book of Revelation. Alas, even this man turned out to be the devil in disguise. Satan was so sacrilegious that he even tried to pose as Christ through a possessed body.[6]

This was the state of sacred vision and the body of Jesus in the colonial world that would become the United States. While slave and free, male and female, young and old professed under oath to interact with demonic forces, none was immediately saved by the Son of God. While the devil used physical costumes aplenty as he tried to lead away Salem's sheep, the good shepherd made no corporeal appearance. Jesus was worshiped as a savior. He was preached as a power. But for Puritans, he was physically absent.

There were no dominant images of Jesus in early colonial America. Spanish and French Catholics, along with their Indian converts, represented Jesus visually, but in a variety of forms. And throughout North America, destroying images of Christ was just as important as displaying them. This was an age marked by destructive iconoclasm. Actively not seeing Jesus by reducing icons to rubble or by excluding images of him from churches defined the era as much as those moments where he was brought across the sea. Throughout the seventeenth century, New World struggles did not revolve around what Christ's body looked like, but whether he should be embodied at all.

Jesus was neither white, nor red, nor black, and all types of people could interact with him. Colonial America was a raucous world where western Europeans, Native Americans, and West Africans (each group with countless differences among themselves) fought, loved, and prayed. Christ was brought into all sorts of discussions and interactions. He was an object of colonialism and confusion, and in the dynamic moments of cross-cultural exchange, he was transformed. In turn, ideas about him remade the many players as they interacted.[7]

A variety of factors account for the relative absence, unimportance, and even annihilation of Christ's physical body in the British colonies. Few of the groups involved had any inclination to create an image of the divine, and few had the manufacturing or distributing abilities to create a prevailing representation. The newness of Native American encounters with Jesus, the lack of freedom and diverse associations between color and divinity among West African slaves, and the radical iconoclasm of the English settlers created an eastern North America where no physical representation of Jesus dominated the landscape.

The white Jesus of European artwork was not a natural import to what would become the United States. For the British Protestants who would control much of America, a white Jesus sanctified neither the white people as sacred because of their whiteness nor the place as holy because of its Americanness.

Whiteness was not made sacred in the form of Jesus, in part, because whiteness itself as a marker of racial identity and power did not yet exist. Loyalties of nation, region, tribe, and religion outweighed other conceptions of identity and muddied the waters of allegiance. Labor demands made any person exploitable. Anywhere from one-half to two-thirds of the first British immigrants were transported against their will. Most were unfree laborers. Moreover, the first English colonists encountered many commanding and skilled Native Americans, while their entry into the West African slave trade was contingent upon powerful African tribes being willing to trade them slaves. English colonists inhabited a world with so many differences of language, faith, and power that they rarely spoke, thought, or wrote in generalized claims of race and racial difference. Concepts of racial hierarchy or white supremacy could not be mapped onto Christ's body, because the racial lexicon and worldview of whiteness had not yet been created.[8]

The lack of a dominant image allowed Jesus to be an active and malleable part of cultural exchange, dialogue, and dissension. He was an unstable symbol in this environment, easily configured and reconfigured by various groups to speak to their changing conditions. The iconographic emptiness would be filled later with a white Jesus, but that conflation of racial supremacy with spiritual identity would be made in the future. Tituba's time was too uncertain and unstable—so uncertain and unstable, in fact, that she, a slave, saved herself in Salem by speaking authoritatively about visions of the devil, not his divine destroyer.

Native First Encounters

Most Americans place the "beginning" of their history with the colonies at Jamestown in 1607 and, two decades later, the Pilgrims and the Puritans in New England. From there, the adventure marches westward in a grand narrative of sweeping expansion across an empty paradise. But the history of Jesus in the lands that would become the United States offers a very different story. Jesus came to Santa Fe, St. Augustine, and Iroquoia before he washed ashore in Virginia or New England. The English used his name in the West African slave trade a full generation before Jamestown was planted. In disparate places, French Jesuits, Spanish Franciscans, English Puritans, Anglicans, grizzled soldiers, diverse Native Americans, and manacled West Africans mixed and matched with each other, killed and saved each other, and in the process created brand-new worlds.

As they swapped spit and stories, their germs and their gods came into contact and created new religious forms. Jesus came with Europeans—but was then transported in time, space, and memory across social, cultural, and linguistic borders. He was a part of New World conquest and contact but was then elemental to new cultural formations and expectations. For the Native Americans who lived along the northern East Coast, their first encounters with Jesus were momentous. Sometimes they embraced him.

Oftentimes they rejected him. But as the decades moved on and the Europeans kept coming, they could not ignore him.

When Europeans arrived in the Americas, they confronted a religious diversity of epic proportions. Each tribe seemed to have its own spirits, its own origin tales, and its own reckoning of the sacred. And none of them spoke Spanish, French, or English. Europeans found Indian beliefs frustratingly ambiguous. They were couched in stories and dreams. They constantly seemed to shift from one informant to another. Of course, many natives felt the same about the diverse Catholic and Protestant faiths brought to them by people who looked and sounded different and told strange tales of a killed and resurrected God-man. Most Indian religions were about right practice, not right belief; they emphasized the practical nature of a plurality of spirits, not right doctrine about one triune deity.

From the eastern coast of North America to the western sierras of New Mexico, Jesus was a potent symbol of colonial encounters. He became in Indian country as diverse as the tribes that encountered him. At times, he appeared as a practical diviner showing the way to the animals. Other times, he served as a symbol of colonial power targeted for desecration. He could also be a new divine presence whose physical suffering spoke to their human struggles. Often natives transformed Jesus into a *Manitou*, a god spirit that could take various forms, interact with humans, and provide them with special powers.

Spanish Catholics were obsessed with carrying Christ to the New World. Christopher Columbus gave himself the title "Christoferens" (Christ-bearer) and believed more strongly over time that his expeditions were marked by God to bring faith to the heathens. Throughout Central, South, and North America, conquistadores and Franciscan priests marched with swords, crosses, and images of Christ in tow. They destroyed indigenous icons and replaced them with images of Jesus—a Christ who usually had brown hair flowing at least beneath his ears and perhaps down his back, brown eyes, and darkened white skin. By the middle of the sixteenth century, Jesus began popping up miraculously among the natives. Mexico's *Cristo Aparecido* was perhaps the most fascinating. "Christ Appeared" first revealed himself to Spanish authorities in the Mexican village of Totolapan in 1543. Carved from the maguey, a plant native to Mexico, and having a green cross against his back, this Christ was less than three feet long. His creation was shrouded in mystery, supposedly delivered to the convent of Totolapan in the arms of an Indian stranger. It has survived as the patron of residents to the present day, in the intervening centuries becoming known for powers of healing and veneration. Similar images migrated to New Spain's northern frontier, where Franciscans (as in California) hoped to fashion a Christ-centered spirituality in the New World.[9]

When Jesus came to eastern North America, he moved furthest inland with French Jesuits. They established mission outposts in the Great Lakes region and later near the Mississippi River from Illinois to Louisiana. Rather than conquer, these missionaries tried to join native communities. The Society of Jesus detailed their adventures in seventy hefty volumes of missionary fund-raising propaganda now called *The Jesuit Relations*. The works bristled with Jesus as a figure of conquest, contact, and transformation. The Jesuits saw themselves, their mission, and French overseas imperialism happening under the figurative and literal image of Jesus. According to one chronicler of the Jesuits celebrating their arrival to Canada, "The figure of Christ, covered with a canopy, was carried about with the greatest possible ceremony, and he came auspiciously into the possession, so to speak of the happy land." As a material object that was part of the long history of Catholic iconography and a new figure for French adventure, this Jesus oversaw the European possession of the land and proclaimed it good.[10]

Conflict and cultural collision came with Christ. The Jesuits encountered natives who were confused by Jesus, and their questions about this man-god showed concerns about relationships among body, spirit, geographical presence, and tribal loyalties. Was he just another holy spirit? Had he walked with the natives on their soil in the past? Could he help them locate animals in the present, and if so at what price? Could he cure disease, or was there something for their souls beyond their pox-marked flesh? As the Jesuits observed, the natives wanted to know exactly how this Jesus fit within their worlds.

For some, Christ was a problem because he had never appeared in North America. "Your God has not come to our country, and that is why we do not believe in him," one native told Father Paul Le Jeune. The Frenchman responded that Jesus could be seen with "spiritual" sight, but this did not satisfy the native. "I see nothing except with the eyes of the body, save in sleeping," he explained, "and you do not approve our dreams." Perhaps pointing out Le Jeune's hypocrisy in trusting his own stories and dreams but not those of the natives, this Indian believed that any reasonable supreme God would appear to all, not just to some.[11]

Others feared Jesus. Some considered both the Jesuits and their savior to be sorcerers (or "jugglers," as the Jesuits often called them). Sorcerers

Novae Franciae accurata delineatio (1657), western portion. Courtesy of the Library and Archives Canada, Francesco Giuseppe Bressani/e008222454.

were ambivalent tricksters for many Indians. They were able to offer guidance but also to take life. "I hardly ever see any of them die who does not think he has been bewitched," noted Father Le Jeune, and the shamans were believed to have done the bewitching. Would Jesus or the Jesuits do the same? Others found the French Catholic visual representations ominous. Paintings of Christ and the Madonna in new chapels purportedly possessed magical qualities. The pictures could supposedly cast illness onto anyone who gazed at them.[12]

To offer a palpable Christ, the Jesuits turned away from miraculous biblical stories and instead created a rich literature of creation, suffering, healing, and martyrdom. Visions of Jesus as a comforter to the mortally ill abounded in the *Relations*, but the Jesuits could never control what natives did with Jesus after first receiving him.

The Jesuits highlighted the power of God over creation, which many natives took and transformed into a belief that Christ could help with the hunt. For the Montagnais, the earliest subjects of Jesuit evangelism, the missionaries translated the word God into "He-Who-Made-All." If God made all, then his son could certainly help them find all. To nomadic hunters, this was an important quality for a sacred spirit. In the winter of 1634, Le Jeune reported on two Montagnais who said, "I have seen thy Manitou, and I thy Jesus. . . . Oh what a good year he promised us! What Beavers, what Elks!" Jesus expected obedience in return. As historian Kenneth Morrison concludes, "Jesus turned out to be a hitherto unknown, but extremely powerful, Master of the Animals."[13]

This exchange of religious ideas showed that these natives understood Jesus as a man-god, a figure familiar to them in their own religious symbology. He was an immediately practical spirit who could intervene in important functions of everyday life. Jesus made game and fish appear, while the sorcery of native tricksters held no such power (or at least so said the Jesuits). "Heads of animals once offered to the manitous at feasts were now offered to Christ," Morrison explained of the change. Indians were therefore "not so much being converted to Christianity as Christ was being converted into a Manitou."[14]

The Jesuits experienced their earliest success among the Hurons, a tribe under siege from disease and from their Iroquois enemies. Jesuits hoped that tales of spiritual salvation overcoming physical suffering would appeal to the natives. They constructed hagiographical accounts of Indian saints and martyrs who in death for Jesus experienced new and everlasting life. "Sometimes she had such great heaviness of heart and such vivid impressions of the sufferings of Jesus Christ, that she seemed to suffer a death that was harder than death itself," a Jesuit chronicler wrote of one such devotee of Jesus in the early 1650s. "Her longing to die, in order to enjoy him whom she had seen in such ravishing beauty, kindled in her soul a fire so scorching and so painful, that she could only quench it by another pain. She appeased her love of joy by her love of suffering."

This hagiography and martyrology climaxed with the account of the first recognized Indian saint, Tekakwitha. She was a young woman whose physical devotion to Jesus (including self-flagellation) and then embrace of death by smallpox made her an ideal model. Before she died, Tekakwitha comforted her own ill mother. The daughter encouraged her mother to "bear with love the pains of illness, and to await with joy the moment of death." Her mother told the Jesuits that Tekakwitha practiced what she preached: "After often repeating the prayer, 'Jesus, have pity on me, and take me to heaven when I die,' she had cried out: 'There is Jesus coming to have pity on me. Oh, how beautiful you are, my good Jesus. I thank you. You will, then, have pity on me. Take me to heaven, then, for I am going to die.'"[15]

Expecting to see Jesus upon death enticed converts, as it did for many English Puritans as well, and Catholic iconography became a part of native encounters with Christ. Jesus imagery was fundamental to the Catholic apparatus of evangelism. "One must be provided in this country with medals; small crucifixes a finger in length, or smaller still; small brass crosses and brass rings, also some in which there is the figure of some saint, or the face of Jesus Christ or the Blessed Virgin; wooden rosaries, very black and rather thick, which they wear hanging from the neck or about the head; knives, the very heaviest, etc.," explained one Jesuit. Another Jesuit asked if his French supporters could send him a handsome, beardless Jesus of about eighteen years old.[16]

These objects became icons of adoration and authority. They seemed to contain the power of Jesus within them. Because of Christ icons, St. Francis Xavier was "surprised and delighted" to receive "tokens of endearment" instead of the "hatchet-blows" he expected. Of one Illinois Indian, Xavier admired the "simplicity of a good old man in whose cabin I publicly explained the holy Mysteries of the Incarnation and Death of JESUS CHRIST. As soon as I produced my Crucifix, . . . this good man, moved at the sight, wished to acknowledge it as his God." Although a new god, the native worshiped him in old ways. He offered "the incense of this country. It consisted of powdered tobacco, of which he took two or three handfuls, one by one, and, as if offering the censer an equal number of times, scattered it over the

Crucifix." The native then brought Xavier into the Indian ritual, sprinkling the incense over Xavier. This, he recounted, "is the highest mark of honor that they can show toward those whom they regard as Spirits." Whether Xavier knew it or not, this was not an example of religious conquest or capitulation. It was a dynamic moment of spiritual contact and religious exchange.[17]

Numerous other accounts in the *Relations* marveled at the power of the icons. Jesuits expressed joy at the "esteem manifested by this new Church for all the outward signs of our holy Religion. Crosses, medals, and other similar Articles are their most precious jewels." As well, the Jesuits delighted in the adoration extended to Christmas cradles with representations of the baby Jesus: "They gave the infant Jesus proofs of their gratitude and love by Singing. It was impossible to resist the persistent requests of those who are still infidels to be allowed to enter, and gratify their Curiosity by gazing for a long time at everything that rendered the spot agreeable to their eyes." Those who thought of the Jesuits' mission field as "thoroughly sterile and unfruitful" would be instructed by a visit to Lorette, explained one father in 1710. There, in the evening, "all gather in the chapel, where prayers are offered up in common for the whole village. Each family also recites prayers privately at home, after which each one, with a pious kiss, venerates the most holy wounds of Christ."[18]

To the Jesuits, language mattered just as much as imagery. When Jesuits translated biblical concepts into the Illinois language, they couched their descriptions of Jesus in native words of understanding. As rendered in Illinois, "Jesus has two fathers and a mother. Jesus is the only son of the great spirit of creation who lives in the sky and who commands fear and respect in those who obey him. The beautiful spirit of light comes down to earth and makes Jesus man through Mary, the pure nubile girl, who gives birth to him so that he can come into the world, where he suffers, dies, returns to life and his father in the sky, and becomes chief of all Christians." The story was told in the present tense. It instilled a sense of immediacy and conformed to traditional Illinois methods of storytelling. The name Jesus was translated as "our chief." But since Illinois chiefs ruled with assent and input, this invited Illinois Christians to view Jesus as a "potentially powerful leader in both spiritual and human terms and to develop a relationship in which the leader and his followers could introduce their own very personal expectations." Even in translation, Jesus' power came into native frameworks of negotiating with the gods.[19]

The name of Jesus could also be rendered as "warrior." One member of the dominant Iroquois confederation announced: "I am talking now of one who bears the reed mat of war, Jesus. He's returned to the sky. He goes about overcoming them, killing the spirit and with it bringing the death of all sinning. . . . Jesus, the master, will help us. . . . Onnontio [the French governor] will overcome the Seneca when he goes with his troops. . . . We should congratulate Jesus, our master, as he overcame them. It would encourage our forces, so it would be certain that he will overcome the spirit who bears us ill will. . . . He goes about seizing them, making them disappear, when he overcomes them." The reed mat contained the beaks of ravens and the talons of hawks. For these natives, a leader who used one first threw a feast and then led a raid.

Indians invoked the warrior Jesus for tribal conflicts. A Christian Huron elder in 1672 urged, "Let us fear our enemies no more; Jesus in glory has us under his protection." Their enemies, the Iroquois, had offended God, and Jesus would hasten to save the remnant of surviving Huron. "Jesus is too powerful to let thee snatch it from his hands; and the blessed Virgin, his Mother, who had graciously designed to make her abode among us in this Chapel, prays him too urgently to protect us. He will never forsake us or suffer us to fall a prey to thy cruelty." Jesus had become a spirit figure of war who would help Indians against one another.[20]

When the Jesuits brought Jesus to the natives of the East Coast and further inland, they and local natives made him a central player in their conflicts, exchanges, and negotiations. He was there in spirit. He could be seen in icons. And Jesuits and natives expressed him through language and ideas. The Jesuits did not dominate the religious landscape, so they could not make their Jesus into a standard image. When they brought Jesus into the situations of first contacts, the Jesuits accepted that Jesus would be changed in name, in ritual, and in meaning. Rather than teach Jesus as a universal savior, they offered him (or accepted his re-creation) as the Master of the Hunt, a warrior, or a chief. In the hands, languages, hearts, rituals, and dreams of natives, Jesus was a malleable power: sometimes threatening, sometimes the irrelevant god-man of another people, and sometimes a helper when all seemed lost.

An Age of Iconoclasm

But for every Indian that the French or Spanish convinced to adore Jesus, there were those who hated the figure of Christ. Iconography came to symbolize Catholic intrusion, and when some Indians violently rose against the invaders, they set out to destroy Christ too. Ritual iconoclasm, in fact, was probably more common than ritual veneration, and assaults upon the body of Christ were part of the attack against colonial subjugation. Not seeing Jesus was a means of beating back the colonists.

Indians who interacted with French Jesuits understood the power of destroying abstract symbols of Christianity. Revisiting the Illinois country where crosses had formerly reigned, a missionary reported that the Christian symbols had been smashed into small pieces. Even worse, local Indians claimed credit for a missionary's demise: "They gathered around the cross that he had erected, and there they invoked their Manitou,—each one dancing, and attributing to himself the glory of having killed the missionary, after which they broke the cross into a thousand pieces."[21]

Native peoples in New Mexico, moreover, fixated on Jesus figures in the most successful counterattack against European conquerors in American history. The Pueblo Revolt of 1680 expelled the Spanish and their man-god from their northernmost colony for thirteen years. At the pueblo of Sandia (just north of present-day Albuquerque) on August 26, 1680, a Spanish delegation found a convent "deserted and destroyed, the cells without doors, and the whole place sacked." The church's images had been removed, and "everything had been stolen and profaned by the rebellious traitors."

It was a rampage of iconoclastic defilement. One account described how "images of saints were found among excrement, two chalices were found concealed in a basket of manure, and there was a carved crucifix with the paint and varnish taken off by lashes." The destruction, a Spanish observer perceived, demonstrated the "hatred" natives felt for the "holy faith" and provided "sufficient reasons for war being waged against them without mercy, and for declaring all those who may be captured slaves for a period of ten years, in the manner which was done formerly." Another observer found remaining at the convent of Sandia only a former guardroom turned into a "seminary of idolatry," with kachina masks attached to its walls.[22]

Derision and dismemberment were part of the rebellion. The Franciscans complained bitterly of the "scoffing and ridicule which the wretched and miserable Indian rebels made of the sacred things, intoning the alabado and the other prayers of the church with jeers." Even some icons the Spaniards had buried were "opened by the apostates and the images taken out." In the sacristy "was found a crown of twigs and two pieces of the arm of a holy image of Christ; and in the cloister were the skeletons of two dead persons." In the plaza of this pueblo rested the "entire thigh, leg, and foot of a holy image of Christ, in one piece, all the rest of the divine image being burned to charcoal and ashes." These Puebloans refused to bow to Christ or to Spaniards. Instead, they taunted, tortured, and tore him, just as the Romans had done centuries ago and just as the Spaniards had done to them in more recent times.[23]

Iconoclasm had many faces in early America. The Spanish had destroyed indigenous icons; Indians had desecrated Catholic representations of Jesus in New Mexico and further north and east. But no group was as dedicated to destructive iconoclasm as the small band of English men and women who came late to the game. A bundle of contradictions and anxieties, English Puritans would settle along the colonial East Coast of North America. They loved Jesus but hated visual representations of him. They longed to share the gospel but feared being tainted by diversity of opinion or by Indians or West Africans. They knew they were right but wondered if they were damned. The English settlers brought Jesus to their America tentatively and in the process discovered that their theologies, laws, and customs were insufficient for the New World of red, white, and black. The new contours of human interaction forced their faith to be remade, but the Puritans were not sure how. Their uncertainties, coupled with their confusions about Christ, left an empty space in their dream to become a city upon a hill and a spiritual darkness in their desire to be a light to the world.

What the English Brought and Broke

English settlers in North America could respect indigenous attacks on Catholic iconography. They too had raged against images of the divine, destroyed them, and fled from them. From a different shore and a distinct theological position, the first English settlers shared this vitriolic hatred for Catholicism and its images of Christ's body. Although the smallest and one of the latest groups to arrive in what would become the United States, the Puritans became one of its most powerful. They arrived in small numbers, a couple hundred here and a couple hundred there. They died in staggering numbers, especially in the southern colonies. Most who came were convict laborers, indentured servants, or forcibly exiled homeless children. Those who came on their own accord brought with them a ferocity for religious freedom for themselves.[24]

What the Puritans did not bring was a white Christ. The white Jesus could not be found aboard Puritan vessels (unless somehow hidden by closet Catholics or high Anglicans); he was not a natural and inevitable creation of English colonists, who merely created him in their own image.

The birth of the white Christ in America and his promotion by Protestants actually contradicted early Puritan religious sentiments. The first British colonists in the New World were radical iconoclasts living in an age of radical iconoclasm. They left the realm of divine imagery unclaimed and hence untamed. Common people developed their own ways of seeing good and evil, Jesus and the devil. At times, their sacred visions spun society out of control, as in Salem in the 1690s.

Unlike the Franciscans and Jesuits, English settlers considered it blasphemous to depict Jesus visually. They did not know what Jesus looked like. They did not want to know. And they celebrated not knowing. As part of the Protestant Reformation, colonial Puritans thought that the Catholic representations violated the second of the Ten Commandments, which forbade the worship of material objects or images. From Zurich, Switzerland, to London, England, art was removed from churches and banned as part of worship. Swiss reformer Ulrich Zwingli gloated that "in Zurich we have churches which are positively luminous; the walls are beautifully white." Under Catholic and Protestant leaders, English monarchs oversaw the destruction and removal of hundreds of depictions of God, Jesus, and the sacred. The visual arts, as historian John Dillenberger has written, "were largely absent from the lives of people generally."[25]

The same was true in the outlands, deadly swamps, and snow-covered fields of British North America. Iconoclasm was serious business. In New England, colonists positioned altars toward the east (the supposed direction by which Christ would return) but made sure to have plain walls on their meetinghouses. It remained this way for 200 years. Church children learned the stories of faith without pictures of Christ. In the early twentieth century, church architect Ralph Cram lamented this artistic desolation. With the Reformation and in colonial America, "for the first time in the history of the world, organized religion turned against art, and . . . devoted itself to the destruction of what it had created." From the seventeenth through the nineteenth centuries, "Art was gone." "We threw it all away, once, in our blindness of heart . . . leaving the few churches we did not destroy barren, empty, desolated."[26]

Reading and literacy replaced visual iconography. According to historian David Hall, "to read was to see; to read was to feel." This shift from images to words was especially apparent in alphabet primers published in New England to teach children how to read (and how to fear God and convert before their imminent deaths). In English versions of the primers, the letter "J" had a small picture of a crucifixion and the stanza "Sweet

Jesus he / Dy'd on a Tree." But not in the New World. New Englanders re moved the cross and replaced the story about Jesus with a rhyme about Job: "Job feels the rod / Yet blesses God." The letter "Z" was also notable for its absent Jesus. English editions had Zacheus, the biblical character who climbed a tree to see Jesus, seated on a branch and peering into a crowd where Jesus preached. The accompanying rhyme read: "Zacheus he / Did climb the Tree / His Lord to see." Not in Puritan America. Zacheus and the tree remained, but Jesus and the crowd were nowhere to be found.[27]

Puritans and other British Protestants regarded claims about Christ's appearance as fabrications. This was particularly true of the fraudulent "Publius Lentulus letter." Puritans read their Bibles, and they knew that the gospels said nothing about Christ's physical appearance. They knew that what Jesus actually looked like was unknown and had been unknown for centuries. A beard, brown hair, ruddy skin, a perfect nose—all of this was probably false. For the most part, the Publius Lentulus forgery was disregarded as a fake.

In terms of visualized sacred figures, the demonic dominated Puritan vision. The number of times Jesus appeared paled in comparison to that of Satan and his minions. To some in Britain, the entire New World was a land of devils. Popular poet Michael Wigglesworth deemed New England,

A Waste and howling wilderness,
Where none inhabited
But hellish fiends, and brutish men
That devils worshipped.

Cotton Mather associated Indians and blacks with the devil in "A Discourse on the Wonders of the Invisible World." "*Swarthy Indians*" were often in the company of "*Sooty Devils*," and Satan presented himself as "a small *Black man*."[28]

But removing pictures could not stop colonial Protestants from hoping to see the holy. Many Puritans wanted to know and see their God. Icono-clastic theology seemed to do little but confuse and disorient visual desires. Samuel Sewall, a merchant of Massachusetts who kept an extensive diary, longed for a "glimpse of Christ" but recorded sadly that he found "none."[29]

Protestants were caught in a conundrum. Many desperately wanted to see Christ but felt that to do so would mean certain death. As one British picture book put it, "Twixt two extreames how my rack't fortunes lie? / See I thy face, or see it not, I die."[30] The only answer was death; it promised to resolve the spiritual problem of life. Just as Tekakwitha had died happy that she would now see Jesus, Puritans longed for the same. And just as was the case with Tekakwitha and her people, one of the reasons may have been the ubiquity of death all around the Puritans. John Rogers, an English Protestant martyr burned in 1555, was immortalized in thousands of English and American primers with his last words to his family:

> I hope Redemption I shall have,
>   and all that in him trust;
> When I shall see him face to face,
>   and live among the Just.[31]

When these early Americans considered the visage of Jesus, they were influenced far more by the biblical descriptions of Jesus in the Book of Revelation, in which Jesus was described in terms of fire and sunlight, than they were by the Publius Lentulus letter or European artwork. For his popular poem *The Day of Doom* (1662), Michael Wigglesworth cast Jesus in light, not white:

> All stand before their Saviour
>   in long white Robes yclad,
> Their countenance full of pleasance,
>   appearing wondrous glad.
> O glorious sight! behold how bright
>   dust heaps are made to shine,
> Conformed so their Lord unto,
>   whose glory is Divine.[32]

When the first English settlers arrived in North America, they resisted images of Jesus. When they first created communities, established churches, and built homes, they did not include paintings or drawings of Christ. When they saw demons in the forms of dogs, when they hoped for angels to rescue them, and when they prayed and prayed to see God's son, they caught, at best, glimpses of him. They saw what the biblical Book of Revelation taught them to see—a blinding light. But most often, they nothing. Whether during witch hunts or lean times, Jesus as a physi- sence or embodied representation was nowhere to be found in this America.

A Ship Named *Jesus* and a Nightmare Named America

Before the Puritans arrived in New England, West Africans had been part of the English Atlantic world. West Africans encountered Jesus within the matrix of New World contact and conquest decades before the British established either Jamestown or Massachusetts Bay Colony. Although impossible to know for sure, it seems that these first African Americans neither conceived of Jesus as white nor had fixed associations between color and the divine.

Two of the first English ships to carry West Africans to the New World had ominous names: *Jesus* and *Minion*. In the slave trade, it surely seemed that the forces of heaven and those of hell were one and the same. Both ships served the same purpose. They hauled hundreds of West Africans thousands of miles away from their homes to be sold for their labor. "The good ship *Jesus*," as it was sometimes called, was part of John Hawkins's fleet, and it was a gift from Queen Elizabeth I. The vessel left England for Sierra Leone in 1562, fifty-eight years before the Pilgrims set sail for the New World.[33]

Forced aboard *Jesus*, African men and women probably had no idea that the ship bore the name of a man who had been crucified fifteen centuries earlier. They probably had no idea that the vessel outfitted with guns, chains, and dungeons was named for the "prince of peace" who had come to "set the captives free." On board, the West Africans may have overheard the preaching of quartermaster William Sanders, the self-proclaimed "greatest Lutheran in all of England." Even if they could understand his English, they would have learned little of Jesus. Sanders's sermons were mostly anti-Catholic rants—perhaps ones that denounced the Jesus iconography of the Catholics for its violation of the Second Commandment.[34]

From the fifteenth century to the middle of the nineteenth century, African slaves and their descendants would learn to associate the name of Jesus, as well as his presence and image, with horrific death and new life. In the process, they created something new from something old. They took shattered lives, communities, and traditions and built vibrant forms of Christianity. New faiths that bore the name of Jesus, in part, helped them endure and disturb the systems of their oppression. Their faith brought democracy to a land of tyranny, justice to a land of misery, and dreams to a land of nightmares. But this change happened gradually, and not until after the seventeenth century. And it happened through their crucifixions.

A great myth of Western white civilization has been that Africans had feeble or backward religions of little consequence. In fact, African peoples of the fifteenth and sixteenth centuries held a host of religious beliefs that had been changing for centuries. Both Islam and Christianity had made marked inroads into the continent. They had interacted with tribal faiths almost 500 years before the beginning of the slave trade to North and South America.[35]

Although the sources come from oral histories after the age of enslavement, it seemed that Africans of this age held a variety of beliefs about the sacred and supernatural. Some tribes considered God to take physical form. God could show up as a lion or a python or in lightning. Just as some European Christians worried, some Africans thought that to see God meant certain death. There was also no clear color to the sacred. The Kikuyu viewed God as the "Possessor of Whiteness," while the Galla referred to God as "black" when the sky was overcast. Some in the Masai tribe believed that there were four gods originally. The black one was "very good." The white one was "good." The blue one was "neither good nor bad." And the red one was "bad." Only the black God survived, though. Others were adamant that God could not be manifest. One tribal hymn, for instance, proclaimed:

Who can make an image of God?
He has no body.
He is as a word which comes out of your mouth.
That word! It is no more,
It is past, and still it lives!
So is God.[36]

Whether following Christian, Muslim, or tribal tenets, there were no uniform ideas of what God or Christ looked like physically. Probably like most Protestant Europeans, West Africans had no definitive depiction of Jesus or God.

The transportation of West Africans to the New World began in the early fifteenth century, hit its full stride in the sixteenth and seventeenth centuries, and continued throughout the eighteenth and nineteenth centuries. Anywhere from 10 million to 15 million slaves were imported.[37] The conditions were dreadful. Crammed into tight quarters, shackled, surrounded by feces, blood, and germs, these "black cargoes" were treated as commodities. No wonder that some West Africans felt so depressed that they simply died of emotional loss. Some West Africans feared being eaten by white cannibals or crushed into gunpowder or oil. For many, this evil could only come from witches who were out for power and wealth. Just as the English and their colonists saw witches and devils all around them, so too did West Africans. The main difference was that the English had the power to try, convict, and execute those thought to bewitch them. West Africans did not.[38]

The paucity of sources from Africans in America in the seventeenth century makes it difficult to observe clearly the religious transition from West Africa to North America. Historians usually look to white observers for help, but these sources are untrustworthy guides. When Europeans and white colonists wrote about Africans, they either denounced them for being heathens or debated whether they could (or should) be converted to Christianity. It is hard to take seriously the reflections of white missionaries to African Americans, since many of them agreed with this bishop, who stated in 1784, "Despicable as they are in the eyes of man [they] are, nevertheless, the creatures of God."[39]

What did God look like to West Africans in the holds of the slave ships? Did any think of Jesus or imagine him along the journey? Did God, Jesus, ancestral spirits, or evil forms appear in the holds or on the decks? Like so much in the slave trade, these answers too are lost. It would be in the New World where some Africans would meet the image of Jesus and adapt it in creative ways. British Protestants did their best to destroy visual images of their God for themselves, while West Africans in America searched to create religious meaning amid such tragedy and loss. For men and women of African descent, what their gods looked like in their new worlds seemed just as much up for grabs. The places and the experiences were new—so too would be Jesus.

Puritans in Red, White, and Black

Try as they might, the Puritans were never alone in the wilderness. They were never a secluded city upon a hill. They were never a unified community free of theological conflict. In part, they chose diversity and difference. They knowingly ventured into a land full of Indians. Seals advertising for colonial Massachusetts and Virginia, in fact, graphically depicted Indians beckoning to the English for help, while Jesus—in good Puritan fashion—was nowhere to be seen. The English also imported West Africans and their descendants, first in small numbers and then in droves. Colonial New England was another Atlantic world creation, where European, Native American, and West African sentiments and bodies mingled, fused, and made something wholly new. The English brought to the mix their particular views of and relationships to Christ, but the situations compelled changes to their theologies, laws, and customs in subtle and more obvious ways.[40]

Never as missionary-minded as Spanish Franciscans or French Jesuits, Puritans carried Christ to the natives in their own unique fashion. They brought Jesus to the natives not to conquer (as the Spanish had) nor to join (as the French had). Instead, the Puritans entered ambivalently. Theirs was a stop-and-go enterprise full of desire and fear. Puritans never gave themselves wholeheartedly to sharing Christ with Indians or West Africans, and their halting attempts spoke to their own confusion about Christ and his relationship to human difference and diversity.[41]

Led by John Eliot, New England Puritans created special "praying towns," to be inhabited by those who became Christians. In the early 1650s, Eliot oversaw the formation of four praying towns, beginning with Natick, Massachusetts, and then founding more in the subsequent decade. These communities would be distinct from Indian tribal villages and Puritan towns. They would be new realms where the so-called Christian Indians could live, work, learn, and worship.[42]

Good Puritan that he was, Eliot distinguished his mission from French Catholics by focusing on words, not on images. He offered the Indians a *"thorough-paced Christianity,"* not one with the idolatrous "art of coyning Christians, or putting Christs name and Image upon copper mettle."[43] Instead of presenting icons, Eliot and his disciples fixated on words. They translated the Bible into native languages. Eliot reasoned that what was good for white Puritans would be good for red Puritans. Bible reading would allow the natives to "see most cleerely what Jesus Christ was."[44]

Eliot also sought to display native Christianity to Europeans through the written word. His missionary tracts were a confusing array of supposedly authentic conversion narratives and explicitly fictionalized dialogues. With his colleague Thomas Mayhew, Eliot published *Tears of Repentance* in 1653. It featured twenty-three conversion narratives recorded from fifteen Christian Indians. Two decades later, Eliot produced the *Indian Dialogues*. It was fictional as well, with Eliot inventing Indian inquirers who posed questions to imaginary native missionaries who were to provide answers. Eliot produced his final narratives of Indians "dying in Christ" with his aptly titled tract *Dying Speeches*. This volume contained the final words of eight praying Indians.[45]

46

Jesus was at the center of Eliot's *Indian Dialogues*, but he was more a confusing presence than he was a converting power. In this dialogue of questions that natives supposedly had of Indian missionaries trained by the Puritans to carry the message to their own people, Jesus was a problematic deity. One native believed that language irrevocably separated Indians from Christ. "He prayed in vaine," this Indian lamented, "because Jesus Christ understood not what *Indians* speake in prayer." Since the English knew Jesus, and since they prayed to him in the English language, it stood to reason that Jesus was a "stranger" to Indian languages.[46] The fictional questions were penetrating, while the answers often left much to be desired. To the question of "whether English men were ever at any time so ignorant of God and Jesus Christ as themselves," the response was that Indians should "know Christ, and love Christ, and pray to Christ." Another group asked how "the English [had come] to differ so much from the Indians in the knowledge of God and Jesus Christ, seeing they had all at first one father."[47]

These questions exposed the limits of Puritanism and its ability to bring Christ to the colonies. How could Indians know that the Puritans were right? And how could Puritans know they were right, if they had never truly met or known Jesus? One question perhaps spoke to the geographical and genealogical distance between English Puritans and the Jesus they worshipped. "What Countrey man Christ was," wondered one native, "and where he was born?"[48] Perhaps embedded in this question was another question: If Jesus was not an Englishman, then how could the English claim to know him?

It all amounted to a profound mistrust of the Puritans on the part of the natives. The fictionalized Indian "Kinsman" summarized the sentiments Eliot must have heard time and again: "But how shall I know that [what] you say [is] true? . . . Are you wiser than our fathers? May not we rather think that *English* men have invented these stories to amaze us and fear us out of our old customs, and bring us to stand in awe of them, that they might wipe us of our lands, and drive us into corners, to seek new ways of living, and new places too?"[49]

Even with these reservations, some Indians did convert under Puritan missions. Those who did sounded very similar to English Puritans in published accounts, and they invoked elaborate metaphors of spiritual blindness and grace-given sight. In one narrative, a literate Indian resisted Christ's call to "gather a church at Natick." Put simply, "My heart disliked that place." But then he drew to mind the gospel tale of Jesus restoring

ight to a blind man who had asked, "Lord, open my eyes." Jesus had answered and "gave him sight, and he followed Christ." It troubled this native's heart, "for I thought I still believe not, because I do not follow Christ,
nor hath he yet opened mine eyes. Then I prayed to Christ to open my eyes,
that I might see what to do, because I am blind and cannot see how to follow Christ."[50]

This account—and the others collected by Eliot—should have been sufficient for Puritans. In them, native Christians related conversion accounts
of their depravity, God's intervention through Christ, and belief in Jesus
as the Son of God. But red Puritans were held to new, harsher standards.
Puritans ratcheted up the examinations normally required of converts.
They brought in ministers from surrounding churches to question "a good
number of Indians about their attainments, both in *knowledge* and in *ver-
tue*." Their oral "*confessions* of their faith in God and Christ" were "taken in
writing from their mouths by able interpreters" and "scanned by the people
of God." Perhaps colonists distrusted natives because they spoke of skepticism, sinfulness, and insufficiency, but these were common themes for
Puritans to express depravity before experiencing God's grace. Or perhaps
Puritans despised people whose tribes, brothers, and fathers had waged
war on the settlers and had not given them everything they desired.[51]

Some Puritans were moved by these accounts. Related in Cotton
Mather's classic *Magnalia Christi Americana*, the well-known minister
Richard Mather criticized those who would "make light" of the praying
Indians. He insisted that to witness the Indians lift their hands to God in
prayer, confess "the name of Jesus Christ, and their own sinfulness," and
do it all with "sober countenances" and "tears trickling down" their cheeks,
"much affected our hearts."[52]

But Puritan anxiety far outweighed acceptance. Indians always seemed
to the colonists to be more closely aligned with the devil than with Jesus.
(To be fair, oftentimes colonists saw their fellow colonists as closer to
the devil than to God too.) Eliot, for instance, explicitly published *Dying
Speeches* to counter the view that "all Indians were instruments of Satan."
Try as he might, though, Eliot could not overcome the association of Indians
with the demonic. This was especially pronounced after the bloody uprising known as King Philip's War of 1676 left colonial New England shaken to
its core.[53]

Jesus was unable to bridge the gaps of difference, greed, war, and faith
in colonial New England. After King Philip's War, many Puritans thought
Christianizing Indians a hopeless and foolish pursuit. Embattled New En-

glanders increasingly viewed the project with scorn. After all, they had witnessed their villages burned and their fellow Puritans dragged off as war captives. As one Puritan wag of the time put it, Eliot's *praying* Indians had better be termed *preying* Indians, for they had "made Preys of much English Blood." They were savages beyond the reach of Jesus.[54]

At this juncture, Puritan settlers definitively shifted a focus of their faith from freedom to bondage. As communities of believers, the Puritans were convinced that religious oppression against them was wrong. That was one of the reasons they fled to the New World. But by the end of the seventeenth century, Puritans were attaching their faith to control. Interacting with Indians, Puritans metaphorically compared civilizing them to breaking an animal, putting these "heady Creatures" in the "yoke of Christ" and teaching them to "bridle their savage instincts."[55]

In the New World racial mix, Puritans disconnected their faith from freedom and reattached Christ to constraints. This was even more apparent in their interactions with West Africans. If Puritans were skeptical about missions to Native Americans, they were downright hostile to sharing Christ with West Africans and their descendants. In part, this was because of the enduring problem of enslaving coreligionists. For centuries, Europeans had wondered if it was acceptable for a Christian to hold another Christian in bondage. Another reason was the belief that Christ had liberating powers and that if slaves learned some biblical teachings, they might resent and oppose their enslavement. Puritans knew that there was more in the Bible than directives to slaves to obey their masters, and they worried about what slaves would do with passages from Exodus, for instance. If Puritans were to preach the good news of Christ crucified and resurrected to West Africans, the colonists might undermine their fiscal investments. And black bodies were too badly needed in the New World to cook, clean, and cultivate the land.[56]

Confronted with the possibilities and realities of slave conversions—and with sexual and social interactions between Europeans and Africans—the colonists of the seventeenth and early eighteenth centuries made some concrete moves in their laws and customs. What would become of a slave who converted to Christ and was baptized in his name? Would she or he be emancipated? What would the status be of a newborn whose one parent was free and the other enslaved?

Colonists answered by disassociating faith from freedom and by setting slavery above Christianity and patriarchy. When Elizabeth Key sued for her freedom on account of converting to Christ, the Virginia assembly responded with an act "declaring that baptisme of slaves doth not exempt them from bondage." Moreover, local courts rendered sexual relationships with African Americans as dishonoring and shameful for white Christians and then made interracial marriage illegal. Finally, colonists undermined a hallmark of English law: patriarchal authority. The British understood the rule of men and fathers as divine. As John Milton put it in *Paradise Lost*, man was created "for God only, she for God in him." But in the colonies, patriarchy lost some power through new laws that declared that status would follow slavery, not paternity. A Maryland law from the early 1660s not only deemed an individual a slave if either of his or her parents was enslaved but also forced into slavery any white woman who married a slave. In this legal configuration, slavery overwhelmed faith, freedom, and paternal power.[57]

It would be in the eighteenth century that Christ in America would be reattached to freedom. During this age of visions, awakenings, and revolutions, Jesus would become for many an agent of liberation. Those Native Americans and African Americans who put their faith in him took it upon themselves to reconnect Christianity and Christ back to the importance of freedom. White colonists, too, would embrace Jesus as a "God of liberty," but in name only and as the exclusive property of white men. Through it all, Jesus had yet to achieve a dominant face or form.

IN THE EIGHTEENTH CENTURY, English Protestants more and more shared Jesus across lines of difference and status. Increasingly, they brought him to slaves and Indians. This process, coupled with colonial expansion, religious awakenings, and revolutionary fire, transformed Jesus and the players involved. What happened during religious, social, and cultural exchanges was out of the control of the Puritans. Native Americans and African Americans wrestled with Christ and made him a power in their own circumstances. In their hands, he came to trouble the emerging world of white citizenship and supremacy.

Almost one hundred years after Tituba had been tried, had testified about spiritual forces, and was then released in Salem, another slave in Massachusetts set out to explain how the sacred invaded her world. This time, the devil was not the main player. This time, it was Jesus.

Phillis Wheatley too had had a long path to New England. She was born in West Africa, captured as a child in the early 1760s, and shipped to New England aboard the *Phillis* (hence her first name). In Boston, the Wheatley family purchased her (hence her last name). Africa's loss was America's gain, for Wheatley became one of its finest poets. Her work radiated with light and emotional depth. She rarely referenced the devil, but the power of Jesus leapt from the pages. In one poem, she was thrilled that

> 'Twas mercey brought me from my *Pagan* land,
> Taught my benighted soul to understand
> That there's a God, that there's a *Saviour* too.[58]

One of her finest pieces brought a new meaning of Christ to enslaved Africans, and she did it in the most brilliant manner. Through a eulogy for the English evangelist George Whitefield, a revivalist preacher who had riveted the colonies in the 1730s and 1740s to become the most popular figure in the Americas, Wheatley crafted a new Christ and wrapped it in the words of Whitefield. Wheatley recounted how Whitefield had taught a radical and inclusive Christ, a god-man who reached out to all and who wanted to love and be loved by all.

Status meant nothing to this Christ. He cried out to men and women like her, Africans and slaves whose lot in life was to serve masters and mistresses. "Take HIM ye *Africans*, he longs for you," Wheatley imagined Whitefield preaching (words that no one else claimed to have heard him speak):

> Impartial SAVIOUR, is his title due;
> If you will chuse to walk in grace's road,
> You shall be sons, and kings, and priests to GOD.[59]

Wheatley spoke her vision of Christ through Whitefield, giving it power and authority. This Jesus was remarkably different from the whites around her, and he was unlike anything the Puritans knew. This Christ longed for Africans, but not to enslave or terrify them. He wanted to make them sons, and kings, and priests. Even more, he offered them the gift of choice. In a world marked increasingly by racial divisions and discriminatory laws, this savior was impartial and slaves could make sacred selections. They could "chuse" to walk with him if they liked. This was a radical departure for women and men like Wheatley who lived in a land with few choices. Even the name given Wheatley and what we call her testified to the power of the master class. But slaves could choose Christ. Rendered this way, the Jesus who still lacked a physical presence in the colonies was anything but a paragon of white power or sanctity.

The line from Tituba to Wheatley was one of wonder and terror in a revolutionary century. The age of destructive iconoclasm died in the seventeenth century. In the eighteenth century, an age of visions was born. Americans white, black, and red started to see Jesus all around them. As Jesus appeared to Indians and slaves, to women and children, to pastors and politicians, his power rose. By the end of the century, calls for freedom and for choices had rocked the New World so violently that a new nation was born—the United States.

Within it, Americans would rage for, with, and against one another as they tried to determine who constituted the nation and whether "all men" really were "created equal." An imageless Son of God was called upon to judge who would be free and who would not be. He was called upon to help determine how the people would be defined and divided. It was in this whirlwind that Wheatley made the dead Whitefield preach about an impartial savior who longed for Africans. He loved them so much that he was willing to offer them the greatest gift of all, a blessing few whites would willingly give to slaves: choice.

CHAPTER TWO

REVOLUTIONARY VISIONS
IN COLONIAL CONFINES

Puritans despised Quakers. Their focus on the "inner light," through which God's spirit could speak to anyone at any time, seemed like theological and social chaos. In the early colonial period, preaching Quaker doctrines was tantamount to witchcraft. It was a good way to be banished from or executed in Puritan dominions. But the shape of the colonies changed rapidly in the eighteenth century. Religious groups of all sorts streamed across the Atlantic. There were Anglicans and Lutherans, Presbyterians and Moravians, Mennonites and Dunkers, and even some Catholics, Jews, and Muslims.[1] Quakers grew in number and respect. They became a power in Pennsylvania, and one of their most talented sons, Benjamin West, embarked on a career that the Puritans would have denounced. He began sketching and painting representations of Jesus.

West saw more of America and the world than did most Americans. He was born in Pennsylvania in 1738, was supposedly taught by Indians to paint, trained in Philadelphia in the 1750s, and then became a successful portrait painter in New York City. He then reversed the usual migratory pattern, traveling east to Europe in the early 1760s. He soaked up the art and architecture of Italy and England and gained fame for *The Death of General Wolfe* (1771) and then decades later for *Death on a Pale Horse* (1817). West joined the European art world by trying his hand at the classic scenes of European Christian art: *The Nativity*, *The Holy Family*, *Christ Blessing Little Children*, *The Raising of Lazarus*, and *The Last Supper*. His most striking design was *Wise Men's Offering* from 1794. An almost blinding light radiates from the baby Jesus, while the three wise men with dark complexions place their gifts at the babe's feet.

As brilliant as he was, West went unappreciated in America. In the eighteenth century, no American on the continent witnessed his Chri art. None viewed the whites, pinks, grays, browns, reds, and blacks that made up the sacred's skin, clothes, and hair. In England, he was heralded by none other than King George III—the "tyrant" against whom the American colonists rebelled. George III commissioned West to develop his most impressive iconography at St. George's Chapel in Windsor Castle. There he created new stained-glass windows of Christ's life, death, resurrection, and ascension. West's experience reflected where Jesus stood as a visual presence in revolutionary America: portrayals of him came from outsiders, and if one wanted to gain notoriety for it, one pretty much had to leave.[2]

There were a host of reasons that West's art was foreign to America. Even as the colonies by the time of the Revolution had expanded in territory to more than 300,000 square miles, had grown tenfold in population to about 2.5 million, and were grinding down some 500,000 slaves with backbreaking labor, the colonies were still colonies. They were still beholden to Great Britain, provincial compared to European cities, and far behind the English in manufacturing and transportation capabilities. There was hardly a leisure or middle class that would have time or money to see such art. Iconoclasm was not dead, either. It remained a powerful force, and many Protestants continued to damn Jesus icons as insidious expressions of the apostate Catholic Church.[3]

But under the river, the riverbed was moving. Puritan iconoclasm was an effort to control religious ideas. It worked for a time but then backfired. With no reigning sacred image, Americans high and low, male and female, red, white, and black created their own. Those who wanted to see Jesus were so desperate that they began witnessing him in their dreams and experiences. An age of visions and visionaries replaced the era of iconoclasm and iconoclasts, and an egalitarian spiritual revolution overwhelmed the colonies just as much as a political one did.

Whiteness never dominated these visions of Jesus, and many of the visionaries were not white themselves. Native Americans and a new set of Protestant missionaries fixated on the redness of Christ, especially his bloodied and broken body. A growing number of African American Christians turned him into a universal and impartial savior who stood beyond and called against the confines of bondage. White Protestants, in turn, transformed him into a God of liberty for themselves, but not necessarily for others.

In this revolutionary age of visions and politics, Jesus had a complicated relationship to the emerging ideas of liberty. Everyone could behold his beauty. When they did, they saw him not in white but in blinding light.

Even when Christ's skin was rendered white, the redness of his blood and the devastation of his body seemed far more prominent. Redness, not whiteness, was what freedom or following Christ would take. Throughout the century and even into the American Revolution, whiteness had not yet become the legal arbiter of freedom or civic standing. African Americans and Native Americans were often the most vocal and courageous advocates of human rights. When they invoked Jesus politically, they demanded liberty with as much passion as Patrick Henry and as much eloquence as Thomas Jefferson.[4]

When white colonists made their political Revolution, Jesus was conspicuously absent—perhaps because he could embody too much liberty. He was brought into the whirlwind of war, but never as a central visual or ideological presence. As an embodied figure, Jesus offered nothing to the Revolution, except perhaps by way of contrast in which Protestant liberty was set against the demonic idolatry of the pope or King George III. For the new United States, a white Jesus was neither a mascot, nor a dominant lord, nor a sacred symbol of white authority. As a symbol of power, Christ's body had yet to take a racial form.

Great Awakenings and the Desire of Sacred Sight

The number of Americans who saw Jesus—either literally or metaphorically—grew dramatically in the eighteenth century. He came in dreams and spiritual experiences and sometimes visually on pieces of paper or canvas. Perhaps the tide turned as colonists encountered Native American spiritual visionaries. Perhaps some kind of insatiable human desire to see cosmic forces drove the shift. Perhaps the fact that icons were deemed off-limits made some colonists hunger for the forbidden fruit even more.

The Great Awakenings of the mid-eighteenth century certainly played a role. During these decades, revival fires swept up and down the American coastline. A new breed of itinerants such as George Whitefield preached a new emphasis on Christ's saving power. They brought their message to new locations such as the outdoors or in separatist churches. The awakeners were even called "new lights." Amid the heightened spiritual intensity, Americans red, white, and black reached out to God. Thousands looked to Jesus and started seeing him in numerous places and with a variety of faces.[5]

The Puritans were never able to contain Christ as much as they wanted. In fact, the fields of sacred vision were so open that several women looked to America as the location where they could proclaim themselves to be Jesus in one form or another. Quaker Jemima Wilkinson, the "universal Public Friend," said she had died and been resurrected. She was, to herself and to her followers, the reincarnation of Christ. Ann Lee, founder of the Shakers, did not exactly claim to be Jesus, but she did claim to be the female half of the messianic figure (or perhaps to be the second coming of Jesus). Pushing the gender boundaries of conceptions of Christ was dangerous work. Lee was imprisoned in 1780 and died shortly thereafter. Wilkinson established a colony in northwestern New York in 1790 but was later shunned by her own followers for being too greedy. These women were followed but were also forbidden.[6]

From the 1730s onward, the colonial world changed dramatically. New Protestant immigrants came who were more open than were the Puritans to visualizing the sacred. Revival fires made heaven seem visible. Desires to behold the sacred spread far and wide. Radical Baptist minister Isaac Backus confided time and again in his diary of his longing to "see" God and that he wanted so badly for the Lord to "appear."[7]

When colonists had visions of Christ and ministers damned them for it, they fixated on blood and violence. Congregationalist Jonathan Edwards in New England was frustrated that some "have had ideas of Christ's hanging on the cross, and his blood running from his wounds." He brushed off these visions. They "have nothing in them which is spiritual and divine." James McGready, a Presbyterian revivalist in the Middle Colonies, recorded similar stories with irritation. He wrote that those who saw Jesus in "something in the form of a man bleeding and dying on a cross" were dupes. "This is no view of Christ, but a deception of the Devil; for in a saving view of Christ, the object discovered is nothing which can be seen by the bodily eye, heard by the ear, or comprehended by the organs of sense; nor yet any ideal formed in the imagination."[8]

Even as he held these visions in contempt, McGready claimed that if one were to see Jesus, one would behold a "face, brighter than the light of ten thousand suns, spat upon, black and mangled, swelled with strokes and red with gore." In McGready's colorful rendering, Jesus was defined by light, black, and red—but not by white. It really did not matter anyway, McGready concluded, for no one would see. "The object is infinite and incomprehensible—only to be seen by the eye of understanding when enlightened by the Spirit of God."[9]

Complaints could not stop the people, though. For many colonial Americans, their visualized Jesus was not the devil in disguise. He was their savior, and proof came in blinding light. New England's James Robe reported that three women believed that they saw Jesus in "a great and glorious light, for a very short time."[10] In 1791, New York's Nathan Culver had a dream of traveling through heaven and hell with Christ as his guide. Jesus had "a bright shining light around him, which appeared brighter than the sun." Lutheran Jacob Ritter recalled a spiritual vision he had as a boy in which "there was no light of the sun or moon, but Christ was the light thereof."[11]

Light was not white. For colonial Americans, purity was not about color. It was about essence. Jesus as light connoted power, goodness, and love. He was, literally and figuratively, the light of the world. The color white, moreover, was not an unambiguous emblem of purity. As a color in dreams, white was considered an evil omen. The *Universal Dream-Dictionary* of 1795 claimed that in dreams, white or pale skin connoted "a sign of trouble, poverty and death." It was a "black face" that meant "long life." According to Jonathan Edwards, white was not even God's favorite color. "Green, being the most pleasing color, and above all others easy and healthful to the eye, is a fit symbol of grace and mercy with which God is surrounded."[12]

The lack of association between Jesus and whiteness left the spiritual terrain open to linking other colors and peoples to the sacred. Quaker John Churchman, in fact, saw the angelic in Native American skin. In 1757, just before he was to travel to a treaty meeting with Indians in Pennsylvania, he had a dream in which he "saw a light before me towards sun-rising, which did not appear to be a common light, but soon observed the appearance of something therein." Within the light was an angel "encompassed with a brightness like a rainbow." It "stood still in the midst of many curious stacks of corn; it was of a human form about seven feet high (as I thought,) and smiling on me." After waking up, Churchman remembered "the complexion of this angelic apparition, which was not much different from one of the Indians clean washed from his grease and filth." Although Churchman revealed his deep cultural chauvinism by associating natives with dirt, he took from the vision two clear lessons: The sacred could inhabit any likeness, and God considered all people equally. "I was made to believe it was not unreasonable to conclude, that the Lord was in them by his good Spirit, and that all colours were equal to him, who gave life and being to all mankind."[13]

Just as many white Protestants reached out with eyes of faith to see Jesus, a growing number of Native Americans and African Americans along the East Coast began to behold Jesus too. Whiteness never dominated their encounters either, and these colonial Christs were far more likely to be seen as bathed in glorious light or in ravaged red. The eighteenth-century American Jesus figures were not emblems of white supremacy but agents of dynamic exchange made through cross-cultural encounters.

Bathed in Blood

Revival fires burned so widely and with so much ferocity that they blazed into Indian territory and created what scholars now call an "Indian Great Awakening." White missionaries of the age believed they were in the midst of a movement that John Eliot would have envied. In these decades, Jesus came in power and might. He also came bathed in blood.

Whites marveled at the advent of Indian conversions. On eastern Long Island, itinerant minister Azariah Horton found Indians ready for him to "show them the Way of Reconciliation by Jesus Christ." He spoke with one woman who communicated "a lively Sense of her actual Sins, and bewailed them exceedingly; a deep Sense of the Plague Enmity of her heart; of the Insufficiency she labored under to help herself; that if Christ did not save her, she must perish; that the Lord Jesus appeared to her exceedingly lovely; and that the Load of Guilt she felt before, was now gone; and that she felt Light." Unlike earlier Puritans, Horton was ecstatic to hear this conversion testimony. He welcomed her into the Christian fold.[14]

Gradually, almost insensibly, the white missionaries and the Indians moved closer together in embracing the kinds of dreams and visions that McGready and Edwards reported on with frustration. Hezekiah Niles admitted that as he led churches of native converts, he looked to the "Guidence of Feelings, Impressions, Visions, Appearances, and Directions of Angels and of Christ himself in a Visionary Way." Joseph Johnson, an Indian convert and minister, recounted a dream in which he saw "the likeness of a lamb that had been Slain, Standing at the foot of my Couch." The sight awakened him, but the lamb was still there. "No sooner I awoke but got directly up, and Dressed me and followed the Blessed Lamb out, and there I worshipped him. It was Jesus Christ." The mysteriously invisible and questionable Jesus of Eliot's *Indian Dialogues* had now become visible.[15]

This Indian Great Awakening produced some of the earliest published Native American theological and autobiographical writings. By writing for themselves in Christian idioms, Indian authors created a new language and means of critiquing English colonialism. They also developed their own ways of explaining who Jesus was for themselves and others. Christ stood at the center of these emerging theologies, literatures, and songs not as a power who upheld white dominance but as a wounded savior of Indian women and men.

The best example was Samson Occom, a Mohegan. He was a pioneer of Native American literature, a defender of Indian rights, and the author of poetry and hymns that spoke to the experience of Christian Indians. Fascinated by Great Awakening preachers, Occom was troubled that he could not read the Bible for himself. So he "began to Learn the English Letters; got me a Primer, and used to go to my English Neighbours frequently for Assistance in Reading, but went to no School." Then, he discovered "the way of Salvation through Jesus Christ, and was enabl'd to put my trust in him alone for Life & Salvation."[16]

Occom's subsequent career was troubled. His erstwhile mentor, Elezear Wheelock, who tutored him when he was a teenager, sent his prize convert on fund-raising missions to England. Occom was there to obtain funds for Moor's Indian Charity School, a college for Indian youths, but later the college moved to New Hampshire, became Dartmouth College, and began admitting whites. Occom felt tricked. The donations were supposed to support a school for Indians, not a college for whites. As he witnessed how whites treated Native Americans and African Americans and as he confronted theological notions that the Bible cursed people of color, Occom began associating the two disempowered groups and turning moral attacks back against whites.

Occom crafted a morality of naming religious hypocrisy in the form of racial mistreatment. He concluded that the spiritual thoughts and physical actions of whites proved their debasement, not that of people of color: "When I come to Consider and See the Conduct of the Most Learned, Polite, and Rich Nations of the World, I find them to be the Most Tyranacal, Cruel, and inhuman oppressors of their Fellow Creatures in the World. . . . They are the Nations, that inslave the poor Negroes in Such Barbarous manner, as out do the Savage Indians in North America, and these are Calld Christian Nations."[17]

Occom may have given up on Wheelock and other white Protestants, but never on Jesus. His Christ was not a white man like the ones around him. Among the subjects Occom studied in England was the emerging art of hymnody. The Great Awakening had encouraged the transition from the older psalmody (where congregations sang the psalms with little passion or change of tone) to more congregational, democratic practices of group singing. Occom trained Mohegans in the art of group hymnody. Occom found that his people were "greatly delighted and edified with Singing."

They have the "most Melodious Voices of any People," Occom explained to one white benefactor, and the "Indians in their Religious Meetings round about here, Sing more than any Christians and they have frequent meetings in all Indian towns." In 1774, Occom published *A Choice Collection of Hymns and Spiritual Songs; Intended for the Edification of All Sincere Christians, of All Denomination*. It included 109 texts of hymns (not including tunes) and was one of the first American hymnals that was not merely a reprint or slight adaptation of an English original.[18]

Occom brought his hymn-singing innovations to the new Christian Indian community he helped to form at Brothertown, New York. Residents sang through the week and during important ritual events such as the corn harvest. Personally authoring the lyrics to at least six hymns, Occom softened the harshly judgmental God of the Puritans and replaced him with a savior who cared for Indians, who embraced them, and whose trials seemed familiar to Indian peoples. As one song rang,

> Jesus laid aside his Robes
> That you may lay aside your sobs . . .
> Come away, come to thy Home
> Come away to thy bridegroom.

"The Suffering's of Christ" may have been Occom's best song. It was subtitled "Throughout the Saviour's Life We Trace," and for it Occom adopted a Mohegan spiritual motif of the beautiful path. Christ's trail ran from Gethsemane to the cross. Occom fixated on the physical details of Christ's suffering—the cold ground of Gethsemane, the chilly sweat, and the "Blood [that] drops through every Pore." According to literary historian Joanna Brooks, for Occom, "Christ's path encompasses experiences familiar to tribal communities: criminalization, forced displacement, and state-sponsored violence." Jesus was bathed in the red of colonization, but he also salved the wounds of that violence. As Brooks concludes, "Occom did not presume to assign colonialist motives to God, or Godly motives to colonialism." He believed that a "strange providence" beyond human comprehension made him an Indian and then made him a Christian too. Only the divinely suffering figure of Jesus could make sense of the contradictions.[19]

Samson Occom and his fellow Christians of New England practiced a relatively restrained spirituality in comparison to the one cultivated, shared, and exchanged by the Moravians and their small band of native converts in Connecticut, New York, and the Middle Colonies. For them, Jesus was a visible presence whose blood brought salvation. When these Protestants arrived in the Middle Colonies, they worked with Indians to fashion a new Jesus. The red of his blood, not the tone of his skin, defined this Christ.

The Moravians were a pietistic Protestant sect persecuted throughout Europe for their rejection of Catholicism and their embrace of everyday people. They first came to the British colonies in 1735 and immediately lit their candles as part of the Great Awakening fires. In Connecticut and the Middle Colonies, they drew native converts with a new message: Christ's salvation could come through touching his physical wounds and drinking the bodily fluids oozing from them. Their "blood-and-wounds" theology was far more successful than anything the Puritans had offered to Indians, and in their encounters with Indians, a red Christ emerged in colonial America.

Moravians never shied from visual representations of Christ or picturesque language in their hymns and teachings. In fact, they delighted in the blood and wounds of the crucifixion. As their "Litany of Wounds," introduced in 1744 in Bethlehem, Pennsylvania, put it, "Hail! Lamb of God. Christ, Have mercy! Glory to the side wound!" "Powerful wounds of Jesus, So moist and gory, bleed on my heart so that I may remain brave and like the wounds."[20]

Indians reached by the Moravians loved the imagery of blood. In the early 1740s, a Mahican sachem named Wassamapah (or, more commonly, Tschoop) described his conversion to the godfather of the Moravians, Count Nicholas Von Zinzendorf:

> My first feeling in my heart was from his blood and when I heard that he was also the Saviour of the Heathen and that I did owe him my heart I felt a drawing towards him in my heart. . . . Untill our teacher came and told us of the Lamb of God, who shed his blood and died for us blind and cursed men. I wondered at it and as often as I heard a preaching of it, I thought, there must be something in it, for my heart got every time warmed by it. I did often dream as if our teacher did stand before me and did preach to me of the blood of our Saviour, and I longed in the morning for his coming to me, that I could tell him my dream.

Later, he came to understand more fully that "I should give my wicked heart to the Savior and let him wash it with blood."[21]

This was a savior bathed in red. His bloody image begged adoration rather than desecration. Tschoop could not forget the words of the brave

Unknown artist, *Crucifixion of Jesus with Brothers, Sisters and Children of the Moravian Church under the Cross* (c. 1750). Aquarelle on paper, 185 × 135 mm. Courtesy of the Moravian Archives, Herrnhut, TS Mp.375.9.

missionary who came to him: "They constantly recurred to my mind. Even when I was asleep, I dreamt of that blood which Christ shed for us." Tschoop's meditation on the blood of Christ led to an awakening among the Mahicans of New York and the establishment of a Moravian Indian community at Shekomeko. The Moravians also successfully won Indian converts in Connecticut. There, hymns translated into the dialect of the Pachgatgoch Indians dwelled lovingly on the blood and wounds of Jesus, which were "warm," "hot," "beautiful," "sweet," "are today still open." They sang in Germanic meter and melody, but with Pachgatgoch words:

> Beautiful wounds of Jesus
> I love you
> Nothing now do I love
> but the blood.[22]

This Jesus paralleled New England Natives' notions of the *Manitou* as a physically and spiritually present higher power. They saw Jesus sitting in trees, guiding hunts, and most of all bleeding his love profusely over his children. Newly baptized Indians spoke of how "my Heart again hungers very much after the Flesh & Blood of our Savr."

One Mahican woman thought Christ's blood could heal her sick baby, and she imagined his blood flowing from her breasts: "When I give my child suck and I think about the blood and wounds of our Savior I feel my heart sometimes very wet and so I think my child sucks the blood of our Savior and I feel the angels look after me and my child." She prayed that the Savior would give fellow villagers a "feeling of his blood and wounds in their hearts."[23]

Bloody breast milk was but one way Christ's redness nourished the natives. The blood was a power, and his torn side was far more vital than his face, hair, nose, or eyes. One woman declared that "her Heart lov'd the Side Hole very much & wish'd to sink yet deeper into it." Another woman brightened on hearing they would travel to the Moravian mission town: "We shall certainly have the Blood of our Savr. there." The thought allowed her to pass through illness and feel restored. She might have sung this verse in Delaware: "Dearest Side-hole! I do covet thy warm Blood above all Things. O thou art the most beloved of all other Wound-hole-Springs. Side-hole's Blood, bedew me! Cover and go thro' me! Take thy Course thro' all my Veins, Heart and Reins, so that nought unbath'd remains." Indian converts of the Moravians composed prayers and hymns in which they yearned to "drink the juice" of his "bloody wounds" and "become strong."[24]

The Moravian message spread to the Delaware and other native peoples in the Middle Colonies. In 1753, Nanticoke and Shawnee warriors visiting Bethlehem, Pennsylvania, "examined pictures of the crucified Christ in the Single Brother's house and responded with awe: 'do look, how many wounds he has, how much blood flows forth! I have also heard lately from the Brethren, that he was very sick, & prayed, & then sweat very much; that his sweat ran like blood from his body." Jesus' blood was a source of physical and spiritual power that could be transferred to human bodies through consumption. Jesus was on the one hand a female figure with a bloody opening that seemed eerily similar to a vagina and on the other hand an "ultimate warrior captive" who sweated blood and remained stoic under torture.[25]

Across the continent, in California, Jesus came in blood too—but this time the blood was spilled and embodied by natives themselves. Beginning in 1769 and extending to Mexican state secularization and dispersal of properties in 1832, a small population of Franciscans and soldiers erected twenty missions stretching hundreds of miles, from San Diego in the south to Sonoma in the north. Their goal was to "reduce" and Christianize the natives, who, in their gratitude, would become a faithful labor force and secure the borderlands of the Spanish empire against European competitors.

The initial leader was Father Junipero Serra. By his death in 1784, he was managing eighteen missionaries and nine missions. His successor, Father Fermín Francisco, expanded the efforts to forty priests and eighteen missions by 1803. The neophyte population tripled from about 5,000 to just over 15,000, but overall the Indians were "reduced" from a population of around 65,000 in the coastal areas in 1769 to 17,000 by 1832. The numbers kept declining, and the result was a near elimination of California Indians.[26]

Serra wanted to create a pristine Christian system in the wilderness that would make way for Christ's second coming. Indians saw it as a choice "between Christ and death." Those who remained outside the missions lived in a world fundamentally altered by the Spanish presence, while those who chose baptism and life in the missions lived in a world of "churchly captivity." They were wards of the missions and children to the priestly fathers.[27]

In this constellation of conquest and engagement, the friars viewed themselves as fathers and the Indians as children. Only through physical discipline could these Indian "sons" be taught the gospel and their rightful place. And the model of accepting divine discipline was the Son of God himself. Submitting to discipline, as the fathers conceived it, mimicked participating in the passion of Christ. "The normal thing for a devout missionary to have done when he wanted a reluctant neophyte to accept a whipping of one or two dozen strokes was simply to point to a Spanish crucifix," historian Francis Guest explained, "particularly one that portrayed the horrors of Christ's death in forceful and graphic fashion. For the neophyte, associating his humiliation with that of Christ in a spirit of penance would have provided him with the religious motivation he needed to withstand the indignity of the ordeal."[28]

Religious paintings and prints reinforced the lessons, but what resulted was a confusing mishmash of religious syncretism. Franciscans relied heavily on image representations of the *via crucis* (stations of the cross). Hung in mission churches and distributed to Indian converts, prints of Jesus and the saints communicated Christ's passion in a way that poorly understood Spanish could not. The friars tried to do the same by placing crosses at the missions and along the roads of Alta California, marking the landscape with sacred reminders of the passion of the Christ. The resemblance of the crosses to the prayer poles of the California natives (akin to the prayer sticks of Puebloans in New Mexico) confused the religious message. Intending to appease the spirit inhabiting the prayer pole so that "it might not be angry with them," Indians visiting the crosses placed broken arrows at their bases and hung sardines and deer meat on the crossbars.[29]

Spanish Catholics could never have imagined that some Latinos, Indians, and mestizos in the Southwest would take the disciplined Christ and refashion him into a badge of brotherhood with Los Hermanos de Nuestro Padre Jesus Nazareno, popularly (and notoriously) known as the Penitentes. Originating probably in the eighteenth century and continuing to the present day, in spite of consistent opposition from church leaders, the Penitentes gained fame for their yearly ritual of men carrying the cross of Christ down roads while lashing themselves in extreme acts of unction. By the early nineteenth century, the Penitentes mystified Mexican colonial religious authorities. When a future bishop of Durango toured New Mexico in 1833, he warned against them: "I prohibit those Brotherhoods of Penance—or more accurately of Butchery." Pastors and church administrators, he ordered, should ensure that "not a single one of these Brotherhoods remains and that there is no storeroom or other place to keep those huge crosses or other instruments of mortification which some men half kill their bodies, which at the same time they take no care of their souls, leaving themselves in sin for years on end." Moderate penance was good and healthy, but illegal Brotherhoods that encouraged bodily excess were sinful: "Let every man whom the Good Spirit calls to do so take up the usual instruments, which bespeak mortification rather than self-destruction; but let them wield them in privacy."

The critics were fighting a futile battle. In many isolated rural communities, the Brothers of Blood (younger Penitente members primarily responsible for carrying out the excruciating ceremonies) and Brothers of Light (older and revered Brothers no longer required to do their penances) effectively were the church. With no priest or perhaps one visiting on occasion, and with many of the other institutions of civil society largely inaccessible to relatively poor and isolated New Mexicans, the Brotherhoods provided communal bonds that were essential. They served as informal courts for law and order, took care of burials, looked after the sick, and negotiated with outside authorities when necessary. Most of all, they expressed a devotion to Jesus that placed the savior squarely within the context of their own culture. In the Spanish Southwest, worshipping the savior involved penance to a Jesus depicted as one who suffered an agonizing death on a cross.[30]

Jesus was a power among Indians, but often still a limited presence. Whether in California, Pennsylvania, or New England, most Native Americans continued to identify with older tribal faiths and had little or nothing to do with Christ. Moreover, by the middle of the eighteenth century, white missionaries began hearing new native origin tales in which "Indians" had separate creations, gods, religions, and heavens from the "whites" or "blacks."

The older view of human and spiritual interaction, in which each tribe had its own origin and in which many different groups of people vied for power, was now being reduced to a few racial categories that were different in this world and would be separate in the next. John Heckewelder, a Moravian missionary, spoke with one Indian seer who said that the Great Spirit allowed him "to take a peep into the heavens, of which there were three: one for the Indians, one for the Negroes, and another for the white people." The Indian heaven was "the happiest of the three," and the white one was "the unhappiest." Whites were being chastised "for their ill treatment of the Indians, and for possessing themselves of the land which God had given to them. They were also punished for making beasts of the negroes, by selling them as the Indians do their horses and dogs."[31]

Before Jesus rose to dominance as a white figure in America, he was red. Bloodied and beaten, the crucified Christ became for many Native Americans a symbol of their experiences. If the sacred bled, then their bleeding could be meaningful as well. In the process, Indians embraced new theologies that challenged the actions of white invaders and oppressors. Beginning to crystallize was a shared sense of Indian-ness, and the role Jesus would play in that new identity would be further transformed in the nineteenth-century battles over land, identity, and autonomy.

African Americans and the Christ of Liberty

As a small-but-significant cohort of Native Americans moved toward Christ, so too did a charter generation of African Americans. Whites were fascinated and alarmed to see so many black Americans reaching out to the Christian God. One critic of the Great Awakenings, Charles Chauncy, griped that among the revivalist exhorters were "indeed young Persons, sometimes Lads or rather Boys: Nay, Women and Girls; yea, Negroes, have taken upon them to do the Business of Preachers."[32] The numbers were impressive, but most slaves were not Christians as of 1800. By 1786, the 2,000 black members of the Methodist Church were about 10 percent of the church in America. By 1797, there were almost 20,000, constituting 25 percent of the denomination. The story and scale were similar among Baptists; African Americans were one out of every four Baptists in the United States.[33]

As racialized chattel slavery rose and as colonial law increasingly associated blackness with perpetual servility, this small group of African American slaves and free blacks turned to Christ and found in him a universal savior. Theirs was neither a white Jesus nor a confining one. They sanctified liberation through Jesus in opposition to the laws of men and society.

Many slaves longed for salvation here and hereafter. John Wesley encountered a slave woman who wanted to know where Jesus was amid their lives. She asked, "When shall the Sun of Righteousness arise on these outcasts of men, with healing in His Wings?" Wesley's answer was the hope of heaven, where, if she put her faith in Jesus, she would "want nothing, and have whatever you can desire. No one will beat or hurt you there. You will never be sick. You will never be sorry any more, nor afraid of anything."[34]

Some slaves did not want to be afraid in this world either. Richard Allen, born a slave in Delaware in 1760, was one of them. He first found "mercy through the blood of Christ" at about age twenty. Immediately, he began talking about Jesus, God, and salvation. He spoke to anyone who would listen—white or black, free or slave. With time (and a new owner who thought religion made slaves better, not worse), Allen accumulated enough money to purchase his freedom. Now the freedom of his body joined that of his soul. For all of it he thanked "my dear Lord," who allowed him to "buy my time and enjoy my liberty." Allen then traveled with Francis Asbury and became a founder of an all-black church in Philadelphia in the 1790s. Allen and his compatriots proudly identified their new denomination with religious and racial markers. As officially christened in 1816, they were the "African Methodist Episcopal Church."[35]

Although never with as much dedication as with Indians, Moravians took their blood theology to Africans and their descendants as well. One well-traveled convert, part of a remarkable set of black Christians from the African diaspora, was Rebecca Protten. Raised on St. Thomas Island in the Caribbean, Rebecca was attracted to Moravianism in the 1730s. Probably like many other slaves, she was drawn to the fascination with blood. Many West Africans and their descendants saw blood as a purifying agent. Her devotion to the wounded savior led her to become the first black woman ordained in Western Christianity. Like Benjamin West, she reversed the migratory pattern and ventured across the Atlantic Ocean to Europe and then to Africa as a missionary. By the time of her death in 1780, Rebecca had ministered on three continents.[36]

Before the nineteenth century, it is difficult to find any African American referring to Jesus as white, or by any particular color. When eighteenth-century missionaries brought the message of Christ to slaves, they did so largely without visual images, and churches catering to slaves had no iconography.[37] Those who had the opportunity to record their views of Christ also avoided whiteness and focused on Christ's brightness. Phillis Wheatley described Jesus as having "auspicious rays" that "shine" around his head.[38] Born a slave in Maryland in 1766, "Old Elizabeth" recalled as a young girl seeing Jesus. A heavenly guide first took her through hell and then up to heaven. She saw Christ and was overcome by light. "I thought I was permitted to look straight forward, and saw the Saviour standing with His hand stretched out to receive me. An indescribably glorious light was *in* Him." Jesus beckoned to her, and at "this moment I felt that my sins were forgiven me." The light of Jesus was transferred to her. "I felt filled with light and love." From that moment, Old Elizabeth began to preach, and in the sixty years following her emancipation at the age of thirty, she addressed black audiences, white audiences, and even a number of interracial ones.[39]

These were the early beginnings of black Christianities in the United States—Methodist and Moravian, disciplined and ecstatic, pietistic and visionary, for slaves and for the free, for women and for men. African Americans looked for some structure or worldview beyond their enslavement. They looked for some power that could stand against the powers of whites. As diverse as they were, many found that power in Jesus.

A Tangible Christ

In this age of visions and visionaries in which so many white, red, and black Americans were seeing Jesus, some began more freely to use and appreciate physical renderings of the Son of God. Those who had the courage to paint or depict Jesus presented him as a suffering savior, as one who bled, agonized, and died. Those Americans who saw visual images of Jesus in the colonial era (and the numbers were few) beheld the divine as devastated. Only occasionally did anyone overtly or explicitly consider Jesus to be white, and that was usually not his main attribute.

Slowly, a few Englishmen and colonists began to hope that the Publius Lentulus forgery was historically accurate. At Cambridge University in England, professor and minister Benjamin Whichcote claimed that the Publius Lentulus letter was "an Eye-witness" account of "the Man Jesus." Several Quakers had copies of the translated Lentulus letter in their libraries, and in the Americas one dissident grew a beard and parted it in the middle. Presumably, he was modeling himself after the letter's description.[40]

Where the Publius Lentulus fraud was accepted, white supremacy was not far behind. Ezra Stiles, a young minister in Rhode Island who would later become the president of Yale University, wrote in his journal in 1772, "This Letter in Latin I have not seen. It is generally considered a Forgery." A fraud or not, Stiles was drawn to the description: "I see nothing in it but what would be natural for an observant Proconsul to write; and it seems to be in the free epistolary way." Just as Stiles wanted a white Jesus, he also wanted an all-white America. Shortly after the American Revolution, Stiles prophesied that there would be neither blacks nor Indians in the new nation: "We are increasing with great rapidity; and the *Indians*, as well as the millions of *Africans* in America, are decreasing *as rapidly*. Both left to themselves, in this way diminishing, may gradually vanish; and thus an unrighteous SLAVERY may at length, in God's good providence, be abolished."[41]

A handful of colonists moved from dreams and visions to tangible Christ art. On these occasions, Jesus was white-skinned but never a dominating hero. He was most often a murdered savior. Scottish Presbyterians, who influenced the founding of the Middle Colonies, were similar to Moravians in dwelling on the physical sufferings of Christ. John Flavel's seventeenth-century book, *The Cursed Death of the Cross Described and Comfortably Improved*, carried a woodcut within it of Christ's crucifixion. In a busy painted woodcut, *Das neue Jerusalem*, German immigrants to Pennsylvania had two visual representations of Christ—one as crucified martyr and the other as heralded king. In neither image were Christ's features easy to recognize, although it was clear he had a beard.[42]

A few painters tried their hands as well. They were principally influenced by European artwork, especially the Italian Renaissance. None, however, gained a large following in the New World. Painter Johann Valentin Haidt emigrated to America in 1754 after spending time in Rome and England. A Moravian, he produced several crucifixion portraits. He bragged that by 1767, "almost all the congregations have some of my work." In Haidt's *First Fruits*, Jesus returned in glory. Light radiated from behind him. He was white and had brown hair and an extremely short beard. He also exposed his chest and stomach to reveal his wounds. An Indian stood at his left hand, while a black man held onto the savior's left leg. On the earth's ground, black men, women, and children stood ready to embrace the sav-

John [Johann] Valentine Haidt, *Lamentation over the Body of Christ* (1758). Oil on canvas, 25 × 30 inches. Courtesy of the Moravian Historical Society, Nazareth, Pennsylvania.

ior. Although white, this savior was bathed in light, embraced by black, and flanked by red.[43]

John Trumbull studied under Benjamin West in London and then in 1793 produced *Christ under the Cross (or Our Savior Bearing the Cross and Sinking under Its Weight)*. Beneath a crowd of Roman guards, prisoners, and grieving women, Jesus falls to the ground. He is pale, dark-haired, and bearded. Unlike the other prisoners, he is clothed and looks faint.

But Trumbull's experience was akin to his mentor's—he was unappreciated in America. Whether being presented with the sophisticated paintings of West, Trumbull, and Haidt or the cruder etchings of the Moravians or Lutherans, most colonial Americans responded the same. They largely ignored or opposed those images. Most early Americans and artists agreed with painter Washington Alliston: "I may here observe that the universal failure of all painters, ancient and modern, in their attempts to give even a tolerable idea of the Saviour, has now determined me never to attempt it. Besides, I think his character too holy and sacred to be attempted by the pencil."[44]

Throughout the mid-eighteenth century, many American Protestants continued to link their iconoclasm with their religious and political rivalries with Catholicism. Moravian use of Jesus imagery led colonists to worry that Moravians were closet Catholics. In the early 1740s, English officials marched on an Indian community in western Connecticut and cross-examined Moravian missionaries, who allegedly had "the picture of our Saviour in it & the cross." Fearing that the Moravians were Catholics in disguise and that their preaching would inflame native passions against the colonists, the Connecticut General Assembly passed a law "providing relief against the Evil & Dangerous designs of foreigners & Suspected persons." The Moravians stood accused of making "ignorance the Mother of Religion as the Romans." An opponent of the new revivalism put his complaints simply: The approved method of indoctrination started with God's existence, moved to man's sin, "and finally told them 'of Jesus Christ & etc.'" But the Moravians reversed the order. They started with "Jesus Crucifyed" and then moved to sin and justification through faith.[45] By putting the bloody Jesus first in theory and image, Moravians had upset the Puritan order.

The eighteenth-century colonies experienced an age of visions but not one of icons. The population grew, diversified, moved, and mingled. New sects mixed with diverse peoples, and time and again Jesus appeared in visions and dreams. He came in the Awakening and appeared to slaves and the free, to women and men. He came to many Indians bathed in red blood, and to others he was defined not by white but by light. A few artists began painting him and were influenced by European traditions, but their number was small and their impact even smaller. Then in the 1770s, Jesus took backstage as the fires of revolution consumed British North America.

The Christless Constitution

The American Revolution was a momentous event, and Jesus was both part of and limited in the action. Anti-Catholic iconoclasm was brought into the political whirlwind of the 1760s and 1770s. Shortly after the Boston Tea Party, a Connecticut pastor declared that a Catholic conspiracy was behind the new British taxes and controls. If the British succeeded, disaster would strike. The colonists would have their Bibles taken from them, and they would be compelled to "pray to the Virgin Mary, worship images, [and] believe the doctrine of Purgatory, and the Pope's infallibility." There was no way the heirs of Puritanism would stand for such political oppression and idolatrous villainy.[46]

Throughout the colonies, fears abounded that the British were trying to "enslave" the colonists and lord over them with tyrannical laws. In response, about one-third of the colonists banded together, declared their independence, and set the world afire in a fight for independence. Jesus was part of the Revolution and the formation of the United States, but not as much as one might expect. As a physical presence, he was almost completely absent. And in the language of law and legislation for the new republic, he was virtually nonexistent. In comparison to how prominent Jesus would become in the United States of the nineteenth and twentieth centuries, the Revolution and the founding of the new nation were profoundly Christless.

Without doubt, Jesus was an important presence in the revolutionary age. During the Great Awakening, a stamp distributor in Philadelphia complained that revivalist preachers were defying British rule and preaching that they would obey "no King but King Jesus." After the Boston Massacre, one minister told his congregants that they should be willing to fill the "streets with blood" because their rights came not from Parliament but from the "blood" of Christ. During the war itself, chaplains encouraged the troops to remember that it was "Christ Jesus, who came to give freedom to the world." Jesus was there, too, among political thinkers. Philadelphia's Benjamin Rush, a friend to many of the other founders, wrote that he "always considered Christianity as the *strong ground* of Republicanism."[47]

To many of the founding fathers, as historian Stephen Prothero has shown, Jesus was an "enlightened sage." His moral teachings and selfless examples instructed Americans in a political code of how to make their new republican government survive and thrive. Thomas Jefferson considered Christ's moral message so profound (although buried under centuries of church dogma) that he constructed his own gospel. He took scissors and literally clipped out the miraculous and supernatural stories of the New Testament. What remained in Jefferson's Bible was a pieced-together tale of Christ's ethics and morals.

But for Jefferson, this was addition by subtraction. It was construction by destruction. He thought he could have more of the true Jesus by having fewer of the stories presented in the Bible. Jefferson also kept this enterprise hidden—yet another of his many life secrets, which included sexual liaisons and children with slaves he owned. The removal of passages and the clandestine nature of Jefferson's Bible were emblematic of the nature of Jesus in the Revolution. Christ was limited, often at a distance, and even removable.[48]

In considering the political forces operating around them, colonists seemed far more likely to consider the Antichrist than the Christ. The Antichrist was the ominous presence in the Book of Revelation whose mayhem came before Christ's second coming. As the British tried in vain to tax and legislate the colonies, many Americans bristled that the Antichrist was working its wickedness through Britain. At first, Protestants mindful of the end-times thought the French carried the spirit of the Antichrist. During the Seven Years' War, one American chaplain explained to his troops, "Antichrist must fall before the end comes. . . . The French now adhere and belong to Antichrist, wherefore it is to be hoped, that when Antichrist falls, they shall fall with him." Then British opposition to colonial freedom became attached to the Antichrist. One pamphlet from 1777 determined that the numbers 666 were somehow in the Hebrew and Greek words for "Great Britain" and "Royal Supremacy," while others associated the British with "the beast" and the "whore of Babylon."[49]

Christ was almost completely absent in the core founding documents and places of the United States. He is not mentioned in the Declaration of Independence. Tom Paine never mentioned Jesus in *Common Sense* (1776); neither did the author of *Letters from a Farmer in Pennsylvania* (1767–68). Even the evangelical Patrick Henry failed to speak the name of Christ in his "Give Me Liberty" speech. Jesus makes no appearance in the Articles of Confederation or the Constitution. John Jay, Alexander Hamilton, and James Madison never invoked his name in their Federalist Papers. In the first twenty annual presidential addresses, neither George Washington, nor John Adams, nor Thomas Jefferson uttered the name Jesus or Christ. When the new American capital of Washington, D.C., emerged slowly from the marshes of Virginia, moreover, Jesus was nonexistent as a physical presence. There were no statues or paintings of him there.[50]

Christ did come up in state constitutions, legal battles, and some treaties, but not always in the affirmative. Several new state constitutions mandated that officeholders profess a belief in the divinity of Christ, but a treaty with Tripoli in 1796 declared that "the government of the United States is not in any sense founded on the Christian religion."[51]

If anyone connected Christ with political liberty in the nation, it was African Americans. Charges of white religious hypocrisy animated their political pushes for freedom. In Massachusetts, for instance, a group of blacks petitioned for liberty by using Jesus as Samson Occom had—as a symbol of white hypocrisy. In 1777, they lamented that they lived in the "bowels of a free & Christian Country" but were treated unjustly and cruelly. They rhetorically asked how they could be condemned to slavery by people who professed to follow the "mild religion of Jesus." To them, the answer was simple. True Christians would never enslave others, especially not other Christ followers. And hence, white Americans were not true believers.[52]

These Massachusetts slaves understood not only white hypocrisy but also white avoidance of the presence and teachings of Jesus. The Constitution was Christless. So was the capitol building. So were most founding documents. And even though Thomas Jefferson reduced Christ's teachings to its morals and ethics, he did so only in privacy, and he clearly did not apply the Sermon on the Mount or the Golden Rule to his dealings with slaves.

Jesus was not the mascot of the American Revolution, and he was not a dominant hero visualized with a white face. Jesus was certainly important for the ways some Americans applied his teachings and spirit to their political situations and agendas, but in comparison to other figures and ideologies, he seemed an afterthought at best. If anyone was making the Son of God a son of liberty, it was African Americans and Native Americans.

ALMOST THREE DECADES after the American Revolution, Russian diplomat Pavel Svinin came to the new United States and was amazed to find sacred images everywhere. In homes, in civic spaces, and in businesses, he kept running into the same icon. It was not Jesus, though. It was George Washington. "It was noteworthy that every American considers it his sacred duty to have a likeness of Washington in his home," Svinin explained, "just as we have images of God's saints. . . . Washington's portrait is the finest and sometimes the sole decoration of American homes."[53]

In the new United States, Americans had images of Washington, but not of Jesus. Most had never viewed paintings or etchings of Christ. Their parents, grandparents, and great-grandparents had probably never seen a visual representation of God's son. If they had, it was at most a small and crucified figure with few details. Churches remained without paintings, murals, stained-glass windows, or other visual imagery. The iconoclastic world the Puritans had made was still, in part, with Americans. Benjamin West became a master painter, but not for Americans. When they witnessed Christ, they saw blinding light or fixated on the red blood of his torn body. The connections between whiteness, Christ, and power had yet to be made, mass-produced, and mass-marketed.

The story of how Jesus became an emblem of the nation and white supremacy was one for the nineteenth century. The new white Jesus was supposed to bring unity and Christianity to a young nation growing and defining its citizens, inventing new religions and revealing new sacred stories, building new kinds of roads, inventing new gins to cultivate cotton, enslaving more black people, and pushing red people further west. But on the unsteady terrain that was the infant United States, the white Jesus was torn asunder as the nation itself fractured only eighty years after its independence. The white American Christ born in the early nineteenth century became a figure Americans have been glorifying and fighting over ever since.

CHAPTER THREE

FROM LIGHT TO WHITE
IN THE EARLY REPUBLIC

When it came time to codify his new revelation, Joseph Smith turned to a revolutionary innovation of the American Constitution: religious liberty. "[We] claim the privilege of worshiping Almighty God according to the dictates of our own conscience," he and the new Church of Jesus Christ of Latter-day Saints proclaimed in their 1842 articles of faith. "[We] allow all men the same privilege, let them worship how, where, or what they may." Americans of Smith's era were following the first part but not the second half of this instruction. They robustly embraced the direction of their consciences but then tried to force their faiths down the throats of others. What appeared to some as the flowering of religious democracy was to others nothing more than ecclesiastical chaos and irreconcilable conflict. This was how Smith had felt only a few decades earlier as a teenager. Coming of age in upstate New York, he had struggled with Protestant diversity. "My mind at times was greatly excited," he explained, because each group claimed that it was right and that the others were wrong. The Presbyterians bashed the Baptists and Methodists, while those two "were equally zealous in endeavoring to establish their own tenets and disprove all others."

Smith had only one option: "Ask of God," and in 1820 he did. Like other evangelicals of his day, he trekked into the forest, found a quiet place, and prayed. Then it happened. God appeared. He answered that Joseph should join none of the sects, and even better, God introduced him to Jesus.

Twelve years later, in 1832, Smith wrote, edited, and rewrote the tale of his vision. He strained to find the most accurate phrases, oftentimes crossing out words or including new ones above the line. He saw a "piller of fire." Or, rather, he did not see fire, and crossed that word out, but "light." It was a "piller of ~~fire~~ light above the brightness of the sun at noon day come down from above and rested upon me." Joseph continued to reduce to ink on paper the glory his eyes had witnessed: "I saw the Lord and he spake unto me saying Joseph thy Sins are forgiven thee." That was not exactly right either. He saw the "crucifyed Lord" who actually said, "Joseph my Son thy Sins are forgiven thee." Jesus had come in the brightest of lights, and the Son of God had called Joseph his son.

Smith fine-tuned the tale as the years went on. In 1835, he recounted it this way: "I called on the Lord in mighty prayer, a pillar of fire appeared above my head, . . . a personage appeared in the midst of this pillar of flame which was spread all around, and yet nothing consumed, another person-age soon appeared like unto the first, he said unto me thy sins are forgiven thee, he testifyed unto me that Jesus Christ is the Son of God." Seven years later, the "official" church description of the vision was published. It had Smith claiming that from the "pillar of fire" he saw "two personages, whose brightness and glory defy all description, standing above me in the air."

This all changed in the mid-1840s. The indescribable became describ-able. Blinding light was edited into pristine white. Smith told a follower in 1844 that the Jesus he beheld had a "light complexion [and] blue eyes." An-other new believer, Anson Call, also saw a blue-eyed Jesus. Christ came to him with "light and beautiful skin with large blue eyes, a very full forehead and his hair considerably black." What had been painstakingly penned as blinding light, as a consuming fire, as defying all description, was now put in the form of a white man with blue eyes. In less than twenty years, Smith's account of seeing Jesus had shifted from one of lightness to one of whiteness.[1]

Smith was in many ways an outsider. He founded a new church with new teachings and scriptures. His people were pushed from one area to another and persecuted intensely as they moved further and further into the frontier. Smith was then assassinated in 1844 for his religious vision and his bid for the U.S. presidency.

In his rendering of Jesus, though, he and his church were part of a broad and sweeping transformation. They were present at and participated in the birth of the white American Christ, an advent that paralleled the birth and rise of the white male citizen as the embodied figure of civic inclusion in the United States. All throughout the United States of the early nineteenth century, being a white man was becoming a marker for political status, power, and opportunity.

The transition from light to white could be seen all throughout America. For whites, blacks, and Native Americans, Presbyterians, Baptists, Method-ists, and Mormons, Jesus was becoming a white man, not just in visions but also in pamphlets and prints. During the initial years of the nineteenth century, Americans for the first time mass-produced images of Christ and sent them throughout the young and expanding nation. A robust industry of Jesus imagery emerged. The pictures stamped onto American minds the notion of an embodied, white Jesus. It was in these years of defining who was (and was not) a citizen, of expanding the market economy, of growing the southern cotton kingdom, and of pushing Native Americans to the west, that Jesus was first fashioned into a white sacred symbol within the United States.

These years also witnessed a number of swift and ingenious responses to white Jesus imagery. Several new religious movements, particularly that of the Mormons, fixated on his body and used it to further their teachings. On the frontier and in the West, Native Americans struggled to comprehend how white men of the present killed Indians to take their land, while another white man of the past supposedly had died to save Indians. In the South, African Americans took the servant Jesus that was taught to them and transformed him into a small, suffering white man. With him, many found a power to confront their bondage and civic exclusion.

The transformation of Jesus from light to white in the young United States made him, on one hand, a cultural icon of white power. But, on the other, his universal love, compassion, suffering, and triumph over death contradicted the dominance and control of white people. His holy whiteness could be used to trouble the waters of white supremacy. Indians could make it a marker of the immorality of whites—that they killed their own God. African Americans could look to him as a holy white man who betrayed the tenets of white society and taught a higher law of love and liberty. Jesus became white in this land, but white power was never able to overcome all notions of right and wrong or divine justice.

Mass-Distributing the White Jesus

The United States experienced political turmoil in its first decades as the nation tried to define and defend itself. Americans fought out their differences from the frontier to the Supreme Court. Always in the back of their minds, the former colonists worried about their national experiment. Increased warfare with Indians on the interior and the presence of the British, French, and Spanish surrounding young America left the new nation anxious that it could be gobbled up at any moment.

As a new and separate nation, the United States had to determine who was a citizen, who could become a citizen, and what that status conferred. For purposes of compromise, the Constitution counted enslaved individuals as three-fifths of a person. No one knew for sure if that elevated or lessened the status of slaves. It certainly did not stop slaves from pursuing freedom, and throughout the North their petitions slowly destroyed slavery in that region. Then, the Naturalization Act of 1790 declared that any "white" individual who resided in the country for two years could apply for and become a citizen. Compared to European nations of the time, this was not only an easy route to citizenship but also an expansive view of whiteness that included all types of Europeans, including Catholics and Jews.[2]

And then there were massive and disorienting religious changes. The Constitution declared that there would be no national church and that the federal government would respect the religious opinions of free individuals. Most states were in the process of eliminating state-sponsored denominations, and new churches, prophets, and visionaries popped up all over. Doubt and skepticism ran high and low too. In 1800, Americans elected Thomas Jefferson president, a man who had publicly led the disestablishment charge while privately taking his scissors to the Bible. The rhetorical hero of the Revolution, Tom Paine, now told readers that it was common sense to join the "age of reason" and ditch religion. A wave of Catholic immigrants—many of whom were poverty-stricken from Ireland—came after 1830 and further muddied the waters of citizenship and identity. Some native whites likened Irish Catholics to blacks and deemed them to be a racial group outside the parameters of whiteness.[3]

Many white Protestants feared that their country was going to hell, and fast. They needed to do something. Their Puritan forefathers and their iconoclasm had failed to build a city upon a hill. The visionaries of the eighteenth century had inspired a revolution, but never harmony or unity. And in the early nineteenth century, everyday Americans seemed awfully ignorant about Christ. One evangelical reported that just outside Princeton, New Jersey, a local had never even heard of Jesus. Another woman thought her biography of George Washington was actually a Bible.[4] This was clearly not yet a "Jesus nation," at least not in the ways evangelicals wanted. In an effort to make Jesus lord of all Americans, a group of white northern Protestants created, mass-produced, mass-marketed, and mass-distributed images of a white Jesus.

The shift from light to white was key, but it was not all about race. Information and transportation revolutions made cultural power possible. New publishing houses, printing and marketing strategies, and mass distribution possibilities joined the new extensive road and canal building to allow for the expanding distribution of tracts, engravings, Bibles, almanacs, and newspapers. Spatial range and visual imagery marked this new print culture. Suddenly, engravings and etchings found their ways into churches, homes, schools, and outhouses.[5]

The mass-produced visual depictions came from a set of new Protestant organizations that were dedicated to creating a strong and unified "America." The American Bible Society (ABS) was founded in 1816; the American Sunday School Union (ASSU) followed in 1824; and the American Tract Society (ATS) was in place by 1825. Amid an era of rising anti-Catholicism, these Protestants leaned in a decidedly Catholic direction. Using technological improvements of stereotyping, steam-powered presses, and machine papermaking, they inundated American society with Bibles, religious tracts, picture cards, and educational material. The ASSU listed only twenty-five titles in its 1825 catalog. Forty years later, the catalog had almost 1,000. In only ten years, the ATS sold 2.4 million books and gave away millions of tracts and its agents visited almost half of the American population. In one century, the ATS distributed more than 800 million tracts and its team of agents visited more than 25 million families.[6]

These organizations so inundated the American public with ephemera that Mark Twain joked about them in his comic and tragic autobiography, *Life on the Mississippi*. On the Mississippi River, steamboat clerks carried "a large assortment of religious tracts with them." When annoying skiff boats got too close, "the clerk would heave over neat bundles" of them. Angry skiff crews then turned to the name of Jesus, but not in the way evangelicals liked. As Twain so humorously put it, "The amount of hard swearing which twelve packages of religious literature will command when impartially divided up among twelve raftsmen's crews, who have pulled a heavy skiff two miles on a hot day to get them, is simply incredible."[7]

The Protestant organizations were no jokes, though. They were innovative pioneers in printing, marketing, and using visual engravings and woodcuts. Many of the four-to-eight-page tracts contained pictures of families, of little girls playing, or of scenes from the Bible. The organizations trumpeted their images as crucial to reaching all Americans—white and black, rich and poor, North and South, East and West. They especially targeted the young and impressionable.[8]

Jesus became a hallmark image—but not as the battered, bloodied man the Moravians had worshipped. For the ATS, Jesus made his tract appearance in the mid-1820s on the cover of "Sin, No Trifle." In it, a hulking Jesus carried the cross on his back. Hunched over, with huge arms, a long beard, and a full head of hair, he was a powerful man even in the face of persecution. The annual almanacs too had pictures of Jesus. In one from Kentucky, a brown-haired and fully clothed Jesus stood tall while teaching his seated followers. One tract for children, *Mary at the Feet of Jesus*, had two images of Jesus, and the narrator implored child readers or listeners "to suppose that we are in Capernaum, in the house of Simon the Pharisee."[9]

Presenting Jesus was still a touchy subject, and iconophobia had a long life. Artist Horatio Greenough, a Unitarian who sculpted busts of George Washington, Lucifer, and Christ, admitted in the 1830s, "I am not aware that any American has, until now, risked the placing before his countrymen a representation of Our Saviour. The strong prejudice, or rather the conviction of the Protestant mind has, perhaps, deterred many from a representation of the Saviour." Only a few years later, when William Page presented his painting *Ecce Homo*, critics complained that Jesus could not be rendered in human form. One grumbled, "It is so *human*. . . . That character conflicts with all our preconceived notions of the Being he has represented. There is nothing Godlike—nothing of the divinity—nothing of the high mission on which he was sent, which ought to make his face sublime."[10]

The tract societies seemed to know deep down that their actions defied the theological convictions of their predecessors. They made another fascinating turn. In a move that paralleled the shift in representations of slavery from a necessary evil to a positive good, the societies now rendered allurement a positive trait, not a sinful one. In 1824, the ATS general council announced that a good tract "*should be entertaining*. . . . There must be something to allure the listless to read." "Be careful to call attention to the *publications for children and youth*," instructed the ATS later to its agents, "which are so beautifully printed and illustrated by engravings as to tempt every eye." Perhaps they were trying to beat the devil at his own game; they used temptations not to sell out God—as Satan would—but to sell for God.[11]

To avoid charges of idolatry, they engaged in a brilliant tactic of misdirection. Tracts raised the specter of idolatry in other faiths and other lands to diminish the possibility of being charged with it themselves. *A Pretty Picture-Book* was a case in point. Printed in 1830, it contained an image of two boys selling sacred sculptures and shouting: "Come, buy my images!" But idol worship violated the Second Commandment, the author insisted. "In India, and other parts of the heathen world, the people buy images and set them up in their houses, and worship them. Can you repeat the Second

LETTER from PUBLIUS LENTULUS, to the Senate of Rome concerning

JESUS CHRIST.

William S. Pendleton, *Letter from Publius Lentulus, to the Senate of Rome concerning Jesus Christ* (1834). Courtesy of the American Antiquarian Society.

Commandment?" On the very next page, there was an engraving of Christ's white, bearded face. Right after reciting the commandment that led Puritans to their iconoclasm ("thou shalt not make unto thee any graven image, or any likeness *of any thing* that *is* in heaven above, or that *is* in the earth beneath, or that *is* in the water under the earth"), children were expected to gaze reverently on an image of Jesus.[12]

Visualizations of Jesus grew by leaps and bounds. New "Illuminated Bibles" with woodcut engravings were sold, the most expensive and popular being *Harper's Illuminated and New Pictorial Bible*. It was printed in installments between 1843 and 1846 and had more than 1,500 engravings. The entire volume cost more than twenty dollars, or about twenty days of labor for a carpenter working on the Erie Canal (or twenty-eight days of work for a common laborer). According to *Hunt's Merchant's Magazine*, "This is by far the most elegant specimen of printing ever produced in New York." In New York City, P. T. Barnum capitalized on the growing regard for Christ's body by placing a life-size wax figure of him in the American Museum.[13]

The new Jesus depictions were indebted to European artistic traditions and to the Publius Lentulus letter, which gained considerable cachet in Great Britain and the United States during the century. Even when admitting it was a fake, some longed for it to be a true description. English traveler and author E. D. Clarke, for instance, trekked through the Middle East and found in Nazareth numerous paintings of Christ. Of one painting, he claimed that it "seems to have borrowed his notions for the picture from the spurious *Letter of Publius Lentulus* to the *Roman Senate*; which is so interesting, that, while we believe it to be false, we perhaps wish that it were true."[14]

For John Colby, a preacher in Rhode Island in the 1810s who recorded his visions in 1838, the Publius Lentulus description was exactly what he saw when he beheld Christ. To those who wondered if it were true or false, he stated flatly: "This biographical sketch, given of Jesus Christ, by the Governor of Judea, corresponds very well with the description given of him, by the ancient inspired writers, as recorded in Solomon's Songs, the books of the Prophets, and the history given of him by the Evangelists, and his immediate followers." Of course, Colby never pointed out exactly where the gospel writers Matthew, Mark, Luke, or John ever referenced Christ's hair length or skin color, but he did not have to. Art was providing what the Bible had not.[15]

By the late 1830s, renowned artist Rembrandt Peale told budding painters that the Publius Lentulus description was a true "Portrait of Christ." The Andover Theological Seminary in Massachusetts had a copy of the Lentulus letter in its library by 1838, while one newspaper described Jesus as "tall and elegantly shaped; his aspect amiable and reverend; his hair flows in those beauteous shades which no united colors can match, falling in graceful curls below his ears . . . parting on the crown of his head . . . ; his forehead is smooth and large; his cheeks without either spot, save that of lovely red; his nose and mouth are formed with exquisite symmetry; his beard is thick and suitable to the hair of his head, reaching a little below his chin and parting in the middle like a fork; his eyes are clear, bright and serene." The Publius Lentulus myth edged closer and closer to fact.[16]

The field of Jesus visualization was bolstered by an influx of Catholic immigrants, a demographic shift that also fired Protestant nativism and questions of whiteness. In 1789, there were fewer than 40,000 Roman Catholics in the new nation. By 1830, Catholics made up about 1 million of America's 13 million people. Then the numbers exploded, mostly because of Irish immigration. In the 1830s, more than 200,000 Catholics emigrated; in the 1840s, with the Irish potato famine, more than 700,000 arrived. Another million washed ashore in the 1850s, and by the time of the Civil War, Catholics were about 10 percent of the population (or 3 million among 30 million Americans).[17]

Never opposed to iconography, European Catholics brought with them a host of spiritual art. They put images of Jesus in their cathedrals and homes. When it came to Jesus, the "Sacred Heart" was the most popular. Its standing, white-skinned Jesus with brown hair held a visible heart at his midsection. He gestured to the heart to encourage faith, to remind the viewer of how much he loves her or him, and to inculcate the idea that the heart is meant for God.[18]

New religious movements also made use of the new sacred visual culture and embodied visions of Christ. The drive to see Jesus hit a fever pitch in the 1830s and 1840s, when William Miller determined with his intricate biblical calculus that Christ was about to come back. The Millerites found evidence of Christ's return everywhere. An expansive movement emerged, fearing and desiring the coming of Jesus. It spawned speakers, newspapers, and new religious leaders. The main journal of the movement, *Signs of the Times*, used simple cartoons to depict prophecy and to portray God and Jesus. The descriptions typically focused on the surroundings of the sacred. When they dealt with Christ's appearance, they quoted the Old Testament book of Daniel (one of the places Miller focused his prophetic mathematics), in which God is visualized in terms of light, the sun, and pure white wool's hair. With the "Great Disappointment" of 1844 (when Jesus failed to show up), most followers of Miller's biblical reading fell away.

Some held on. Ellen White, co-founder of the Seventh-day Adventist Church, had a vision shortly after the Great Disappointment in which she saw "light and glory poured upon Jesus in rich abundance. . . . I could not long look upon the glory. No language can describe it." White saw light. She could not see for long, but still she could see—even if it was indescribable.[19]

No new American religion was as successful, as reliant upon sacred interventions, or as committed to a white Jesus as Mormonism. Joseph Smith's upstate New York was an enchanted wonderland. God and Jesus appeared to him and so did an angel named Moroni. He came on several occasions and even showed up multiple times on one night, repeating himself each time. Smith found special stones to translate new revelations from God and produced a new set of scriptures.

Jesus was central to Smith's new teachings, not only for what he looked like but also for where he appeared. When Smith translated the new scriptures that he had discovered buried in upstate New York, he was amazed to learn that Jesus was not as distant from America as the Puritans had thought he was. In fact, Christ had been here. He had come hundreds of years before the Pilgrims or Columbus. After his crucifixion and resurrection in the Middle East, Jesus had walked among the peoples of North America. He taught them, shared God's love, and ascended to heaven. By locating Christ on American soil, the Book of Mormon sanctified the American landscape. Jesus was not removed. He had been physically immanent centuries ago, and he was spiritually immanent for Smith now.[20]

Mormon teachings offered explanations for the pressing racial questions of the day: Where did Native Americans come from, and what did God feel about people with dark skin? Smith and his followers built upon the widely held idea that Indians were members of the Lost Tribes of Israel. According to Mormon teachings, around 600 years before Christ, a group of Jews left the Middle East and eventually sailed to America. In the New World, they split into two rival camps: the Nephites and the Lamanites. The Nephites were light-skinned and literate and maintained a close relationship with God. The Lamanites neglected God, and the Lord cursed them with darkened skin. As Mormon theology developed, dark skin represented sin that was present before an individual was born. Immorality darkened one's skin, while moral lives whitened the skin. Over time, the dark Lamanites decided to destroy the light Nephites.[21]

In this racial mix, and given the political climate of the day, it was obvious and imperative that Jesus would be white. At the same moment that the state of New York was redefining its elective franchise by opening it to all white men while making it much harder for free black men to vote (a privileging of whiteness that was happening all over the North), Mormonism privileged whiteness as a marker of sacred inclusion and damned blackness as a marker of sacred exclusion. Even before Smith altered his narrative of viewing Jesus as white (rather than as light), the writing was on the wall—or rather, the golden tablets. Mary, the mother of Jesus, was described in one Mormon text as "exceedingly fair and white." Then, when the Church of Jesus Christ of Latter-day Saints printed its first images of Christ, it was sure to depict Jesus as a white man with dark hair and clear blue eyes. Unlike other American visions of Jesus at the time, the Mormon Christ's blue eyes designated him as whiter and more American than other descriptions in the young nation—perhaps to bolster Mormonism's own whiteness as the church moved beyond the Protestant canopy.[22]

Joseph Smith was not the only New Yorker claiming divine revelations and tying them to the body and appearance of Christ. Robert Matthews also tried his hand at creating a new faith, but he was not as successful. Probably murdering his wealthiest disciple was not the best strategy for getting ahead religiously in antebellum America. Matthews was an aspir-

ing young man in the 1820s, but the economic and religious transformations reshaping the North frustrated him. He was a failure in both the new
market economy and the new family-centered faith of evangelicalism.
Matthews was a terrible husband who repeatedly beat his wife; he lacked
professional skills and regularly ran business ventures into the ground. So
Matthews became a spiritual entrepreneur. He fashioned himself into the
"Prophet Matthias," declared himself a "Jew," preached a doctrine of patriarchy and agrarian plenty, and grew out his hair and beard.

He gained a small following, including the wealthy merchant Elijah
Pierson. Then it all came crashing down. Pierson died and Matthias was
charged with an assortment of crimes. In an exposé of the "Kingdom of
Matthias," inventor and writer Gilbert Vale looked to uncover what hap-
pened through the testimony of a black servant within the community,
Isabella.[23]

Vale wondered how Matthias's followers were duped into believing that
he was from God. One of the explanations was the similarity between Matthias's appearance and that of the Christ in tracts and engraved Bibles. Vale
reported that since Isabella had grown up a slave in New York, she "was
of course very ignorant, not being able to read." To learn about Jesus, she
looked to pictures. She found them in Bibles and tracts. Again according to
Vale, she judged "by the pictures in the large family Bibles she had seen"
that Jesus was "a great Man, like Washington." Isabella also saw God and
Jesus. "Who *are* you?" she exclaimed when Christ came to her. "The vision
brightened into a form distinct, beaming with the beauty of holiness, and
radiant with love. She then said, audibly addressing the mysterious visi-
tant—'I *know* you, and I *don't* know you.'" Then somehow she was able to
speak his name. "It *is Jesus*."[24]

Vale believed that the Christ images in Bibles and Isabella's experience
led her to see Matthias as Jesus incarnate. Matthias's "aspect," Vale continued, "was certainly much like the engravings of Jesus Christ in the family
bibles." So on May 2, 1832, when Isabella first met Matthias, she could not
help but think it was Jesus. Vale recounted: "On opening the door she, for
the first time, beheld Matthias, and her early impressions of seeing Jesus in
the flesh, rushed into her mind." Isabella became convinced that "God had
sent him to set up the kingdom."[25]

The body of Jesus was a prominent feature in the Kingdom of Matthias.
After becoming a member of the kingdom, Elijah Pierson connected the
long beard of Matthias to that of Jesus. "Jesus Christ wore a long beard
when upon the earth," Pierson explained to a visitor trying to talk him out

of the cult. "We are commanded to follow his example in all things." For Pierson, Matthias, and presumably Isabella, the bodily form and presentation of Jesus had become a part of "his example."[26]

Following his trial, Matthias fled New York and met up with Joseph Smith's wandering band of Mormons on the Ohio frontier. After hearing each other preach, both Smith and Matthias declared the other a tool of the devil. Looking like Jesus, it seemed, was not enough. The beardless Smith kept his followers, while the bearded Matthias skulked off, never to be heard of again. Isabella was heard again, just not as Isabella. She changed her name to Sojourner Truth and became one of the most powerful voices for abolition and women's rights in the North.

Just as in the eighteenth-century age of visions, Jesus seemed everywhere in the early nineteenth century. But this era was different. While Moravians and Native Americans had fixated on the blood of Jesus, now Americans were beginning to obsess over his skin tone, beard, and eye color. Amid a nation increasingly defining its citizenry by whiteness and its economy by market production and consumption, Jesus too was made white and sold as a material object. During these years, Jesus moved from an object of dreams and visions to a presence on paper. Found now in tracts, almanacs, and Bibles, his physical body became an object of presentation and discussion. New prophets fashioned themselves in this new image or shared visions of seeing the divine with white skin. Jesus had once again taken human form, and Americans—red, white, and black—had to respond to the presence of his visualized body.

"He Did Not Die in Indian Land but among the White People"

When the American colonists defeated the British, one of the new freedoms they won was the liberty to move west across the Appalachian mountain range. As they went, they brought war and land struggles with them. Native Americans were compelled to respond to an ascendant Anglo-American power, and from the 1790s to the 1830s, they carried on increasingly desperate struggles for protection of their lands, communities, and traditions. Some Indians responded with religious revitalization movements that sanctified their own traditions; others brought Christianity into their communal lives and created new syncretic traditions; and for many by the time of the Trail of Tears, Jesus was with them. The Son of God wept once more as they moved toward the sunset.

Far from the new United States, but close enough that it would become part of the country by mid-century, the Spanish Southwest found Indians and Spaniards locked in continued struggles and Jesus at the center of the action. During the Chumash revolt of 1824, the largest rebellion of the California mission period, one Indian was trapped in a chapel. He grabbed a crucifix and spoke to this miniature god in the language of everyday, informal conversation among social equals: "Now I will know if you are god almighty as the padre says. Carrying you completely hidden so that no one will see you, I am going alone to fight against all of the soldiers. If they don't kill or shoot me, I will serve you well until I die." He left the church, shot some arrows at nearby Spanish soldiers, returned to the chapel, and lived to tell his tale. Surviving a hail of fire, he was persuaded and kept his promise to Jesus. He worked at the mission until he died.[27]

Crucifixes in the Spanish borderlands became malleable symbols of local power and protest. One in a San Jose church spawned numerous stories about its origin. This Christ was dark brown and is frequently referred to as *el Cristo negro de imuris* (the black Christ of Imuris). The icon was said to have healing and magical powers that were linked to its blackness. According to one account of its turning black, a "very pious farmer" prayed each day to the white crucifix. "At the end of his prayers, he would kiss the feet of the crucified Christ and go about his business." An evil man knew this and smeared poison on Christ's feet. When "the good man finished his prayers, he tried to kiss Christ's feet but was prevented by a mysterious force." The color of Christ intervened. "Looking up, he saw the toes, then the feet, then the entire statue turning black. Due to this warning, his life was saved."[28]

Spanish, Mexican, and white American authorities did not like what natives were doing with Christ. They did not appreciate Christ being rendered black or encouraging rebellions against their rule. Even though they were bitter rivals, Catholic and Protestant missionaries united to mock and replace these Christ figures with new ones. They brought new prints with white Jesus images and removed the older woodcuts of browner saints. In northern New Mexico, French Catholic bishop Jean-Baptiste Lamy described native art as "grotesque" and outlawed the penitentes as a heretical sect. A Baptist minister in 1853 sarcastically described the celebrations surrounding one penitente ritual in Santa Fe as involving "the farce of crucifying the Savior."[29]

Further east, where white Americans were transforming the frontier into a constant battleground over land, rights, autonomy, and resources,

Native Americans felt compelled to deal with not just whites but also the new white icon of Jesus. Religion came to resistance movements with thunder. The emerging white Christ became a foil, a means to denounce white hypocrisy, a religious symbol to inspire resistance, and a cosmic frustration for people who kept wondering how long they would have to endure pain, migration, and tears.

To beat back Anglo-American invasions, a number of natives tried to create Pan-Indian alliances. Tribes that had long seen one another as rival and distinct peoples were now advocating an overarching "Indian" identity. New intertribal ceremonies became instances of tenuous bonding for new allies and for natives to practice what they preached—ritual cleansing and the recapturing of sacred power through proper ceremony. Pan-Indian alliances relied upon notions that Indians had wrongfully adapted to whites' ways and that God had made Indians a category of humanity distinct from whites. A group of Cherokee traditionalists explained that the "great spirit is angry with them for adopting the manners, customs, and habits of the white people who they think are very wicked." They kept alive the notion of a separate and distinct creation as well: "You yourselves can see that the white people are entirely different beings from us; we are made from red clay; they, out of white sand."[30]

For some, the white Jesus became an object of ridicule and an example of whites' hypocrisy. Several Indians took literally the whitening of biblical figures and scoffed at whites for killing their own god. "He did not die in Indian land but among the white people," a follower of the Shawnee prophet Tenskwatawa said. Shawnee warrior Tecumseh posed this question to William Henry Harrison: "How can we have confidence in the white people when Jesus Christ came upon the earth you kill'd and nail'd him on a cross." If Europeans and Americans were so foolish to have killed their own god, why would Indians trust anything they had to say?[31]

Others simply rejected Jesus and Christianity altogether. Red Jacket of the Seneca mocked whites for their treatment of "so good a man as Jesus." Whites, Red Jacket reportedly claimed, "ought all to be sent to hell for killing him." Indians were blameless when it came to the crucifixion, for they "had no hand in that transaction, they were in that matter innocent."[32]

Yet, increasingly, Jesus was coming with force to native leaders and prophets. Although widely separated in time and geography, common visions and dreams united Indian prophecies and prophets. Each of them took dream journeys and reached forks in the road along the way. Narrow roads led to paradise, while wide roads went straight to hell.[33]

Along the way, some met Jesus. This was the case for Handsome Lake of the Seneca. His messages melded Iroquois lore and the Christian beliefs he had first learned from Quaker missionaries. "Our lands are decaying because we do not think on the Great Spirit," he wrote to President Thomas Jefferson; "but we are now going to renew our Minds and think on the great Being who made us all, that when we put our seeds in the Earth they may grow and increase like the leaves on our Trees." In one vision, Handsome Lake and his companions met the red and bloodied Jesus that the Moravians and their Indian converts had adored so much. Christ had nail-scarred hands and blood flowed from his wounded side. Jesus told the dreamwalkers that his own people had put him to death and that "he would not return to help them 'until the earth passes away.'" Jesus concluded with this warning: "Now tell your people that they will become lost when they follow the ways of the white man."

Handsome Lake told his brother Cornplanter about the story, and they were both intrigued. Could it be that Jesus had come? Could it be that the savior was to guide and help them? They asked a Quaker missionary about the vision, and he assured them that it could have been real. The Senecas celebrated with dancing and feasting. Cornplanter now rendered Christ as theirs and whites as the evil killers of god. He explained to a missionary that it "was the white people who kill'd our Saviour."[34]

Native Americans in the Southeast faced massive and aggressive white expansion. Some Indians Christianized and acculturated to white patterns; some engaged in trade with Anglo-Americans but otherwise maintained their own cultural practices; others resisted American expansion under the leadership of messianic individuals. Regardless of their choices, the outcomes for the vast majority were forcible removal from their lands, repression of religious practices, and exile to the West.

Georgia became a key battleground. The state legislature of the 1820s and 1830s used every means necessary to clear out lands so that whites could grab mineral resources and drive coffles of slaves to raise cotton there. When missionaries among the Cherokees refused to move, they were arrested and eventually took their case to the Supreme Court. In the landmark case *Worcester v. Georgia* (1832), Chief Justice John Marshall ruled in the Cherokees' favor. He suggested that the state of Georgia lacked the legal authority to disperse them and enforce laws within the bounds of Indian lands. But President Andrew Jackson refused to act on the Court's decision. He knew that military force, not Supreme Court doctrine, would carry the day.

American Protestant missionaries were furious. Jesus was moving in Indian territories, and forced removal was not only immoral but also destructive to Christ's cause. For them, Christian rights trumped white privileges. They had made inroads among southeastern Indians and especially with children at institutions like Brainerd school in Chattanooga, Tennessee. The first Indian convert there, a young woman named Catharine Brown, arrived at Brainerd in 1817. She underwent a conversion process and drew from both Cherokee and Christian traditions. Brown dreamed that a hill stood before her that was "almost perpendicular." This was frustrating because she "had to go to its top," and she "knew not how to get up." Brown became weary and feared she would fall. She saw a bush and reached to grab it. Then "she saw a little boy standing at the top, who reached out his hand." Brown grasped his thumb and at that moment "was on the top and someone told her it was the Saviour."

The dream was an amalgam of Cherokee and Christian imagery. Jesus appeared in a manner akin to the Cherokee Little People, who, in some Cherokee stories, were there to guide children and healers through important spiritual passages before returning them to their parents. Stories like this ran throughout the American Southwest as more Indians reached out to Jesus.[35]

Politically and ideologically, the Cherokee removal became a contest over differing conceptions of Christianity. In his State of the Union address of 1830, President Andrew Jackson broke tradition from previous presidents and overtly referenced Christianity. He upheld removal by juxtaposing unsettled and unchristian Indians with settled and Christian whites. "And is it supposed that the wandering savage has a stronger attachment to his home than the settled, civilized Christian?" Jackson asked rhetorically. By gently removing Indians, the president explained, the government was treating natives "kindly" because the alternative was probably "utter annihilation."[36]

Many Cherokee and their missionary allies hoped to destroy the assumed links that tied whiteness to civilized Christianity and redness to barbaric heathenism. The Cherokee "civilized" themselves in a host of ways. They created a written language; they established a newspaper, the *Cherokee Phoenix and Indians' Advocate*; they wrote a constitution and laws; some bought slaves just as leading southern whites did; and many became Christians.

Stories in the *Cherokee Phoenix and Indians' Advocate* highlighted the Christianity of the Cherokee. It carried conversion narratives and sermons and reprinted accounts of missionary work. One dying Cherokee boy urged his family to "weep not for me[;] I go to my heavenly Father's house, my Savior's arms;—there I hope to see you." He warned that failing to follow Christ's commands would make the separation permanent. In this case, faith trumped lineage as Christianity (not tribal or kin relationships) determined life together after death. At a "Revival among the Choctaws," missionary Loring S. Williams described a camp meeting led "chiefly by converted Indians themselves," which showed that "verily the Lord Jesus is raising up a people here to show forth his praise. . . . O such a wrestling in prayer, such a yearning over sinners, such floods of tears, I myself never witnessed in any land." The paper regularly hoped that a revival among them would save their nation.[37]

Cherokees and other embattled Indians split over removal and over Jesus. While some rejected this new god and efforts to move them west, others tried to prove their civilization through Christianity and keep the land. Another group determined it was best just to bring Christ with them into the West. Clearly, white Christians and white politicians were not on the same page. One report lamented that the ministers and missionaries who might have "administered to them the consolations of Religion, have been arrested, chained, dragged away before their eyes, tried as felons, and finally immured in prison with thieves and robbers."[38]

Whatever the efforts of missionaries and Jesus on their behalf, the Cherokees, the Choctaws, and other southeastern Indians experienced removal and dispossession. The white American hunger for land and military power overwhelmed the Indians and their allies. None of this stopped the march of Jesus or his movement into Indian cultures. Through the middle of the nineteenth century, missionary efforts aimed at bringing civilization to tribal groups continued. Missionary idealists trusted that conversion to the religion of Jesus would bring the blessings of civilization to noble-but-savage peoples. Proselytizing successes among the Ojibwas in the upper Midwest and particular bands of "civilized tribes" in Oklahoma and Arkansas drew special attention from Protestant and Catholic leaders vying for the religious affections of these groups.

Just as before, Indians continued to bring their religious cultures to their encounters with Christ. Vision quests linked with conversion stories to account for the presence of Jesus. Dakota minister Artemas Ehnamani "saw a great light." He thought this light was Jesus, and he put it succinctly: "I saw I believed." Henry Roe Cloud, who later became a Presbyterian minister for the Winnebagoes, converted at a boarding school in Nebraska. Introduced to Jesus at Sunday school, he experienced "a strange constraint to accept this new spirit-friend." As friends, he understood that Jesus "was to defend me and I was to defend him." Another devotee was reported to have sown her grain "in the form of a cross, having implicit confidence that our Lord, who died on the cross, would fructify it." The cross symbol was her way of reuniting the heaven and earth, which had been so painfully disunited by man's transgressions.[39]

The forced migration of the Cherokee and other native tribes from the American Southwest made room for the expansion of the southern kingdom of cotton and slaves. These African Americans too had encounters with new forms and faces of Jesus. The Jesus many came to worship through song and story had unique powers. They took the white servant Jesus offered to them and fashioned him into a suffering white man who undermined white authority. By shrinking him and focusing upon his suffering, they made this Jesus upset the world the slaveholders were trying to make. Just how a small white Christ could give hope in a hopeless world was a mystery, one that slaves hid in plain view with rhythmic and sonorous codes, secretive stories, and masterful misdirection.

The Son of God in the Cabins of Slaves

There was once a game called "Where Is Jesus?" It was fun, exhilarating, and depressing all at once. It was played after the sun went down and darkness enveloped the slave cabins of the South. While white middle-class homes of the era were beginning to place engravings of the white Jesus in their parlors, these cabins were lucky to have even a chair or a bed. They had dirt floors and barren walls. The game began when someone asked, "Where is Jesus?" Another person answered, "Here is Jesus," and the participants ran to the place of the voice. Not finding him, they shouted, "He is not here." Then from another place in the cabin, a voice hollered, "Here is Jesus." And the pattern would repeat. The game could last all night, as men and women, children and adults, looked for the light of the world. As a community, they searched for a savior amid the dirt and darkness. They heard he had arrived, only to be disappointed. It was a game of perennially searching and almost finding, a beautiful and tragic metaphor for so many experiences of African Americans in the age of bondage.[40]

This game was part of a Jesus revolution that happened in the early nineteenth century. As African Americans turned to him, he became a central part of their songs, their dreams, their debates, their wounds, their whippings, and their hopes for freedom. Certainly not all of the roughly 4 million slaves living in the United States by the time of the Civil War were Christians; but, as one spiritual announced, "Everywhere I go, / Somebody's talking about Jesus." In their hands, the Son of God became a power greater than state or national laws, customs and traditions, and even the mighty slave masters.[41]

Black slaves embraced a white Jesus similar to the one mass-produced and distributed by white Protestant organizations, but this savior affirmed blackness in slick and subtle ways. They saw him as a little man who made big changes. He was a suffering savior who communed with suffering slaves. Black slaves took the new white Jesus, shrank him, and made him into a trickster of the Trinity—a white master who would work with black men to subvert the world that other white masters were making.[42]

White southerners first reached out to slaves in earnest in the early nineteenth century. A group of new white missionaries thought they had a Jesus that would appeal to slaves and slave masters. They presented Christ as a servant who labors. In sanctifying service, the missionaries hoped that slaves would become Christians and better servants—a win-win scenario for slaveholders. Lowcountry Georgian Charles Colcock Jones (known widely as the "Apostle to the Negroes") became the most effective advocate for slave missions. He was convinced that obedience to masters would not be "felt and performed . . . *unless we can bottom it on religious principle.*" So he offered "great spiritual good . . . through the knowledge of a Redeemer." He used Scripture cards of biblical scenes, including white Christs, along with slave catechisms to teach about Christianity. "The eye," Jones maintained, "greatly assists the memory." The whole project aimed to sanctify servile work. Jesus, he instructed, "came into the world and labored."[43]

Southern white ministers stressed the universality of God's love through Christ and the importance of service. Right Rev. William Meade explained to Episcopalians in Virginia that God "sent his Son to taste death for every man" and that "our glorious Emmanuel chose the form of a servant, became the servant of servants, illustrating its blessed doctrines by his own meek, patient, suffering life." The image of Jesus took the form of a servant.

Whites hoped that the servant Jesus would reinforce the structure of slavery. Reassuring whites of the safety of the mission to the slaves, Meade noted how Jesus had "adapted all his precepts and promises and doctrines to the poor, and those who were in bondage." Jesus never counseled "pride, discontent, or rebellion." Instead, "the whole spirit of the Gospel" teaches "us to feel that the poorest and most oppressed condition upon earth is too good for such sinful beings as we all are." The words and example of Jesus would speak to servants, for they were "admirably calculated to soothe a wounded spirit and reconcile to any hardships of their lot."[44]

At least one slave viewed his master's power as akin to God's. "I really believed my old master was almighty God," Henry Brown recalled, "and that his son, my young master, was Jesus Christ." When older, Henry Brown realized the metaphorical half-truth of his apprehensions, for slaveholders acted like gods on the plantation. By that time, though, Brown had proven that earthly gods were far from omnipotent. Brown had literally boxed himself up and had the postal service unknowingly deliver him to freedom in Philadelphia. As a free man and abolitionist orator, he took the new name Henry "Box" Brown (the box, by the way, was three feet long and two feet wide).[45]

Southern whites never contained Christ. As one enslaved man explained, the whites could keep them out of church, "but dey couldn't law 'way Christ."[46] In a brilliant shift, African Americans took the Jesus presented to them (a servant of servants), attached it to themselves as servants who suffer, and then focused on how Jesus triumphed over both suffering and servitude. The suffering Jesus became their analogue and invested them (not the whites around them) with sacred value. While white Americans had the time and capital and the access to new media technologies to create visual images of Jesus and while Native Americans were constantly on the move in response to white land grabs, the vast majority of African Americans were stuck. They had little time or goods to produce engravings or paint crucifixion scenes. They had precious little money or autonomy to start newspapers or journals or publish tracts with drawings or lithographs.

But they did have opportunities to dream, to see visions, to sing songs, and to preach. Free people of color, and those who fled to their freedom, also had opportunities to speak and write. As increasing numbers of African Americans turned to Protestant Christianity, they crafted new religious worldviews in which Jesus was their friend, mentor, guide, king, master, and liberator.

Slaves gravitated to stories of Jesus' humble birth, his miraculous deeds, his gruesome execution, and his glorious resurrection. He labored and suffered, but he also prevailed. They associated his poverty and oppression with their own:

Poor little Jesus boy
Made him to be born in a manger
World treats him so mean
Treats me mean too.

He was a king who identified with the poor. Jesus could have come majesti-cally if he had wanted, a slave minister told his congregation. But "did he come only to the rich? . . . No! Blessed by the Lord! He came to the poor! He came to us, and for our sakes!"

Slaves brought Jesus to their present day and made him active in their daily affairs. They placed the crucifixion, resurrection, and triumph of Jesus in the present tense: "Dey nail Him to de cross. . . . Dey rivet His feet. . . . Dey hanged him high. . . . Dey stretch Him wide."[47] Jesus became to many slaves an active friend who encouraged a reciprocal relationship of conversation, disagreement, and affection. In 1836, one black abolitionist claimed that "the slave has a friend in heaven, though he may have none here," while one song announced that "Mass Jesus is my bosom friend."[48]

The guidance of Jesus could be the literal difference between life and death. Along the underground railroad, that makeshift and ever-changing route of homes, roads, and burrows where slaves could steal themselves to freedom, conductors sang out the name of Jesus if all was clear:

Jesus, Jesus will go with you;
He will lead you to his throne;
He who died has gone before you,
Trod the wine press all alone.

Jesus was a man to whom slaves could talk, with whom they could walk, and to whom they could turn. They sang out, "Jesus is our fr'en, / He'll keep us to de en' / An' a little talk wid Jesus makes it right."[49]

With the divine, friendship contradicted the main structures of slave society. It entailed the right and ability to speak freely, openly, and even contentiously. In a society where talking back could earn a whipping, the call to speak was rebellious. Slaves were known to remark of their experi-ence with God: "The Lord unlocked my jaws and cut loose my stammering tongue." They may have had to go "in de woods" to "talk wid Jesus," but with Christ, they were able to speak. One song even bragged about believ-ers who were "gwine to argue wid de Father and chatter wid de son." In front of whites, African Americans had to "wear the mask" and become masters of emotional misdirection. With the contours of their faces and the utterances of their tongues, slaves could never let their masters know what was really hidden deep within them. But with Jesus, they could pour out their minds, hearts, and spirits.[50]

Jesus was a friend but also a master, and this spiritually reordered the entire structure of ownership. He might be "Massa Jesus," but he was a good master, as opposed to evil ones. With him, ownership became a two-way street. One spiritual rang out, "I found Jesus over in Zion an' he's mine." When Jesus came into the equation, masterhood became a reciprocal relationship between God and man, in which the Son of God was tethered to the slaves as much as they were tied to him.[51]

Slaves did not just sing new renditions of Jesus. They saw new visions too. As a suffering savior, Jesus was immanent in their worlds. He intervened actively in their everyday lives, and on some occasions they could intervene in his. Christ became seeable and touchable. He walked on earth like a man, a suffering servant who channeled God's power and came to slaves.

Slaves felt and saw Jesus suffer. Some would have answered "yes" when asked in verse, "Were you there when they crucified my Lord?" Peter Randolph remembered when the "eyes of my mind were open, and I saw things as I never did before." Before him, he "could see my Redeemer hanging upon the cross for me." Randolph described how slaves linked their suffering savior with their own hardships. "The slaves talk much of the sufferings of Christ; and oftentimes, when they are called to suffer at the hands of their cruel overseers, they think of what he endured." This teaches them "patience and consolation from his example."[52]

Octavia Victoria Rogers Albert grew up in a Catholic plantation household in Louisiana. There slaves sang:

O brother, where was you
When the Lord come passing by?
Jesus been here,
O he's been here;
He's been here
Soon in the morning;
Jesus been here
And blest my soul and gone.

According to her account, Catholic masters jailed slaves like her who refused to attend Mass. In the jail, "Jesus did come and bless me in there."

Her mistress's religion would not suffice, for it did not make her happy like the slaves' religion did: "I was a poor slave, and every body knowed I had religion, for it was Jesus with me every-where I went. I could never hear her talk about that heavenly journey."[53]

Perhaps the most poignant encounter with the suffering Christ came from Martha Griffith Browne, a former slaveholder who became an abolitionist. In an all-too-real fictional account, a slave named Ann refused to hold her master's hand. The overseer cracked his riding whip against the back of her head, and Ann fell to the ground "half-lifeless." Then, at her master's command, an elderly slave bound Ann and dragged her across the ground to the whipping post. Within the dust, Ann wondered: "Does God look down with kindness upon injustice like this? Or, does He, too, curse me in my sorrow, and in His wrath turn away His glorious face from my supplication, and say 'a servant of servants shalt thou be?'"

Then she could see him. Jesus was in the distance. "Far way I strained my gaze to the starry heaven, and I could almost fancy the sky breaking asunder and disclosing the wondrous splendors which were beheld by the rapt Apostle on the isle of Patmos! Oh, transfiguring power of faith!" Ann was transported from hell on earth to heaven above, from the terror to the triumph. She could see Jesus, and they were alone together. Now, she "stood in the lonely garden of Gethsemane. I saw the darkness and gloom that overshadowed the earth, when, deserted by His disciples, our blessed Lord prayed alone." Jesus was not abandoned by all. Ann was there; she was there when he prayed, when he was crucified, when he rose again. She was the apostle who would not sleep or leave him or deny him. The soon-to-be-crucified Savior and the soon-to-be-whipped slave were in the same place.

The point was that, just like her, Jesus was an outcast and neither would abandon the other. Just like her, Jesus was brutalized. Just like her world, his was full of gloom. This connection with Jesus powerfully indicted slavery. In her account, Ann declared, "This same Jesus, whom the civilized world now worship as their Lord, was once lowly, outcast, and despised." Jesus was "born of the most hated people of the world, belonging to a race despised alike by Jew and Gentile." Ann's Christ was not white or a representative of a master race. He was despised just as African Americans were.

No matter what happened, she counseled, "trust in Him who calmed the raging tempest; trust in Jesus of Nazareth!" "Look beyond the cross, to Christ," she told her fellow enslaved. The vision helped Ann withstand the brutality of slavery. It brought her "cheer," and although her body was whipped for rejecting her master's sexual advances, her soul flew. Years later her feet would fly as well—to freedom.[54]

When Jesus invaded the physical space of northern and southern African Americans, he did so in ways similar to the experiences of many whites and Native Americans. At first, African Americans described Jesus with the language of lightness and brightness. It was not until the early nineteenth century that he was viewed as white. But even then, African Americans saw a distinct Jesus—one that whites could hear about but whom they would never understand. The white Jesus for African Americans entered the world of whiteness, turned it on its head, and sometimes dismantled it.

Unlike earlier slaves who saw Jesus in blinding light, those born from the 1830s to the 1860s routinely described Christ as white. It is clear that the newly mass-produced and mass-distributed images of the white Jesus influenced these visions. One preacher explained, "I saw the Lord in the east part of the world, and he looked like a white man. His hair was parted in the middle, and he looked like he had been dipped in snow, and he was talking to me." Another black man recalled, "I seen Christ with his hair parted in the center. He was white as snow."[55]

White and with hair parted in the center, this Jesus looked a lot like the Publius Lentulus description and the artwork produced by northern tract societies. But there were subtle differences, and slaves seemed to be bending whiteness in ways that dissociated it from privilege and the oppression of people of color.

The physical size of this white Jesus was distinct. On almost all occasions, the sacred was small. Repeatedly, former slaves reported seeing "a little man" who was God's herald. One remembered, "God came to me as a little man. . . . He was dressed in dark, but later he came dressed in white." Former slave Peter Randolph tried to explain the fascination with sacred smallness. "They think Jesus to be inferior to God in size; and that the reason why He is so small is, that He once dwelt in the flesh, and was so badly treated as to hinder his growing large!"[56] Usually diminutive and usually white, this savior had a powerful impact on those he visited. When Christ crossed the color line, he did so to help, not hurt. Here was a white man who wanted to save them, not to sell them.

Several African Americans recounted feeling emboldened by these encounters. One former slave, who had long been whipped by his master and who trembled in his sight, recalled that after being visited by the divine, "my master came down the field. I became very bold and answered him when he called me. . . . I told him that I had been talking with God Almighty, and that it was God who had plowed up the corn." The master was confused and seemed to sense that his slave "no longer dreaded the whipping I knew I would get." The hierarchy of the slave system was inverted: the slave was brave and the master afraid. As this narrator boasted, "My master looked at me and seemed to tremble."[57]

The smallness of Jesus was remarkable and unprecedented. It was an unheralded theological invention of brilliance and creativity. In mass-produced images of Jesus in the United States and Europe, the adult Jesus was almost always tall. When standing, he almost always rose above his fellows. Even when seated, the Christ seemed larger than those surrounding him. Not so in the sacred encounters of many slaves.

Size mattered. Akin to the Brer Rabbit tales, in which smallish and seemingly weak animals outwitted and outmaneuvered bigger and stronger foes, accounts of a white Jesus were deceptive. The white messiah could sneak past white masters. He could talk and walk with slaves. He could teach them to speak back, to have dignity, and perhaps to run to freedom—all in his name. Through it all, he had tricked whites into thinking he was making slaves into better servants. What he was really helping to make was an unstable situation. And when given the right opportunity, when perhaps a national crisis and an invading army would open up fissures in southern society, African Americans would rise up, believing that King Jesus was among them and on their side. For that unlikely event, some biblical figure like John the Baptist or Father Abraham would have to appear in the present and pave the way.[58]

From the age of the middle passage to the expansion of the cotton kingdom in the American South, Jesus rose in the minds and lives of black Americans. Without power to produce in mass quantities, without spaces of freedom or autonomy, and without luxuries of time or leisure, African Americans dreamed of a distinct Jesus. Even wrapped in white flesh, their Lord did not sanctify white supremacy; he short-circuited it. He was a friend who crossed the color line, a master who could be owned, and a suffering servant who was resurrected and ascendant. This was the future they longed for, not just in the next world but in this one as well.

BY THE MIDDLE OF THE nineteenth century, it was easy for many Americans to assume that Jesus was white. There he was in almanacs, Bibles, and tracts. Maybe the Publius Lentulus letter was not a fraud after all; it certainly sounded like something that could have been written in ancient

times. Whiteness meant power and privilege, and who was more empow-
ered or privileged than God's only Son?

But all was not as it seemed. Before the generation passed, the first explicit challenges to the whitening of Jesus were raised too. A small group of
red, white, and black artists, reformers, and authors confronted the coloring of Christ. They boldly proclaimed that Jesus could not be white. For
them, American whiteness was linked to power, greed, and exploitation,
and Jesus would never condone it. They came to believe that a "higher law"
and a nonwhite Christ stood against the racial privileges whiteness offered
in this world and allegedly in the next. And it would not be just African
Americans or Native Americans who would challenge the whiteness of
Christ. An array of white Americans joined the attack. With the Bible in
one hand and a pen in the other, white abolitionists assaulted the idea that
God's Son sided with masters and overseers. To these radicals, if the spirit
of Christ was anywhere in this land, it was in the experiences of slaves.

PART TWO

CRUCIFIED AND RESURRECTED

CHAPTER FOUR

BODY BATTLES
IN ANTEBELLUM AMERICA

William Apess was certain that Jesus was not white. The Son of God did not look like the visual images circulating throughout antebellum America, and Apess wanted white Americans to see this truth. To show them, he built a window: not a literal one, but an essay carved from theological insight, social commentary, and racial perspective. He titled it "An Indian's Looking-Glass for the White Man" (1833) and published it in a book of sermons and essays. Apess was a Pequot, his mother had been a slave, and he lived in the Northeast near the epicenter of the new white Jesus production. He was also the first American to explicitly criticize the whiteness of Christ and its links to American racism.

Apess berated whites for a number of their hypocrisies. They taught the Golden Rule of Christ but lived for the greed of gain. They counseled love but barred whites and Indians from marrying each other. They taught that Jesus died for all but enslaved others and segregated people by race and status. And, worst of all, they made the Son of God into their own image. He declared, "You know as well as I that you are not indebted to a principle beneath a white skin for your religious services but to a colored one."

How did Apess know that Christianity came from colored skin? Jesus Christ was his answer. "Christ as Jew is recalled as a man of color," Apess announced, and the apostles "certainly were not white." This meant that the true Christians of the ancient world were akin to contemporary Native Americans. Whites were then the backward ones, Apess continued, for in the age of Jesus, "were not the whites the most disgraced people on the earth at that time?" But "skin, color, or nation" should not matter. These were obsessions of the current day. Christ and his disciples "never looked at outward appearance."

Being an Indian and a Christian was perplexing for Apess, who lived in an era when whiteness was increasingly attached to civility, citizenship, and Christianity. He was a committed Christian who had converted to the faith in his teenage years. It was a sermon like the Moravian ones of old that had caught young Apess's attention. The preacher awed Apess with his words about Christ's pierced side and how the blood could heal all wounds. But the racial sins of white America cut deeply into Apess. He was barred from Methodist class meetings, a form of Christian racism that wounded this self-proclaimed "son of the forest." As he later wrote, "How hard it is to be robbed of all our earthly rights and deprived of the means of grace, merely because the skin is of a different color; such had been the case with me." Apess proudly wore the mantles of Christian and Indian, and it was crucial for him to embrace his own sacred Indian-ness and Christ's non-whiteness. In the face of all the oppression, "I chose to remain as I am, and praise my Maker while I live that an Indian he has made."

When he published a new edition of his sermons, visions, and hymns in 1837, however, Apess removed "An Indian's Looking-Glass for the White Man." Perhaps he or his publisher wondered if his calling Christ a "colored" man would hurt sales. Perhaps his discussion of Christ's color and his challenge to opponents of interracial marriage cut too close to the core of white supremacist spirituality and sexuality. Perhaps, in an America more and more dedicated to market sensitivities and to the white Jesus as a visual commodity, the essay was a casualty of market considerations.[1]

These were years when white American Protestants used renditions of and ideas about the body of Jesus to redeem and control the United States and its people. They were hoping to make the United States a Jesus nation. In many ways, they succeeded. Conversions skyrocketed; churches filled up; thousands and then millions of African Americans and Native Americans turned to Christianity. White Protestants altered the visual and material culture of the nation as they began to inundate the land with visual images of Christ. But as Apess and others testified, there were problems.

By using white Jesus images as sacred figures, the makers of the American white Christ relied upon an unstable and malleable symbol, just as whiteness was a confused and conflicted category that was strained when it came to Irish Catholics, Latter-day Saints, and even later southern and eastern European immigrants. Just as the Declaration of Independence's insistence that "all men are created equal" caused havoc in a nation built upon slavery, the whitening of Christ generated a host of conflicts and contradictions. How could a savior who proclaimed liberty to captives become an ideological spokesman for enslavement as a positive good? How could the same man who said the meek shall inherit the earth be grafted onto whites' violent demands for land and gold in Georgia's Indian territory?

The idea of Jesus as an outsider, as a servant who sanctified humility and befriended slaves, or as an impoverished member of a despised race emerged to disrupt white power. In the hands of some Native Americans, African Americans, and white reformers, the new white American Jesus was fashioned into a looking glass for whites to see and confront the various evils of white supremacy. If only they had the courage to look, they could see Christ for who he really was—and was not. The challengers forced heated debates over Native American rights, slavery, and Christ's identity. Who Jesus was, who he was not, what he said, what he did not say, and what he looked like became prominent features of the struggles that were slowly and painfully tearing the new nation apart.

The Great Slavery Debates

When Americans looked around their nation from the 1830s to the 1860s, they saw not only images of Jesus but also how Jesus ignited religious and political conflict. Protestants and Catholics battled on the streets. Mormons struggled with white Protestants and then on the frontier with Native Americans. Slavery, especially the problem of slavery in the West, became the most explosive issue. With westward expansion and the absorption of Texas, California, and the Southwest after the Mexican-American War, the United States became a house divided.

As an increasing number of northerners questioned or attacked the institution of slavery, many southern whites became defensive. They joined new proslavery ideas that bondage was a positive good to older ideas that slavery was a necessary evil. They found passage after passage in their Bibles to support slavery. When it came to Jesus, though, they were flummoxed. Although most proslavery spokesmen were biblical literalists who denounced abolitionists for their slippery and historically contingent readings of the Bible, the voices for bondage abandoned common sense when approaching Jesus. They focused on what Christ did not say or demanded that Americans attune to the circumstances and surroundings of his life.

Abolitionists, in turn, easily made Jesus their own. They pushed Christ so close to the oppressed that some even began locating the spirit of Christ in and among slaves. Culturally and ideologically, black men became surrogate figures for Jesus. Proslavery minds may have won the battle over the

Bible, as historian Mark Noll has claimed, but antislavery activists won the joust for Jesus.[2]

When it came to Jesus, proslavery voices first turned to an argument of absence. Jesus never denounced human bondage, they boasted. One southern woman commented, "Neither the Bible, nor the Apostles, nor Jesus Christ, ever condemned the institution of slavery as a sin." Up north, Massachusetts's own Daniel Webster used this line of reasoning to defend strict fugitive slave codes. He reminded his fellow northerners that Jesus had never spoken a word against slavery but that Christ did counsel his followers to heed the laws of the land. Thus, northerners should stop harping on slavery and instead help the government return runaways.[3]

Another tactic was to accuse antislavery voices of replacing Christ with politics. Following the idea that Jesus never denounced slavery, any minister who did so must be moving outside of his sacred circle. In one parody of a "Political Preacher," northern writer J. H. Van Evrie had a fictional minister express the difference between his preaching and the teachings of Jesus. "And then I forsook Christ and took up politics," the preacher confessed. "And I taught people to hate each other. And I taught my church to hate the men of the South; to hate other denominations; to hate, and vilify, and slander, and abuse; . . . I preached the negro and Abolitionism instead of Christ and salvation." This fictive minister knew the difference between Christ and culture but did not care. "Christ never preached hate, envy, discord, malice, &c., as I have for years; but this is American religion; it is popular; it is the kind that pays. Christ is out of mind now."[4]

When forced to focus on Jesus, the voices of white supremacy seemed perennially on the defensive. The Sermon on the Mount bedeviled them. Christ's interactions with the suffering troubled them. His parables and the Golden Rule vexed them. The Golden Rule needed a special dose of proslavery revising. Van Evrie racialized the Golden Rule, claiming it only applied within one's own race. Its teachings referred to "all men—that is, all who belong to the race or species—having the same nature and designed by the Creator for the same purposes, the same rights and same duties." One of the most influential southern ministers, James Henley Thornwell, did not go that far, but he preached that to take the Golden Rule literally would lead to the "grossest wickedness." Jesus did not mean that a Christian should treat another as she or he wanted to be treated. "Our Saviour directs us to do unto others what in their situations, it would be right and reasonable in us to expect from them." Even after the war, the former vice president of the Confederacy (who was elected as a representative to Congress from Georgia), Alexander Stephens, made this point when opposing new civil rights legislation. Rendered this way, the Golden Rule should take into account status, power, and position.[5]

Although Jesus was hard to make an advocate of bondage, he was easy to bring into the antislavery camp. With Christ's words and teachings, abolitionists had a treasure trove of texts. They read, saw, and felt in Christ an intense opposition to slavery. Joseph Story, for instance, denounced slavery in 1820 by turning to Christ's teachings and the Golden Rule: "We believe in the Christian religion. It commands us to have good will to all men; to love our neighbors as ourselves, and to do unto all men as we would they should do unto us."[6]

Freedom's Journal was the first American newspaper owned and operated by African Americans, running from 1827 to 1829. It regularly heralded the Golden Rule as an antislavery edict. One letter to the editors shrugged off the seemingly proslavery culture of the Old Testament and defended the antislavery cause with the "single law, which fell from the lips of Him . . . 'As ye would that men should do unto you, even so do ye to the them.'" To this writer, the Golden Rule "leveled the odious system of slavery forever."[7]

Before he was an American hero, Jesus was a crusader for abolition. Captured in Boston in 1854 only to become a cause célèbre among locals who opposed the harsh Fugitive Slave Act of 1850, Virginia runaway Anthony Burns reported to the *New York Tribune* that as a young man he learned "that there is a Christ who came to make us free." That inspiration led to his flight. Frederick Douglass went to great pains to distinguish between his deep love for Christ and his hatred for proslavery Christianity. To him, the categories "Christian" and "slaveholder" were incompatible. To Douglass, it was clear which side Christ was on: "I love the pure, peaceable, and impartial Christianity of Christ: I therefore hate the corrupt, slaveholding, women-whipping, cradle-plundering, partial and hypocritical Christianity of this land."[8]

In this context, at least one northern black imagined a messiah beyond whiteness. Around the same time that William Miller was making his predictions about Christ's return, Joseph Smith was meeting angels in upstate New York, and William Apess was writing his essay about a colored Christ, Robert Alexander Young prophesied that a messiah of ambiguous racial classification was about to bring "universal freedom." In *The Ethiopian Manifesto* (1829), Young attacked slaveholders as "monsters incarnate" and quoted the biblical God as saying, "Surely hath the cries of the black, a most persecuted people, ascended to my throne and craved my mercy;

now, behold! I will stretch forth my hand and gather them to the palm, that they become unto me a people, and I unto them their God." The Lord had sent a new savior in the form of a mixed-race messiah. He would have "long and flowing hair" and would appear to be a "white man." But he was actually "born of a black woman." The new messiah would "call together the black people as a nation in themselves," and they would wreak havoc on the South.[9]

David Walker did not predict a new messiah, but he did prophesy holy vengeance if whites did not change. His *Appeal to the Coloured Citizens of the World* (1829) was a stirring indictment of white Christianity in the name of a militant black faith. Walker ran a clothing store in Boston and was active among local abolitionists. He had no objections to militant resistance. Walker denounced whites as "pretenders to Christianity." They were an "unjust, jealous, unmerciful, avaricious and blood-thirsty set of beings, always seeking after power and authority." In the United States and the world, Walker maintained, blacks were the only hope for true Christianity. "It is my solemn belief, that if ever the world becomes Christianized . . . it will be through the means, under God of the *Blacks*." If whites did not repent, the result would be a holy bloodbath, in which men and women of color would strike against their oppressors. Unlike Miller's or Young's prophesies, this one came true.[10]

Something new was happening to Jesus. Only a few years after white Protestants had distributed images of white Jesus figures throughout the nation, the Son of God was becoming aligned with the slaves of the South. Just as slaves were claiming direct and personal relationships with Jesus, abolitionists were conflating the southern slave with Christ. These voices started to declare that Jesus in America was a fettered slave.

For many black and white abolitionists, Jesus had most in common with the enslaved. Preaching in Philadelphia, Richard Allen defied those who supported slavery by turning to Jesus: "The meek and humble Jesus, the great pattern of humanity and every other virtue that can adorn and dignify men, hath commanded to love our enemies; to do good to them that hate and despitefully use us." Allen followed with a threat. "God himself hath pleaded their cause; He hath from time to time raised up instruments for that purpose, sometimes mean and contemptible in your sight." In another sermon, Allen proclaimed that "the real poor and needy are Christ's representatives."[11]

The slave became an analogue for Christ, most spectacularly so in Harriet Beecher Stowe's famous and infamous novel, *Uncle Tom's Cabin: Or,*

Life among the Lowly (1852). The beating and death of the pious Uncle Tom mimicked the crucifixion, even including two slave thieves moved to tears at the sight. Tom was a redemptive figure. Before his own death, he saw a vision of the dying Christ and sang a hymn about eternity: "The earth shall be dissolved like snow, / The sun shall cease to shine; / But God who called me here below, / Shall be forever mine."[12]

Stowe saw African Americans as closer to Christ than were whites. "It is to be remembered," she admonished in *The Key to Uncle Tom's Cabin*, "that Jesus Christ, when he came to found the Christian dispensation, did not choose his apostles from the chief priests and the scribes[;] . . . he chose twelve plain, poor fishermen." Stowe felt moved by stories of African Americans witnessing the divine, and to her it showed that African Americans possessed a racial spiritual sense that whites did not. "The vision attributed to Uncle Tom introduces quite a curious chapter of psychology with regard to the negro race," she continued. "Their sensations and impressions are very vivid, and their fancy and imagination lively. In this respect the race has an Oriental character, and betrays its tropical origin. Like the Hebrews of old and the Oriental nations of present, they give vent to their emotions with the utmost vivacity of expression."

To Stowe, if white Americans desired to learn true Christianity, they needed men and women of color. The "Anglo-Saxon race," which she viewed as "cool, logical, and practical," had trouble comprehending Christianity because "God gave the Bible to them in the fervent language and with the glowing imagery of the more susceptible and passionate Oriental races." To the question of how whites could ever see Christ, she had this answer: join the abolitionist crusade and learn from black Americans.[13]

The character of Uncle Tom has not fared well in the American imagination. He has been seen as too passive and too pious. His faith let him be brutalized, and Stowe's form of "romantic racialism"—according to which a racial category is assigned positive qualities as a group—only gestures at appreciating African Americans. It actually set them up as uniquely distinct from white Americans and slyly justified their political exclusion. In this view, their sacrificial deaths were necessary to atone for the sins of white Americans.[14]

Criticisms of Stowe and Uncle Tom may be accurate, but for many black Americans of the age, identification with Christ was a means to transcend the nation and its legal codes. Nineteenth-century black theologian Edward Blyden portrayed Jesus not only as a mediator and savior for suffering African American people but also "as a blessed illustration of the glorious fact that persecution and suffering and contempt are no proof that God is not the loving Father of a people—but may be rather evidence of nearness to God, seeing that they have been chosen to tread in the footsteps of the firstborn of the creation." Being like Christ made African Americans a special and holy people.[15]

By the time the Civil War came, a host of white Americans directly connected Jesus to the slave. "The Christ of American civilization is the Slave," a writer for William Lloyd Garrison's *Liberator* concluded. "His heart is with the bleeding heart of humanity, whether under the slaveholder's lash or the tyrant's law," another northerner explained. "He cannot be dragged into the service of slavery, nor can his religion. A slaveholding Christ and a slaveholding Christianity is a false Christ, and a spurious Christianity, no matter how scrupulously the one is worshipped and how loudly the other is professed." Then, during the war, when one abolitionist missionary trekked south to teach former slaves, she found that it was there she first met Christ:

No more talks about our Lord
No more searchings for his word,
No more longings of his grace,
She hath seen him face to face.[16]

All of this exasperated southern whites. They had tried to claim Christ but had failed. And now abolitionists were equating the Son of God with the slaves of the South. One exclaimed, "We have understood that one popular clergyman at the North (an abolitionist) has gone so far as to say that Jesus Christ was a Negro! To what folly and extravagance will not wickedness subject its slaves!"[17] It did not matter, though, what the Apostle Paul counseled or that ancient Hebrew scriptures included slavery, for Jesus was on the side of the slaves.

Christ was taught to slaves as a servant who serves; slaves made him a servant who suffers. Abolitionists took Christ's teachings and ethics, applied them to the American context, and concluded that if the Son of God were here, then he would be a slave (or at least spend most of his time with slaves). Proslavery apologists battled back—but when it came to Jesus, they made arguments about absence or historical contexts. They bowdlerized passages like the Golden Rule and abandoned their literalist and commonsense readings of the Bible to defend the peculiar institution. By the time Abraham Lincoln was elected, if Jesus could be considered a hero in America, he was an antislavery hero.

Battles over Bodies and Bibles

Uncle Tom was not the only Christ figure in *Uncle Tom's Cabin*. Jesus was there too—in the artwork. By the age of Abraham Lincoln, the United States was fast becoming a land awash with images of Christ's body. In the context of the great slavery debates, politically violent conflict erupted among Protestants, Catholics, Mormons, and Native Americans. The body of Jesus and books about him became important markers of human similarity and difference. Although not as prominent or as explosive as struggles over slavery, other racial, religious, and citizenship struggles engaged presentations of Jesus as well.

Some whites challenged directly and indirectly the whiteness of Jesus. Not all were convinced that the Publius Lentulus letter was truthful or that beautiful skin meant divine presence. When confronted with statues of Christ as lovely, one fictional character in a *Knickerbocker* story of 1838 responded: "As in the human form and face, beauty is often but a lie, covering over a worse deformity than any that ever disfigures the body, so it may be here." A few years later, when one Protestant lashed out at fiction reading, he zeroed in on the myth of Publius Lentulus. Fiction that masquerades as fact could have an awful impact, he wrote. One prime example was the "reputed letter of Publius Lentulus, a forgery of the tenth or eleventh century, which has been received as a genuine and true description of the person of Jesus Christ by the procurator of Judea." According to this writer, fictive frauds—whether sensational novels or claims about Christ's appearance—could lead to frustration, uncertainty, insanity, and even suicide.[18]

For reformer and religious radical Ralph Waldo Emerson, it was the Jewishness of Jesus that marked him as distinct from contemporary images. As a Unitarian and then transcendentalist, Emerson approached Christ as a model for man, not as the divine Son of God. Emerson lauded Jesus for his "sublime sympathy," his courage, and his tenacity. Emerson was clear to trumpet Christ's Jewishness as well. "When the Word was made Flesh," Emerson preached, and when "the revelation of God was cloathed with a human form," he "was born of a Jewish woman, and sent out into the light of worldly life to have the sympathy and influence, the love and the hatred, the tears, infirmities, fear, and death of man." Then, in another sermon,

Emerson heralded Jesus as "a despised Hebrew; among men reputed a carpenter's son; born in a manger; a man of sorrows and acquainted with grief."

Emerson's embrace of Christ's glorious example and his Jewishness contrasted with Emerson's more frequent paeans to Anglo-Saxonism. As historian Nell Irvin Painter has shown, Emerson did a great deal to further the mythology of Anglo-Saxon supremacy. But when it came to the sacred god-man, Emerson adjusted his racial hierarchies. If God could come in a Jewish form, a despised form, and a sorrowful form, then perhaps the "revelation of God" subverted assumptions about the power and place of dominant whites.[19]

Embracing Jesus' Jewishness, however, did not necessarily mean embracing real-life Jews. Emerson regularly denounced present-day Jews as usurers. His fellow abolitionist William Lloyd Garrison depicted Jews as enemies "of Christ and Liberty" and as those "who nailed Jesus to the cross."[20] In the racial and religious realm of antebellum America, defenders of one kind of liberty sometimes mongered other forms of hate.

Anti-Semitism would become a crucial factor in how Americans represented Jesus after the Civil War, but in these earlier decades the context of Christ's visual creation was westward expansion, rising numbers of slaves, and political links of citizenship to whiteness. The visualized Christ moved as far as the new roads and canals of the age could take him, and increasingly when Americans saw Jesus, they saw a white man. The critics rose almost immediately. Whether it was Native Americans chastising whites for being so foolish as to crucify their own God or William Apess declaring that Jesus was "colored," whether it was slaves claiming they owned "master Jesus" or Martha Browne reminding them that he was a member of a "despised race," the new white American Jesus was conflict-ridden from his beginning.

Protestants were not very friendly to Catholics either. They attacked the religious minority over just about everything during the first half of the nineteenth century. They clashed in the courts of law, in courts of public opinion, and on city streets. Oftentimes, the struggle was over which translation of the Bible to use. Protestant nativism crested in the 1850s, when the combination of Irish immigration and political instability sent many white Protestants in search of scapegoats.[21]

Protestants continually lashed out at Catholics, especially Irish Catholics, as racially degenerate and politically corrupt. One proof of their otherness was their idolatry. When discussing "Black Nunnery," the classic and fraudulent memoir of "Maria Monk" made sure to mention the wax figurines of Jesus that the nuns had in and around their chapels and rooms. Symbolic parts of these *Awful Disclosures*, icons helped mark Catholics as distinct and devilish. Out west, Protestant-Catholic conflict helped to stoke the Mexican-American War. Some Protestants hoped that by destroying Mexican Catholics, they could rid the continent of Jesus imagery. An agent for the American Bible Society looked forward to the day when the Catholics would be defeated and when "the valley of the Rio Grande will be peopled with those who obey the second commandment in the letter and spirit."[22]

John Hughes, archbishop of New York, crafted clever responses to these charges of Catholic idolatry and love for liberty. He cast Catholics, particularly Irish Catholics, as the true destroyers of idolatry. In a sermon for the 1835 celebration for Saint Patrick—that one-time slave who helped transform Ireland into a Catholic kingdom—Hughes described old Ireland as a place where "idolatry" and "the rites of druidism" were the faith of the country. "It remained for the hand of Patrick to pluck up the pagan superstitions of the land," Hughes remarked. He did so at great peril, for "kings, and people, and princes" of the land were against Patrick and "his Christ." Patrick was a saint because he destroyed the icons of paganism and replaced them with "Christ and Him crucified."[23]

Increasingly, however, middle-class northern white Protestants were joining Catholics in the use of sacred imagery (although these Protestants would have claimed they did not worship or venerate the images as Catholics did).[24] Once-forbidden images were now displayed in parlor rooms and churches, in Bibles and P. T. Barnum's American Museum. Advice books, novels, and tracts offered guidance for where and how to display portraits of Jesus. Horace Bushnell, the leading Protestant thinker on the "Christian nurture" of children, advised that art should be placed in sanctuaries and homes. A "new Christian art," he maintained, would implant Christ in the minds and hearts of young people. Tract societies included drawings of domestic scenes in which religious artwork could be seen on families' walls.[25]

By the mid-1860s, teaching faith meant using pictures. In *Dutch Tiles: Or, Loving Words about the Saviour*, Emma Babcock placed nineteen tiles around a fire to tell the story of Christ's life, death, and resurrection. Flora and Willie, the children of the story, marvel at the "row of beautiful little pictures. They were smooth and shiny." Allured, the children desperately want to know what they mean. After the nineteen lessons, the children now conflate Jesus and the images. "Every time I come to the fire-place," Willie boasts at the end, "I shall think of Jesus, and love him."[26]

When Joseph Smith and his followers looked around America, they too thought about Jesus. The nation was, for them, both sacred and terrifying, and Smith regularly asked God to tell him when and where Jesus would return. Amid the whirlwind of conflicts, Mormons tried to carve out new theological and physical space. They agreed with abolitionists that slavery was wrong but also joined with white supremacists in believing that blacks should be subservient to whites. Mormons conceived of America as a holy land but also prophesied that God would drench the nation in blood for failing to follow the new revelations.

Of course, Mormons had every reason to be conflicted. White Protestants largely rejected Smith's new faith and bullied his people from place to place. After trying to build homes in Missouri and Illinois, the majority of Mormons moved far away, to the Utah Territory, where they practiced their faith, criticized the North and the South for failing to reach some kind of agreement over slavery, purchased Native Americans as slaves so they could convert them to the faith, and practiced their own "peculiar institution" in the form of plural marriage.

Heading west, Mormons were excited to share their new faith with Indians. The Book of Mormon begins with a dedication to Indians that they "shall be restored . . . to the knowledge of Jesus Christ, which was had among their fathers." Mormon missionaries referred to Indians as "brethren," and when some white Mormons were touched by the spirit, they actually spoke in Indian languages. To Joseph Smith's followers, Indian removal to the West was a godsend, for it would further the creation of a "local, Indian Israel."[27]

Mormons in the West focused much more on their new scripture than on their visions of Jesus. The first Mormon artists painted landscapes and portraits of pioneers but never of Jesus. Missionaries to Indians spent hours explaining how God had revealed to Joseph Smith a new book but little time on Jesus, what he looked like, or that he had walked in America. When James Brown went to the Shoshone, he passed around the Book of Mormon. It baffled and entranced the Indians (at least according to Brown's recollection). The chief chastised his brethren for failing to see the power and truth in it. It was clear that God favored whites, and proof was in this book and in what whites could make. "Picking up a Colt's revolver," he explained that "the white man can make this, and a little thing that he carries in his pocket, so that he can tell where the sun is on a dark day. . . . This is because the face of the Father is towards him, and His back is towards us. But after a while the Great Father will quit being mad, and will turn His face toward us. Then our skin will be light."[28]

When it came to African Americans, Mormons were far less interested. They were pretty confident that God's plan for blacks was perpetual servitude. In December 1860, as one Utah diarist recorded it, Brigham Young preached of slavery in much the same way as Alabama governor George Wallace would speak of segregation a hundred years later: "Touched on Slavery; said it always was so and would be. The inferior would always be in subjection to the superior."[29]

As Mormons hit the frontier, they joined Catholics and Protestants in the raucous competition for Indian converts. Each group claimed to be converting Indians in droves and in the process rebuked the other faiths. "The Indian Convert," an 1852 story from a Methodist magazine, highlighted one Indian who after turning to Christ "took my images, the gods of my father, and I did burn and destroy them." For Protestants, iconoclasm marked true conversion. This Ojibwa convert traveled around the region of Lake Superior in Michigan and reported how converted tribesmen "all brought their images and bad medicines to me. I took them all, and piling up those images and bad medicines, I did burn and destroy them before their eyes."[30]

The 1850s, however, were not the 1650s. In the 1850s, Protestants were happy to have new sacred images replace the older Indian icons. One missionary reported how a Lakota named Red Owl refused to attend church. He did, however, gaze daily at a picture "of that sweet, sad face of the Saviour," and then asked, "Who is that? Why is he bound? Why is there blood on his face? Why are the thorns on his head?" According to this account, when he was dying, he requested that a cross be put over his grave "so that when the Indians see it, they may know what was in Red Owl's heart."[31]

The growing American fascination with Jesus imagery ran directly into the slavery debates as well. There, the embodied white Jesus became a complicated symbol of resistance and passivity. Visions and images of Jesus were part of the antislavery crusade. Harriet Beecher Stowe was inspired by a visual connection she imagined between slavery and Jesus. While taking communion in Maine, she had a vision of a black male slave being whipped. It was a poignant moment for her. While eating and drinking the "body and blood" of Jesus, she beheld the scourged body and dripping blood of a black man. This experience led directly to her writing *Uncle Tom's Cabin*.

117

Jesus disapproves of a slave whipping in Harriet Beecher Stowe, *Uncle Tom's Cabin; or, Life Among the Lowly*, illustrated edition, original designs by Hammatt Billings (Boston: John P. Jewett and Company, 1853). Courtesy of the American Antiquarian Society.

While the association of the suffering slave and the suffering Christ powered *Uncle Tom's Cabin*, drawings of Jesus offered another layer of sacred symbolism for the first illustrated edition of the novel. The images came from the hand of northern artist Hammatt Billings. In *Uncle Tom's Cabin*, Billings had Tom kneel before a bearded, mustachioed, and tall white Jesus. In another scene, the white Jesus disapprovingly wags his finger at the white overseer, who has directed two slaves to whip the man. Jesus looks almost like an apparition. He stands behind the whipping post not physically but in spirit. He admonishes the evildoers but does nothing to stop them.[32]

Billings's Christ entered William Lloyd Garrison's *Liberator* as well. After 1850, this leading abolitionist newspaper had the white Christ at the center of its masthead as a symbol of justice and brotherhood. He beckoned to a kneeling black slave with his right hand and scolded a white slave owner with his gaze.[33]

The rendering of a white Jesus who was morally opposed to slavery but physically unable to do anything about it was far more disturbing than the behavior and choices of Uncle Tom. This was nineteenth-century white romantic racialism at its most egregious. Most abolitionists were ethically on the side of oppressed blacks and antagonistic to the slave regime but ultimately unwilling to take or inspire a physical stand against it. By having black men kneel before a white savior, Billings set the stage for sculptors after the Civil War to place black men beneath white redeemers—whether in the form of Jesus, Abraham Lincoln, or Union soldiers.[34] This approach showed how powerful racial thinking permeated white reformers' world-views. Even some of the most open-minded whites found African Americans inherently different and hoped white otherworldly actors would somehow overcome this-worldly forces of white authority.

In the decades before the Civil War, Jesus was never rendered visually as a black man. He could symbolically be a slave and he rhetorically could be called "colored," but when created in an embodied form, he had white skin, brown eyes, long hair, and a straight beard. This showed another limit to how far some of the most radical whites would go. They could side with black Americans; they could befriend them; they could advocate for them politically. But when thinking about the Son of God, they could render him only as white. And then the war came.

ONLY ONE GENERATION after the birth of the white American Christ, the Civil War tore the nation in two. White men would kill white men at epic rates, and the suffering slaves of the South would be called upon to save the nation with their blood and guts. Jesus found himself embroiled in it all. He could be seen in the camps and in the slave cabins. His name rang out as cannon fire shook the ground. In their war against slavery, abolitionists located the spirit of Christ among slaves. In their war against the Union, Confederates located his spirit among the suffering white South. Mormons in the West hoped that the war and the arming of slaves were proof that their assassinated leader was God's prophet and that with Christ's return they would be vaulted from national outsiders to justified insiders. When emancipation came, it forever altered the nation, its laws of citizenship, its religious terrain, and its sacred connections between racial categories and religious icons. Emancipation cut the chains legally linking blackness and enslavement, and in so doing opened new discussions about Christ and his relationship to whiteness. The war was so devastating that, like the American nation, Jesus too would have to be reconstructed.

CHAPTER FIVE

CHRIST IN THE CAMPS

Abraham Lincoln had a lot to deal with. Even before he took the presidential oath of office in 1861, the nation had splintered apart. He entertained an endless line of job seekers while in the White House, and Mrs. Lincoln was often depressed and dressed in black (understandably, since their young son had died). The nation's most popular general, George McClellan, constantly demanded more troops, yet he refused to attack with his superior numbers. And then there were the letters: hundreds and hundreds of them. Lincoln's secretary estimated that he read fewer than one in fifty. But only one month after signing the Emancipation Proclamation in 1863, the frightening notes of George F. Kelly gained the president's attention. "We see that you are surrounded by Spies and men of evil intentions," Kelly opened. He worried that the president was losing courage amid the carnage. Perhaps the president wondered "if God has forsaken us." "He has not," Kelly declared, but he also reminded Lincoln that "God is just."

He called on the president to "adopt the plans called, Radical," which would emancipate former slaves and bring full racial equality to the nation. "I have Seen in 'visions,'" Kelly concluded, and "I wept for joy when the Angels, Showed me how God would destroy their power and Save the Nation." God was about to redeem the nation as he had done in older days—through his Son. "Have not the honest hearted been longing for the Second 'Jesus' to Save this nation and the world—Doesent the times look like he was wanted even *now*." He was wanted now, and he had returned. A day of thanksgiving must be called, and the people must rejoice. The savior was back.

The second Jesus was on an abolitionist crusade. He had returned to restore the Union and to slay the serpent of white supremacy. "Have ye not heard that in one of the New England States 'God has raised him up in "humble life'"—did He not do even So with His former Servant; who toiled with the people more than thirty years." In two weeks, Christ would reveal himself. Kelly's Christ was a New Englander who had most likely worked on a farm. He probably looked like the hundreds of thousands of white Union troops who were camping, marching, loading rifles, and dying to save the nation.

Lincoln was not impressed. Although he often wondered about God's purposes for the war, the president had little time for visions. Unlike Kelly's or Joseph Smith's, Lincoln's world was not an enchanted one. These were not "the days of miracles," the president told two ministers who pressed him for emancipation in 1862, "and I suppose it will be granted that I am not to expect a direct revelation."

To Lincoln, Kelly's letter was not prophecy. It was lunacy. On the front of one envelope, Lincoln wrote sarcastically, "a vision." Then, months later, when Lincoln's secretary of state received another letter from Kelly (this one regarding land claims in California and failing to address the lack of Christ's return), Lincoln merely wrote on the envelope: "G. F. Kelly—Crazy Man."[1]

Kelly may have been crazy, but he was far from the only American hoping to see Jesus. It was not surprising that Kelly thought Jesus would return; what was shocking was that his Christ was like John Brown—a white New Englander dedicated to violently overthrowing white supremacy. Kelly's Christ was wrapped tightly within a New England body, committed to saving the suffering, and ready to use his power to kill slavery and save the Union.

In the age of Lincoln, Christ was brought to the conflict on all sides. He called men to combat, ate hardtack with them in the camps, inspired them to fight to defend slavery and oppose it, and challenged the nature of their actions. West from Appomattox, Mormons brought their new Jesus history and imagery into the frontier. They were hard-pressed to prove their American loyalty and their whiteness, while hoping that bloodshed over slavery would demonstrate their religious rightness.

Jesus became a fractured symbol in a divided land, a white deity who could be deployed for and against various forms of white supremacy. When the war ended, his ethics and body remained points of contest. He became a central focus in how the nation would reunite. Former slaves hailed the new era as the age of King Jesus, who had come to liberate, just as he said he would. Former masters tried to take Jesus back from the slaves and associate him with their own crucifixion during Reconstruction. A host of northern whites dreamed an impossible dream—that somehow Jesus could make the nation a land of both racial justice and sectional harmony.

What ultimately occurred was a great reversal and resurrection. By the end of the century, the American Christ who had come to identify with slaves was transformed into a messiah of former slaveholders whose disciples wore white robes, burned crosses, and terrorized people of color. George Kelly's vision of a white Jesus who fought for black people faded, and in its place arose a neo-Confederate Christ who subjugated black people in the name of liberty and democracy. Jesus as an overt physical symbol of white supremacy was born only after dreams of Confederate independence died and after Reconstruction had severed the legal ties between whiteness and citizenship.[2]

Wars and Rumors of Wars

In 1858, Americans began singing a new hymn. It was a call to militancy and courage; it was a summons to "stand up for Jesus, ye soldiers of the cross." The new hymn implored Christ's faithful to march from "victory unto victory." The end would be victory: "His army shall he lead, / till every foe is vanquished, / and Christ is Lord indeed." The song presaged a holy war between North and South, and perhaps just as fittingly, it originated from death. The words were the dying ones of Rev. Dudley Tyng, and the lyrics came from Rev. George Duffield after Tyng's funeral.[3]

During these decades, Jesus and his followers did indeed go to war, and slavery brought them there. The peculiar institution was predicated on violence. It took coercive means to keep individuals in bondage, and northerners grew more bellicose as slavery grew and expanded. In the South, rumors of uprisings unsettled whites. Southern blacks were even more terrified of whites who could and would exact tremendous revenge for any challenges. In the western territories, those who wanted free states and those who wanted slave states armed themselves and began holy wars in Missouri and Kansas. When the Civil War came and millions of Americans took up arms to kill other Americans, Jesus was drafted into both armies.

Within the confines of southern slavery, it was difficult to confront directly the slaveholders' conception of Christ. One man who did was Nat Turner. One early August morning in 1831, Turner led a band of fewer than one hundred slave rebels against the whites of Southampton County, Virginia. By the time his group had been defeated, it had killed more than sixty whites. We will never know how many innocent African Americans were murdered afterward, but rampaging southern whites were dead set on making sure this never happened again.

Nat Turner was eventually captured, and while he was imprisoned he was interviewed by Thomas Gray, a white attorney. Turner (in Gray's rendition) claimed to be led by God, and he forthrightly likened himself to Jesus. He told Gray that "the spirit spoke" to him with words from Christ: "Seek ye the kingdom of Heaven and all things shall be added unto you." Turner had a vision of spirits fighting, and the good ones were the "lights of the Saviour's hands, stretched forth from east to west." Turner saw drops of blood on some corn, and he interpreted these natural signs as Christ's call for rebellion. "For as the blood of Christ had been shed on this earth, and had ascended to heaven for the salvation of sinners," it "was now returning to earth again in the form of dew." To Turner, it was clear: "The great day of judgment was at hand."[4]

After listening to Turner's tales of his enchanted world, Gray asked Turner, "Do you find yourselves mistaken now?" Turner answered simply: "Was not Christ crucified." Turner knew that death was not necessarily defeat, and that judgment was not necessarily justice. Nat Turner died as Jesus had, executed by a state that oppressed his people. Turner's execution sentence declared that he would "be hung by the neck until you are dead! dead! dead and may the Lord have mercy upon your soul."[5]

Nat Turner's revolt, plus the South Carolina nullification crisis of the next year, left Joseph Smith expecting violence. In 1832, he offered another prophecy, one that would dominate Mormon thinking during the age of Lincoln. The "days will come that war will be poured out," Smith wrote of the United States. It would begin with South Carolina and envelop the entire nation. "For behold, the Southern States shall be divided against the Northern States." Nat Turner's spirit would take over, and "after many days, slaves shall rise up against their masters, who shall be marshaled and disciplined for war." Amid the death and destruction, God's Latter-day Saints would rise up too. The "remnants who are left of the land will marshal themselves, and shall become exceedingly angry, and shall vex the Gentiles with a sore vexation." Thus "with the sword" God would bring his vengeance to the United States.[6]

Smith's revelation seemed even more probable decades later when a white man was executed for his violence against the slave regime. Like Nat Turner, John Brown too thought Jesus had called him to a holy war. Brown's raid of Harper's Ferry in 1859 shocked the nation; white men and black men united in taking up arms to assault a federal fort. The plan was to steal weapons, distribute them to the slaves who would certainly rally, and bring war to slaveholders. For Brown, a militant Jesus led the way.

The operation failed miserably. The first person Brown's company killed was a free black man. Then, after overtaking the arsenal, Brown stalled, and the military showed up. Two of Brown's sons were killed, and Brown was quickly apprehended. He was imprisoned from October until his December execution. Like Turner, he never stopped believing he was right, but unlike Turner, Brown wrote for himself about his religious sentiments. From his cell, Brown penned letters to family, friends, and supporters to assure them that he was a true follower of the crusading Christ. Brown felt personally tied to slaves through the teachings of Jesus, especially the Golden Rule. "Christ told me," he wrote to a northern minister, "to remember them that are in bonds, as *bound with them*, to do towards them as I would wish them to do towards me in similar circumstances." He also explained that his violence followed biblical guidelines: "You know that Christ once armed Peter. So also in my case I think he put a sword into my hand, and there continued it so long as he saw best, and then kindly took it from me." And, finally, Brown comforted his family by comparing himself to Jesus, just as Turner did: "Remember, dear wife and children all, that Jesus of Nazareth suffered a most excruciating death on the cross as a felon, under the most aggravating circumstances."[7]

Many northerners were riveted by Brown, the man Herman Melville called the "meteor of the war." Not a traitor, lunatic, or heretic, Brown was heralded as a Christlike martyr. Rev. Edwin Wheelock claimed, "The gallows from which he ascends to Heaven will be in our politics what the Cross is in our religion. To be hanged in Virginia is like being crucified in Jerusalem. It is the last tribute that sin pays to virtue." Only a few years later, Union soldiers sang that "John Brown was John the Baptist, of Christ we are to see, / Christ who of the bondmen shall the Liberator be."[8]

These were only preludes. The Civil War that began in April 1861 and ran for four years until 1865 forced the entire nation to confront mass bloodshed, violence, and horror. More than 600,000 Americans died, and the entire nation was transformed. Jesus appeared on the battlefields and in the camps, the music, and the laws. Americans north and south, white and black, all marched in Christ's name, albeit for different reasons and often trying to kill one another.

Confederates seized the opportunity to reclaim Jesus. With a war that they considered one of "Yankee aggression," Confederates looked to Christ as a warrior who experienced mortal pain. They grabbed the Jesus of the slave imagination, grafted it onto their national agenda, and created a new hybrid. Jesus would be in the South, but not as a slave. He would be there as a Confederate captain.

Determined to have God on their side, the new Confederate government put the Lord front and center in its new national constitution. Invoking "the favor and guidance of Almighty God," the Confederacy's constitution implicitly critiqued the moral failing of the United States Constitution. But even to some southerners, this was not enough. They complained that by failing to name Jesus, the document was spiritually superficial.[9]

Confederates militarized Jesus. His power would lead them to kill and be killed, to charge and to hold the line, and to march on without shoes in winter. Becoming "good soldiers of Jesus Christ" meant learning how to kill and to die. One Confederate soldier from Tennessee believed that "he who kills the greatest number of abolition thieves and their abettors is the best Christian." For others, it was learning how to die or cope with death that mattered just as much. Jesus was a rugged leader of troops but also a tender warrior who could comfort the afflicted. On the battlefield, many of the badly wounded could be heard softly moaning "Jesus." Mildred Lynch wrote in her diary of attending a church service at the war's beginning at which the preacher made the congregants feel "the rest through Jesus, that remains for the people of God, and we were *comforted*. Oh! May the brave soldiers return to us, not only victorious, but may each one enlist under the banner of the Cross, and at last be enabled to say I have fought the good fight."[10]

Following the prince of peace while making war was sometimes easier said than done. Eliza Frances Andrews in Georgia confided in her diary that she refused to believe that "when Christ said, 'Love your enemies,' he meant Yankees."[11] As the war dragged on and as the more than 1 million-man Union army defeated the Confederate forces, white southerners faced their greatest fear: The Confederate nation was killed and with it the institution of slavery. When it all came tumbling down, Ella Gertrude Clanton Thomas of Georgia was brought to her knees. As the pious former slaveholder was just beginning to realize, abolition had shown her "how intimately my faith in revelations and my faith in the institution of slavery had been woven together—true I had seen the evil of the latter but if the *Bible* was right then slavery *must be*—Slavery was done away with and my faith in God's Holy Book was terribly shaken. For a time I doubted God. The truth of revelations, all—everything."[12]

Here was the dilemma, and Confederates seemed to know it. Jesus of the Bible was a suffering servant (and this was the Jesus taught to white and black alike). Yet the sufferers of the South were black and enslaved, not white and free. Add to this the fact that the militant Jesus had, by 1865, failed to lead them to victory. All this left white southerners deeply troubled. How could Christ be on their side if they lost the fight and if they were not the worst afflicted? Maybe they were wrong even about slavery. "I some times think that this is rong to one [own] a slave for the Bible ses that a man shal eat bred by his swet of his brough," one Confederate from North Carolina wrote to his sister. White southerners worried that perhaps Jesus was not on their side after all.[13]

The Union was not going to be beaten either on the battlefield or in claims to Christ. Northerners too enlisted Jesus into their armies, sang new patriotic songs about his presence and absence, and, in his name, made the South "holler." Northerners might have disagreed on how and when slavery should be abolished and whether black people should have any rights, but most seemed to agree with a private from Maine who wrote that "theology that sanctions slavery savors too strongly of Satan to be tolerated. The religion of Jesus Christ has nothing in common with the auction block or the lash."[14]

Yankees claimed Christ as vigorously as southerners did. In 1865, the United States Christian Commission published its own history with the title *Christ in the Army*. One Unitarian minister preached that the war served as a national "atonement by blood." Union martyrs shed their blood "with that of the great Redeemer of mankind." Sometimes the experience of battle drove soldiers to Christ and brought hopes to be with him afterward. One soldier professed faith in Christ after being wounded twice: "Jesus owns me, O, how sweet to feel that if we fall on the field of strife, we only fall to rise to higher and more perfect bliss than this world can give. My object is to live for Heaven."[15]

Perhaps the most popular and enduring linkage of Christ and the northern military was Julia Ward Howe's "Battle Hymn of the Republic." She wrote it after viewing a Union army regiment along the Potomac River. Sleeping in Willard's Hotel in Washington, D.C., she awoke "in the gray of the morning twilight." The tune of "John Brown's Body" raced through her mind, and she scribbled a new song for the Union effort. She invoked a series of religious images—from the "Mine Eyes have seen the glory" of Isaiah to the "Let the Hero, born of woman, crush the serpent with His heel" of Genesis.

The entire song built upon the idea of Christ's presence in the Union army. "I have seen Him in the watch fires of a hundred circling camps," Howe sang. But while the spirit of Jesus was present, he was also distant. Jesus was not an American. God was not one of us. "In the beauty of the lilies Christ was born across the sea," the second-to-last stanza intoned, "With a glory in his bosom that transfigures you and me." The notion of Christ from beyond the sea—both literally and figuratively—punctuated the song.

The otherness of Jesus, however, did not mean that his ethics should not be followed. In a war for emancipation, his spirit could move from across the sea to the American battlefields. In the end, Civil War soldiers should follow his example and become like Christ: "As he died to make men holy, let us die to make men free."[16]

If Jesus was originally from beyond the seas, some northerners wondered too about his presence in the war. Pacifist religious groups like the Mennonites, Quakers, and Shakers struggled to avoid war and the Union juggernaut that so inextricably tied faith to patriotism. One Indiana soldier simply shrugged that the war could not be made Christian: "Read all Christs teaching, then tell me whether *one engaged in maiming and butchering men—made in the express image of God himself—can* be *saved* under the gospel."[17]

Although this soldier thought patriotic war could not be squared with Christ's name, a group of Protestants in 1864 believed just the opposite. They concluded that the only way to save America was to bring Jesus to the center of the nation's identity. The new National Reform Association proposed to Lincoln a revision of the Constitution. Its members could fix the "godless Constitution" and out-Jesus the Confederacy with these simple words added to the preamble: "Humbly acknowledging Almighty God as the source of all authority and power in civil government, the Lord Jesus Christ as the Ruler among nations, his revealed will as the supreme law of the land, in order to constitute a Christian government."[18]

Lincoln pocketed the proposal. He gently explained that he liked the "general aspect" of this movement but thought that changing the Constitution "should not be done hastily." The president was probably dissembling when he said he appreciated the idea. Lincoln showed little interest in Jesus for the vast majority of his career. While he routinely talked about the mysterious ways of Providence, he rarely mentioned Christ. His most famous speeches—his Lyceum Address of 1838, the Temperance Address of 1842, a eulogy for Henry Clay in 1852, the Cooper Union Address of 1860, his First Inaugural of 1861, the Gettysburg Address of 1863, and his Second Inaugural of 1865—made no explicit mentions of Jesus. Even his House Divided Speech, whose title came from Christ's words, omitted any mention of Jesus as a person. Like so many leaders of the American Revolution and in the early Republic, Lincoln wanted to acknowledge the divine without being trapped by the particulars of Jesus.

Much to Lincoln's chagrin, the people who elected him brought Jesus front and center to their interpretations of the war. Those who wrote to Lincoln considered Jesus a very real presence amid them. Several implored Lincoln to put his faith in Jesus, while Benjamin Talbot was thrilled to hear rumors that Lincoln had placed his trust in "the Saviour, that you 'do love Jesus.'" And then there were the prophets, the cranks, and the would-be Christs who sought Lincoln's attention. One demanded of Lincoln half a billion dollars and he would "at my Pleasure . . . Reveale, Christ, Jesus." Lincoln gave this envelope the same notation he gave the one from George Kelly: "Crazy-man." God even wrote to Lincoln through Lydia Smith (although God's penmanship looked remarkably similar to Smith's). Through Smith, God informed Lincoln that "now I choose to take the affairs into my own hands and keep and conduct them." The Lord had sent "my instrument the Messenger of Peace the Christ of this day." Lincoln could find this neo-Jesus "at Mrs Fitzgeralds 476 Pennsylvania Avenue." Coincidentally, Lydia Smith also was staying at Mrs. Fitzgerald's.[19]

The Emancipation Proclamation elicited millennial joys from many northern whites and African Americans. A group of Reformed Presbyterians cheered Lincoln for it and implored him to keep following Jesus. "Jesus Christ is above earthly rulers" and "through [him] alone either nations or individuals can secure the favor of the Most High." An enlightened Unitarian preacher shocked his congregants when he told them that they had much in common with other Americans who "in the commotions of the time, hail the second advent of Christ, and the coming of his kingdom." Although Unitarians did not believe in "any personal appearance of Christ," they now saw his return in the principles of freedom. "He comes a second time in his principles, in his truths. . . . He comes in new thoughts, higher disclosures of duty, fresh manifestations of the glory and safety of his Gospel. He comes, blessed be God, in the captive freed; in manacles broken; in systems of cruelty and wrong shattered; in the new kingdom of righteousness, freedom, justice, and humanity."[20]

Mormons too were ready for Christ's return. They saw the national schism and arming of slaves as proof of Smith's 1832 prophecy. Even before South Carolina initiated the military conflict in 1861, Mormons rejoiced in Lincoln's election. "There is tremendous excitement prevail[ing] in the U.S. concerning the Election of Lincoln," one Mormon wrote in his diary. "The south is angry; the North is no better and from what I can see they are both hastening to fulfill the Prophecy of Joseph Smith Jr." Time and again, diarists cheered the war as evidence of the end-times. "There has been many severe Battles fought between the North and South at Gettysburg, Chattanooga, Chickamaugua, and other places," one diarist penned in September 1863. "Many thousands have been slain. . . . In fact as far as I can judge every thing is working out right for the redemption of Zion and the onward progress of God's great Kingdom in the last days."[21]

Southern slaves prepared for the kingdom to come as well. King Jesus had promised to deliver them. As the game "Where Is Jesus" shifted from the slave cabin to the entire slave South, African Americans moved from one place to another looking to find him, freedom, and their families. With certainty, gratitude, and a willingness to fight and die, slaves followed their friend, master, and king as he led them to victory.

When news of freedom came to one slave, she could barely contain herself in front of the master: "I jump up and scream, 'Glory, glory hallelujah to Jesus! I'se free! I'se free!'" She crouched to the ground, kissed the free earth, and felt "so full o' praise to Masser Jesus." A new joy could be heard in slave songs all throughout the South. Charlotte Forten, a black northern missionary in the Sea Islands, heard the "rich tones" of black boatmen singing in "sweet, strange, and solemn" voices:

> Jesus makes de blind to see
> Jesus make de cripple walk;
> Jesus make de deaf to hear.
> Walk in, Kind Jesus.

And another, featuring warm greetings in Gullah dialect with a physically present King Jesus:

> In de mornin' when I rise,
> Tell my Jesus Huddy oh!
> I wash my hands in de mornin' glory,
> Tell my Jesus Huddy oh![22]

White abolitionist and commander of a black regiment of the Union army Thomas Wentworth Higginson recorded some of the finest testimony of Christ's presence among African Americans. Although Higginson believed that slave theology exhibited nothing "but patience for this life,— nothing but triumph in the next," the songs revealed a belief that King Jesus was here today. "Ride in, kind Saviour!" the men sang by the light of the campfire:

> No man can hinder me.
> O, Jesus is a mighty man!
> . . . .
>
> We're marching through Virginny fields.
> . . . .
>
> And he has his sword and shield,
> . . . .
>
> O, old secesh done come and gone!
> No man can hinder me.[23]

Just as the Jew would "look hopefully for the Messiah," a South Carolinian commented at the war's end in 1865, "so has the negro for forty years been looking for the man of universal freedom, and, when his eager ear caught the sound of his voice thundering at his prison-door think you that the watchfulness of years was to be drugged into fatal sleep by the well-meant kindness of his keeper."[24] The Christ of the slaves and of the abolitionists had come to the South. Sometimes he met them alone in the fields; sometimes he came in cannon fire; sometimes he came in song. The point was that he came, and they were free. Just as the slave Ann had told them after her encounter with Jesus at Gethsemane, all they needed to do was look past the cross and behold Christ victorious.

The white South had been militarily defeated. Slavery had been destroyed. Neither Jehovah nor Jesus had saved the Confederacy. Former slaves were ecstatic. Freedom had come, and they could thank themselves, Abraham Lincoln, the Union army, and the Master Jesus for the dawning of a new day. Mormons in the West were confused. Their prophet had predicted the events but not the outcome. Would Jesus still come, even though they had not stepped in to save the nation? Northern whites now dreamed that the South and the nation would be rich with peace, liberty, justice, and harmony. They knew no politician could bring such a world, but some looked to Jesus to inspire such a revolution.

Reconstructing the White American Jesus

When the Civil War ended in the spring of 1865, it appeared that the United States was marching to the beat of sacred time. Robert E. Lee surrendered on Palm Sunday. Abraham Lincoln was then assassinated on Good Friday. The years that followed were harrowing and confusing. About 4 million individuals were legally transformed from slaves to free women and men. The southern states reentered the Union with new state constitutions. The national Constitution was revised, not with a preamble dedicated to Christ but with three new amendments. The Thirteenth Amendment abolished slavery; the Fourteenth Amendment ensured citizenship rights to individuals regardless of former slave status; and the Fifteenth Amendment offered black men the right to vote. The legal tie of whiteness to citizenship had been dealt serious and potentially fatal blows.

Northern whites and African Americans had a new Christ figure when Abraham Lincoln was shot on Good Friday, April 14, 1865. It became commonplace to compare him to Jesus as both liberator and reconciler. Upon hearing of Lincoln's death, one slave in South Carolina reportedly said, "Lincoln died for we, Christ died for we, and me believe him de same mans." Herman Melville lamented that Lincoln was killed "in his pity" and praised the fallen president as "the Forgiver." A Methodist minister implored northerners to push for peace. If "anything that you read or hear in these sad days, breeds within you a single revengeful feeling, even towards the leaders of this rebellion," he proclaimed, "then think of Abraham Lincoln, and pray God to make you merciful. Think of the prayer of Christ, which the president said, after his Saviour, 'Father, forgive them, they know not what they do.'" Others commented that perhaps Lincoln was too Christlike and too forgiving.[25]

Mass freedom and citizenship rights for African Americans meant the possibility of an entirely new world. Former slaves now had the power to name themselves and their children, to establish their own households without fear of being sold away, and to practice religious liberty. Within years of the war's end, the vast majority of African Americans religiously voted with their feet. They exited hierarchical biracial churches and joined all-black congregations.[26]

Freedom led to a material question of imagery: What pictures should African Americans use in their homes and churches? As early as 1862, black abolitionist T. Morris Chester called on African Americans to take down pictures of white politicians, leaders, and military heroes. He wanted them replaced with images of powerful African Americans of the past and present, including Frederick Douglass and Richard Allen. Chester made no specific reference to Jesus, but he figured Bible pictures into the mix. Chester cautioned that black Americans should avoid any image that coded black with evil and white with good. Instead he thought American history proved that if God had a color, the sacred was black. "As it is a mere speculation what is the color of the inhabitants of the celestial and infernal regions, I am confident that if the developments of the two races are an index to their complexion, that God and his winged seraphs are black, while the Devil and his howling imps are white." If you "want a scene from the Bible, and this cloven-footed personage is painted black, say to the vendor, that your conscientious scruples will not permit you to support so gross a misrepresentation, and when the Creator and his angels are presented as white, tell him that you would be guilty of sacrilege, in encouraging the circulation of a libel upon the legions of Heaven."[27]

The spirit of Chester's words would be felt again in the twentieth century, but in his era, they were impractical. African Americans did not have the consumer power or the production capabilities to mass-distribute black icons. Cash and land poor, embattled throughout the South, and uncertain of the future, most African Americans had little time, energy, or money for new religious imagery.

The white Jesus could still be deployed on the side of racial justice, but northern whites also wanted him to oversee national harmony. He made a notable visual appearance in a busy print simply titled "Reconstruction." Distributed in 1867 just after Congress passed the Fourteenth Amendment, this political cartoon imagined a sacred transformation of the United States. The reconstructed nation would be built upon new pillars of justice, liberty, and education. Friendship would flourish where once fratricide had reigned. Northern and southern whites would shake hands on the earth below, and in the sky above, whites from the nation's past would populate heaven. Universal education would link blacks and whites in games and grammar. Universal suffrage would enfranchise African American men, and black and white children would be treated equally. In the center, a white Jesus with long flowing hair offered political, social, and religious instruction for the reconstructed nation: "DO TO OTHERS AS YOU WOULD HAVE OTHERS DO TO YOU."[28]

Southern whites objected strenuously. Northerners were not going to tell them what Jesus meant, and they were sure the Golden Rule did not mean civil rights. Former Confederates were not going to shake hands cordially with northerners or with African Americans; the sons of the South did not like emancipation; they certainly did not endorse citizenship for all blacks and suffrage for black men; and they did not want Jesus associated with racial justice.[29]

Confederates and their children found an answer to their Jesus problem by reclaiming the mantle of suffering. What had been a theological conundrum for the white South became the solution for the white South. Southerners transformed Jesus back into a sufferer and themselves into the ones who had truly born the cross. If white southerners, in the famous argument of C. Vann Woodward, had experienced the human realities of loss and defeat in a way that was unlike that for white Americans generally, then Jesus could bind their wounds. Defeated Confederates created in Jesus a suffering savior who sanctified their warriors of the past and the Lost Cause theology of the postwar present.

Southern ministers frequently connected the suffering South to the dying Christ. From the hundreds of Confederate monuments setting in biblical relief the major southern war heroes, to the addresses at yearly Sons of Confederate Veterans and United Daughters of the Confederacy meetings, to the inscriptions on the monuments themselves, Jesus sanctified the myth of a unified white southern people who had fought for him. Nashville Presbyterian James I. Vance, for example, explained that "his enemies could nail Christ to the cross, but they could not quench the ideals he embodied. His seemed to be a lost cause as the darkness fell on the great tragedy at Calvary, but out of what seemed Golgotha's irretrievable defeat has come the cause whose mission it is to save that which is lost." One southern Catholic cleric noticed his niece gazing at an image depicting Christ's death, and he asked her how Jesus had come to his martyrdom. She replied, "'The Yankees' had crucified him."[30]

John William Jones's *Christ in the Camp*, first published in 1887, outlined the major tenets of the religion of the Lost Cause. It ensured that Jesus and revivalism defined southern memory of the war as much as political concepts of liberty or fighting for their homeland. As southerners remembered the war, to receive Jesus prepared southern soldiers to fight for "freedom," and, for them, to see Jesus was to envision victory in the here and the hereafter. The ferocity of the war itself naturally turned men's thoughts to the divine. After revivals swept their camp, soldiers stationed for battle in Orange County, Virginia, steeled themselves for war with praises of Jesus. One correspondent cheered that "the stately steppings of Jesus are heard in our camps" and that the men were "enlisting under the unfurled banner of King Immanuel." Amid the storms of war, the men felt "safe in the arms of the Lord Jesus."[31]

Whiteness never defined this Jesus—just as racial categories were not explicitly used in new southern laws of the 1880s and 1890s that circumvented the Fourteenth and Fifteenth Amendments and effectively undercut black male voting and other civil rights. Instead, Confederates described Jesus in terms of warmth, comfort, and compassion for their suffering. When they saw Jesus, they beheld "Glorious brightness," which came "straight from my Saviour's countenance." One account described standing "by the bedside of one of the heroes who are daily offering themselves as sacrifices upon the altar of their country." As he "gazed upon the thin, emaciated form" of the soldier on the cot, he thought, "Jesus, the King of kings, dwells here, and I had rather be this poor soldier than to be the tenant of a palace."[32]

Key to the postwar mythology was the exalting of southern war heroes as Christian evangelical gentlemen. The United Confederate Veterans and the United Daughters of the Confederacy, for instance, heralded the Civil War as one baptized by the consecration of "Christian knights of the South whose proud names and glorious fame shall endure forever."[33]

They even transformed Robert E. Lee and Jefferson Davis into Christlike figures. As a symbolic Christ figure, morally spotless but betrayed by the sins of lesser men (General James Longstreet usually standing in for Judas in this story), Lee showed how a character could be honed to perfection by pain. He embodied how the South "had transformed the shame of its worldly failure into a glorious, metaphysical triumph." Lee was emblematic that "God's greatest gift to a race and a time is some one man in whom that race shall see the embodiment of its highest ideals." Lee lived not for himself but for his fellow men, for "the sign of the Cross was upon his life." At the dedication ceremony for the newly constructed Lee chapel at Washington College (later renamed Washington and Lee University), Senator John W. Daniel of Virginia called Lee "the Priest of his people," who drank "every drop of Sorrow's cup." The chapel, where Lee's remains rested, was transformed into a "holy place."[34]

Most amazing was the resurrection of Jefferson Davis. Throughout the war, Davis was often vilified for political ineptitude. He was disgraced at the war's end, too, when he was supposedly caught fleeing in a woman's dress. But he was brought back from political death to become a Christ of the white South. Called to Atlanta in 1886 for the unveiling of a Confederate memorial, Davis received a rapturous greeting. He arrived in a car bearing this inscription: "He was Manacled for Us." Davis was the "chosen vicarious victim," said the rector of Baltimore's Memorial Protestant Church, for northerners had "laid on him the falsely alleged iniquities of us all." A southern poet in 1923 made the connection most explicitly:

> Jefferson Davis: Still we honor thee!
> Our lamb victorious, who for us endur'd
> A cross of martyrdom, a crown of thorns,
> A soul's Gethsemane, a nation's hate,
> A dungeon's gloom! Another god in chains.[35]

By the end of the nineteenth century, Confederates and their children had brought Jesus into their fold. Although they had lost control of Christ's meaning and importance in the antebellum period, Confederates took him back by merging the warrior with the sufferer. In this way, the white South became like Christ crucified. Turning death into life was Christ's supernatural trick, and through the Lost Cause, southern whites hoped to find strength after sorrow. "When our Divine Master perished on the cross, did the doctrines for which he died perish with him," asked the former South Carolina general and politician Wade Hampton in 1892. The answer for him and for them was clear and simple, "No."[36] Jesus became a southerner first in his suffering. He became a white southerner only after Confederate failure during the Civil War.

For Mormons out west, Reconstruction was a disaster, and they needed a savior. Not only had Jesus failed to return at the time of the national schism, but the Union's victory led to new rights for black people and renewed attacks on Mormons. They were bitter that civil rights were offered to former slaves. Brigham Young assailed northern Republicans for establishing "schools for the freedman," while the *Latter-day Saints Millennial Star* complained that "in making the Black man think he is equal of White unleashed his savage and crual [*sic*] nature, hence trouble in the South. This is a violation of the laws of nature."[37]

Eastern Republicans seemed to be helping blacks and more vigorously targeting Mormons. Just before the war, an army doctor described the children of polygamous Mormon marriages as physically a new and deformed race: "The yellow, sunken, cadaverous visage; the greenish-coloured eye; the thick protuberant lips, the low forehead, the light, yellowish hair, the lank, angular person, constitute an appearance so characteristic of the new race, the production of polygamy, as to distinguish them at a glance." This doctor reported to Congress that Mormons would "eventually die out."[38]

Then, just after the war, anti-Mormon writers warned that the Latter-day Saints were latter-day traitors. "The elements of a second rebellion are in active progress in Utah," prophesied one voice in 1866, "and, as in the case of the slavery rebellion, the great danger lies in the failing to place a proper estimate upon the power of those elements for mischief, and to take the proper precautions in time. Religious fanaticism is more active, and, when hostile, more dangerous, than political ambition; hence the arrogant and intolerant spirit, and the bitter hostility of the Mormons, are more worthy [of] the serious attention of our statesmen than would be the opposition of so many mere political traitors."[39]

Anti-Mormonism united northerners and southerners, Democrats and Republicans, Protestants and Catholics, whites and blacks. In the 1860s, 1870s, and 1880s, Congress, the president, and the Supreme Court joined to outlaw plural marriage. President Grover Cleveland, a Democrat and no friend to civil rights for blacks, contrasted in his 1885 annual address the miserable "homes of polygamy" with "our homes, established by the law of God, guarded by parental care, regulated by parental authority, and sanctified by parental love."[40]

Mormons could not believe what was happening. Black people—the people whose skin showed their sin so evidently—had rights that Mormon true believers did not. Because of polygamy, Congress denied Utah statehood until the 1890s. This meant that the Mormon haven did not have congressional representation and could not send votes to the Electoral College. Thus, black men throughout the South who used to be slaves had more political power in federal elections than white men in Utah (some of whom had owned slaves in the past).

Mormons responded by abandoning one aspect of their revelation for another. In 1890, their leadership rejected polygamy and in the following decades looked to Jesus. They did not produce their own art—not quite yet. Mormons at the turn of the century took European artwork of white Christ figures and placed them prominently in their newspapers, magazines, and books. They avoided images of defeat or sadness, though, and the crucifixion or portraits of Jesus that appeared overly feminine were largely absent. Instead, they selected artwork that showed Jesus as vigorous, vibrant, and manly. Although Mormons were still a relatively small group and were still embattled legally and politically, they slowly became some of the most powerfully committed to Jesus' (and their own) whiteness and strength.[41]

When the twentieth century came, the West and the South united to create a new Christ for America. Unlike the one of the Civil War era, this one supported white supremacy. He was a white man who strengthened white men, subjugated people of color, heralded the Ku Klux Klan, and did it all in the name of sacred liberty. This white Jesus had his vocal critics and competitors, and the decades following Reconstruction witnessed another round of intense competition for the soul and body of Jesus. If Harriet Beecher Stowe defined a suffering servant Jesus, one closely identified with the slave, her brother pioneered a new way of conceiving of the life and face of Jesus, one that rhetorically claimed no race for Jesus but visualized him as white.

FOR MANY BLACK AMERICANS, nothing symbolized the shift in their fortunes more than the career of Harriet Beecher Stowe's brother, "the most famous man in America": Henry Ward Beecher. Before the war, he had been an abolitionist. He had heralded black soldiers as heroes of the age and thought the spirit of Christ rested in the abolitionist cause. Almost immediately after the war, however, he embraced the white South with open arms. He became, in the sarcastic words of Frederick Douglass, an "apostle of forgiveness."[42]

What went unappreciated at the time (perhaps because Beecher was embroiled in a sex scandal in 1873) was that in the early 1870s, he set in motion a new way of representing Jesus in the racial and political reconfiguration of America. He established a rhetorical and visual shell game in which white Americans could claim Jesus as their own without words. Beecher worked this magic on Jesus by joining a century-old debate in Europe over whether the life of Jesus could be put into a biography.[43]

Beecher's *The Life of Jesus, the Christ* (1871) was the first American biography of Jesus. An important wrinkle was what Jesus looked like, for any good biographer would describe his subject physically. Beecher admitted that it was impossible to know truly the contents of Christ's countenance. Beecher was biblically honest: "There is absolutely nothing to determine the personal appearance of Jesus. . . . To his form, his height, the character of his face, or of any single feature of it, there is not the slightest allusion." Text was one thing; art was another. Beecher included five visual heads of Christ on one page. All were from European artists and all featured a white Jesus with brown hair and brown eyes.

With text and image, Beecher set up Jesus so that white Americans and Europeans could claim him rhetorically as a universal, nonwhite savior,

1. EARLIEST KNOWN, FROM CATACOMBS OF ST. CALIXTUS.

2. FROM EMERALD INTAGLIO OF EMPEROR TIBERIUS.

3. AFTER FRANCISCO DI FRANCIA.

4. AFTER ALBRECHT DÜRER.

5. AFTER PAUL DE LA ROCHE.

Five depictions of Christ by various artists in Henry Ward Beecher, *The Life of Jesus, the Christ* (New York: J. B. Ford and Company, 1871).

but visually as one of their own. It sounded similar to the ways Americans could claim to be liberty loving while functioning in the world as agents of oppression. As had Beecher's sister, he too distanced Jesus from whiteness by claiming they were of different races. "He was of the Shemitic race; we are of the Japhetic." These racial differences, Beecher insisted, spoke to differences of mind, spirituality, and worldview. "The orderliness of our thought, the regulated perceptions, the logical arrangements, the rigorous subordination of feeling to volition, the supremacy of reason over senti-ment and imagination, which characterize our day, make it almost impos-sible for us to be in full sympathy with people who had little genius for ab-stractions." For white Americans, Beecher concluded, the gospel of Christ "seems like a glittering dream or a gorgeous fantasy."

Then Beecher put another spin on it. In a spiritual sense, Christ was a man of all nations and peoples. "As Christ spiritually united in himself all nationalities, so in art his head has a certain universality. All races find in it something of their race features." Together, the visuals, the racial other-ness, and the universalism added up to a singular mix of racial similarity and difference, spiritual closeness and strangeness. Read together, the pic-tures and the text showed Beecher taking racial particularity (whiteness), wrapping it in religious particularity (Protestant Christianity), and claim-ing it as human universality.[44]

This was an innovative move, one that would not be matched until the twentieth century and only after the modern civil rights movement had challenged the grand claims of white supremacy. Rhetorically, Beecher ac-knowledged Jesus as nonwhite but visually rendered him white. By offer-ing separate and conflicting messages from the text and the image, Beecher began the process by which whites could embed whiteness into their sa-cred worldviews without having to say it out loud, just as southern whites would try politically.

These complicated maneuvers were ahead for America after the Civil War. During the war, when Lincoln was still alive, when George Kelly was prophesying that Jesus had returned to set the captives free and save the Union, when Confederates struggled to figure out whether Jesus had for-saken them, and when Mormons thought they were certain that Joseph Smith's prophesies were coming true, it appeared that Jesus had invaded the American landscape. From proslavery forces bending their biblical readings to suit their slaveholding desires to abolitionists cheering Jesus as a slave, from political redefinitions of the Golden Rule to Nat Turner and

John Brown speaking with courage from prison that Jesus had led them to violence, Christ had been a mighty presence. Americans enslaved and killed one another in his name. More than 600,000 died; more than 3.5 million African Americans won their liberation. And the white Jesus went marching on.

CHAPTER SIX

NORDIC AND NATIVIST IN AN AGE OF IMPERIALISM

Fifty years after he was assassinated, Abraham Lincoln was back in the White House and about to be shot again. It was 1915, and film director D. W. Griffith's cinematic masterpiece *Birth of a Nation* was being screened by Woodrow Wilson and his presidential staff. The film begins with Lincoln on screen as the South's best friend, a magnanimous victor who longs for national unity. Booth's bullet, though, unleashes a reign of racial terror in which black men and radical Republicans rule the defeated white South. The movie tells the gripping saga of how men who burn crosses and disguise themselves in white sheets band together to save and unite the nation. Ku Klux Klan vigilantes are the heroes in this travesty of a historical narrative, and they even pave the way for Christ's return. As the film concludes, a brown-haired, brown-eyed, white-robed, and white-skinned Jesus appears on screen to bless the United States.

Birth of a Nation was a technological marvel that heralded the birth of modern motion pictures. Filmed in southern California and more than three hours long, it features close-ups and panoramic shots, action sequences, and hundreds of extras. It was "history written with lightning," according to one U.S. official. President Woodrow Wilson loved it. So too did members of his cabinet and the Supreme Court. White crowds all over the nation were riveted. They gasped when white actors in blackface pursued white women to rape them. They cheered as Klansmen rode to avenge the South. And they experienced relief when Jesus stretched his hands over the nation the Klan had saved.[1]

This white Jesus seemed to offer his approval to the varied forms of white supremacy—from President Wilson's segregating of the national capital to the many lynchings of black men. His holy whiteness seemed to nod in agreement with the electoral disfranchisement of African Americans and the policing of bodies and minds. *Birth of a Nation* was so inspirational that it led to the resurrection of the actual Ku Klux Klan. The twentieth-century Klan expanded hate. Its members targeted anyone considered un-white and un-American, including Catholics, Jews, socialists, Communists, immigrants from Asia and eastern Europe, and, as usual, blacks. They did it all in the name of Jesus.[2]

Black Americans were appalled. The newly created National Association for the Advancement of Colored People led a charge against the racist spectacle of the silver screen. One picketer carried a sign that challenged the Klan's Christ with the Jesus of the abolitionists and the reformers: "Put the Spirit of Christ Back in the Making and Execution of Law."[3]

Griffith was chagrined. As a midwestern Methodist, he could not believe that anyone would think he was a bigot. He responded the next year with a film about real intolerance, aptly titled *Intolerance* (1916).

It was a long, winding tale of four different intolerance scenarios, and Jesus was a main storyline. Actor Howard Gaye had played Robert E. Lee in *Birth of a Nation* and now was recast as Griffith's Christ. Performing as Lee, Gaye's hair was gray. As Christ, his hair was darker, longer, and parted in the middle to look like the Publius Lentulus description. White and tall, Gaye had eyeliner caked on his now-sacred face. He taught compassion, acceptance, and love. For this he was hated and crucified by the Jews. Holding Jews responsible for Christ's death, Griffith trafficked in centuries' old Christian anti-Semitism. The innovative film director had accomplished quite a lot in just a two-year span. He had attached the white Jesus to both white supremacy and anti-Semitism, and he had done it all in the name of American liberty and with the new tools of Hollywood cinema.[4]

These were profound changes from Lincoln's time. The white Jesus of the abolitionist vision had been transformed into a compatriot of Klansmen, and the prosouthern Jesus had swung from a regional symbol to a national icon. This white Jesus was then distanced from his Jewish roots and portrayed as a paragon of democracy. The supposed whiteness of Christ was joined to his ethics, words, and actions to symbolize and define white authority. Attaching principles of grace, love, liberty, and power to Christ's whiteness, whites could dominate while claiming to be democratic, and they could mistreat while thinking they were doing ministry.

There were a number of reasons for the change. Extensive legal, economic, demographic, political, and religious shifts redefined and limited whiteness, and subsequently Christ's whiteness was reconstructed. First, the abolition of slavery cut the legal ties between blackness and enslavement and the association of whiteness with freedom. This left white supremacists scouting around for new resources to assert their authority. The whiteness of Christ and the southern Lost Cause attachment to him became two important sources. Second, industrialization allowed Americans to import, export, and mass-produce images of Jesus. Third, American imperialism at home and abroad expanded white racism, provided markets for Jesus imagery, and set the stage for Americans to imagine Jesus as a militarized and imperial big brother over people of color. Fourth, waves of new immigrants led nativist Americans to tighten the parameters of whiteness and Christ's appearance as a white man. The parameters of whiteness were shrunk so dramatically that Congress limited the immigration not just of Asians but also of eastern and southern Europeans.

This confluence of factors led white Americans to embrace new images of Christ displayed in new ways. They sat spellbound and then cheered *Birth of a Nation* as a white Jesus blessed Klan members old and new. They shook their heads at the villainy of Jews in *Intolerance* who crucified the powerful-yet-compassionate savior. The new and rigorously restrictive perspectives on whiteness then led some Americans to reimagine Jesus with blond hair and blue eyes. By the 1920s, a Nordic and nativist Christ had been created who sanctified national unity through more rigid racial hierarchies and inspired international glory through military adventures.

Yet just as Griffith's films had their opponents, each new white form of Jesus and each use of him to advance and reorient white supremacy had its critics as well. The opposition tried just about everything. Some called out the Publius Lentulus letter as an evil fraud. Others deployed racial, geographical, and historical logic to point out that since no whites had lived in the Middle East during Christ's time he could not have been white. One black artist who had been to Palestine presented Jesus as mystical, cloaked, and clouded. Another black leader who had been neither to the Middle East nor to Africa declared himself the president of Africa and proclaimed that black people, if they ever wanted to be free of colonialism, must stop viewing Jesus as white. On the bloody western frontier, an Indian revival asserted that Jesus had returned. This time, he came with red skin, had the power to make it rain, and promised that the buffalo would roam the plains once again. The ritual dances that followed were too much for whites, and it took the United States military to defeat the religious revitalization.

The critics had one main problem: power. The makers and followers of the white Christ had it in a variety of forms, and the opponents did not. For every voice of opposition, scores of new white Jesus images were manufactured. The growing number of challengers simply amplified just how powerful the racial images and the associations were. Every counterclaim to the reworking of Christ's whiteness seemed corralled by police forces. The opponents had fewer resources, outlets, paint brushes, and guns. But they had courage, and they set the stage for battles for the control of Jesus in word and image.

Producing and Consuming the White Jesus in a Global Market

The United States forged itself into a global power in the decades after the Civil War. Industrial, commercial, and banking giants such as Andrew Carnegie, John Wanamaker, John D. Rockefeller, and J. Pierpont Morgan invented new corporate styles, fashioned new links among business, capital, and consumerism, and amassed staggering wealth. Telephones, phonographs, motion pictures, and lightbulbs brought light to the night, movement to the still, and voices to the distant. New consumer practices, including department stores and mail-order catalogs, altered how Americans purchased and desired goods. All of this led the United States to become a mass world producer and consumer.[5]

Visual representations of Jesus were part of the production and consumption revolutions that tied Americans into the world economy. Some of the early British settlers had fled Europe 300 years earlier, hoping to avoid iconography. Now, north to south, east to west, Protestant, Catholic, and Mormon, Americans joined a transatlantic exchange of Jesus imagery and began collecting European artwork.[6]

Contemporaries noted the sea change in America's church and religious material culture. According to one art historian of the age, "It is within the memory of the present generation that so much as a stained glass memorial window has been admitted into the churches of the dissenting denominations." He boasted, "Examples of fine quality are now found in the churches of the Unitarian, the Baptist, the Presbyterian and other sects." Methodists still were "noticeably aloof," but even they evinced a "more liberal spirit in the use of colour in the decoration of their recent churches . . . even to the introduction of works by masters who wrote wholly under the inspiration of Roman Catholicism." For this critic, the use of visual imagery allowed Americans to become "a whole religious people."[7]

In Philadelphia, John Wanamaker brought religion, business, and art together in unprecedented ways. In 1876, he purchased the Philadelphia

Railroad Depot and invited evangelist Dwight Lyman Moody to hold a huge urban revival there. Then, within months, the savvy salesman refurbished the building into one of the nation's first department stores. As a depot and then as a revival site, just about every Philadelphia resident had been there. It was a brilliant strategy to link the location of one's salvation with the place of one's spending. In the 1880s, Wanamaker's began displaying art. As religious educational leader Cynthia Pearl Maus wrote, European paintings of Christ were displayed each season of Lent "for the purpose of deepening the spiritual appreciation of men and women of the significance of Easter and the Risen Christ in the lives of all those who follow their Master in devoted service to mankind." With Christ artwork, Wanamaker baptized consumerism in the cleansing waters of education and spirituality.[8]

The importation of European sacred imagery was not done by the rich alone. Millions of Catholic immigrants came to the United States and brought with them treasure troves of iconography. Between 1850 and 1906, Catholics rose from making up less than 10 percent of the total population to more than 15 percent—from roughly 1 million to 7 million. They came from all over Europe, spoke Italian, Polish, and other languages that were relatively unknown in the United States, and moved from a marginal religious tradition in the nation to a central one. Catholics brought, bought, sold, produced, and venerated countless images of saints, Madonnas, and Jesus himself. From the streets of New York to the pastures of the Midwest, European artwork of Christ as an adult or as a baby with his mother populated the nation at a rate even faster than the immigrants themselves.[9]

For those who were not from Europe, could not make it there, or could not get to Wanamaker's department store, new books carried Americans on imaginative sacred journeys across the Atlantic Ocean, throughout Europe, into the Middle East, and beyond to the divine. Frank Milton Bristol's *The Ministry of Art* (1897), for instance, had a chapter dedicated to the "Art Galleries of Europe." Bristol recommended that tourists see art galleries in the morning. Spiritual art was more enjoyable when an individual was full of energy. For those who could not make it to Europe, Bristol offered thoughts on the images and a few engravings. He proclaimed that art and religion were intimately connected. Art "set forth her doctrines, portrayed her saints, and even her very God and Savior. . . . Art has been a teacher of things divine."[10]

Then, in the late nineteenth century, French artist James Jacques Joseph Tissot's watercolor exhibition *The Life of Our Saviour Jesus Christ* captivated thousands of Americans. It presented Christ as a virtuous Victorian—his light skin and Anglo appearance contrasting with the sinister hook-nosed Jewish characters who challenged him. Tissot's contemporaries praised his images of Christ for being "luminous," for showing an "incandescence," and for having a "certain awfulness of light and whiteness." Tissot's Anglo-Saxon Christ figures made their way into American prints and the early film industry, and the image of a white Christ was everywhere by the early twentieth century.[11]

Whiteness dominated the new imagery. Unlike the eighteenth century's age of visions when Jesus came in blinding light and the Publius Lentulus letter was largely unknown, Jesus now conformed to that myth. For these Christians, he appeared almost uniformly as a white man with brown eyes, a beard, and long straight hair parted in the middle. Even more, his white-ness became embedded as part of his moral and ethical identity.

Before World War I, the Publius Lentulus letter rose to become either a desired truth or an accepted reality. One Chicago publishing company printed numerous editions of the Lentulus letter as a pamphlet, "The Cru-cifixion, by an Eye-Witness." The associate dean of the Bible Institute in Los Angeles considered it authentic, while biographers of Jesus referenced it when describing him physically. A collection of more than 800 poems, stories, and anecdotes that supposedly made the hearts of common Ameri-cans "throb" contained as its culminating entry a picture of a white Jesus with the Publius Lentulus letter printed in full.[12]

Jesus imagery may have had its greatest impact in American Sunday schools, where the whiteness of Jesus became a religious fact in the psyches of children long before they could experience conversion. Beginning in the 1880s, the Providence Lithography Company published thousands of bibli-cal scenes as posters and lesson cards. The cards measured three-by-four inches. A year's supply of fifty-two cards cost only ten cents, so even the poorest churches could own them and most Sunday schools could have multiple sets. The cards had a fully colored image on the front and a lesson plan on the back. A generation of children first visualized Jesus and other biblical characters from these cards.[13]

Although Jesus looked somewhat different in each card, he was always white, with brown hair, brown eyes, and a ruddy face. Sometimes his beard was short; other times it was long. But always it was like his hair: straight. Adam and Eve were both white, as well, with Eve having long blond hair. There were some darker characters in the deck, too. Figures from the Old Testament had darker complexions than those of the New Testament, with the exception of David (from whom Jesus had biologically descended).

146

TRUE BLESSEDNESS

Matt. 5:1-16.

GOLDEN TEXT:—Blessed are the pure in heart: for they shall see God.

Matt. 5:8.

"True Blessedness," Sunday school lesson card, January 23, 1910, published by the Presbyterian Board of Publication and Sabbath School Work. © 1909 Providence Lithograph Co. Courtesy of the Presbyterian Historical Society, Presbyterian Church (U.S.A.), Philadelphia, Pennsylvania.

One New Testament figure was black—an Ethiopian who converted to Christianity in the Book of Acts. Interestingly, the Ethiopian's servant was even darker, perhaps to represent the assumed link between darkness and servility.[14]

Sunday school instructors loved the images and encouraged others to use them. Pictures of Jesus, one advocate exalted, "help us in the practical realization of the character of him who though we now see him not is yet present with us."[15]

Mormons could not agree more. One Mormon artist explained, "Art causes us to feel that Christ was a man, that He lived a physical existence,

Minerva K. Teichert, *The First Vision* (1934). Oil on canvas, 102 × 78 inches. Courtesy of the Brigham Young University Museum of Art.

that He was mortal, sympathized with sinners, moved among beggars, helped the infirm, ate with publicans and counseled with human beings for their immediate as well as their future spiritual welfare. It is to art that we turn for help in seeing the reality of the facts of the religious teachings of this divine human." Then, in 1913, Joseph Smith's first vision was made into stained glass in Salt Lake City. Fair-skinned with full brown hair parted down the middle, Jesus stood next to God as Smith knelt before them. Christ was fairer than the white Jesus made around the same time for Sixteenth Street Baptist Church in Birmingham, Alabama, but the two looked more similar than dissimilar.[16]

Protestants marveled at the power of imagery over children. In one popular short story, "The Talking Picture," a mother instructs her son to head to an art gallery and behold Jesus. When the boy opens the door to one room, he sees a beautiful man kneeling and praying. The boy shuts the door to allow the man his solitude. Minutes later, the lad peeks into the room again. That beautiful gentleman is still praying. Then the boy figures it out—it is not a real person. It is a painting. He sits down in front of the image and stares. He is so moved by the painting of Jesus that he brings his mother to the gallery the next day.[17]

New religious groups were also drawn to the whiteness of Jesus. Even Mary Baker Eddy and her Christian Science followers described Jesus as white. This was particularly paradoxical since a main tenet of Eddy's doctrine was the falsehood of material matter—that there was only spiritual energy and that the physical was a delusion. One of her New York disciples, Augusta E. Stetson, wrote to Eddy in 1909, "Let me continue to follow, and obey and adore the white Christ, fall at the feet of Love, and leave behind me all that is false and unreal." Stetson often encouraged her students to adore the "white Christ" and wrote to church officials in Brooklyn that she longed to gaze "on the white Christ through tears, trials, toils, tribulations, and persecutions."[18]

Assumptions of Christ's whiteness became so powerful that they even reverberated into legal arguments about citizenship for immigrants. When Syrian immigrant George Dow faced a challenge to his eligibility for American citizenship in the 1910s, the Syrian American Association rallied to his defense with Christ. They endeavored to establish Dow's and their whiteness through Christ's. Syrians were not "Asiatic," they protested, unless one described Jesus, "the most popular man in history," as "Asiatic." The community reasoned that "if Syrians were Chinese then Jesus who was born in Syria was Chinese." Of course, neither American whites nor American judges by this time believed that Jesus was Chinese. Only through his whiteness had Jesus saved Dow. He won the case and remained in America, white and free.

A contrasting case may be found in the saga of Bhagat Singh Thind, a Sikh who in 1920 sued for citizenship under the claim that he was scientifically classified as a Caucasian and was, therefore, white. But in his case, science lost where Jesus previously had won, for the Supreme Court unanimously ruled against him on the grounds that whiteness was equivalent to assimilability, and that, therefore, a "Hindoo" (never mind that he was a Sikh) was not in anyone's actual working definition of whiteness. Unlike Dow, Thind had no Jesus defense; and like obscenity, apparently, the justices could not define whiteness, but they knew it when they saw it—and it did not include anyone with a turban on his head.[19]

Critics of the White Christ

Perhaps the greatest indication of the emerging power of the white Christ was the steadily growing number of challengers the image had. A diverse group began to contest explicitly the notion that Jesus was white. Several were appalled to hear the Publius Lentulus myth treated as fact, while civil rights activists zeroed in on the white Jesus as a racial problem in a nation being defined by racial segregation and discrimination.

Publius Lentulus never existed, and many Gilded Age Americans knew it. An 1879 review of several new Protestant books in *Catholic World* scolded one author who "gravely tells the reader that 'Publius Lentulus, who was Governor of Judea in the time of Christ, wrote to Tiberius Caesar' a minute description of the personal appearance of our Saviour, and he quotes, as if it were a genuine epistle and not a coarse and impudent forgery." David Gregg, a Presbyterian in New York City, rebuked the letter, the portraits based upon it, and the racial logic that emerged from having a white Jesus: "The conventional heads of Christ are the manufacture of the merest fancy," he told his congregation in a sermon from the 1890s. According to Gregg, it was God's design that no original physical descriptions of Christ existed. "God set Christ forth as a man, and not as any particular man, that He may not be localized, or nationalized." Gregg concluded that to give Jesus a race would do damage to other racial groups. It would drive a wedge between him and others: "If He were particularized and localized— if, for example, He were made a man with a pale face, then the man of the ebony face would feel that there was a greater distance between Christ and him than between Christ and his white brother." Jesus, instead, opposed all racial differences: "As it is, there is neither white nor black in Jesus. He is a man. That is all. And wherever you find a man, black or white, Christ is his brother."[20]

Albion Tourgée offered one of the most blistering attacks in his fascinating novel of 1890, *Pactolus Prime*. Born and raised in Ohio and then serving with the Union in the Civil War, Tourgée was a radical par excellence. He supported civil rights and opposed the Klan; he drew up the first antilynching law in America; he was the lead attorney in the *Plessy v. Ferguson* (1896) segregation case; he opposed American imperialism; and he brought it all together in his attack on the whiteness of Jesus.[21]

Pactolus Prime was born a slave, but as a son of the interracial South, he appeared to be white. During the Civil War, he was mistaken for a Confederate soldier and taken prisoner by the Union. In freedom, Prime became a bootblack in the nation's capital. Even though Prime made good money, he was angry. He was mad at a world that looked down upon him because of his supposed race. He was mad at God for allowing such a world to exist. And he blamed the white Jesus.[22]

"The birthday of the white Christ!" sneered Prime when a white clerk wished him Merry Christmas. Prime went on to juxtapose the egalitarianism of Santa Claus with that of the white Christ. Santa "might not be troubled at my complexion—might be color-blind, you know, but the Christ, . . . your *white* Christ, don't ever make such mistakes." The white Christ was synonymous with all of the evils of America's racist society. "And what was slavery," Prime asked and answered, "only another name for the worship of the white Christ!" Then, later, Prime wedded an economic and historical critique to his moral one: "I feel as if Christianity—the followers of the white Christ—had robbed my people of two hundred and fifty years of bodily tool and rightful opportunity, taking the proceeds to add to their own wealth, their own luxury, the education of their children, the building of churches and colleges."[23]

Prime had a deep impact on those he met. After hearing him, many were, for the first time, willing to question Jesus' race. His assistant wondered "what welcome the Saviour would receive should he come again to earth without the pomp of an angelic following, and clothed in a fleshly garment of dusky hue." One minister was particularly shaken by Prime's claim. The preacher asked himself if "the followers of the Christ have made Him seem to be only the friend and Saviour of the white man? Is Prime right in calling Him the 'White' Christ?" The minister entered a church and "brushed aside a tear." He found no consolation, though, only more of the white Christ. "The hymns and the prayers seemed full of the idea of the 'White' Christ! His heart stood still with horror." This led to another thought: what if he or Christ were black. "He thought what would have been his own religious status had the *Man* Jesus Christ been black, and the circumstances of his life and that of Pactolus Prime been reversed." The minister left with no answers—just questions and possibilities.[24]

Arguments like Prime's appeared often enough to constitute a counter theme to the dominant white Jesus image. In 1893, the editor of the *Cleveland Gazette* announced with a headline: "Christ Jesus Not White." Just as abolitionists had positioned Jesus in America as a slave, this paper now suggested that Jesus would suffer the shame of segregation. "Christ was not of the Caucasian race or races, but, if He were living in Kentucky to-day, would be cooped up in the 'Jim Crow' cars."[25] Some new black Pentecostals of the South agreed. In Wrightsville, Arkansas, William Christian of the Church of the Living God created a catechism that tied biblical characters to black America. Unlike antebellum slave catechisms that sanctified service, Christian now divinized blackness. He taught that Job, Moses' wife, and even Jesus were black. "Q: Was Jesus a member of the black race? A: Yes."[26]

Willard L. Hunter turned to biblical genealogies to prove this in 1901 with a book that certainly set out to shock anyone who saw the title: *Jesus Christ Had Negro Blood in His Veins*. Hunter sought to connect Jesus to African Americans as a way to combat segregation, the lynchings of black men, and the rapes of black women. Charting biblical genealogies, Hunter concluded that "Jesus Christ came nearer being a black man than a white man, or at least a very dark man." This meant that whites unknowingly worshipped a black deity. He wondered what they would think when Jesus returned in black flesh. "Now, the thought that presents itself to us is, what will the negro-hating white Christians do when He comes to take charge of His church, and they find that He is a black Savior? Will the white man worship a black Savior? Yet, that is what they do every day in the week, and must forever do or have no Savior at all, for we have proven in this chapter that the incarnate Savior was nearer a black than a white man, and if He was living in the United States of America to-day He would be called a negro."[27]

Refined and middle-class blacks took aim at the white Christ too. Their critiques were usually less strident and more covert. The first African American to receive a doctoral degree from Harvard and a founder of the National Association for the Advancement of Colored People, W. E. B. Du Bois, described Jesus as "a dark and pierced Jew" in his magisterial *The Souls of Black Folk* (1903). Du Bois also claimed that segregation placed African Americans somehow curtained behind a "veil," the kind of veil that in biblical times hid Moses' face after he spoke with God or that separated the holy of holies from the most holy. The veil hid the sacred from the profane, and so it was to Du Bois that African Americans were sacred in American culture.[28]

The imagery of a darkened or perhaps veiled Jesus became a hallmark of the artwork of Du Bois's friend Henry Ossawa Tanner. The son of an African Methodist Episcopal bishop, Tanner was the most decorated black artist of the early twentieth century. Born in 1859 and raised in Philadelphia, Tanner first attended art school at the Pennsylvania Academy of the Fine Arts before sailing to Paris in 1891. He was inspired by Jesus, writing on scraps of paper in his studio: "Wednesday—I invited the Christ spirit to manifest in me." Then on Friday, "I follow the star (high ideal) that leads me to the Christ."[29]

Tanner's Jesus often had dark skin, a black beard, a moustache, and dark eyes. In his gripping *The Resurrection of Lazarus* (1897) and his elegant *Christ and Nicodemus on a Rooftop* (1899), Tanner showcased Jesus as tall and commanding. His face was far darker than those in Sunday school prints and his beard was almost black. Tanner's *Savior* (c. 1905) even veiled the face of Jesus with layers of dark and brown paint. Although one can make out dark hair and a beard, it is difficult to discern most of Christ's facial features. It would be nearly impossible for anyone to consider him white. The effect was riveting. It was as if the veil described by Du Bois that hid African Americans also cloaked the savior.[30]

Tanner's Christ figures looked distinct from any previous American artist. His Christ looked Mediterranean. Perhaps this was because unlike most American artists, Tanner had toured Palestine several times. Perhaps this was also because Tanner employed Jewish men and children to pose for his paintings.[31]

Tanner's work was a hit in France and the United States. His compositions were reproduced in *Harper's Weekly* and the *Ladies' Home Journal* and exhibited in New York City, Chicago, Philadelphia, Cincinnati, Buffalo, St. Louis, Pittsburgh, San Francisco, Los Angeles, Washington, D.C., and Boston.[32]

Most often, reviewers drew attention to the mystical darkness and "Oriental" feel of the paintings. Some noticed the importance of shadow and veils. After an exhibition in 1911, the *Chicago Daily Tribune* commented upon the "shadowy greenish tone," and later the *New York World* concluded that his work contained mostly "heavily swathed figures, bathed in an unearthly light." Years later, one art critic remarked, "Tanner's colors . . . are usually those of the late afternoon, dusk, and evening. His use of blues is striking whether in his earlier works or the later paintings of blue/green tones."[33]

Tanner was not the only one giving Jesus an "Oriental" face. Throughout the late nineteenth and early twentieth centuries, a small but active set of Asian immigrants brought their Hinduism to the West Coast. Some cosmopolitan white Americans showed a keen interest in these faiths, particularly after Swami Vivekananda's speech at the World's Parliament of Religions held in Chicago in 1893. In San Francisco, the first Hindu temple in the United States commissioned a white Catholic artist to depict

Jesus as a "yogi." This Christ had long brown hair that was matched by his straight brown beard, but his skin was darker than most Jesus figures made in America. He was also seated in a half lotus position to meld Christian teachings with Hindu meditation.[34]

These new Christ figures gave visual expression to the emerging critique of the white Jesus. The challengers used ink and paint, novels and sermons, commentaries and histories. They were sometimes subtle, as in Tanner's art or Du Bois's *Souls of Black Folk*. They were sometimes abrupt, as in Christian's catechism or Prime's accusations. The emerging picture was clear, though. From novels to social commentaries, sophisticated artwork to Pentecostal catechisms, the mass-produced white Jesus was going to have to fight to carry the day.

And fight his supporters did. For every act of resistance, there were thousands of white Christ figures produced, sold, and gazed upon by white, black, and red Americans. The opponents, moreover, could do little to stop the deadly combination of gospels and Gatling guns that led Americans to crusade through their own continent, across their hemisphere, and into Asia in a new set of imperialist adventures. As they advanced through the American West and then overseas, white Americans made their white Jesus into a big brother who sanctified their behavior, whether the "little brown brothers" of William McKinley's imagination liked it or not.

Imperialisms Near and Far

The white Jesus could be found far and wide in the culture of militant expansion, and his presence cloaked particular national, racial, and economic interests under a sacred canopy of universal care and compassion. As imperialism stretched from the American West to overseas ventures, the white Christ became a big brother figure who sanctified concepts of white racial adulthood and nonwhite racial childhood. He was made into a supposedly universal savior, but one who privileged white authority and dominance.

With the end of the Civil War, the nation's attention and its military turned from east to west. Northerners grew fascinated by the drama of cowboys, Indians, and expansion into lands controlled by "wild" Indian tribes. Violence both physical and cultural was at the core of white interactions with Native Americans. Missionaries and military men bought into the motto, "Kill the Indian, save the man." Jesus in this environment became an agent of imperialism through his supposed individualism. Soldiers, missionaries, and politicians teamed up to take land but give Native Americans in return the white Jesus as their personal savior.[35]

Individualism and personal salvation became the mantra of whites toward Indians and the West. Historian Frederick Jackson Turner became famous for noting the importance of the frontier in shaping American democracy and juxtaposed the white Christ of liberty with the autocratic gods of the Prussian empire. "The Prussian discipline is the discipline of Thor, the War God," Turner commented, while "the discipline of the White Christ" made American individualism and freedom in the frontier.[36]

Christ's individualistic discipline destroyed Indian communities with a benevolent violence. Members of the Indian Rights Association, founded by white activists in 1882, thought it impossible for the Indian as a tribal member to survive the "aggressions of civilization." But, they suggested, his "individual redemption from heathenism and ignorance, his transformation from the condition of a savage nomad to that of an industrious American citizen, is abundantly possible." Since Christ touched the individual, he could be the backbone of making good individual citizens. As one leader claimed in 1893, Indians could only be "redeemed from evil" by breaking up the "mass," and as "we get at them one by one, as we break up these iniquitous masses of savagery, as we draw them out from their old associations and immerse them in the strong currents of Christian life and Christian citizenship, and as we send the sanctifying stream of Christian life and Christian work among them, they feed the pulsing life-tide of Christ's life."[37]

Jesus and individualism were knotted together, allowing whites to take Indian tribal lands. The Dawes Act of 1887 was the legal lever that made it happen. Written by Massachusetts senator Henry Dawes, the act divided tribal lands into individual "allotments." Male heads of families received 120 acres, and sales of leftover "surplus" lands funded Indian boarding schools. The best known of these schools, such as Carlisle and Pratt, uprooted Native American children from widely scattered locales. Often wrested forcibly from their families, the children were punished in the schools for "talking Indian," dressing in traditional clothes, or engaging in "heathenish" practices. It was also there that they were indoctrinated with images of the white Jesus.[38]

He was a ubiquitous presence in the boarding schools. According to novelist Rupert Costo, "When the Christians took the Indian children off to boarding schools, the minister used to lead the children into the chapel and

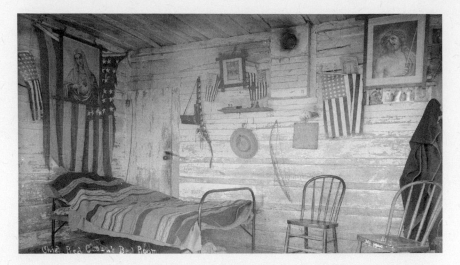

Clarence Grant Morledge, "Interior of Red Cloud's House—Pine Ridge Agency, South Dakota" (1891). Courtesy of the Denver Public Library, Western History Collection, x-31433.

point up to the picture of Jesus, with long flowing hair, and tell the Indian children that they were going to learn how to be just like that man, Jesus. After this statement, the minister would send all the Indian boys off to get their hair cut short." Curiously, becoming more like Christ meant looking less like him. Short hair, not long hair, was somehow civilized.[39]

As in previous white-Indian religious encounters, some adopted the new savior as their own. Henrietta Chief's single mother was unable to care for her on the plains of the early twentieth century, so Henrietta was sent to Tomah Indian School in Wisconsin. There she learned about Jesus and saw him. She converted to Christianity after viewing slides prepared by the school superintendent that depicted "Jesus on the cross, with his arms outstretched. . . . And right then and there I accepted Jesus as my Lord and Savior." Recounting this event sixty years later, Henrietta remained "happy, just as I was when I was converted."[40]

Happiness and hope were elusive on the frontier, but in the final decades of the nineteenth century, a new messianic challenge emerged to promise salvation, the return of the buffalo, and the removal of whites' sins. In the ghost dance movements (usually referred to as "crazes" by uncomprehending and patronizing whites), a new Jesus seemed poised to storm onto the prairies. The modern dances originated among the Bannock and Shoshones in southern Idaho, found their way to Nevada by the 1870s, and became a deep part of Indian life among a variety of groups in the Rocky Mountains and upper plains.[41]

In the ghost dances, the American West became a sacred geography of Christ's presence and return. The Paiute prophet Wovoka was its most spectacular representative, and his religious innovations reflected his mixed cultural and racial heritage. His Paiute father died when he was a teenager, and he was then raised by David Wilson, a white farmer, in Nevada. He took the name Jack Wilson. In the late 1880s, suffering from illness and despair, he experienced a series of transformative visions. He took from his native background ideas about controlling the weather, beliefs in dreams and visions, and practices of ritualistic dances.

From his white father's Presbyterianism, Wovoka drew resurrection images of the dead in heaven and the leading role of a charismatic preacher figure. Around the time of the solar eclipse of January 1889, he had a near-death experience and a new revelation. Wovoka was, one white testified, "a Simon pure, yard wide, all wool Christ . . . who advised peace and performed miracles which made all people feel good." Ethnologists of the age saw him as fitting the Plains Indians idea of *waneika*, a Christ "returned to Earth to benefit Native Americans and to punish whites on a second sacrificial go-around."[42]

Wovoka played a kind of shell game with his sacred identity. Normally he rejected direct connections of himself to "the Messiah," but on a photograph of himself taken in 1917, he wrote, "I am the only living Jesus there is. Signed, Jack Wilson." Wovoka most often claimed the mantle of a prophet preaching the rituals necessary for pan-Indian renewal. One western agent explained, "He tells them he has been to heaven and that the Messiah is coming to earth again and will put the Indians in possession of the country."[43]

His power seemed too great for Wovoka to be a mere prophet, though. Many hoped that he was their new Christ. In 1891, Captain Josephus of the Indian police around the Walker Lake Reservation encountered Jack Wilson. Josephus tested Wilson's power, and when the rains came, concluded, "I am a strong believer in the unnatural powers of the new Christ." Decades later, when Wovoka passed away, one woman was shocked: "How can he die?" It seemed that Christ had come to this place of so much pain and agony.[44]

Local whites were fascinated and unsettled. They described Indians as anxious but seemed themselves to be the nervous ones. In his study for the Bureau of Ethnology, pioneering anthropologist James Mooney recorded one curious Indian observer noting that those living in Paiute land were "anxious to see Christ. Just before sundown I saw a great many people, mostly Indians coming dressed in white men's clothes. The Christ was with them. They all formed in this ring around it. . . . I had always thought the Great Father was a white man, but this man looked like an Indian." He instructed everybody to join "the Christ singing while we danced." One Indian, according to Mooney, thought he was beholding the risen Jesus: "I had heard that Christ had been crucified, and I looked to see, and I saw a scar on his wrist and one on his face, and he seemed to be the man."[45]

Jesus was back. He was an Indian, and he stood in judgment of whites. Mooney recorded an ominous letter in his book, one that supposedly came from the Indian Messiah. The letter revealed and concealed Christ's return and that righteous judgment was about to come: "Do not tell the white people about this. Jesus is now upon the earth. He appears like a cloud. The dead are all alive again. I do not know when they will be here; maybe this fall or in the spring."[46]

New hope for Indians brought attention from the government. Soldiers from the U.S. Army warily eyed Indians who danced continuously for days, fell into trances, and foresaw the deaths of their enemies and the re-creation of an Indian world. As white fears spread, the military determined that one force could stop this new religious uprising: violence. In late December 1890, the heavenly ghost dance turned into a hellish bloodbath. When federal troops led by Colonel James Forsyth attempted to disarm Sioux warriors in South Dakota—warriors who claimed to have no arms—U.S. forces opened fire on women, men, and children. Four days after Christmas in 1890, that celebration of the "white Christ," as Pactolus Prime sneered, almost 200 natives died for living their faith. Wovoka was not dead, but in many ways his movement was.[47]

What happened in America did not stay in America. Missionary and military action expanded in the late 1890s as the nation shifted its imperialist arm from the frontier to islands and nations abroad. These new imperial ventures took Americans to places as near as Cuba and Puerto Rico in the Caribbean and as far as the Philippines, Hawaii, and China in the Pacific. It inspired Theodore Roosevelt to have a bully time as a rough rider and Admiral Thomas Dewey to become an American hero. And it led the United States to have, for the first time, real power throughout the world. Imperialist expansion was part of an American racial patriarchy rooted in previous approaches to Native Americans and African Americans. This racial patriarchy imagined whites (embodied in the "white nation") as adults and men and women of color (either within the United States or outside of it in other nations) as children. Jesus became an imperialist emblem as a white big brother to the "half devil and half children" foreign peoples, as Rudyard Kipling so ominously wrote.

Missionary language of the period helped drive imperial impulses. In 1894, the newly formed Student Volunteer Movement took as the theme for its national convention "The World's Conquest for Christ." Unlike eighteenth-century Moravians who focused on the violence committed against Christ, white Protestants now fixated on the violence committed for Christ. An article in *Century* magazine declared that Jesus was a man of violence who had used physical force to clear the temple in Jerusalem.[48]

At the height of the excitement to evangelize the world in this generation, several religious writers expressly connected Jesus to whiteness. They did so as part of a new white supremacist theology that presented whites as the only true children of God. Rev. G. C. H. Hasskarl, for instance, penned a series of articles declaring that Jesus was part of "a white Nation holding servants." He warned that empires rose and fell based on their ability to separate whites from blacks socially and sexually. Jesus' teachings, he continued, applied only to whites. When he told his followers to "go, and teach all nations," Jesus meant "'all' white 'nations,' for, history knows of no Negro 'nations.'"[49] Another writer translated Christ's whiteness into God's whiteness by asking and answering: "Did He come in the form and likeness of either one of the inferior races? He presented Himself to us in the image of his Father, clothed upon with all the paraphernalia that indicated a direct descent from Adam. Christ was the God-man, a true Caucasian of the blushing race, the highest type of the original creation."[50]

Christ's white physical attributes became another defining feature of his glory. One Protestant writer claimed that Jesus was clearly God and white because he was "endowed with beauty of person, symmetry of form and feature, . . . his brow beaming with intelligence and his heart melting with compassion." Northern evangelical minister A. J. Gordon commented: "There are negroes in central Africa who never dreamed that they were black until they saw the face of a white man; and there are people who never knew that they were sinful until they saw the face of Jesus Christ in all its whiteness and purity." Taken not as fictitious or just representative, the white Jesus now seemed true and historical.[51]

A new song and a new painting forged Jesus into an imperial big brother. "Jesus Loves the Little Children" was first written during the Gilded Age. Set to a popular Civil War tune, it was in many ways a song of sacred inclusion. Jesus loved, died for, and rose for all the children of the world, "red, brown, yellow, / black and white." All of them, regardless of laws, social practices, or cultural mores, were "precious in his sight."[52]

But by the 1910s, when the song took graphic form, it was one of racial hierarchy. Harold Copping's *The Hope of the World* (1915) became a staple in Sunday schools in the United States and around the world. It had five children seated beneath a white, adult Jesus. What was striking in the painting was not racial connection, but racial disconnection. The various children all touched the white Christ except for one child: a nude black boy. The other children were all clothed and either stood by Jesus or were held by him. No part of the black boy's body touched the savior. In Tennessee, one black educational leader looked at the painting and asked, "Why is it . . . that the only one of these children of the world who is not touching Jesus is the little black lad in the foreground?" Responding, the head teacher, who was white, claimed, "Because your race is one of the most backward of all the race of the children of men."[53] The art marked not only the sacred status of whiteness but also the profanity of blackness.

Imperialism troubled many Americans, and religious arguments exploded from those who thought it a moral travesty. Mark Twain was one of the most outspoken voices of protest, and he even poked some bitter fun at believers in Christ's whiteness. Throughout the late 1890s and into the twentieth century, Twain castigated "Christendom" for "playing it badly." It was bringing violence everywhere in the name of the prince of peace. Twain even began writing stories in which Satan was not just the lead character but also the most admirable figure with his wit and wisdom.

In private, Twain chided family members for thinking that Jesus and his mother were white. On one occasion, his imperious daughter, Jean, told him it was "sacrilegious" to say that "the Mother of the Saviour was *colored*." Twain smirked and shot back: "Sac—oh, nonsense!" He then made an argument from racial and historical logic: "In her day the population of the globe was not more than a thousand millions. Not *one-tenth* of them were *white*. What does this fact suggest to you?" Jean was not sure, so Twain continued the lesson: "It most powerfully suggests that *white was not a favorite complexion with God*. Has it since become a favorite complexion with Him? . . . There is nothing important, nothing essential, about a complexion. I mean, to me. But with the Deity it is different. He doesn't think much of white people."[54]

This was Twain at his sarcastic and sardonic best. Theologically, Twain connected the "colored" incarnation of Jesus to God's preference for nonwhite people. Twain even positioned himself as morally above God—that he, Twain, was colorblind. God had racial preferences, just not the same ones that white Americans had.

Twain could toy with these ideas in private and find humor in it all. He was not black or oppressed. Marcus Garvey did not consider white colonialism so amusing, and he rose to attack it and its white Christ. Born in Jamaica, he came to the United States to study under Booker T. Washington. Finding Washington dead but white American and European colonialism alive and well, Garvey set out to make himself a messianic figure for black people throughout the world. Only through racial and global solidarity could they challenge the powers of colonialism and imperialism. Garvey hoped his new organization, the Universal Negro Improvement Association, could unite black people, liberate Africa, and transform the entire world.

Part of Garvey's anti-imperialist thrust was to divest Christ of his whiteness and comprehend the sacred through the eyes of black women and men. He blasted the notion of a white Jesus. Part defiance to white supremacy, part embrace of blackness, Garvey's organization demanded that his people "never admit that Jesus Christ was a white man, otherwise he could not be the Son of God and God to redeem all mankind. Jesus Christ had the blood of all races in his veins . . . from which Jesus sprang through the line of Jesse[;] you will find Negro blood everywhere, so Jesus had much of Negro blood in him."[55] Garvey's followers were convinced: "Jesus Christ was not a white man; we know that well." When depicting a man with "the blood of all races," Garvey's followers represented Jesus as black. One 1924 edition of the *Negro World* ran the headline "Jesus Was a Negro by Blood" and had a "picture of Jesus as a colored man with wooly hair."[56]

Garvey and his Universal Negro Improvement Association staff reversed the racialized sacred past imagined by whites. In the organization's race-based biblical history, whites crucified Christ while blacks supported him. "Oh Jesus the Christ, oh Jesus the Redeemer, when white men scorned you, when white men spurned you, when white men spat upon you, when white men pierced your side out of which blood and water gushed forth, it was a black man in the person of Simon the Cyrenian who took the cross and bore it on heights of Calvary." Ultimately, "the Cross is the property of the Negro in his religion because it was he who bore it."[57]

Garvey's spiritual dream faltered, much like Wovoka's had. It fell prey to government surveillance, financial malfeasance, and black opposition. In Garvey's case, the military was not involved, but the predecessor to the Federal Bureau of Investigation, the attorney general's office, and the United States Postal Service were, all of which joined forces and eventually convicted him of mail fraud. The government sentenced him to five years in prison and then deported him. Garveyism never died, but his organization foundered. When liberation theologians exploded onto the American scene in the 1960s, many of them claimed it was Garvey's voice they echoed with pride. And before then, Garveyism deeply influenced black political opposition, from the family of Malcolm Little (later Malcolm X) to the father of Rosa Parks, who trained a daughter in race pride; that daughter took those conceptions into her struggles against sexual violence perpetrated by white men against black women in the 1940s, more than a decade before her "tired feet" became an icon of the civil rights movement.[58]

A Nordic Warrior Christ

By the time Americans entered World War I, Christ's whiteness had been profoundly reshaped by the destruction of chattel slavery, the industrial revolution, immigration shifts, and the rise of segregation and imperialism. He had become an emblem of a white supremacy that was being redefined and becoming more limited. Civil rights activists recognized this image as a powerful and dangerous one, particularly after he had been militarized and southernized, not to mention shed of his Jewishness. This set the stage not only for D. W. Griffith's cinematic renderings of Jesus, which positioned him as a non-Jewish lover of freedom who blessed the Ku Klux Klan, but also for Americans to embrace for the first time a painting of Jesus Christ as blond-haired and blue-eyed. The Nazis would call him "Aryan." American white supremacists called him "Nordic."[59]

In the decades surrounding the turn of the century, Americans longed for and despised immigrants. The new Statue of Liberty invited women, men, and families from the world to join the American experiment, but nativist attacks upon what they called an "immigrant problem" ranged from legal briefs to violent assaults. Whether Klansmen, members of Boston's elite Brahman class, or esteemed New York City attorneys, a growing number of white Americans denounced the new immigrants from eastern and southern Europe as racially and religiously unfit for citizenship. Nativism was so widespread and ran so hot that by 1924 Congress passed a new immigration law that virtually closed the doors to individuals from these lands.[60]

Jews were particularly deemed as less-than-white and denounced as non-Christian. As more than 1.5 million Jews immigrated to the United

States from eastern Europe from 1890 to 1914, anti-Semitism rose sharply. In 1893, a Baltimore minister declared that Jews were a "veritable Shylock who loses every sentiment of humanity in his greed. Of all the creatures who have befouled the earth, the Jew is the slimiest." During the Easter season, Protestant and Catholic children accused Jews of being "Christ killers." In Malden, Massachusetts, in 1911, a group of teenagers viciously attacked a group of Jewish Americans, shouting "Beat the Jews" and "Kill the Jews." The police did little to stop it. Four years later, enraged whites in Georgia lynched pencil factory owner Leo Frank, while the police stood by.[61]

For some, the whiteness of Christ and his Jewishness became incompatible, and distancing him from Judaism became part of efforts to redefine and limit whiteness and American citizenship. Madison Grant helped lead the way. A refined New York attorney who preferred a black suit to a white robe, he thought American whites were far too tolerant. In his influential *The Passing of the Great Race* (1916), he claimed that the millions of "new immigrants" flooding into the United States during the previous thirty years would spell doom for America. To avoid "race suicide," as Grant called it, white Americans needed to protect those at the top of the racial ladder, "Nordic whites." Americans needed to learn to see blond hair and blue eyes as evidence of group strength and prevent imposters from entering the white camp. Grant's work provided Congress with the rationale, statistics, and racial limiting of whiteness to pass its immigration restrictions of the 1920s.

For Grant, Nordic supremacy was spiritual as well as material. "Mental, spiritual and moral traits are closely associated with the physical distinctions among the different European races," Grant explained, and this meant that Jesus must have been Nordic and thus not Jewish. Grant grounded his proof in how biblical Jews responded to Christ: They "*apparently* regarded Christ as, in some *indefinite* way, non-Jewish." Grant then applauded the history of European art for painting Jesus as Nordic. "In depicting the crucifixion no artist hesitates to make the two thieves brunet in contrast to the blond Savior. This is something more than a convention, as such quasi-authentic traditions as we have of our Lord strongly suggest his Nordic, possibly Greek, physical and moral attributes."[62]

Grant also invoked the Publius Lentulus letter, which he read as a description of Jesus as Nordic. Grant knew the letter was false but wanted the myth of the white Jesus to be considered a fact. After admitting that the Publius Lentulus letter was a fraud, Grant continued: "It is interesting . . . in showing the popular attitude to the traits in question, and in attributing these Nordic characters to Christ."[63]

Religious writer Robert Warren Conant also wanted to distance Jesus from Jews, and he wanted to make Christ more masculine in the process. Conant was frustrated by the effeminacy and weakness he perceived in American men. Unlike Grant, though, Conant found little to praise in Christian art. He damned its Christ representations. "From lovely illuminated church windows and from Sunday-school banners he looks down upon us," Conant complained, "'meek and lowly,' with an expression of sweetness and resignation, eyes often down-cast, soft hands gently folded, long curling hair brushed smoothly from a central parting—all feminine, passive, negative."

What Americans needed was a tough and rough Jesus. They desired a savior more like Theodore Roosevelt and less like a teddy bear. They needed a Jesus with "a strong tonic of Virility." "The men of a strenuous age demand a strenuous Christ," Conant proclaimed. "If we want to win modern *men*" to the church, "we must quit preaching the 'meek and lowly Jesus' and substitute the Fighting Christ."[64]

The fighting Christ was an un-Jewish Christ. "Why is it that we never think of Christ as a Jew?" Conant asked and then answered. "Because he was more occidental [western European] than oriental [Middle Eastern], and more cosmopolitan than either." To Conant, in temperament, intellect, and attitude, Jesus had much more in common with Anglo-Saxons. "Born of a race which has always been characterized by great excitability and volubility, he was more like the best type of the modern Anglo-Saxon in his perfect self-command, his cool, steady eye, his capacity for reticence, and his love for brevity." So Jesus was white, tough, and not Jewish.[65]

Conant and Grant had a problem, though, and that problem was the Bible. Since there were no biblical physical descriptions of Jesus, Conant and Grant had to build their arguments upon half-truths, fraudulent letters, and speculations. And whatever Jesus looked like, the genealogies seemed to make it pretty clear that he was descended from Jews. Grant did not have good evidence, and he knew it. Jews "apparently" viewed Christ as different, and the artistic tradition was "quasi-authentic." Conant also admitted, "There is no contemporaneous picture of Christ and no direct description of his appearance. . . . All sorts of descriptions and representations have come down to us along the centuries, often contradictory, sometimes ridiculous." Even more, Conant at other times asserted the nonwhiteness of Jesus. "It is to be remembered that he was an Oriental speaking to Orientals."[66]

Even as they acknowledged Christ's nonwhiteness, Conant's and Grant's insistence on him somehow still being white showcased just how powerful racial ideologies had become and how weak their foundations were. The white Jesus was needed to sanctify whiteness, but white supremacists could not prove it, so they turned to assumptions about character, conduct, self-control, and moral temperament. None of that, though, could be shown to come from hereditary or physicality, especially not Christ's.[67]

By the time Conant and Grant were writing, the idea of masculinizing the white Jesus had gone into overdrive. Psychologist G. Stanley Hall wrote a series of articles and books denouncing the passivity of Jesus in art and calling for a more vigorous Christ. Likewise, Mormon writers denounced the tendency for artists to paint Jesus as a "somewhat effeminate and sentimental young man with long flowing locks, a weakling in body and with few traces on his face of the strength of character within. All this is wrong."[68]

During World War I, Jesus went marching to war as a symbol of the allied effort. War propaganda depicted the American army as a new crusading arm of God's hand in the world while vilifying the Central Powers as demonic, barbaric Christ haters. American soldiers regularly associated themselves with Christ's sufferings and triumphs. In one cartoon from *The Stars and Stripes* in 1918, German leaders laugh and mock a crucified Christ in the background: "Oh, Look Papa!" one says to the other as he motions at the crucified white Jesus: "Another of those Allies!" One pamphlet calling for American volunteers linked the white Christ with the war effort directly: "The great Comrade in White is seeking recruits for an invincible and conquering company of Comrades of the forward-looking, Comrades of His holy cross, Comrades of His coming Kingdom."[69]

While nativist Americans had a problem with Jews, Jewish Americans had a problem with Jesus. He was not their messiah. They did not follow a holy calendar around his birth, death, and resurrection. They did not have or want images of him. And although his followers in the United States treated them far more kindly than those in eastern Europe were treated, new Jewish immigrants had to contend with Jesus as part of their dilemmas of assimilation. For the vast majority of Jews and their children, though, Jesus was a foreign presence, a name by which they were oppressed, mistreated, and despised. Although several Jewish leaders of the age pressed for Jesus' Jewishness to be honored, most American Jews kept their distance from Christ.[70]

Pastor-turned-novelist Thomas Dixon Jr. had little concern for Jews—except for his hatred for those who became political radicals in northern cities or for how their biblical history could be appropriated, molded into a story of sacred racial domination, and mapped onto the United States to justify white supremacy. "We believe," one of his fictional white characters explained, "that God has raised up our race, as he ordained Israel of old, in this world-crisis to establish and maintain for weaker races, as a trust for civilisation, the principles of civil and religious Liberty and the forms of Constitutional Government." The weaker races in the modern world were the blacker ones, and Dixon took it upon himself in the 1890s to redeem the South by resurrecting the Ku Klux Klan. He set out to convince the nation that Klan members were the real protectors of God's racial plan for the United States and the world.

Dixon was a popular novelist of the age, and his novels helped transform the suffering savior of the Lost Cause into a herald of American power. Dixon's most famous works, *The Leopard's Spots* and *The Clansman*, trafficked in an unabashed sanctifying of white supremacy. His stories were filled with notions of "righteous wrath," where death was preferable to dishonor and where God ordained white American supremacy. His rage was based on his belief that "the love which filled the soul of Christ was a consuming fire, and before it evil must be burned up." Dixon determined that the Anglo-Saxon family was the core of the American nation and God's plan to redeem the world. To protect the family (and especially white women's reproduction), Americans should go to any length. If the government would not do it and the church would not do it, then a new "Invisible Empire" must. In Dixon's historical imagination, the Ku Klux Klan was a new church, formed "for their God, their native land, and the womanhood of the South." The white, militant Christ of the suffering South had become an American emblem of segregation and white supremacy.[71]

Through Dixon, the cross became the ultimate symbol of the Klan. Before him, Klan members of the 1860s and 1870s rarely used crosses on their outfits or in their attacks. They were more likely to present themselves as demons or as the ghosts of Confederate dead. Now they became champions of Christ. Illustrations in *The Clansman* showed Klan members and their horses with large crosses emblazoned on their robes. At secret ceremonies, Klan members raised flaming crosses to proclaim their allegiance to Christ and white supremacy. D. W. Griffith picked up on these images and inserted them directly into *Birth of a Nation*. Klan members in the film have large crosses on their chests, and one of the film's promotional posters was taken almost directly from the novel. Atop a rearing and powerful horse, a Klansman thrusts the "fiery cross of the Ku Klux Klan" into the air.[72]

When the new Klan formed after *Birth of a Nation*, members of its very visible Empire placed Jesus and the cross squarely at the center of their white supremacist culture. The opening prayer of the officially prescribed Klan ritual of the 1920s called members to adopt "the living Christ" as the "Klansman's criterion of character." One Texan put it simply: Jesus "was a Klansman." Christ's act upon the cross perfectly symbolized the Klan's turn to Jesus as the emblem of suffering, pain, service, and sacrifice. "Since Jesus's wounded body bore the sins of the world," a Klan historian explained, "a member should follow Jesus's example. . . . It was not necessary to sacrifice one's life, but to sacrifice one's selfhood for the greater body of Klan membership."

The white robe, its symbols, and burning crosses became emblems of the Klan's claim to Christ. As one minister in the movement surmised, "I think Jesus would have worn a robe." A Klan newspaper explained, "Pure Americanism can only be secured by confidence in the fact that the Cross of Jesus Christ is the wisest and strongest force in existence." The Klan's cross had united faith and nation in one symbol: "Sanctified and made holy nearly nineteen hundred years ago by the suffering and blood of the crucified Christ, bathed in the blood of fifty million martyrs who died in the most holy faith, it stands in every Klavern of the Knights of the Ku Klux Klan as a constant reminder that Christ is our criterion of character." Illustrations from Klan histories of the age had Klansmen in the place of Christ's disciples. They helped him pass out bread and fish to the multitudes without food. On another occasion, Jesus distributed the "Tenets of the K.K.K." as spiritual and civic nourishment for "100% Americans."[73]

And this new Klan (and its various female auxiliaries) did not hide in secret and attack at night in the South. Instead, Klansmen now marched in public from Atlanta to Chicago, from Newark to Los Angeles. From the end of the Civil War to the early 1920s, Jesus in the United States became a symbol of white supremacy, and his whiteness partly defined his essence. Further, his whiteness suggested racial adulthood, imperial dominance, martial power, anti-Semitism, and a Ku Klux Klan that was now all-American.

THE IDEA OF JESUS as non-Jewish, Nordic, and masculine received a visual representation right after World War I. *The Nazarene, or Christ Triumphant* was Henry Stanley Todd's greatest artistic accomplishment. He was previously known as a New York City portrait artist, and he had painted Theodore Roosevelt, William McKinley, and Mary Baker Eddy. He was also known for playing the drums while his "Negro servants" played guitars. For

Henry Stanley Todd, *The Nazarene, or Christ Triumphant* (1932).
From Cynthia Pearl Maus, *Christ and the Fine Arts* (New York:
Harper and Brothers, 1938).

years, Todd had considered painting Christ, and after the Great War, he did
it. White Americans hailed it as a marvel.

The Nazarene, or Christ Triumphant was a simple head of Christ, but the
savior now had a resolute look, pale skin, blond hair, and clear blue eyes.
Todd displayed it to the crowds as part of the Hall of Religion at the 1933
World's Fair in Chicago. From that point on, *The Nazarene* was a hit and
was shown throughout the country. It received praise from Presbyterians,
Lutherans, the Federal Council of Churches, and a host of other religious
groups. *Time* and the *Literary Digest* featured Todd for his remarkable new
vision of Christ.[74]

Viewers saw in it the tough, masculine, and Nordic Jesus they had desired. Art critic E. C. Sherburne heralded Todd's painting as "an Original
Conception. . . . Here we have THE TRIUMPHANT CHRIST." Sherburne
loved the new blond hair and blue eyes. "While the Christ in art [is] so

often depicted as a Latin type, Colonel Todd's painting is startling at first in its divergence from convention. . . . This Nazarene has golden hair and blue eyes." Sherburne claimed that recent biblical scholarship had established that Jesus came from a group of blond Israelites, and hence his painting was historically accurate. Another pastor claimed that "its light hair and blue eyes transported me into another world."[75]

One enthusiastic reviewer believed that the painting was uniting Americans around a manly symbol. He exclaimed that "Protestants and Roman Catholics alike agree that it is a marvelously new conception of the face of Jesus." No longer would Americans worship a "man of sorrows," but now they would have "a man whose strength of character and mystical power has overcome sorrow and triumphed over all the problems of life." Authority was in his whiteness. "The picture shows Jesus as a blonde, blue-eyed, with a determined mouth, and an air and color of virility, perfect manhood, fascinating expression, and loving nature."[76]

Madison Grant finally had his wish and immigrant restriction had a sacred face. Todd's Jesus was Nordic with blond hair and manly with blue eyes. So much had been reversed from the days when abolitionists proclaimed that Jesus was a slave or when George Kelly believed that Jesus had come back to set the captives free. So much had changed since eighteenth-century New Yorkers saw Jesus in blinding light or Puritans witnessed devils all around them. Reconstruction, economic development, reworkings of whiteness, internal and external imperialism, and a southern literary renaissance had helped transform Jesus into a totem of white supremacy.

Yet this newly ascended white Jesus was in trouble from the start. The first half of the twentieth century found Jesus in danger on all sides. When Americans north and south, east and west, conservative and liberal, red, white, and black sought to save him, they often did so once again by reframing his body. According to the Bible, before Christ ascended into heaven, he gave his followers a "Great Commission" to make disciples of all nations. Americans of the early twentieth century wanted to do this. But as they fell into the Great Depression, they more and more disagreed over which Christ they were to spread.

PART THREE

ASCENDED AND STILL ASCENDING

CHAPTER SEVEN

THE GREAT COMMISSION IN THE GREAT DEPRESSION

Upton Sinclair was best known for his muckraking exposure of the Chicago meatpacking industry, but he wrote a lot more about Christ than he did about cattle. In perhaps his best novel, *They Call Me Carpenter: A Tale of the Second Coming* (1922), Sinclair conjured a tale of Jesus visiting Los Angeles at the beginning of the roaring twenties. The tale begins with a conversation about movies and Jesus. Three years after World War I, the narrator, Billy, and his friend Dr. Henner are on their way to watch a German-made film. They discuss the fate of the still-young film industry and its uncertain future. Dr. Henner uses the pain of the early Christians as a prophecy for the modern cinema. "Is not that the final test of great art, that it has been smelted in the fires of suffering?" he asks, and then he answers, "All great spiritual movements of humanity began in that way; take primitive Christianity, for example."

Henner warns that Americans might do to movies what they have done to Jesus. The people "have taken Christ, the carpenter," and made him into "a symbol of elegance, a divinity of the respectable inane." Billy mentions that Americans had merely joined Europeans in this redefinition, but the traveling partners agree that the lowly workman Jesus had been reconstructed into an American icon of affluence and banality. Their prime example is the stained-glass Jesus at St. Bartholomew's Church, where Jesus was "dressed up in exquisite robes of white and amethyst." This Christ looked eerily similar to the white Jesus at the Mormon Temple in Salt Lake City, Utah, some 700 miles to the east. It also looked eerily similar to the one another 2,000 miles across the continent at Sixteenth Street Baptist Church in Birmingham, Alabama.

These ruminations are ruined when a mob attacks. An anti-German crowd assails the theater and its guests, forcing Billy to take cover in St.

Bartholomew's. He marvels at the "gleaming altar," where Jesus has "a brown beard, and a gentle, sad face, and a halo of light about the head." Distraught, Billy places his head down on the railing. Then a miracle happens. Jesus steps out of the window, stands beside Billy, and puts his reassuring hand on Billy's shoulder. It is the second coming, and Jesus is an agent of his own iconoclasm. He leaves a "great big hole" in the window, which they fill with the portrait of a banker (no one even notices the switch). Billy nervously inquires: "I thought you belonged in the church?" Jesus replies, "Do I? . . . I'm not sure. I have been wondering—am I really needed here? And am I not more needed in the world?"

Jesus wants to see America through Los Angeles, a young city seething with class and racial tension. Christ, or as he likes to be called, "Carpenter," first goes to the rich. T. S. is an immigrant filmmaker who cannot stop looking at Christ's "soft and silky brown beard" and his "dark eyes." He is captivated by "that face" and knows it could make him a fortune. T. S. offers Carpenter millions to star as himself in motion pictures. "My face?" Christ wonders: "Is not a man more than his face?"

Undeterred, T. S. shifts his temptation from money to missions. Perhaps, "I make it a propaganda picture fer de churches, dey vould show it to de headens [heathens] in China and in Zululand." This does not appeal to Carpenter either, and he tells T. S., "I fear you will have to get someone else to play my part."

Jesus is then drawn to the city's poor, whom the elite treat with disdain. After a car ride with a wealthy family that begins with the young girl complaining to her mother about "horrid fat old Jews" and ends with the automobile crashing into some poor immigrants and the rich family fleeing the crime scene, Jesus joins the downtrodden. He is like the Jesus of the abolitionist imagination, a white man who sides with the stricken. Carpenter heals the wounded and speaks to the Mexican, Italian, Jewish, and other immigrants around him. To these Catholic women and men, Carpenter symbolizes "something serious and miraculous." He tells them that they are better than the rich and that they must not attack their attackers:

> If you kill them, you destroy in yourselves that which makes you better than they, which gives you the right to life. You destroy those virtues of patience and charity, which are the jewels of the poor, and make them princes in the kingdom of love. . . . Let us grow in wisdom, and find ways to put an end to the world's enslavement, without the degradation of our own hearts. . . . Oh, my people, my beloved poor,

not in violence, but in solidarity, in brotherhood, lies the way! Let us
bid the rich go on, to the sure damnation which awaits them. Let us
not soil our hands with their blood!

Carpenter is a socialist and a pacifist, just as Sinclair was in real life.
Jesus was no American icon or hero, though. His invocation of solidarity
and the power of the poor were politically charged items in this day, especially since the Russian Revolution of 1917 had generated a "red scare"
in the United States, which rendered suspect anything that smacked of
left-leaning politics or foreign influence. For his teachings, Carpenter was
repeatedly referenced as a "stranger." His face fit America, but his words
did not.

Jesus eventually drew a following, and the city's elite forces rolled up
against him. The local newspaper denounced his teachings as "the doctrine
of Lenin and Trotsky in the robes of Christian revelation." A group of businessmen commissioned an assassination team. They had to kill him before
his followers killed them. They planned to have Carpenter murdered during a mob riot so that it looked accidental. "See to it that the Carpenter is
lynched instead of being tarred and feathered!" one agent explained to the
group. Billy overheard the plot and set out to save Christ.

Billy devised an ingenious plan. If a mob was going to be used to kill
Christ, perhaps another more powerful mob could be used to save him.
Billy needed one that would receive immediate respect; one that would
not have to prove itself. Then he remembered, Hollywood had produced
several fake mobs for the film industry, and the Ku Klux Klan was fast becoming a national power. Billy brought to mind Griffith's *Birth of a Nation*
and wondered if the studio still had the costumes and if the extras needed
work. They did, and a new Klan was formed. This one would not lynch
someone in the name of Jesus. This one was to save the Son of God from a
lynching himself.

Only the creative mischief of cinema culture could render such a reversal of Griffith's film. As if there were not enough playful wrinkles, this Klan
was led by a female friend of Jesus now donning a white robe. As Sinclair
wrote, "Some fifty figures had descended upon them, and others were still
descending, each one clad in a voluminous white robe, with a white hood
over the head, and two black holes for eyes, and another for the nose."
The lynch mob knelt to the fake Klan led by a woman dressed as a man
and Christ was spirited away. The deception worked. Newspaper headlines
screamed the next day: "KU KLUX KLAN KIDNAPS KARPENTER."

Billy expects Carpenter to be happy, but he is not. He wants to inspire a revolution, not be whisked away by white-robed Hollywood extras. The next day, Jesus is beaten during a random street fight. Enough is enough. He is tired of America and Americans. He fumes, "I meant to die for this people! But now—let them die for themselves!" Carpenter sprints back to St. Bartholomew's Church and leaps into the stained-glass window. This white Christ of the West Coast takes flight. He flees rather than bleeds.[1]

They Call Me Carpenter showcased the perils and possibilities of Jesus in the roaring twenties and the Great Depression. Americans hoped he would intervene and help with their economic, racial, and immigrant dilemmas. They wanted to follow his Great Commission to spread his message throughout the world. But he seemed powerless to stop the class antagonism or the racial violence. Disenchantment led some Americans to wonder if Jesus was relevant at all. But modernity did not kill Christ. From Los Angeles to New York City, from northern white radicals to southern black Pentecostals, and from urbane businessmen to Indian prophets of the frontier, Americans joined Billy in trying to rescue Jesus. From the depths of their frustrations and depressions, they set out to save him, the world, and in the process themselves.

Modernity brought new ways and new places to teach the world a refashioned Jesus. Hollywood's budding film industry used his image to convince Americans of the morality of the silver screen. Films transformed southern California into a new and powerful center of religious production, cultural creation, and political influence. On the frontier, whites and Indians struggled to comprehend Christ's meaning for Indians, who were now being placed on reservations. New ethnographic books that parroted Indian experiences hid and revealed Christ in dynamic and disturbing ways. Along the East Coast, Jesus was being remade in Harlem too. Out of the heart of the Harlem Renaissance, black artists used new graphic magazines and social forums to link Jesus directly to themselves. In this age of jazz and the blues, Jesus was being made and remade, sacrificed and saved.

Invariably, Americans located their frustrations, hopes, and missionary-mindedness on physical representations of Jesus. When they bemoaned his ineffectiveness, they zeroed in on the physical weakness or banal whiteness of his depictions. When they sought to resurrect and display him to the world, they did so with new visual incarnations—new bodies and faces that were somehow more relevant and more sacred. From the abyss of great depression came even greater depths of spiritual understanding.

During these years, as Native Americans, black Americans, and working-class whites hoped against hope, new theologies of liberation were born that painted Jesus beyond whiteness. It was amid great pain that Jesus gained a darkened visual face of racial liberation.

Depressed about Christ

By the roaring twenties and the Great Depression, many Americans were finding that the white Jesus shown to them in Sunday schools or displayed for them in sanctuaries was unable to address their most fundamental problems. The old Jesus had few answers for modern consumer capitalism or the politics of worker solidarity. He had little to say about the manliness of new business practices or whether he was honored or horrified by strikes. On reservations in the West, Native Americans wondered how to experience Jesus in a frontier without buffalo, open ranges, or communal rituals. Neither the ghost dance, nor Wovoka, had brought them back to power. And no matter how often black Americans sang to him, called out his name, or even put white versions of him in their churches, Jesus did not stop segregation or mass violence. In the face of the Great Depression, Jesus seemed particularly powerless. Where was he as Americans choked on the Dust Bowl or stood despairingly in breadlines with billboards above them featuring families out for an evening drive and living the "American Dream"?

Modern consumer and entertainment capitalism posed a number of problems for Jesus that sounded similar to the ones debated before the Civil War. With whom did he align: workers or owners? If he was as manly as imperialists wanted him to be, then how was he a friend to middle-class businessmen who sat at desks and surveyed insurance forms? If he was a working man and triumphed over his enemies, then why were laborers losing in their struggles?

Several white businessmen critiqued older Jesus images as feminine. When portrayed as too womanly, Jesus seemed antagonistic to modern capitalism. Filmmaker Cecil DeMille bemoaned the Sunday school Jesus and saw it as a religious handicap. "All my life I wondered how many people have been turned away from Christianity by the effeminate, sanctimonious, machine-made Christs of second-rate so-called art."[2]

DeMille shared a common vision of what Jesus was and what he was not with Bruce Barton, an advertising executive who became one of the most popular religious writers of the 1920s. In *The Man Nobody Knows* (1925),

Barton cast a new vision of Christ. His Jesus did not speak in "thee" and "thou," but in "buy" and "sell." His savior was an expert businessman who had created the world's most powerful corporation from a group of ragtag fishermen and tax collectors. Barton discovered his probusiness Jesus only through disgust for the effeminate Jesus of Sunday school art. He remembered as a child being indoctrinated with a weak Christ. "The little boy looked up at the picture which hung on the Sunday-school wall. It showed a pale young man with flabby forearms and a sad expression. The young man had red whiskers." This Jesus was a bore, a killjoy, and a weakling. "Jesus was the 'lamb of God,'" and this "sounded like Mary's little lamb. Something for girls—sissified. Jesus was also 'meek and lowly,' a 'man of sorrows and acquainted with grief.' He went around for three years telling people not to do things."[3]

Questions of Christ's usefulness and his manliness hit Mormons too. In Utah, as Mormons created their own Jesus art and placed the new works alongside imports from Europe, some began to wonder if it squared with the Bible and their scriptures. An editor for *Deseret News* admitted that the gospel writers "studiously avoided to draw any picture of the physical features of the Master." This did not mean artists should stop painting Jesus. It just meant they must be careful. They should avoid "mean and repugnant" depictions that cast Jesus as poor or degraded and instead capture his "strength, and endurance, and dignity, and electric influence."[4]

Part of the new image problem was that working-class Americans had drawn Jesus to their side by portraying him as a "rebel" and "revolutionary" who in his oppression sided with the "poor and lowly." Radicals like Upton Sinclair and Terrence Powderly, the son of Irish immigrants and head of the Knights of Labor, depicted Jesus as foreign in America and in American churches. They linked his injuries to theirs. Powderly kept above his desk a picture of the crucifixion, "representing the world's greatest, most sublime agitator." Christ's death reminded Powderly of the price paid for love and justice. One day in despair, he wrote two lines at the feet of the cross: "Work for self and humanity honors you, / Work for humanity and it crucifies you." This Jesus inspired him: "When through my agitation abuse came to me from press, pulpit, and those I tried to serve, I could always look on the picture of the crucified Christ and find consolation in the thought that a divine example had illuminated nineteen hundred years of the world's history, that it shone as bright as on its first day, and that duty to fellow men called for agitation in their interests."[5]

Jesus as a working man. "The Carpenter of Nazareth Was 'A Workman That Needeth Not to Be Ashamed,'" In Bouck White, *The Call of the Carpenter* (Garden City, N.Y.: Doubleday, Page, and Company, 1913).

When workers gave Jesus a visual expression, he was white but distinct. Socialist artist Arthur Young created a mock "wanted poster" of Christ on which Jesus was wanted for "Sedition, Criminal Anarchy, Vagrancy, and Conspiring to Overthrow the Government." Although white with brown hair, this Jesus was unlike the Publius Lentulus description. Jesus had deep lines in his face, darkened skin, and a hardened brow. The working-class Jesus was neither middle class nor pretty; he was tough and gritty.[6]

For African Americans in the South and the thousands moving north as part of the Great Migration, Jesus was a particularly perplexing problem. Black churches that could afford images had put white Christ figures in their sanctuaries. The white Jesus in black churches was so iconic, in fact, that when young artist Jacob Lawrence painted his masterful *Great Migration* series, his portrayal of a black "storefront" church in Chicago featured black worshipers bowing before a gigantic white Jesus portrait. Yet life seemed to get worse and worse. By the 1890s, segregation and lynching were crushing black communities. From 1890 to 1940, lynch mobs had cut short the lives of several thousand African American men and wreaked social, psychological, and spiritual havoc throughout black communities.[7]

This was an age when lynchings became gruesome public spectacles that tied premodern execution rituals to modern culture's new tools of consumerism. New rail lines and special train cars carried whites from cities to lynching events. Photographers snapped pictures and sold cheap postcards of the murders. Newspaper reports predicted the deaths, demonized blacks, and lionized white mobs. Body parts became souvenirs from the events just as baseball cards became collectibles from watching professional ball games.[8]

Lynching created a crisis of faith. "God seems to have forgotten us," lamented the lead character in one dramatic play written about lynching. The head of the Colored Women's League, Mary Church Terrell, confided in her autobiography that lynching "came near upsetting my faith in the Christian religion." She could not comprehend "how a crime like that could be perpetrated in a Christian country, while thousands of Christians sinfully winked at it by making no protest loud enough to be heard or exerting any earnest effort to redress this terrible wrong." Some went beyond Terrell and rejected Jesus. After one character in James Baldwin's *Go Tell It on the Mountain* (1953) mentions Christ's teaching to love one's enemies, another figure shouts, "You can tell that puking bastard to kiss my black ass."[9]

Frustrations sometimes centered on the racial representations of the sacred. After overhearing his mother whisper prayers when a mob was about to murder her brother, James Yates asked, "Mama, why didn't the Lord create some Black angels? In all the Sunday School books and the bible all you see are white folks." Years later and only days before the Japanese attack on Pearl Harbor, in 1941, Charles Jenkins wrote to President Franklin Roosevelt, "If there is such a thing as God, he must be a white person, according to the conditions we colored people are in."[10]

Philadelphia became an epicenter of black rage toward the white Christ. Known on the streets by friend and foe alike as Prophet Cherry, F. S. Cherry was an aged and weathered black man. He had gray hair and a large mole on his chin. On his wrist was a golden bracelet and by his side was a staff. Cherry had emigrated from the Deep South, "a hell of a place," as he described it, in the same years the new Ku Klux Klan was rising. At some point, God touched him and told him to speak.

Cherry had a lesson for whites and blacks of the 1930s: Jesus in the paintings and on the picture cards was a false idol. Cherry stormed into

African American churches, pointed at paintings or prints of white Christs, and laughed. He shouted at congregations: "I'll give anybody one thousand dollars tomorrow night who can tell me who the hell that is!" Sometimes he upped the ante to $1,500. One observer noted, "He will pull out a so-called picture of Jesus suddenly and scream to his followers, 'Who in the hell is this? Nobody knows! They say it is Jesus. That's a damned lie!'"[11]

Later in the century, Malcolm X followed Cherry's lead. When Malcolm X told his personal story through the writer Alex Haley, he presented himself as knowing even before his conversion to the Nation of Islam that Jesus was not white. Malcolm X recalled a story from prison in which he quizzed a Harvard seminary student who was there to lead a Bible study. Malcolm X asked, "What color was Jesus? . . . He was Hebrew, . . . wasn't he?" The white and black convicts "sat bold upright." The question had never occurred to even the toughest of criminals, and no one seemed "ready to hear anybody saying Jesus wasn't white." The instructor had no answer and eventually replied, "Jesus was brown." Malcolm X was feeling good, so he "let him get away with that compromise." Malcolm X had shown that America's best and brightest whites were no match for an unbrainwashed black man.

In later sermons, Malcolm X was not about to compromise. He attacked African American "Uncle Toms" as any person "not interested in any religion of his own. He believes in a white Jesus, white Mary, white angels, and he's trying to get to a white heaven. When you listen to him in his church singing, he sings a song . . . 'Wash me white as snow.' He wants to be—he wants to be turned white so he can get to heaven with a white man."[12]

Prophets from Cherry to Malcolm X were not the only ones blaming Sunday school imagery and racialized hymnody. Renowned sociologist E. Franklin Frazier was too. For one of his projects on the state of black America, he and a partner asked dozens of youth: "Is God a White Man?" The data he assembled was part of a study commissioned by the American Council on Education to assess the personalities and experiences of African American children. These types of studies bolstered the case that racial segregation hindered the mental development of African Americans. This point, more than legal precedent or constitutional amendments, ultimately persuaded the Supreme Court to declare segregated education unconstitutional in the landmark decision *Brown v. Board of Education* of 1954.[13]

What Frazier heard troubled him. Black youth bought into the great lie of white supremacy—that God and Jesus were white. The answer of one twenty-one-year-old was indicative of how most answered the question of

Jesus' race. "I've never heard of Him being a Negro," the young man maintained, "so He must have been a white man. People would think you were crazy if you told them He was a Negro, especially white people."

To Frazier, a belief in a white Jesus led to low self-esteem and poor group image, a point psychologists Kenneth and Mamie Clark made through their now-famous doll tests. Frazier blamed Sunday school cards and mass-produced images of blue eyed, brunet Christs. He also held blacks accountable for displaying these images. "Paradoxical as it may seem," Frazier contended, "the Negro church, an institution which is the product of Negro leadership and cooperation, does little to give Negroes a sense of personal worth and dignity in a world where everything tends to disparage the Negro. . . . The religious ideology of the Negro church tends to perpetuate such notions as a white God and white angels, conceptions which tend toward the disparagement of things black."[14]

Educator and interracial church leader Howard Thurman agreed wholeheartedly. He explained that the religious iconography of segregation led blacks to disparage themselves. In *Jesus and the Disinherited* (1949), Thurman reasoned that if segregation was considered "normal," it was then "correct; if correct, then moral; if moral, then religious." To be considered valid as a social system, segregation needed the divine to be white. God "is imaged as an elderly, benign white man." Angels "are blond and brunets." Satan "is viewed as being red with the glow of fire. But the imps, the messengers of the devil, are black." Thurman found that the "implications of such a view are simply fantastic in the intensity of their tragedy. Doomed on earth to a fixed and unremitting status of inferiority, of which segregation is symbolic, and at the same time cut off from the hope that the Creator intended it otherwise, those who are thus victimized are stripped of all social protection. . . . Under such circumstances, there is but a step from being despised to despising oneself."[15]

From the 1920s to the 1940s, voices of spiritual protest called for new forms of Christ. These voices ranged from African Americans frustrated with his whiteness or his inability to restrain Judge Lynch or Jim Crow, to white businessmen irritated with the sissy Jesus of Sunday school art. And with the new media of the age, including movies and magazines, Americans remade Jesus to fit with their modern times. They spoke to the racial, economic, and religious sagas of their days with new physical renderings of his body. For many, fresh representations of his body renewed his message for the modern world.

Movies and Missionaries

Innovation arose from desperation. Complaints about how Jesus was represented led to a massive outpouring of new Jesus types. From Harlem to Hollywood, Americans generated a whole new set of Jesus images. No single representation rose to cultural dominance, but the vigorous efforts to remake him revealed that Americans were searching for new spiritual directions. Out of all of this came new debates about how Christ should be physically rendered and the first lives of liberation theologies.

The white Jesus was most spectacularly brought into the world of consumer capitalism through the newest media technology of the day: filmmaking. There, he leapt from Sunday school pictures and imported European artwork onto the silver screen. During the twentieth century, his whiteness was refashioned as Americans became obsessed with cinematic beauty and highly stylized presentations of bodies and scenery. At first, the new film industry needed Jesus to legitimate its questionable morality. But with time, Jesus relied on the film industry to spread his message within the United States and also throughout the world.[16]

Through Jesus, the American film industry became a new creator of perpetual spiritual commodification, with southern California becoming a surrogate sacred geography that could mimic the Middle East. Southern California was an idyllic place to make movies: it rarely rained, and the area boasted a remarkable topographical diversity that ran from sunny beaches to desolate deserts to snow-capped mountains. As home to new biblical movies, Hollywood provided the scenery, the geographical backdrop, and the actors for Christ's adventures.[17]

Modern motion pictures were invented with an eye toward Jesus. They were developed in the late nineteenth century as inventors realized that by piecing together translucent images, running a light through them, projecting the images onto another surface, and moving the images rapidly one after another, they could make objects appear to move. In 1885, an Episcopal rector and part-time chemist in New Jersey devised a way to coil translucent film into one long strip. He wanted to be able to show Bible pictures cleanly and smoothly. For their first motion pictures, Protestants looked to the artistic images they knew best, especially James Tissot's paintings.[18]

With celluloid film, American Protestants took the pictures they had grown to love and put them into motion. They began with short Passion plays, which focused on the final days of Christ and his crucifixion. The most famous live Passion play was held every ten years in Oberammergau, Germany. Since the early seventeenth century, locals there had staged the final days of Jesus, and then in the late nineteenth century Americans flocked to the tiny village to watch Jesus in German flesh. They wrote avidly about the "Miracle-Play" across the ocean. "When Christ makes his appearance," one penned, "all your soul is concentrated on that one figure. You never take your eyes off him. I can shut my eyes and see him now." Then, in the 1920s, the three-time Jesus of the play, Anton Lang, came to the United States to raise money for the village. Keeping his hair long to look the part, this German Jesus met with President Calvin Coolidge, who thanked him for the "great influence for good which you have been to all the world." In this regard, Coolidge had something in common with Adolf Hitler, who only a few years later wore a trench coat to watch the play.[19]

The most popular early full-length film of Christ's life was *From the Manger to the Cross* (1913). Directed by Sidney Olcott, it starred Robert Henderson-Bland as Jesus. Especially noteworthy at the time and unlike other silent Passion films, this one was filmed in the Middle East. It promised audiences a more authentic visual experience, where geography, trees, and terrain were supposed to bring viewers closer to Christ. An English actor, Henderson-Bland played the role looking almost exactly like the Publius Lentulus description. His hair was long, flowing, and parted in the middle. He sported a short but full beard. Henderson-Bland toured the nation, meeting with churches and Sunday schools to talk about what it was like to play Jesus. The press heralded the seventy-minute film as a "sublime work." It promised to make the Great Commission much "easier."[20]

Just as before the Civil War, media innovators targeted children. To the language of temptation and allurement, religious organizations now added action and cunning. One 1911 essay emphasized the importance of the movies for appealing to boys: "Some boys will attend Sunday school and some will not. All boys, however, will and do attend moving picture shows." Sure, they would rather see "scenes of battle, murder and sudden death, but if they can see the 'Passion Play,' 'Life of Christ,' or the 'Story of the Good Samaritan,' told in the roll of pictures they will remember them far more accurately than if the stories were told them by an indifferently interested teacher on a sunshiny Sabbath morning." Time and again, religious advocates of film highlighted its emotional appeal, drawing on newly popularized psychological concepts. "The motion picture strikes into the minds of people through the eye. . . . No wonder that skilled psychologists and educators see in the motion picture an incomparable force and potentiality!" Another advocate explained, "It appeals to people primarily as an amusement and relaxation but cunningly weaves into such hours of play thrills, thoughts, emotions, the elements for imagination, instruction, and culture."[21]

Not all Christians liked what they saw. At a time when Protestantism was fracturing along theological, political, social, and geographical lines in what would come to be known as the Modernist/Fundamentalist debate, movies became a lightning rod for the culture wars. Fundamentalist Christianity was never a unified movement, but its adherents tended to dislike a number of "modern" inventions, such as the teaching of evolutionary theory in school, rampant consumerism, flappers who wore short dresses, bobbed their hair, and smoked, and liberal interpretations of the Bible.[22]

Many vigorously opposed movies too. Notions of idolatry informed their disdain, but so did the despicable content of other films. "The picturing of the life and sufferings of our Savior by these institutions falls nothing short of blasphemy," wrote one concerned Christian. "Just think of it, one day the horrible scenes of crime and murder are pictured, and the next day by the same men, the same instruments, in the same building, for the same purpose, and in the same cold irreverent way, the sufferings of Christ are presented." The Second Commandment still mattered to this writer. "Even God the Father is represented in the form of an old man . . . a direct violation of the second commandment, which forbids us to make any image whatever of the infinite Being." The modern technology of choice for many Fundamentalists was the radio (even though some worried that it too was of the Antichrist), where the word could be heard but not seen.[23]

Over time, Fundamentalists came to embrace films, and missionary activity was one of the reasons. Missionaries and their supporters aggressively promoted religious films and in so doing became key exporters of the white American Jesus. The International Student Missionary Movement showed films for free in Japan and China, and so many missionary groups were using films that as early as 1916 the Federal Council of Churches could proclaim, "In *mission work* the motion picture has found a place."[24]

Film could be a part of imperialism by extending the white Jesus as a big brother who could lead foreign peoples to higher standards of civilization. One 1916 piece in *Motion Picture Classic* highlighted the positive effect motion pictures had "on heathens," while Ernest Dench believed that missionaries should use Jesus movies to teach nonwhite and non-European peoples the ways of Western civilization. "'The Life and Teachings of Jesus' and the standard stories of the Bible should be displayed . . . to set forth the fundamental moral and religious conceptions of Occidental [Western] civilization. By use of motion pictures . . . the entire Asiatic population would be unconsciously swept into the circle of our Occidental life."[25]

Hollywood had a neighbor and Fundamentalist friend in Aimee Semple McPherson. While other Fundamentalists railed against films and turned instead to radio airwaves, Sister Aimee preached the "old-time religion" with the most modern of modern technologies. A Canadian faith healer and Pentecostal with a penchant for marital problems, McPherson set up camp in Los Angeles in 1918. She knew that a huge demographic of Americans was on the move to southern California, and she would be waiting for them. Thousands flocked to her flamboyant preaching and show-woman stunts. McPherson did just about anything to draw attention to herself and her church. Only two decades after the Wright brothers' first successful airplane flight, she boarded a small plane to fly to northern California. It was a brilliant media stunt. Pictures and reports of the daring Sister Aimee flooded local newspapers. Her huge Angelus Temple opened in 1923 as one of the nation's first megachurches. Her pulpit was a stage with lions and tigers and bears as props. In 1924, she constructed a two-hundred-and-fifty-foot radio tower to broadcast her sermons and lessons. Inside she had a forty-foot mural of a white Christ returning from heaven. Along the walls were huge stained-glass windows that showcased the life of Jesus.

When "talkies" took the nation by storm in the 1930s, McPherson jumped on the bandwagon. She lost forty pounds, got a face-lift, and endeavored to become a cinema star. She explained to one reporter, "The talking picture is the greatest agency for the spread of the Gospel since the invention of the printing press."[26]

Hollywood made its first big stab at representing Jesus with *The King of Kings* in 1927. Heralded as "the most important picture ever made," it was directed by Cecil DeMille, produced in black-and-white, filmed just off the coast of southern California on Catalina Island (where the Cubs had spring training practices up to World War II), and displayed Jesus in several dynamic ways. Viewers first witnessed Christ through the eyes of a blind girl healed by the savior. Before Jesus appeared, she and the audience sat in darkness. Then they saw a great light as a hazy form come into focus. The screen faded to the white face of Jesus, smiling with a halo behind his head. This Christ was both familiar and unfamiliar. He had white skin, was tall, and had a full beard. Yet his hair was distinct. It clung closely to Christ's head and barely reached his shoulders.

At the film's end, when Jesus was brought back to life, he returned in color. To punctuate the resurrection, DeMille turned to the innovations of the Technicolor Motion Picture Corporation. The screen now filled with vibrant reds, sandy browns, and dark purples. Jesus emerged from his tomb with blinding light behind him. As he stepped toward the camera, his pristine white skin, rosy cheeks, and almost blond hair lit up the entire dark theater. Now in color, the Nordic Jesus had become a star.[27]

H. B. Warner played the role of Christ. Born in England in 1875, he hailed from an acting family. Warner moved to the United States in the early twentieth century, where he starred on Broadway before venturing to southern California to work in the budding film industry. Before he was a cinematic savior, Warner was best known for playing the crook Jimmy Valentine. DeMille recognized that the Christ role was "literally a superhuman assignment" and that only Warner could pull off the combination of strength and tenderness. Warner, however, was in his fifties and seemed quite a bit older than Jesus was before his crucifixion.[28]

DeMille knew that he had a tough challenge. He wanted to please those who loved Hollywood and those who worshipped Jesus, and this was no simple task. "The church people would be up in arms at the irreverence of the very idea," DeMille remembered later, and "the people who were indifferent to religion would be monumentally indifferent to a picture [in] which, presumably, sanctimonious characters would walk around in long robes." To grab both audiences, DeMille turned to the fame of D. W. Griffith. He asked Griffith to visit the set and to shoot a scene from the crucifixion. DeMille even shot promotional films of the two working side by side. Advertisements for the film compared *The King of Kings* to *Birth of a Nation* for their riveting storylines and visual displays.[29]

DeMille also wanted to avoid religious or moral tension. He employed Protestant and Catholic advisers, including Bruce Barton. Days opened with interreligious prayer services that featured Christians, Jews, Muslims, and Buddhists. Actors' contracts for the film contained clauses that demanded "exemplary conduct" on and off the set.

The center of the sacred atmosphere was Warner. He was treated as more than a man. Only DeMille was allowed to speak to him when in costume, and he was "veiled" or driven in a closed car from his dressing room to the set. The reverence on the set and in the film paid spiritual dividends. Years later, according to DeMille, a minister told Warner: "I saw you in *The King of Kings* when I was a child, and now, every time I speak of Jesus, it is your face I see."[30]

Warner's portrayal never became a dominant image of Jesus, but reviews of the film revealed how Christ's body had become an important part of how Americans imagined the Son of God. Several were frustrated that Warner's Jesus looked so unfamiliar. "The generally accepted conception of the appearance of Christ is that his hair was long," one reviewer complained. If DeMille wanted to get the visual right, he should have consulted the Publius Lentulus letter, which was now considered "genuine" by "expert antiquarians" for its description of Jesus as Nordic or Aryan with "blond" hair, "pink" skin, and "blue" eyes.[31]

Other reviewers marveled at how the recent history of Jesus artwork had transformed American perspectives on visualizing the sacred. "Christ in the movies? Sacrilege!" maintained Gilbert Simons in *The World's Work*. Or at least that is what Protestants would have said ten years earlier. But "it is not to-day because, in a decade, the moving picture as an art has grown vastly in prestige." "To many minds it seems a sacrilege to represent Christ on the stage or on the screen," editorialized *The Outlook* in its review. Yet if Christians brought paintings and pictures of Jesus into their homes and churches, why would not they accept moving pictures? "Intrinsically, there is no reason why one art as well as another should not depict and interpret the life of Christ."

This reviewer was especially pleased that Warner's Jesus was the manly example the modern world needed. Invoking the same criticisms as Bruce Barton, he declared that this cinematic savior was better than the artistic ones, because it "is a manly Christ that is depicted, masculine, gracious, restrained, and dignified."[32]

The King of Kings was unsuccessful at the box office but a smash hit for missionary organizations. They carried it, or re-edited the film and unused footage to create a version that focused more on Christ's divinity, all over the world. The titles were translated into Chinese, Turkish, Arabic, Hebrew, and Hindustani. One film reviewer prophesied, "It is my guess that *The King of Kings* will girdle the globe and that the multitude will still be flocking to see it in 1947." He was right. *The King of Kings* traveled far and wide, and it—like *Birth of a Nation*—could be seen in American theaters throughout the 1930s, 1940s, and 1950s. DeMille himself boasted late in life, "Its statistical history can be summed up in the fact that it has been playing steadily somewhere in the world, I believe without a day's interruption, ever since." The only other American film that could boast the same was *Birth of a Nation*.[33]

"I Have Come to the Conclusion That Jesus Was an Indian"

Just as American audiences were watching DeMille's portrayal of Jesus, they were also keeping a close eye on spiritual developments on the frontier. Ever since the ghost dances, white Americans had become fascinated by and fearful of Indian faith expressions. Congressmen worried about what Indians were doing on the reservations, and as new forms of Indian Christianity incorporated peyote, the U.S. government wondered if it needed to intervene. When the New Deal came, it meant another legislative turn in the approach to Indian religion. This one was based for the first time on freedom.

Whites became avid consumers of Indian religious narratives and fundamental shapers of those tales. Through varying degrees of manipulation and with new ethnographic studies, whites tried to control Jesus among the Indians. Whites published new books about Indian religion that concealed and revealed native interactions with Christ. For all their efforts to exploit Indian faith, though, whites could not hold back Indians from identifying Jesus as their possession and property. Unlike antebellum Native Americans who had denounced whites for being so foolish as to crucify their own savior, new voices proclaimed that Jesus was actually an Indian.

For centuries, as part of their religious rituals, natives in Mexico and the Southwest had taken peyote buttons or pills derived from cactus flowers. Christianized peyote religion in the late nineteenth century spread northward through Texas and established its strongest base in Oklahoma. From there it traveled to the nations on the Great Plains and to the Northwest. Peyote religion, in its varieties and with its traveling "road men," integrated Christian doctrine and practices with Indian cultural ways. Hymns, homilies, and Jesus imagery joined healing rituals in the taking of peyote buttons. In acts of communion, Indians consuming peyote imagined themselves to be ingesting Christ's spirit.

Around the same years that Congress entertained Madison Grant's theories on Nordic whiteness and his proposals to restrict immigration, they also heard testimony on Indian peyote use and wondered if they should outlaw it. Francis LaFlesche, an Omaha reporter for the Bureau of American Ethnology, studied the use of peyote among the Osage, Poncas, and Omahas. He testified that he had expected to find "gloriously drunk" Indians. Instead he found joy and Jesus. At one ceremony, a leader asked peyote practitioners what they saw, and one responded, "We expect to see the face of Jesus, and the face of our dead relatives." Another said, "I saw the face of jesus and it made me happy." LaFlesche was "thoroughly convinced that these Indians are worshipping God in their own simple way, and if their religion is interfered with by the government or anybody else, and it is suppressed, the consequences will be very grave."[34]

New institutions emerged from these visions. John Wilson, a Caddo Indian from Oklahoma, created a branch of the Native American Church in 1918. As related to his nephew, he consumed about fifteen peyote buttons, which led him into the sky realm. He was shown the "celestial landmarks which represented the events in the life of Christ, and also the relative positions of the Spiritual Forces, the Moon, Sun, Fire, which had long been known to the Delawares." He saw the grave of Christ and the road from Jesus' tomb to the "moon in the Sky which Christ had taken in his ascent." Peyote instructed him to walk in the path of this road. Eventually, he would reach the door of the moon and be led into the "actual presence of Christ and Peyote." Wilson led followers into what became known as the Big Moon ceremony, part of a peyote ritual that involved symbols of Jesus, the crucifix, and the Bible. Wilson evidently drew much of this from his Catholic background.[35]

Charles Whitehorn, one of the first "road men" for peyote religion, also taught a version of the new Big Moon ceremony that made Peyote and Jesus co–sacred powers. A specially decorated tipi featured a cross representing Calvary, and at one ceremony an Indian agent described how "a large cross was painted on the altar tent, and they had a big picture of Christ hung up in a prominent position." As expressed by a Delaware tribesman, "God made Peyote. It is His power. It is the power of Jesus. Jesus came afterwards on this earth, after Peyote. . . . God (through Peyote) told the Delawares the same things that Jesus told the whites." Father Peyote led these Indians to see Jesus and had been with the Indian ancestors and prophets.[36]

A growing number of Indians were viewing Jesus as one of them. The experience of Charles Eastman showed vital aspects of this transformation. Taken as a boy in the late nineteenth century to the Presbyterian Santee Training School in South Dakota, Eastman later received degrees at Dartmouth and Boston University's School of Medicine. He was a medical missionary at the Pine Ridge reservation during the Wounded Knee massacre, and he traveled widely among western Native Americans. While cordially received, his religious message met with skepticism from natives who saw that the white man did not "follow the example set by his brother Christ."

Eastman listened sympathetically as Indians of various nations responded to his efforts "to set before them in simple language the life and character of the man Jesus." One man explained that his Jesus "was opposed to material acquirement and to great possessions. He was inclined to peace. He was as unpractical as any Indian and set no price upon his labor of love. These are not the principles upon which the white man has founded his civilization. It is strange that he could not rise to these simple principles which were commonly observed among our people." This native explained: "I have come to the conclusion that this Jesus was an Indian."[37]

What Eastman witnessed and recorded was a birth of liberation theology. Just as Marcus Garvey taught his followers in New York that Jesus could not be white and just as Wovoka's followers believed he was Jesus returned to bring restoration, the Indians Eastman heard were convinced that Jesus could not be white. The Son of God condemned the material greed and racial oppression that seemed to animate American whiteness. When Christ was translated into modern racial categories, "Jesus was an Indian."

By the Great Depression, native life in the United States reached new lows in numbers of people, economic prospects, and cultural vitality. In the 1920s, the federal government went on the attack against Indian religious practices. In 1921, the Office of Indian Affairs declared that ceremonies such as Sun Dances, annual rituals of plains' Indians that often brought together various tribes in united ceremonies, were to be considered "Indian Offences." This criminalized "any dance which involves . . . the reckless giving away of property . . . frequent or prolonged periods of celebration . . . in fact any disorderly or plainly excessive performance that promotes superstitious cruelty, licentiousness, idleness, danger to health, and shiftless indifference to family welfare." Indian dances continued, in part, because of the demands of the tourist trade, but the Bureau of Indian Affairs would have halted them completely if it could have. Legislatively and administratively, it was one of the most explicit denials of religious freedom in American history.[38]

The Indian Reorganization Act of 1934, commonly called the Indian New Deal, shifted the terrain of interactions between Indians and the U.S. government. Although in other arenas the federal government took on unprecedented powers with the New Deal, in this case it actually relinquished some direct control. The driving force behind the Indian New Deal, John Collier, attacked the Dawes Act and other governmental schemes of "civilization." The Indian New Deal reinstated tribal and communal rule as a basic foundation for Indian life and governance and permitted (even encouraged) Indian ceremonial customs. In Circular 2970, "Indian Religious Freedom and Indian Culture," Collier insisted: "No interference with Indian religious life will be hereafter tolerated. The cultural history of Indians is in all respects to be considered equal to that of any non-Indian group." Circular 2970 also prohibited compulsory attendance by Indian children at religious services in boarding schools without parental permission. Collier was protecting, as Franklin Roosevelt would in response to Nazi aggressions as part of his "Four Freedoms" speech, the freedom of worship.[39]

The Indian New Deal inaugurated a new era of modern Indian religious practice. Native traditions gradually emerged again in more open ways. By this time, it was nearly impossible to separate "native traditions" from aspects of Christianity, and younger Indians taken to boarding schools often knew as much or more about the religion of Jesus as they did about the customs of their tribe. A majority of Native Americans identified with some Christian denomination. Indians wore Christian crosses to Sun Dances; they pronounced prayers in Jesus' name in the Cross Fire ceremony of the Native American Church; they prayed to Jesus and to Kateri Tekakwitha of sainted memory; and they listened to sermons in Cherokee and Choctaw Baptist churches that closely resembled those that could be heard in white Baptist churches.

But even the Indian New Deal and white reformers' appreciation for Indian religions had elements of control. They were based on romantic assumptions that Indians were preindustrial peoples who had not been tainted by modernity. This rendered Indians somehow outside of modern history and thus free of the cross-cultural collisions that supposedly cut off modern people from their ethnic traditions. This approach to native life—which defied hundreds of years of Indian interactions with and transformations by varieties of European and African communities—led whites to render Indian encounters with Christ as somehow strange, mysterious, and exotic.[40]

Black Elk Speaks (1932) was a prime example. Recorded by scholar and poet John Neihardt from the translation of Black Elk's voice from Lakota to English, it became a classic of twentieth-century Indian literature. The work, like a spirit journey or the Bible, was hard to interpret. It is a written text that professed to speak; it is supposedly the words of a native written by the hand of a white man. Recent scholars have pointed out that *Black Elk Speaks* distorts Black Elk's life in significant ways, and some have gone so far as to claim that *Black Elk Speaks* was actually John Neihardt speaking.

At the least, Neihardt's presentation downplays Black Elk's relationship to Christ and the crucial role Catholicism played in his imagination.

Black Elk told Neihardt of one vision during a ghost dance in 1890 in which he saw a messianic figure:

> Then they led me to the center of the circle where once more I saw the holy tree all full of leaves and blooming. . . . Against the tree there was a man standing with arms held wide in front of him. I looked hard at him, and I could not tell what people he came from. He was not a Wasichu [white man] and he was not an Indian. His hair was long and hanging loose, and on the left side of his head he wore an eagle feather. His body was strong and good to see, and it was painted red. . . . He was a very fine looking man. While I was staring hard at him, his body began to change and became very beautiful with all colors of light, and around him there was light.

When Neihardt spoke for Black Elk, he silenced crucial portions of this story. In his notes, Neihardt wrote that Black Elk also drew attention to wounds in the palms of this man's hand, but this detail was excised from the final text. By the time of this vision, Black Elk had been studying Christianity. The vision was clearly a Jesus figure of racial ambiguity. He was perhaps white, but he was painted red. Black Elk looked closely at this figure but could not place him in a people group, and then this holy man shifted into an array of colors. The wounds Neihardt neglected revealed another layer of religious vision that linked Catholicism with Indians, the kind of complicated mixing white Americans did not want to read about.

Black Elk's daughter explained that he and the resident priest "talked about my father's visions . . . and the Sun Dance, and all the Indian ceremonies that my father said were connected to Christianity. My father said we were like the Israelites, the Jews, waiting for Christ. . . . He said all these ceremonies connected. They knew, somehow, that in the future our Lord Jesus Christ would come one day to his people." Before the Sun Dance, participants purified themselves and put on a "sage crown, which resembles the crown our Lord wore. . . . So the Indian, early before sunrise, had to stand there and had to go with the sun—watching it until it went down. That's the suffering, you see. And some of them even shed their blood. Christ did that too, before he died on the cross. That's the way he suffered."[41]

Black Elk's visions inspired later generations of Indian Christians. Native Catholic Marie Archambault had a vision of Jesus "as a Lakota man" after reading *Black Elk Speaks*. As she explained, "With this vision of the Wanekia, standing at the center of the Sundance circle, we see Jesus Christ among Native people, as one of us. His presence made the tree at the center bloom. He was surrounded by light. This was the Christ who caught the imagination of Black Elk."[42]

Black Elk Speaks and the Indian New Deal offered a new moment for Native Americans to reconceptualize Christ, but they were certainly not free from white surveillance or manipulation. Traditions, rituals, and teachings that had, in part, been hidden now reemerged in spectacular fashion, and whites looked to mediate the process, whether through editorial or legislative control. *Black Elk Speaks* was a complicated text with Jesus revealed and hidden. He was strong; his hair was long; he wore a feather in his head; he was difficult to position in one tribe or another; he was painted red; and he was wounded in his palms. Violence shaped Black Elk's vision of Christ, just as violence suffused native-white interactions. Violence also figured centrally in African American restorations of Jesus in America.

Harlem's Great Awakening

While whites could not stop Indians from fashioning Jesus into an Indian and an agent of liberation in the West, a group of black artists in Harlem determined that Jesus could not be a white man who supported white supremacy. If black Americans wanted to redeem blackness, they must redefine the savior toward it. They were vying for a massive cultural revolution, one that would not only oppose whites who sanctified their race through Christ but also defy blacks who had taken white Jesus images into their material lives. To counteract these forces and the violent devastation around them, artists gave Jesus new black faces. He became through the stories, poems, plays, and art of the Harlem Renaissance a black man who invaded the segregated South, sanctified blackness, and liberated the spirits of black folk. They failed to carry the cultural day, but for the first time Jesus in the United States had a black face.

Black liberation theology was born amid the Harlem Renaissance (known also as the "New Negro Movement") of the 1920s and 1930s. This era witnessed an explosion of African American production. New magazines, literature, artwork, and dramatic performances jumped from Harlem to Washington, D.C., Baltimore to Chicago. Poets, teachers, editors, novelists, publishers, activists, painters, and sculptors led the cultural awakening. It was not a secular movement, although it took place outside of churches. Neither was it an all-black artistic uprising, although most of its leaders were African American.[43]

Their great commission was to recast Christ as a lynch victim. African American authors and artists discovered a way to make spiritual life out of atrocious death. They made the early twentieth-century South as the place and space of Christ's second coming. They robed Jesus in a black body and transformed whites into his killers. Although whites justified mob murders with claims of black immorality (usually charges of rape, theft, or murder), black artists characterized the lynch victim as an innocent Christ figure. They converted the lynched African American from an object of disdain into a paragon of sacred virtue. The black man became a potential savior not only for the oppressed community but also for his persecutors, southern whites. Only a black Christ living, teaching, and dying in America, they claimed, could save all the people.[44]

Much of the Harlem revival radiated intellectually, socially, and organizationally from W. E. B. Du Bois. His fictional stories and poems, his networks, and his magazine, *The Crisis*, were the basis for this new sacred vision. Born in Massachusetts in 1868, educated at Fisk University in Tennessee, Harvard University in Massachusetts, and the University of Berlin in Germany, Du Bois traveled extensively throughout the United States and the world. He was a professor in Ohio and in Georgia before moving to New York City to work for the new National Association for the Advancement of Colored People. He was a literary leader, an ideological pioneer, and a culture broker who brought North and South together in his global vision of social justice. He linked readers with writers, authors with artists, historians with activists, and playwrights with theater troupes. Du Bois encouraged an entire generation of poets, playwrights, and essayists to connect Jesus, lynching, and liberation.[45]

Du Bois penned several poems and short stories that related tales of Jesus coming to America. This Christ was usually born in the South and taught messages of forgiveness, love, justice, integration, and economic fairness. Southern whites rejected his teachings, not because they were unbiblical but because he looked black or Jewish to them. When his lessons sounded too radical or his actions too subversive, such as preaching the Beatitudes, hanging out with Communists, or healing white women, Jesus was lynched. Often, Jesus boldly accepted his crucifixion in the place of black men who had been wrongly accused of crimes.[46]

Du Bois's finest story of Christ invading America was "The Son of God" (1933). It spoke to layers of violence in Great Depression America and the power of Jesus to challenge them. Mary, who was beaten by her husband, Joe, has a sacred son. This new black Christ draws attention with his thoughtful sermons and his abilities to cross the color line. White and black, rich and poor all come to hear him speak. With a beautiful re-voicing of Christ's Sermon on the Mount, this new Jesus proclaims a new vision for heaven and earth. It brings Christ's teachings smack into the worlds of poor, disfranchised, and brutalized blacks and whites during the Great Depression. "Heaven is going to be filled with people who are down-hearted and you that are mourning will get a lot of comfort some day," he declares. "It's meek folk who are lucky, and going to get everything; and you that are hungry, too. Poor people are better than rich people because they work for what they wear and eat." He then makes a bold proclamation about the hereafter: "There won't be any rich people in Heaven."

This is too much for the interracial crowd, especially for Joe, who deems it "damned nonsense." The black Christ gets himself into further trouble when he starts "hanging around with a lot of Communists and talking on street corners, and saying things about property that white folks ain't going to stand for." Joe knows what becomes of black men who congregate with white women, or who push too hard and too fast for economic change. And Joe is right. At the age of thirty, God's (and Mary's) son is "seized by a mob and they had hanged him at sunset." No one knows exactly why they killed him. As Du Bois narrates, "The charge against him wasn't clear: 'Worshiping a new God.' 'Living with white women!' 'Getting up a revolution.' 'Stealing or blasphemy,' the neighbors muttered." But everyone really knows that he was crucified not for the company he kept but for the color of his skin.[47]

A team of artists joined Du Bois in recasting Jesus and racially reshaping the religious terrain. His son-in-law, poet Countee Cullen, longed to see God and Jesus as black. In one poem, Cullen wished that

He I served were black,
Thinking then it would not lack
Precedent of pain to guide it,
Let who would or might deride it.

Cullen looked for a God who had "dark despairing features" and "dark rebellious hair." Four years later, he felt commissioned by God to create such a representation with his poem "The Black Christ" (1929).

Written from Paris, Cullen dedicated the poem "Hopefully . . . to White America." It begins by claiming inspiration from "Calvary in Palestine," where "Of trees on which a Man should swing / World without end, in suffering / For all men's healing, let me sing." As the poem-tale proceeds, the lynching of a young black man leads his father to profound religious questions. Perhaps God does not care for African Americans at all: "What has He done for you who spent / A bleeding life for His content?" Perhaps, God forbid, Jesus was a white racist: "Or is the white Christ, too, distraught / By these dark skins His Father wrought?" Resurrection saves the father. When his son returns as Christ, the father casts away all doubts and feels a sense of kinship with Christ. "That love which has no boundary; / Our eyes have looked on Calvary."[48]

Langston Hughes, a close confidant of Du Bois's, had a particularly conflicted relationship with Jesus and used his blackness to blanket the South with shame. A leftist who was profoundly influenced by Karl Marx, Hughes usually told Jesus to get out of the way of the social revolution. This was altered, though, in 1931, with the Scottsboro Boys case in Alabama. In March 1931, two young white women riding a train accused nine African American boys of assault and rape. One of the women later recanted her story, but trials, appeals, and retrials dragged on for years as the boys languished in prison. They were forced to listen to the executions of other African American men; several of the boys reported terrifying nightmares afterward. Hughes, along with other African Americans and the Communist Party of the United States of America, rallied to attack the judicial injustice. Hughes set about redefining Jesus to expose the hypocrisy of white America. He minced few words in his "Christ in Alabama" (1931). He brings sex, power, and family into the equation, declaring Christ "a nigger, / Beaten and black." His mother is Mary, *"Mammy of the South,"* and his father is God, the *"White Master above."* Jesus is the

Most holy bastard
Of the bleeding mouth:
Nigger Christ
On the cross of the South.[49]

The association of Jesus and the lynch victim ran far and wide. Playwrights, often friends of Du Bois, joined the chorus. For the final scene of her play *Black Souls*, Annie Nathan Meyer instructs stage directors to link the lynching with the crucifixion subtly: "Without too much emphasis there must be a suggestion of the Christ figure, crucified. The emotional effect of martyrdom, of patient suffering, of terrible agony, of helplessness of the victim in the face of the mob spirit." May Miller, a high school teacher in Baltimore, titled her lynching drama *Nails and Thorns* and has one white character denounce a lynching for its widespread effects on all communities. "For generations to come the children will be gathering the nails and thorns from the scene of that crucifixion."[50]

Painters and sculptors moved beyond words and oblique references to give Jesus distinct black faces. Prentiss Taylor, a white artist who established a publishing house with Langston Hughes, created a lithograph for *Christ in Alabama*. In it, a cloudy cross holds an African American man. He is muscular and has short, slightly curled hair. Beneath him, a black woman mourns on one side, while cotton grows on the other.[51]

The tie between Christ and the lynch victim had its most notable visual display in 1935. The National Association for the Advancement of Colored People sponsored an art show on lynching at the Arthur U. Newton Galleries in New York City. These works drew the lynch victim together with Christ in pain and suffering. Prentiss Taylor's *Christ in Alabama* was on display. So too was M. Gray Johnson's *The Crucifixion* and Fred Bucholz's *We Too Knew Calvary*. Julius Bloch, a Jewish artist of Philadelphia, offered a black man with short cropped hair crucified on a tree in *The Lynching*. E. Simms Campbell envisioned a white Christ carrying his cross and a black man hung by the neck meshed together in *I Passed Along This Way*.[52]

The connection between African Americans and Jesus could be heard echoing all over America. Around 1940, poet Robert Hayden joined "the bruised body" of Jesus that was "lynched on the hill of Calvary" with the "charred April body" of a young black man that swung "from a tree in Dixie!" Artists John Biggers and Frederick Felmister continued the visual tradition with *Crucifixion* (1942) and *The Mourners* (c. 1940), while Elizabeth Catlett's 1946 lithograph *Mother and Child* displayed the Madonna and Christ baby as petrified African Americans with a lynching tree behind them.[53]

The new visual iconography influenced a variety of African American artists, both professionally trained and self-taught. Southern black artists blackened Jesus in their environments of racial violence. Painter William H. Johnson depicted a black crucified Christ in *Jesus and the Three Marys* (1939). Jesus is pinned to the cross at the center with a dark-skinned Mary Magdalene and Mary, sister of Martha, underneath. They stretch their arms to him in Pentecostal fashion. Johnson brought his southern

Julius Bloch, *The Lynching* (1932). Oil on canvas, 19 × 12 inches. Courtesy of the Whitney Museum of American Art, New York, New York.

background (he was a native of South Carolina) to his modernist and surrealist artistic training (he studied in Denmark and Scandinavia) to this canvas, as elongated arms and exaggeratedly large hands dominate the center of the canvas.[54]

Southern self-trained artists did similarly. Folk artist Clementine Hunter, a native of Louisiana, mixed the Catholic influences of her state with the reigning Protestantism of the region to create new imagery of Jesus as black. Working her way up from a childhood on a plantation and through many years in Natchitoches, Hunter's own personal and vivid imagery naturally placed Jesus in a context that spoke to her individually. In the 1940s, she began a series of paintings of crucified black Jesus scenes (often set against lighter pastel colors, flowers, and birds). When asked why, she responded: "Everybody always talking Black Jesus." Eventually, she produced more than one hundred pieces. *Cotton Crucifixion* (1970)

199

William H. Johnson, *Jesus and the Three Marys* (1939). Courtesy of the Howard University Gallery of Art, Washington, D.C.

brought Jesus to her contemporary world. A background of white cotton highlighted the central figure of a small black Christ. Anderson Johnson, a Virginia native, painted Jesus with striking black skin, eyes, and beard set sharply against a green background in his *Behold the Man*.[55]

The paintings and poems neither revolutionized black church life nor revised white approaches to race or religion. They did, however, influence Western theology through Dietrich Bonhoeffer. Born in the early twentieth century in Germany, Bonhoeffer became a leading challenger to Hitler and the Nazi Party in the mid-1930s. Eventually he was arrested and executed for his involvement in an assassination attempt on Hitler's life. Through his writing and activism, Bonhoeffer became a saint for twentieth-century Protestants opposed to any tyrannical or oppressive government. Often

Clementine Hunter,
Cotton Crucifixion (1970).
Oil on masonite, 27 × 19
inches. Collection of
Gordon W. Bailey.

overlooked, however, was the profound way African American early theories of liberation theology influenced Bonhoeffer.

In 1930 and 1931, he held a position at Union Theological Seminary in New York City. He met with Du Bois and other black leaders, and he read *The Crisis* and other black magazines. Bonhoeffer ventured to African American churches and experienced a new form of Christ. He found that Christ "goes incognito, as a beggar among beggars, as an outcast among outcasts, as despairing among the despairing, as dying among the dying." Years later, when confronting the Nazi Holocaust, Bonhoeffer brought his new understanding of Christ—as one with the poor and outcast of a society—to bear on events in Europe. "An expulsion of the Jews from the west must necessarily bring with it the expulsion of Christ," he wrote in 1941, "for Jesus Christ was a Jew." Like the fictional Christ lynch victims, Bonhoeffer too was executed for the crime of militant compassion.[56]

It would not be until the modern civil rights movement that large numbers of whites would come to appreciate the righteous rebellion of African Americans. But during the first half of the twentieth century, African American authors and artists of the Harlem Renaissance experienced their own great commission and created new spiritual life by recasting the body, presence, and power of Christ. Presenting him as a lynch victim and placing him squarely in the racial dramas of Jim Crow America, they challenged the association of whiteness with godliness. Christ's words had not changed; his actions remained mostly the same. What was different was how he appeared and what Americans thought about his appearances.

JUST THREE YEARS after Upton Sinclair imagined Jesus invading Los Angeles, reaching out to the poor, being attacked by lynch mobs and saved by Klan extras, and retreating back to his pretty stained-glass window, theologian Shirley Jackson Case noticed that perceptions of Christ were not timeless. All over modern America, Jesus was being refashioned to be made relevant. Case explained, "There is hardly an area of modern religious interest where Jesus has not been himself made the ideal modern man." Increasing religious diversity, he found, led to increasing multiplicity of approaches to Jesus. Reformers saw him as a reformer. YMCA workers saw him as a YMCA worker. Pacifists portrayed him as a pacifist, belligerents as a belligerent. Bruce Barton made him sound like a "typical modern hustler."[57]

Case was right to point out that there were numerous approaches to Jesus and that many Americans molded him to their own purposes. What Case missed, however, was important—how some Americans used Christ's foreignness, his outsider status, and his differences with modern culture to define him. Case did not see that many Americans, especially black Americans, did not think Christ looked like them—or if he did, he could not be sacred. And finally, Case neglected the importance of the body to these renderings. Whether debating his relationship to consumer capitalism, worker solidarity, white supremacy, or land expropriation, race and physical identity had become crucial markers of Christ's spirit.

What Case also overlooked was that some everyday Americans were beginning to realize that culture, power, and racial concepts played a significant role in how Jesus was rendered. Quietly, unexpectedly, and unnoticed by theologians like Case or sociologists like Frazier, some were starting to comprehend the power of presentation and production. This was making the United States ripe for a civil rights movement, not only to challenge and transform the basic structures of white supremacy but also to hear the possibility that Christ's whiteness was made by men, not by God.

If E. Franklin Frazier had listened more closely to the young black men and women he interviewed, he would have found that many recognized that his whiteness was a product of historical and cultural construction. One nineteen-year-old, for instance, thought that Jesus was "a white man" but quickly added, "Negro or white, by the time white people got through, they made Him white, too." Another invoked the slippery problem of Jewish racial identity and spoke to the ambiguity of Christ's categorization. "As a Jew, He might have been dark," explained one boy, "but Jews are supposed to be white, so I guess that makes Him white, too." One college freshman saw behind the pictures and the power: "All the pictures I've seen, He was a white man. If by any chance He was anything else, the white people have taken great pains to make Him a white man throughout these many, many years."[58]

Beneath the dominant images of white Christ figures and beyond the artistic renderings of Harlem Renaissance painters, these teenagers were trying to come to grips with a history they could sense but could not pin down. They had learned enough about the Bible, geography, and contemporary racial politics to recognize that the race of Jesus was a complicated issue that had little, if anything, to do with what he actually looked like. They knew that whites' social, cultural, economic, and legal power played a role, but also that confused and malleable racial categories shaped approaches to Christ. And they understood that there were limits to what people of color could say or claim. They were unsure of Christ's appearance but grasped that the questions and answers could not be untied from their nation's history and the contemporary political climate. Finally, many may not have wanted Christ in their racial image, because they had experienced what a racial group could do with the belief that they were of the same race as Christ.

As these teenagers grew to maturity, their generation transformed America and Christ once again. Only a decade after Frazier's findings, black women and men—perhaps some of those he interviewed—swept the nation into a civil rights revolution. They stormed the citadels of white power: schools, courts, libraries, buses, churches, synagogues, and department stores. In the process, new battles over the meaning and color of Christ emerged. Yet underneath the public spectacles, high-profile court cases, and television attention, Jesus received a new and dominant face from a man who lived a million cultural miles from Hollywood and Harlem.

Printed, purchased, and consumed by hundreds of millions, it traveled to the most distant shores and the deepest recesses of the mind. Americans came out of the civil rights era open to the intellectual idea that Jesus could be nonwhite, but they were swept away visually with the unspoken conviction that he was in fact white.

CHAPTER EIGHT

CIVIL RIGHTS AND
THE COLORING OF CHRIST

In 1957, Martin Luther King Jr. received a letter to his syndicated "Advice for Living" question-and-answer column that cut to the heart of concerns about racial identity and God's work: "Why did God make Jesus white, when the majority of peoples in the world are non-white?" King answered with the essence of his political and religious philosophy. He denied that the color of one's skin determined the content of one's character, and for King there was no better example than Christ. "The color of Jesus' skin is of little or no consequence," King reassured his readers, because skin color "is a biological quality which has nothing to do with the intrinsic value of the personality." Jesus transcended race, and he mattered "not in His color, but in His unique God-consciousness and His willingness to surrender His will to God's will. He was the son of God, not because of His external biological makeup, but because of His internal spiritual commitment."

Try as he might to downplay race altogether, King could not avoid the color of Christ. In his attempt to separate Christ's body from his soul (and thus whiteness from godliness), King inadvertently upheld the assumption that Jesus was white. The Son of God, King continued, "would have been no more significant if His skin had been black. He is no less significant because his skin was white." Jesus had white skin, but it did not matter to King; it was Christ's spirit that made all the difference.

Another of King's readers was "disturbed" by this assumption: "I believe, as you do, that skin color shouldn't be important, but I don't believe Jesus was white." He then asked, "What is the basis for your assumption that he was?" Only twenty years since E. Franklin Frazier had found most black teenagers accepting the whiteness of Christ, now black folk challenged the idea in public even when it was subtly made by one of their leaders.

William Gale Gedney, "African-American Boy Sitting on a Float Dressed as a King below Picture of Jesus" (1967). Courtesy of the William Gedney Collection, David M. Rubenstein Rare Book and Manuscript Library, Duke University.

King never replied. Just like so many other Americans, King had no biblical basis for his assertion that Christ's "skin was white." He just assumed that somehow, someway, Jesus had been a white man. Like other Americans of his age, King inhabited a world populated by images of white Christ figures. These representations and racial assumptions possessed such power that they did not have to be proven or defended. They just were.[1]

In the middle decades of the twentieth century, King and his civil rights allies set out to remake America. They imagined a world where character mattered more than skin color, where righteousness was worth more than racial categories, and where souls could soar above social mores. Their efforts relied upon Jesus. It was King's genius and the brilliance of his colleagues that took back Jesus from white supremacists. Directly defying the ways Jesus had been tethered to white power in film, law, art, and politics, the civil rights activists moved to render Jesus as a universal savior who cared for all peoples. They then redefined Christ's service and his suffering. In their hands, he became the first nonviolent protester whose moral strength could overwhelm whites' social power. In this way, Jesus was a civil rights crusader whose skin color was irrelevant. His actions and ethics put him on the side of freedom and justice. For a season, it seemed as if King and his fellows were winning the struggle over Jesus.

King and those who rallied around him had every reason to dream and to believe the nation could change. The 1950s and 1960s were decades of immeasurable civil rights success. From *Brown v. the Board of Education* of 1954 to the Voting Rights Act of 1965 to the Indian Civil Rights Act of 1968, it seemed that freedom struggles were finally yielding freedom victories. "We shall overcome" was shifting from prophetic song to legislative reality. They felt so close to the mountaintop of racial justice that it seemed they could see the summit.

Yet resistance came from many sides. Sometimes it was overt massive resistance, like fire hosing, threats, bullets, and bombs. Sometimes it was moderate, like requests to "slow down" or to understand how white people felt. Sometimes the resistance was covert and contractual, like housing restrictions and lending policies.[2] Resistance also came from Native American and African American communities, which alternatively felt that King and his protégés were moving too slow or too fast, that they did not have the right political plan, or that they were theologically brainwashed. From all directions, the civil rights Christ came under attack. His body, which King tried so hard to rise above, once again became a lightning rod for conflict and a site of new creation.

Debates over Christ's race, physical appearance, and political identity animated conflicts within American society and the civil rights movement itself. White southerners who opposed desegregation turned even harder toward a white Jesus who sanctified white bodies. At the same time, some African Americans rejected Jesus altogether, while others bemoaned white Christ figures in black churches and created alternatives by rendering him as black. Some Native Americans struggled to move beyond Christianity as well, while others took the notion that "God is Red" and applied it to Christ. It became so commonplace to reform the body of Jesus that by the end of the 1960s just about every group in America was reframing Christ in its own image and generating new conflicts with each sacred manifestation.

As King and his colleagues tried to redeem the nation, a small midwestern publishing house was quietly reshaping the face of Jesus in America and throughout the world. This white Christ was not a religious relic from ancient days or simply a fraud from medieval European art. It was a mass-produced, mass-consumed image that rose to previously unimaginable visual dominance and was drafted into the Cold War as an icon of American freedoms and free markets. For every civil rights speech or protest, and for every question of whitened sacred images, this one was distributed or shown a thousand times or more. For millions of Americans, and for untold numbers across the globe, it became the literal face of Jesus.

Warner Sallman, the Cold War, and the Globalization of American Sacred Imagery

When white, black, and red Americans of the 1920s and 1930s complained about older Christ figures, none of them could have expected what happened in the 1940s. The new and dominant Jesus image did not spring from Hollywood directors or from Harlem artists. It did not arise from self-taught painters of the segregated South or from working-class radicals enamored with the New Deal. Instead, it came from the Midwest, was drawn for Fundamentalist Christians, was deployed against Communism in the Cold War, and became the most recognizable face of Jesus in the world.

Warner Sallman's *Head of Christ* (1941) revolutionized Jesus imagery. Sallman was born in the 1890s to the children of European immigrants. His religious art went global but had local roots. He was inspired by a professor at Moody Bible Institute, an evangelical Bible college in Chicago, who asked for a more "manly" Jesus. Sallman's new head originated as a charcoal sketch in the 1920s, the decade Congress determined to restrict immigrants, and was then printed in a small evangelical denomination's magazine. The painted version exploded into national and world consciousness like no other piece of American art.[3]

This new Jesus had smooth white skin, long flowing brown hair, a full beard, and blue eyes. He wore a white robe, and the image stopped just beneath his shoulders. A profile of Jesus, this Son of God looked into the distance and away from the viewer. Light from behind his head brightened his face and hair. The background was simple brown with no geographical markers or landscapes.

Almost immediately the image became extraordinarily popular. By 1944, it had sold more than 14 million prints, as it became a staple of evangelical churches and Sunday schools. Americans placed the picture in living rooms or bedrooms as if he was a member of the family. Christian publishers and entrepreneurs marketed Sallman's work in every conceivable fashion, plac-

Warner Sallman, *Head of Christ* (1941). © 1941 Warner Press Inc., Anderson, Indiana. Used with permission.

ing it on bookmarks, calendars, Bibles, plates, stickers, buttons, and even lamps. Religious groups supplied World War II soldiers with wallet-sized prints that looked like baseball cards, and GIs carried them on their war journeys to Europe and the Pacific. Victorious abroad, they returned home and sang "I surrender all" to gigantic billboard versions of him at Billy Graham's massive revival services.[4]

Christians encountered this Jesus as the true Christ, and for some the image had supernatural powers. Many fixated on his eyes and the "radiance" of his face. "I have had visions of our Lord Jesus Christ and his painting is a very close resemblance," a letter to the editor of *Christianity Today* stated in 1958. One woman from Iowa wrote that the one in her living room turned literally "from paper to living flesh." In the 1980s, art historian David Morgan collected several hundred letters from individuals on their interactions with Sallman's painting. Oftentimes, writers referred to it as a "photograph," and one elderly woman claimed that it was "an exact likeness of our Lord Jesus Christ." Children saw the image as authentic too. When first seeing it, one two-year-old exclaimed, "That's Jesus," and others remarked, "That's Him" or "There He is."[5]

The painting comforted anxious souls at mid-century, a pivotal and unsettled moment of religious debate, postwar prosperity, and the possibility of nuclear Armageddon. Sallman's Christ protected Americans in the midst of duck-and-cover anxiety. At the end of the 1953 film adaptation of *War of the Worlds*, for instance, a white family crouched inside a church and looked to a painting of Jesus near the altar. His blond hair and blue eyes provided solace and safety in a nuclear world gone mad. In the real world, one Chicago Lutheran went on a crusade to put wallet-sized Christ images in every Christian's pocket. He wanted "card-carrying Christians" to stand against "card-carrying Communists." In this case, the physical picture of Jesus became a sign of religious and political identity. Proof of Christian faith was now reduced from behavior or belief to the possession of a material artifact.[6]

Jesus imagery also addressed issues of child development, home life, and suburban comfort. When an evangelical magazine juxtaposed "broken homes" with Christian ones in an article, Jesus made all the difference. On one side was a photograph of street boys gambling and smoking. On the other was a young white boy teaching his family about Jesus by holding a print of Christ before them. Dressed in a suit, the boy stood in front of the family's fireplace as his parents and sisters looked on, listened attentively, and gazed at Jesus before their eyes.[7]

The rise in popularity of Sallman's *Head of Christ* showed that everyday Christians, not just church leaders or theologians, were the prime movers of faith's material culture. Mothers and fathers, Sunday school teachers, and new Christian entrepreneurs were the ones who made Sallman's Christ ubiquitous. They did so in spite of the contrary teachings of the day's theological and aesthetic experts. Trying to keep pace with suburban growth in the 1940s and 1950s, Christians and Jews built thousands of new churches and synagogues. One of the most influential liberal theologians, Paul Tillich, recommended that new churches incorporate art but do so wisely. They should favor "abstract, nonrepresentational works," and if compelled to have a crucifix, the figure of Jesus should not be "realistic." Church organizers published a spate of new books on how to plan and build these churches. They paid attention to features big and small: carpet colors, parking lot sizes, shrub placements, and bank loans. But they did not draw much attention to Jesus or art. One who did, Katherine McClinton, devoted a chapter in her book, *The Changing Church* (1957), to "Art in the Church." Sacred artwork should have a "persistent strangeness to the human figures that lifts it above the natural."[8]

But when it came to Christ, most Americans did not listen to McClinton or Tillich. There was nothing strange or abstract about Sallman's Christ. In fact, it was just the opposite. His easy familiarity made him more approachable and hence a savior who spoke to their circumstances.

American Catholics welcomed Sallman's *Head of Christ* into their large fold of sacred art. In the 1930s, one Catholic organization asked Sallman to provide a pastel picture of Jesus for their Scripture Text Calendar, and Catholic leaders in Oklahoma supported Protestant efforts to flood the state with Sallman's paintings. A new Catholic seminary in Oklahoma City requested and received a gigantic *Head of Christ* to display on campus.[9]

Sallman's Jesus looked awfully similar to the Catholic Sacred Heart, and his shared use by Protestants and Catholics was part of strengthening relationships across the religious divide. The Cold War united Protestants and Catholics as comrades against atheistic Communism, and the children of immigrants who had once been deemed nonwhite were now becoming emblems of America and its faith. The election of John F. Kennedy in 1960, who convinced voters that his American identity, not his Catholicism, would shape his political decisions, was another watershed moment of that religious rapprochement.[10]

By the 1990s, Sallman's *Head of Christ* had been printed more than 500 million times and had achieved global iconic status. Those who wrote to David Morgan in the 1980s testified to the sense of comfort it gave them amid confusing times. One woman wrote that the image "has offered me a comfort through just looking at it." Another complained that her husband worked too much and never listened to her. Her pastor handed her a wallet-sized *Head of Christ*, pointed to the ear of Jesus, and said, "it is always turned to you, he is willing to listen anytime you care to talk." This woman had kept the picture in her wallet "ever since." Many recognized that this Christ was not an authentic depiction of Jesus, but they did not care. "I know Jesus probably doesn't look like the picture," one claimed. "It doesn't matter. I thank Mr. Sallman for giving me this image to hang onto." Another woman who had traveled to Saudi Arabia and feared it as a "dark spiritual land" kept Sallman's *Head of Christ* close by because it brought her "comfort and security." It held at bay "the dark forces."[11]

King and the King of Kings

Sallman's Christ was not the only one battling "dark forces" or rising to sacred status. By the 1960s, black activists from every walk of life assaulted the legal, social, and economic structures of white power. When it came to Jesus, Martin Luther King Jr. and his followers tried to fashion the Son of God into a universal savior who taught love and justice for all people. Just as anthropologists, sociologists, and scientists of the age were showing how notions of permanent racial difference were myths and that humans shared traits across cultures and skin features, civil rights activists took the focus off of Christ's body and placed it onto his soul.[12] They tried to transform his moral example into a grassroots political program of everyday defiance. Theirs was a grand effort to redeem Jesus and America from racism and discrimination. Living in the American racial nightmare, they dreamed of a colorless redeemer.

Without Christ, there would have been no King. Sitting in his kitchen late at night on January 27, 1956, almost two months into the Montgomery bus boycott, which was to occupy the next year of his life, the not-yet-thirty-year-old King was depressed. Discouraged by constant threats and setbacks, he considered giving up his leadership role in the young movement. Early negotiations with the city had soured, and he feared for his family's safety.

King felt alone, and even his faith seemed to fail him. As he later acknowledged, he had "grown up religious," and the church was real to him. "But it was a kind of inherited religion and I had never felt an experience with God in the way you must . . . if you're going to walk the lonely paths of this life." Around midnight, another threatening phone caller barked, "Nigger, we are tired of you and your mess now, and if you aren't out of this town in three days, we're going to blow your brains out and blow up your house."

What happened next was life changing. King had a transcendent experience that steeled him for the difficult days to come. He realized the burden was on him alone. He had to "call on that something in that person that your Daddy used to tell you about, that power that can make a way out of no way." At this moment, "religion had become real to me, and I had to know God for myself." King bowed his head and prayed. "But Lord, I must confess that I'm weak now. I'm faltering. I'm losing my courage. And I can't let the people see me like this because if they see me weak and losing my courage, they will begin to get weak."

King then heard a voice. It commanded him to "stand up for righteousness. Stand up for justice. Stand up for truth. And lo I will be with you, even until the end of the world." It was the "voice of Jesus saying still to fight on. He promised never to leave me, never to leave me alone." His fears diminished, and his "uncertainty disappeared." Three days later, local whites tried to destroy his home, but King emerged unscathed. His encounter with the voice of Jesus settled him. Just as Joseph Smith's visions had inspired a faith that would walk from east to west amid persecution and just as Sojourner Truth had heard God's call to speak amid a society that wanted her to remain silent, King now felt strength for a battle. It was a new kind of strength, the "strength to love." It consumed and then took his life.[13]

Time and again, King credited Christ as the political, social, and spiritual architect of the era's new approach to civil rights activism. "Love is the only way. Jesus discovered that," King told an audience in 1957 while reflecting on the power of nonviolence to overcome discrimination. Visions of the past Christ inspired strength for today: "Yes, I can see Jesus walking around the hills and the valleys of Palestine. And I can see him looking out at the Roman Empire with all of her fascinating and intricate military machinery." He could hear Jesus rejecting the use of violence to defeat violence, and King urged his audience to march in the face of potential martyrdom as Jesus did.[14]

Jesus was such a powerful force that when civil rights activists borrowed the dynamic innovations of Mohandas Gandhi from India, they transformed him into a Christian and Christ figure. Early members of the Fellowship of Reconciliation, for instance, called Gandhi "one of the greatest Christians of all times" and "the Christ of our age." According to King, more than anyone else Gandhi had "caught the spirit of Jesus Christ and lived it more completely in his life." He took the "love ethic of Jesus Christ and made it effective as a sociopolitical force and brought about the transformation of a great nation and achieved freedom for his people."[15] Through Gandhi, American civil rights leaders showcased their emphasis on soul over body. Christ's ethics could claim anybody (even one that was not white), anywhere (even outside the United States), and of any faith (even beyond Christianity) and make them useful and meaningful in the American context.

King identified with the physical trauma of Christ's experiences. He spoke frequently about "bearing the cross." "When I took up the cross," he explained, "I recognized its meaning. The cross is something that you bear and ultimately that you die on." After repeated death threats and a stabbing, he reminisced how he had "learned now that the master's burden is light precisely when we take his yoke upon us." King could now humbly yet proudly say, "I bear in my body the marks of the lord Jesus." His parishioners in Montgomery seemed to recognize it too. Shortly after his arrest for violating Alabama's antiboycott law, King entered Montgomery's Holt Street Baptist Church to tumultuous applause. A platform speaker introduced him as "he who [was] nailed to the cross for us this afternoon," while several audience members compared King to "Jesus himself."[16]

Many Americans responded by identifying King as a new Christ figure himself. A "fellow Sufferer" from Sixteenth Street Baptist Church in Birmingham wrote that black mothers had "prayed that God would send us a leader such as you are. Now that the Almighty has regarded our lowly estate and has raised *you* among us, I am indeed grateful." Recalling the student sit-ins in Nashville in 1960, student leader John Lewis recited the rules they followed: "The whole idea, matter of fact, came from the Montgomery Bus Boycott. This was telling people what to do. Don't talk back. Sit straight up. Don't laugh out. Don't curse. And at the end of the rules, it said something like 'Remember the teachings of Jesus, Gandhi, Martin Luther King.'"[17]

Then with his assassination in 1968, King rose to messianic status. Answering the question of whether King's martyrdom was foreordained, one of King's mentors, Benjamin Mays, answered that it was inevitable, not because God willed it, but because "any man who takes the position that King did . . . if he persists in that long enough, he'll get killed. Now. Anytime. That was the chief trouble with Jesus: He was a troublemaker." Pope Paul VI remarked that King's death was part of "the tragic story of the passion of the Christ," and decades later King's friend Ralph Abernathy said that he could never forget "Martin, for he lives in my soul, like Gandhi and Jesus Christ." In the 1980s, the government honored King with a national holiday in his name, the only American other than George Washington to have such a distinction. The Irish rock band U2 then shifted a song originally about Ronald Reagan and the notion that "pride comes before the fall" to one that likened King (as the man who "came in the name of love") to Christ (as the man who was "betrayed with a kiss") in their pulsating hit "Pride (In the Name of Love)."[18]

King died because of his efforts to remake Jesus and America. He and the civil rights movement around him tried to present Christ as a universal savior whose life showed what current science and anthropology were revealing—that skin color bore no relationship to innate qualities and that racial categories were created by societies. Christ's actions, ethics, and words mattered. His skin tone, hair length, or eye color did not. The effort to take back Jesus from the prosouthern, prowhite, and proimperialist representations that dominated previous decades was a tall order, but in some ways they were successful. Most Americans after the civil rights era would agree that Jesus was not a friend to segregation or racism.

The Wrongs of the Civil Rights Christ

But at a deeper level, King failed. The history of racial division and the power of Christ imagery were too much to overcome. Racial categories had assumed so much authority that neither scientific studies, nor anthropological insights, nor the ethics of Jesus could seem to convince Americans that race was not real or that his color was insignificant. Fashioning Jesus into a particular and visualized body made it impossible for any universal savior to rise above the conflicts, and his having an individual body made it nearly impossible for Americans to avoid giving him shape in a racial form.

King and his colleagues relied on the supposed King of Kings to dampen down differences of political opinion, social vision, and religious values. But the Jesus center could not hold. The notion of Christ as one who transcended race gave way to a series of racial contests over sacred icons. These disputes led white supremacists, students, hippies, Mexican Americans, Native Americans, and Jewish Americans to make their own racial claims about Christ.

White supremacists focused their energies on taking Jesus back. Segregationist authors asserted the whiteness of Christ's blood as part of their defense of the justness of segregation. Carey Daniel, a White Citizens' Council leader and pastor of the First Baptist Church of West Dallas, Texas, authored a widely reprinted pamphlet, "God the Original Segregationist." In it, he rehashed the familiar racial genealogy that linked African Americans to the Canaanites, "the only children of Ham who were specifically cursed to be a servile race," and whites to the lineage of Israel and Christ. God so hated racial integration that he commanded his people to destroy other groups when mixing seemed possible. Then, Daniel joined antebellum defenders of slavery by turning to an argument of silence. The burden of proof rested with those who believed Jesus was not a segregationist, for God's Son never specifically repudiated the system. Instead, Jesus had run money changers out of the Temple, just as "we had good reasons to keep those [civil rights] agitators out of our Church," as a Methodist laywoman in Georgia insisted to her bishop.[19]

Debates over the church as the metaphorical "body" of Christ led to discussions about family units and sex between literal white and black bodies. As historian Jane Dailey has shown, white supremacists gave their defense of segregation cosmological meaning through sexuality. They opposed integration for its potential to result in interracial sex, and they deemed intercourse across the color line to be against God's plan for human development. Even liberal southern whites like Baptist T. B. Maston, who opposed segregation with the belief that in "Christ there is neither male nor female, bond nor free, Jew nor Gentile, red nor yellow, black nor white," thought that interracial sex was unwise. He explained that the well-being of the body of Christ was more important than the individual choices of particular bodies. "If by entering into a particular marriage one would lose his opportunity to witness or to minister for Christ, or if his marriage would handicap and hurt the work of Christ, then the marriage would be not only unwise but positively wrong."[20]

In its most extreme versions, white supremacist reliance on Christ turned into terrorism. Mississippi's Sam Bowers revived the state's White Knights of the Ku Klux Klan with the firm belief that "a Solemn, determined Spirit of Christian Reverence must be stimulated in all members." What other white residents called a civil rights "invasion" of Mississippi he referred to as the "crucifixion" of the state. The "empirical fact" of Christ's resurrection, he believed, meant that "the disciple has no alternative but to strive towards that great day when all Christ's enemies will be put under his feet." Jesus Christ himself, Bowers preached, had called him to the "priestly task of preserving the purity of his blood and soil."[21]

This alleged "priestly task" became deadly in the ensuing weeks after King captivated the nation with his "I Have a Dream" speech. In Birmingham, Alabama, Robert "Dynamite Bob" Chambliss and a group from the United Klans of America set more than one hundred sticks of dynamite outside Sixteenth Street Baptist Church. They exploded at about 10:20 A.M. on the Sunday morning of September 15, 1963, killing four girls, blowing out the face of the church's white Jesus, and devastating the hearts of civil rights activists throughout the nation.

The explosion symbolized the difficulties of rendering Jesus as a universal savior in a nation with racialized visual images of his body and a history of violent racial strife. Since the late nineteenth century, the white Jesus and especially his widespread use among African Americans had come under fire. The bombing and the fractured white Christ revealed how King's reliance on a bodiless and universal Jesus failed to answer the racial problems of America or its sacred material culture. Some black commentators, such as novelist and essayist James Baldwin, were relieved that the "alabaster Christ" had been destroyed and hoped African Americans could give Jesus a "new face" and a "new consciousness."[22]

Anne Moody's reaction was to damn God. Her gripping memoir, *Coming of Age in Mississippi*, showcased the spiritual trauma of living through the civil rights era and how these problems orbited around racialized concepts of God and Christ. Her baptism at the age of eleven in 1951 was a big event. Decked out in baptismal white, Moody resented herself for caving in to the pressure exerted by her mother and the other churchwomen to be saved and baptized. Paradoxically, she associated whiteness with purity and, rhetorically, with excrement: "I look at that white dress, those white socks, that white slip, and those white drawers, and thought, 'This shit means I've been washed clean of all my sins!'"

As a college student years later, she threw herself into the civil rights movement in order to purify herself and society. Like many of her generation, the movement became her church and her religion. Moody deified its heroes: "I thought Bob Moses, the director of SNCC [Student Nonviolent Coordinating Committee] in Mississippi, was Jesus Christ in the flesh. A lot of other people thought of him as Jesus Christ, too." She participated in efforts to integrate churches in Jackson, Mississippi, but all the traumatic moments of being forcefully removed or accepted with condescension led her to wonder if God truly was on the side of civil rights: "If they were praying to the same God I was, then even God, I thought was against me."[23]

Jesus of the freedom songs was not enough. When Moody looked at the faces of African Americans singing hymns and spirituals, "I could tell by the way they said the word that most of them had given up here on earth. They seemed to be waiting just for God to call them home and end all the suffering."[24] Then the Birmingham bombing shattered her faith in God. She explained to God that if he was white, she no longer believed. If God was black, then Moody planned to kill him. In either racial configuration, God was dead to her.[25]

The idea that "God is dead" emerged as a playful academic notion for rogue theologians of the 1960s, but it was potentially earth shattering for many African Americans. Faith had been a foundation; it had been a shelter from the storms. Lynchings had led some to wonder about God's relevance to their world, but faith had remained vibrant and strong. Most did not want God dead but cried out for the white Jesus to be crucified, buried, and never resurrected. Renowned boxer Cassius Clay, for instance, remembered how his father "painted murals of a White Jesus in Baptist churches all over town." Clay associated the idea that blacks should be "humble" and "meek" with the "white Jesus." The Nation of Islam, and its rejection of sacred images, appealed to him. He joined this faith, changed his name to Muhammad Ali, knocked out anyone in his path, and refused to participate in white men's wars, like the one raging in Vietnam.[26]

Inspired by both King's civil rights crusade and the ideology of the Nation of Islam, the concept of "black power" grabbed national attention in the mid-1960s. It suggested morals beyond the Christian tradition and images beyond the white Christ. Black power advocates were clear on the white Christ: they wanted him gone.

Critiques of Christianity sometimes created rifts among radical African Americans. When the teenage Cornel West spent time with Black Panthers in California, for instance, their dismissal of Christ became a stumbling block for his participation with the group. He agreed with so much of their economic and social critique but refused to abandon faith. They always "criticized" his Christianity, West acknowledged, but he was determined to follow King's Christ. "My understanding of Jesus Christ went like this: Everything comes beneath the cross—nationalism, tribalism, patriotism, networks, even kinships." As the years went on, West would keep alive King's dream by linking Christ to all forms of social justice that transcended racial categories and perceptions.[27]

Vincent Harding, a protégé of King who grew up in Harlem in the 1930s and 1940s, tried to explain the religious sentiments of black power to white moderates. In a 1967 article for the liberal magazine *Christian Century*, he told white readers that black power was not an outgrowth of Christ's teachings. "Whatever its other sources," he wrote, "the ideology of blackness surely grows out of the deep ambivalence of American Negroes to the Christ we have encountered here." Black Americans were angry that "Christ was painted white and pink, blond and blue-eyed." This was a problem, he continued, "not only in white churches but in black churches as well. Millions of black children had the picture of this pseudo-Nazarene burned into their memory. The books, the windows, and paintings, the filmstrips all affirmed the same message—a message of shame."

The white Jesus signified a gospel of shame. "This Christ shamed us by his pigmentation, so obviously not our own. He condemned us for our blackness, for our flat noses, for our kinky hair, for our power, our strange power of expressing emotion in singing and shouting and dancing. He was sedate, so genteel, so white. And as soon as we were able, many of us tried to be like him." No more would they bow to a white savior. "For a growing edge of bold young black people all that is past. They fling out their declaration: 'No white Christ shall shame us again.' We are glad to be black." In place of shame, the black power movement had a message of righteous judgment. The "redemptive suffering" of King and mainline civil rights activists was a gospel of the past. Now black power would tap into "redemptive anger." It would rain down a judgment of righteous fire on white "arrogance and power."[28]

Harding heralded the destructive and creative birth of modern black liberation theology. His insights had a long and a short history. The long history stretched back to slave renderings of Jesus as a friend, master, and liberator. It moved through novelists, ministers, poets, and painters who refused to believe that Jesus could be white and instead linked him to lynch victims. It ran from the streets of Harlem to the patios of self-taught southern painters, and from the sacred musings of black children looking in mirrors to the highly stylized performances of street prophets.

The short history came from the 1950s and 1960s when a new group of renegade pastors, students, and theologians reread biblical texts from black power perspectives and shifted away from the civil rights focus of integration and toward either racial authority or racial separatism. Joined with "Afrocentric" histories of the birth of civilization, a tradition stretching back to nineteenth-century black historians and authors who had produced "race histories," modern black theology brought the gospel to Africa and proclaimed a black Jesus the true messiah.[29]

For the most part, white and black communities were ill-prepared to hear or see Christ associated with blackness. As a college student at the mostly white DePauw University in Indiana, for instance, Vernon Jordan, from Georgia, starred as the Christ figure in a play entitled *Blackwater*. As a minister hallucinated during a sermon, Jordan was suspended to a cross and a spotlight hit him. And "there I am—on the cross," Jordan remembered. "You could literally hear gasps from the audience, for there was the image of the black man as Jesus crucified by white townspeople." Years later, Jordan became a prominent lawyer and a political aide to President Bill Clinton. But while at DePauw, he was considered a blasphemer for embodying Jesus in a black body. "House mothers across the campus said it was blasphemy to have me on the cross. That was not the only problem. I suspect they hated the mixing of racial symbolism, which equated persecuted blacks with Jesus and prejudiced whites with those who executed Him. It may have hit just a little too close to home."[30]

John Henrik Clarke's fictional short story "The Boy Who Painted Christ

Black" (1940) revealed that whites were not the only ones upset by such renditions. In the story, a boy in Muskogee County, Georgia, astounds his classmates with a "large picture of Christ—painted black!" The boy's uncle, who taught black history classes at the YMCA, said black folks were the "most powerful on earth. When I asked him about Christ, he said no one ever proved whether he was black or white." The boy explains the genesis of the picture this way: "Somehow a feeling came over me that he was a black man, 'cause he was so kind and forgiving, kinder than I have ever seen white people be. So, when I painted this picture I couldn't help but paint it as I thought it was." Clarke distances this fictive drawing from the ones in white and black Sunday schools. This picture "looked much different from the one I saw hanging on the wall when I was in Sunday School. It looked more like a helpless Negro, pleading silently for mercy."

The symbol was opposed immediately. When the supervisor of the school visits, he takes offense at the picture. He asks, "Who painted this sacrilegious nonsense?" The boy responds that he did, adding that blacks had as much right to paint Jesus as black as whites did painting him white. The schoolteacher and his principal had encouraged him, noting that artists targeted particular audiences with their messages. And it made some historic sense to portray Christ this way, for "Christ was born in that part of the world that had always been predominantly populated by colored people." Quite possibly, then, Christ was black, the principal had assured them. The supervisor warns, "There'll be a lot of fuss in this world if you start people thinking that Christ was a nigger." Power prevails. The supervisor reprimands the boy and forces the principal to resign.[31]

Everything changed in Detroit when Albert Cleage Jr. made the black Christ central to his ministry. He crafted into programmatic power what had been in the form of paper and artistic presentations. Cleage had been a longtime proponent of racial integration. His preaching in the 1940s was dedicated to white and black Americans learning to live in harmony. This shifted in the 1950s. Cleage saw Detroit's white community oppose school integration, economic advancement for the poor, and genuine justice or reconciliation. To obtain freedom, he concluded, African Americans must destroy the white Jesus, the white Madonna, and the white God. He had his Detroit church renamed the "Shrine of the Black Madonna" in 1953.[32]

Cleage went back to his Bible and found a tribal, not universal, faith. The new approach was not really that new at all. He remembered his mother, the descendant of white, black, and red Americans from the South, telling him as a theology student that his "New Testament professor was wrong because Jesus was Black." Just as his mother was, Cleage became fed up with the notion that Jesus was white. He declared this idea a grand "illusion." It was nothing less than "the crowning demonstration of their white supremacist conviction that all things good and valuable must be white." Cleage explained to God in a prayer: "Certainly thou must understand that as black people, it would be impossible for us to kneel before thee, believing thee to be a white God." Instead, Cleage contended that God was racially mixed (and therefore a "Negro" by classifications in the United States) and that Jesus was a "non-white leader of a non-white people struggling for national liberation against the rule of a white nation, Rome." Cleage concluded that the only true Christianity for blacks was nationalist and separatist.[33]

His movement went beyond ideas and preaching; it hit the streets. After the city's riots of 1967, black Detroiters painted the hands, feet, and face of a white Sacred Heart Christ with black and brown paint. Local whites then repainted the statue white, only to have it painted black again, a racial swapping signifying another contest over the body of Christ now set within the context of urban strife.

In the late 1960s, Christ's blackness moved from streets and stories to another niche: the university. Primarily through the work of James Cone, liberation theology achieved a scholarly language and discourse. In a series of articles and books beginning in the late 1960s and continuing into the twenty-first century, Cone took it upon himself to reconcile black power with Christianity. As for Cleage, Cone's mother also figured prominently. "I cannot support any revolution that excludes my mother," he once wrote in reference to the atheism of some black power advocates, "and she believes in Jesus." Rather than reject the revolution, Cone sought to reconcile it and his mother. He viewed himself as saving Jesus in a moment of spiritual crisis, and he brought together the theology of Karl Barth, the philosophy of Albert Camus, and the experiences of African Americans, to claim that "Christianity is essentially a religion of liberation," and that God "is the God *of* and *for* those who labor and are heavy laden." Jesus was "an oppressed Jew" who in American society must be rendered only as "black."[34]

Cone launched an all-out intellectual assault on whiteness and the white Christ as its chief symbol. God's revelation on earth, he claimed, always had been "black, red, or some other shocking shade, but never white. Whiteness, as revealed in the history of America, is the expression of what is wrong with man. It is a symbol of man's depravity." Cone cast his venture in terms of sacred imagery: "The white God is an idol, created by racist bastards, and we black people must perform the iconoclastic task of smashing false idols." "It is not surprising that the people who reject blackness in theology are usually whites who do not question the blue-eyed white Christ," Cone continued.[35]

Although Cone was in Michigan when he wrote his first theological works, he was a son of the South, and violence energized his spiritual imagination. Just as it was for Harlem Renaissance artists, lynching took center stage in reframing Christ. Raised in Bearden, Arkansas, Cone came from a family that loved the church. Singing, worshiping, and praying in the segregated South, Cone experienced Jesus as "a significant presence in my life." Integration hopes, however, were thwarted by violence and fear. "We talked about testing the theological integrity of white faith by seeking to integrate one of their churches, but felt that the risks of bodily harm were too great."

In 1954, Cone watched his father stand against lynching. The whites of Bearden were ready to lynch a family friend. Cone's father grabbed his gun, joined his friend, and stayed up all night. "Let the sons of bitches come," Cone remembered his father saying; "they may get me, but they can be sure that I will take some of them with me." The whites never showed up.[36]

White violence, coupled with white counsels on black nonviolence, led Cone to wonder: "Why did we not hear from the 'nonviolent Christians' when black people were *violently* enslaved, *violently* lynched, and *violently* ghettoized in the name of freedom and democracy?"[37]

Cone and his work brought black liberation theology to American universities and church institutions, where academic debate and organizational support fostered interracial exchange and new intellectual achievements. New and old organizations rallied to black liberation theology, such as the National Conference of Black Churchmen, the Southern Christian Leadership Conference, and the Philadelphia Council of Black Clergy. Black and white theologians responded with criticism, admiration, and complication.[38] Cone was hired at the prestigious Union Theological Seminary—home to Reinhold Niebuhr, Paul Tillich, and Cornel West at various moments—in New York in 1970.[39]

Because Jesus and race were central to black liberation theology, art and visual culture were crucial as well. Ministers, theologians, and artists pushed black churches to reject whitened images of the sacred and replace them with sacred symbols that associated blackness with the divine. They called black churches into a new era of iconoclasm. "A Declaration of Black

Churchmen," published in 1967, demanded "the removal of all images which suggest that God is white." Time and again, ministers complained about church imagery that was dominated by whiteness. "Everything they looked at was white, white, white," grumbled one pastor. From the 1970s into the twenty-first century, black liberationists pressed their congregations to visualize Christ as black and to transform their sacred material culture.[40]

When black liberation theology entered the academy, it gained much. It achieved intellectual respect and garnered heretofore lily-white positions of theological and professorial authority. Its graduate classes produced scholars who pushed the theological insights further and deeper.

But the academic version of black liberation theology lost much too. When it sought to explain itself, its spokespeople generated two distinct histories. Neither had the capacity to comprehend or expose the historical construction of Christ's whiteness, and neither was able to harness past resources into a holistic attack upon the ways white supremacy wrapped itself around and within the white Christ. The long history of black theology, Cone asserted, was as old as slavery itself. "It came into being when black churchmen realized that killing slave masters was doing the work of God." Gayraud Wilmore—the first and finest historian of the movement—crafted a narrative arc in his *Black Religion and Black Radicalism* (1972) that began in the dark days of slavery and ended with Cone. It was an all-black story in which white supremacy was an all-encompassing force that never seemed to change its religious face. That whiteness itself was a construct, and that its relationship to Jesus was fraught with contradiction and rooted in a variety of racial complications, were incomprehensible to Wilmore's kind of historical approach.[41]

The more popular history was a short one that placed the beginnings in the North and its power in young ministers of the 1960s. When Wilmore and Cone released a book of primary documents for seminary students on the emergence of black theology, they placed the genesis in 1966 with a statement from the National Committee of Negro Churchmen in support of black power. Signed mostly by ministers from the urban North, the statement appeared prominently in the *New York Times*.[42]

The short history shifted the focus from everyday African Americans to black clerics. It moved from songs, short stories, and creative art to church statements and theological tracts. It failed to remember its southern roots, its artistic lineage, and the vital role of women. In its historical amnesia, black liberation theology became an academic game of logic and reasoning, rather than an emotional and visual power that addressed the entirety of religious experience.

With what it lacked, what it lost, and the powers it stood against, modern black liberation theology could not possibly unseat the white Christ. Theological language games could not match the march of Sallman's *Head of Christ* icon, and long academic treatises could not appeal to children or Sunday school classes. Moreover, black liberation theologians were ill-prepared to integrate their theological insights with those of other oppressed minority groups. The result was that if every oppressed group had Jesus as their representative, then none of them could genuinely lay claim to him. The discrete liberation theologies simply would counteract one another.

A Christ for Every Crusade

Although black liberation theology received the lion's share of attention for its new physical renderings of Christ, a host of other groups in the 1960s and 1970s were refashioning the body of Jesus to suit their own critiques as well. All seemed to agree with the civil rights crusade that if America was to be changed, Jesus would have to be reimagined. They disagreed with the civil rights movement, though, by fixating on the body of Christ as an important element to change (and not simply his soul). The civil rights movements and black liberation theology had shown that they needed a new body of Christ to represent the new corpus of their social critiques.

The new Christ figures spoke to the spirit of the sixties: civil rights activism, young people's cultural movements, and conservative retrenchment and reformation.[43] Although Sallman's *Head of Christ* was printed in increasing numbers, it too became a lightning rod for dissatisfaction. It was seen by some as too white, too bourgeoisie, too feminine, too old, and even too sexual. In 1967, one seminary student in the North Park neighborhood of Chicago overheard another student complain, "It's a white Christ; looks too Swedish!" One Lutheran griped that it was "a pretty picture of a woman with a curling beard who has just come from the beauty parlor with a Halo shampoo . . . [not] the Lord who died and rose again!" Another pastor allegedly refused to have it in his church, because it was "too much of a come-on for the homos in the parish and the community."[44] None of the criticism stopped the image from selling or being used all over the nation and world, but the attacks revealed how representations of Christ's body now served as avenues to express discontent in any and all forms.

The Jesus People, a mashup of evangelicalism, the student crusade, and alternative personal styles and fashions of the 1960s, wanted to have their protests, their rejection of America, and their Jesus too. They remade Christ with new vernaculars of youth protest and media entertainment. Jesus, according to one, was "truly the Cool One because he took the rap for you and me on the cross." They zeroed in on Christ's long hair as sacred proof that it was acceptable for men to do the same, and they joined the Doobie Brothers in 1969, if not in their fixation on marijuana, then in singing: "I don't care what they may say, I don't care what they may do, Jesus is just alright with me." Student protesters updated the older "wanted poster" of Jesus that working-class radicals had used earlier and rechristened Jesus as "a hippie type" of the 1960s whose "insidious" message most appealed to "young people."[45]

The Jesus People got their visual Christ in 1964 with Richard Hook's *Head of Christ*. It became the main rival to Sallman's *Head of Christ*. This time, Jesus stared straight at the viewer. His hair was brown and unkempt. His beard was trimmed, his eyes were blue, and his white skin had been kissed by the sun. This Jesus appeared younger than Sallman's and looked like he could have been a California surfer. Printed by a Lutheran publishing house, Hook's Christ captured the imagination of many young Americans.[46]

The cinema already had been leaning in a youthful and West Coast direction in representations of Jesus. Nicholas Ray's film *King of Kings* came out in 1961, six years after he had directed *Rebel without a Cause,* in which James Dean stunned audiences with his teenage rage. *King of Kings* starred Jeffrey Hunter as Christ. Although in his mid-thirties, Hunter looked much younger, and the studio billed him as a "teen heart-throb." Tall and muscular, blond-haired but with a shaved and toned physique, the film had close-up after close-up of Hunter's face and eyes. To market the movie, the studio raved about his "fan-mag baby-blue eyes," while critics mocked Hunter and the film with the subtitle: "I was a teenage Jesus." Critics did not scorn, though, the film's approach to Jews. Against the grain of hundreds of years of anti-Semitism in presentations of Jesus, *King of Kings* did not explicitly or implicitly hold the Jews responsible for Christ's crucifixion. Nazis had given anti-Semitism a bad name, and the hippie's Jesus wanted nothing to do with that kind of bad rap.[47]

Long before hippies wrestled with Christ's hair length, it was an important topic for Native Americans. Those who went to boarding schools had been presented with a long-haired Jesus as an emblem of civilization but then were told to cut their hair short to be most civilized. To religious thinker Vine Deloria, this was all nonsense. Debates over Christ's hair length, he thought, were part of white America's complete and utter inability to deal with real existence. When people were struggling for hope, what some ancient prophet looked like was another foolish American escape into fantasy. Deloria wanted to find another path—one beyond Christianity or Christ.

Deloria became the architect of a new Native American liberation theology. He deliberately modeled his work *God Is Red* on James Cone's pronouncement that "God is black." The work arrived in 1973 just on the heels of a standoff between Indian activists in the American Indian Movement and federal authorities at Wounded Knee. The activists had occupied the town, in part, as a symbolic redemption of the 1890 massacre there that had killed almost 200 ghost dancers of the plains.

Deloria respected his friend James Cone and the spiritual guide Black Elk but came to different conclusions about the possibilities for melding Indian and Christian traditions. Deloria was unable, as Black Elk was, to make Jesus white and red, Indian and Catholic. Spiritually reared in Indian and Episcopalian ways and educated in a Lutheran seminary, Deloria developed a wide familiarity with varieties of religious thought. He came to reject in the 1960s the Western biblical tradition as beholden to a linear narrative that was time-oriented. This, he suggested, devalued native modes of placing space and geography at the center of religious understanding. Deloria wanted religion and human experience freed from the confines of Western Christian history, and therefore freed of reliance upon Christ in the past and the present.[48]

For Deloria, the fixation on Christ and his body was absurd. He ridiculed debates over the length of Christ's hair, for instance, and the plans to create a "Holyland USA" in Alabama, which would feature a 157-foot statue of Jesus. This "would be bigger than the Statue of Liberty," Deloria scoffed. The Jesus People were searching for a perpetual "high," Deloria remarked, while Billy Graham and his acolytes worshiped the American nation more than they did any lord of creation. The result of all of it was spiritual "chaos." Deloria hoped that Christ would be supplanted and that "a new kind of religion will make itself manifest to us."[49]

Perhaps because of the title *God Is Red*, Deloria was often identified with the "Red Power" movement, as if he was an Indian James Cone trying to reconcile another form of racial power with another form of racial Christianity. But Deloria was not interested in either the political or religious forms of Cone. Deloria was skeptical of Indian activists who operated in a white world of public political protests and sought instead to rekindle the native sacred fires by recapturing Indian tradition. For him, God was Red but Jesus was relevant only as a cultural relic.[50]

Most Native Americans did not move with Deloria. For hundreds of years, Native Americans had been wrestling with the meaning of Christ's lineage, his relationship to racial issues, and his role in individual and group identities. Most were not about to cast him out. He had become a powerful presence that had to be destroyed or deciphered—but he could not be ignored. Making Jesus red was hard work, and it was as perplexing for Native American theologians as it was for Wovoka or Black Elk. But in the effort, native theologians joined James Cone in creating new theologies of the oppressed—theologies that linked Christ to the blood and bodies of Indians.

For many natives, Jesus was simultaneously bathed in the red of violence, colonialism, and salvation. A character in N. Scott Momaday's classic novel *House Made of Dawn* summed up the nexus of Christianity and colonialism as "the whole Jesus scheme." It damaged native communities by wrapping poison in cloths of healing, and only by weaving new and healthy spiritual garments could native communities move forward. This concept also was central to Leslie Marmon Silko's magisterial *Ceremony*. In this novel of self-destruction and healing, the main character, Tayo, has returned traumatized from his service in World War II. Neither modern medicine nor traditional ceremonies can heal him. Midway through the story, he finds the unorthodox healer Betonie, who has created a mishmash of ceremonies, ritual objects, and prayers that promise help. Their sacred vision pictures the time before whites as certain and simple: "The people had known, with the simple certainty of the world they saw, how everything should be."

White Europeans altered the world beyond recognition, and Jesus became the grand symbol of colonialism. "But the fifth world had become entangled with European names: the names of the rivers, the hills, the names of the animals and plants—all of creation suddenly had two names: an Indian name and a white name. Christianity separated the people from themselves; it tried to crush the single clan name, encouraging each person to stand alone, because Jesus Christ would save only the individual soul; Jesus Christ was not like the Mother who loved and cared for them as her children, as her family." Personal and communal reconciliation could not come until the "entanglement had been unwound to the source." Ultimately, Betonie's ceremonies work to transform and heal Tayo. Christian rituals are part of, but not central to, the ceremonial mash up. Jesus is not a communal savior but an individualistic destroyer of harmony and community.[51]

Beyond the novelists were a group of modern native Christian theologians who struggled to locate an approach to Jesus beyond whiteness and white supremacy. "The image of Jesus that we have learned to hold dear is the image of the White Jesus," one remarked. It would be preferable to have Christ beyond color, as Martin Luther King had hoped, but this was impossible, given American history and religious culture. "Of course we have learned to insist with our denomination that Jesus indeed has no color, that the gospel is color blind, and that God makes no distinction among people. Yet if we look closely, the Jesus we have embraced is too often a White Jesus. . . . If we accept a White Jesus, if that is the image we see, have we not also adopted an image of salvation, of health, wholeness, happiness, that also comes to us via a White culture and comes to us with a White value system." Only by rejecting the white Christ and decolonizing the gospel would native peoples have a Jesus who spoke directly to them.[52]

Some Indian theologians merged the two traditions or insisted that Christian and Indian truths could complement one another. "It would seem a terrible loss if these truths did not inform each other," James West wrote about the apparent dilemma. "It would be a loss if a tightly knit tribal and spiritual understanding of life were not challenged by the Christian concept of universality. In like manner, it would be a loss if a nation built on Christianity and its belief in human 'dominion over the earth' was not challenged by the traditional Indian belief that creatures are brothers and sisters and that the earth is Mother."[53]

Others insisted that by decolonizing the gospel, by going "beyond the white gospel," Indians could meet Jesus freed from the chauvinism of white supremacy; they could see him as brother and quiet servant. "Then we will know that the cry of Jesus Christ from the cross was the cry of our people at Wounded Knee, Sand Creek and other places of the mass death of our people," wrote one native Catholic. Jesus was "our companion during these years of our invisibility in this society." One Kiowa elder believed that "we lost our Christianity because we turned towards the White Man's ways."[54]

Native communities were struggling with many of the same dilemmas African Americans had. They had experienced hundreds of years of oppression, and a white Jesus had come to stand symbolically for that mistreatment. But he had also been an agent of love, compassion, cross-cultural care, and salvation. While experiencing him in universal terms was an ideal, it was also impossible. The weight of history and of sacred symbolism was too heavy, and somehow he would have to be reckoned with in red, white, and black.

Jews never experienced the level of oppression that African Americans or Native Americans did in the United States, but they were certainly in touch with the ramifications of discrimination and violence. All of the talk about Jesus, his identity, and his relationship to civil rights and social inclusion offered Jewish Americans a new, yet dangerous, way to address their place in the nation. In the early 1940s, President Franklin Roosevelt had included "freedom of worship" and "freedom from fear" as part of his "Four Freedoms," and Jewish Americans wanted to make Christian America live up to it. The horror of the Holocaust, moreover, opened the eyes of many Christian Americans to their own anti-Semitism. Will Herberg may have complained in his pathbreaking study *Protestant-Catholic-Jew* (1955) that each group had succumbed to a banal glorification of the United States, but a key point was that each was respected as an American faith. It even became commonplace for Americans to accept the new linguistic construct of "Judeo-Christian," which linked and subsumed Judaism into Christianity, just as "Irish-American," "Italian-American," and other hyphenated American identities did years later for immigrant groups.[55]

The Jewishness of Jesus became a focal point in the 1940s, and it stood as an identity problem for many Jews. As part of the same moment when Jewish Americans were being folded into the broader contours of whiteness, Jews were hashing out what it meant to be American for where they lived, whom they married, and how they celebrated their faith. The assertion that "Jesus was a Jew" had been gaining traction in American Jewish defenses of their communities since the early twentieth century. During World War II, one Jewish soldier mentioned to his comrades "that Jesus was in fact Jewish and of presumed Jewish parentage." His friends were not interested: "The immediate and united stiffening of the entire circle of white faces was an instantaneous warning that they had never been told this before and did not want to be told it now, or ever. Even my closest pals bristled." Christ was both a problem and a possibility for Jews like this. He could be used to claim inclusion, but in doing so Jewish Americans had to accept another faith's savior and to overlook all that had been done against them in his name.[56]

In the 1960s, with every group claiming Christ and with Americans increasingly obsessed with movies and television, one Jewish writer deployed Jesus to mock it all. He created a theatrical satire of a popular television show to expose racial and religious hypocrisy in the nation. Malcolm Marmostein's play *Will the Real Jesus Christ Please Stand Up?* parodied the television game show *To Tell the Truth*. First airing in the mid-1950s, the show toyed with the dynamics of appearance, truth, questions, and intuition. The game show's two contestants had to determine which of the three characters before them was telling the truth about her or his identity. The authentic individual would be matched with two other characters, each of whom was a con artist trying to convince the contestants that he or she was the actual person. At the show's end, the announcer would ask, "Will the real [person] please stand up?"

Marmostein's play was set in a television studio where a company was casting for a new Jesus. Five Christ figures vied for the part, with four of them costumed in robes, long brown hair, and beards. As these would-be Christs jockeyed for the position, they congratulated one another for looking "very authentic." The actual Jesus spoke and acted like the biblical Jesus taught—he allowed others to go before him and treated everyone with respect. Appearance and performance mattered, though, not morality or words. The real Jesus did not get the part, in the end, because "he looked too Jewish."[57]

Christ's Jewishness became especially important for a new small group of Jewish Americans who were deeply inspired by the Jesus People. Jews for Jesus were organized in the mid-1970s. They joined a broad American search for ethnic identity, a "roots revival" that had the nation cheering new cinematic heroes like the fictional boxer Rocky Balboa, the "Italian Stallion."[58]

Jews for Jesus wanted to be Jewish and American and followers of Christ. But to accomplish this they had to create a brand-new identity—one that was not accepted by most Jews or Christians. James C. Hefley's book *The New Jews* (1971) revealed how the new identity would take new marketing tools. The young Jews for Jesus defined themselves by contrasting "old Jews" (who viewed Jesus with either disdain or frustration) with "new Jews" (who embraced Christ as their messiah). Members told new conversion narratives, in which they first had to overcome anti-Semitic treatment from Christians, the teaching that Jesus was foreign to them as Jews, and the ostracism from parents or prior communities. Through faith in Jesus, they claimed to "become *more* Jewish than they ever were."[59]

The new Jewish identity also played into popularity, sporting culture, and beauty. The most famous convert was Barry Leventhal, a star football player for UCLA. Described as a "husky Californian," Leventhal found Jesus through a series of encounters. First there was a door-to-door evangelist who presented himself as a Christianized Jew. Then there were friends and teammates in high school and college. Then there was his college sweetheart, who viewed Jesus as her "buddy" and could only marry a man who had Jesus as a "buddy" too. Then Leventhal met Hal Lindsey, co-author of *The Late, Great Planet Earth* (1970), the best-selling book of prophecy that Christ's return and the end of the world were near. Encouraged to read the Bible for himself, Leventhal expressed to Lindsey his new regard for Christ using the new student vernacular of the age: "One thing, for sure: this guy took a bum rap. He was innocent. But what I can't figure out is, why did he do it? He could have gotten off the hook." Captivated by Christ, Leventhal became a Jew for Jesus. He lent his name and fame to the crusade, focusing especially on college campuses.[60]

When the spirit of the 1960s crashed into questions of Christ's color, Jesus found himself made over physically time and again. For the West Coast sports star Barry Leventhal, discovering the Jewishness of Jesus let him experience his own Jewishness. For James Cone, a northern theologian and son of the segregated South, the language of Western theology and the faith of his mother allowed him to craft a black Jesus with the pride of a panther. Hippies on the West Coast could walk, talk, and surf with their buddy Jesus with sun-tanned skin, while defenders of segregation tried to protect the purity of his paleness as they did their schools and families. To Vine Deloria, it was spiritual chaos. To Martin Luther King Jr., it was another manifestation of how the color of one's skin wrongfully rose above the content of one's character. But so it was, that by the end of the 1960s the body and racial identity of Jesus animated political, social, and cultural struggles throughout the nation.

PERHAPS NOTHING exemplified the dominant place of racial conflicts over presentations of Christ more than the making of and responses to Andrew Lloyd Webber and Tim Rice's film *Jesus Christ Superstar* (1973). Originally a popular musical in London and New York City, it was radical for its focus on popularity, on the centrality of Judas as a moral element of the narrative, and on the erotic links between Jesus and Mary Magdalene. Perhaps most noteworthy was the way the film brought together varied genres of music. *Jesus Christ Superstar* begins with raging guitar riffs, fades into dreamy love ballads like Mary Magdalene's "I Don't Know How to Love Him," walks into folksy new hymns like "Hosanna," and transgresses into high camp in "King Herod's Song," in which Herod teases Jesus to "walk across my swimming pool."[61]

The cinematic version threw Jesus into the world of civil rights and popular youth movements. The notion that Jesus was brown-haired and blue-eyed was so prominent that when Ted Neeley, a young actor who was starring as the "deaf, dumb, and blind" teenage pinball wizard of The Who's *Tommy*, tried to convince director Norman Jewison to cast him as Christ, Neeley showed up at Jewison's hotel room wearing a fake beard to "look the part." When Jewison saw the now-bearded, blue-eyed, young Neeley, he knew he had his man. According to writer Tim Rice, Neeley "just looked the part."[62]

Neeley was only thirty when the film was released. He had a rich tan and his hair was dirty blond. Reviewed in every major magazine and newspaper, *Jesus Christ Superstar* was slammed for Neeley's portrayal of Jesus. Reviews described this Jesus as a "wishy washy figure with a whine to his singing." One called him "a puny college pacifist." Another damned Neeley as "a dead ringer for all those sentimentalized figures one sees in second rate religious art."[63]

While reviewers chided Neeley, the casting and characterizations of Judas sparked a controversy. The directors selected Carl Anderson, a budding African American singer and actor, for the role of Judas. With an Afro, dressed in red and exposing his chest, Anderson was a powerful cinematic presence. He was trying to save Jesus from the seduction of superstardom, to keep Christ's ethics alive rather than his cult of personality. Interestingly, at the end of the film, after Judas has hung himself from a tree and Jesus has been crucified, it is Judas who returns from the grave. Judas is alive, singing and dancing in Israel.

Following on the heels of the rise of black power movements and the assassination of Martin Luther King Jr., the casting of an African American for the traditional role of Christ's betrayer caused a fury. Writer Tim Rice disclaimed any interest in race, saying decades later that the directors merely chose the "best guys for the part." Reviewers at the time loved Anderson's voice, but some black Christians were upset. A group of black Baptists protested and were told by the studio producers that the choice of a black Judas was not racial but "aesthetic." The Baptists countered: "If it was only a matter of aesthetics," why could not Jesus "have been black."[64]

Curiously, Mary Magdalene drew little controversy. Throughout the film, she and Christ interact in highly eroticized moments. She fans him and caresses him; they gaze into each other's eyes; Mary seems to be the one closest to Christ's heart and soul. Played by Yvonne Elliman, a Hawaiian with Japanese and Chinese ancestry, this pair hint at an interracial relationship. Only six years earlier, in *Loving v. Virginia* (1967), the Supreme Court had declared unconstitutional state laws that banned interracial marriage.[65]

Jews were dismayed by the film's presentation of Jewish leaders as menacing, evil, and cruel. These Pharisee figures care nothing for Christ's message of good works but only want to thwart his growing popularity. They sing in low, gruff tones and wear black. For the American Jewish Committee, it was as if Americans had learned nothing from World War II, let alone the longer history of European and American anti-Semitism. They called it a "clear and present danger." It "type-cast" Jews "as villains" and equated them with "the Satanic and perfidy."[66]

By the 1970s, explicit racial questions, criticisms, and conversations surrounded depictions of Jesus. The Holocaust, the civil rights crusades, and the various expressions of liberation theologies had rendered all divine representations questionable. The long history of red, white, and black interactions with Jesus had set the stage for various types of Americans to display Christ in their own fashion. When millions of new immigrants came to the nation after immigration reform in 1965, the number of distinct Christ figures jumped by leaps and bounds. But none of this slowed down the juggernaut of the mass production of white Christ images. Even though white Protestants dropped their rhetorical claims to Christ's whiteness, they retained the power to control the mass production of imagery and material artifacts. In this way, white America imbibed the simple lessons of the civil rights era without taking its most potent pills. By divorcing rhetoric from the visual, conservative white Protestants were able to step in line with notions of freedom while upholding older models of power and structures of hierarchy.

CHAPTER NINE

A DEITY IN THE DIGITAL AGE

Before Barack Obama was elected president of the United States in 2008, claims about the race of Jesus and the sanctity of the nation almost upset his campaign. For Obama, religion, race, and immigrant status made him a candidate unlike any previous one. His name was more Islamic than Christian; his phenotype was darker than prior presidents; some opponents spread rumors about his supposed birth outside the United States; and his pastor in Chicago sparked a firestorm with the words "God damn America," which almost cost Obama the nomination.

The media bombshell exploded in March at the height of the primary elections, and the collateral damage included vigorous debates about the color of Christ. Obama's minister, Rev. Jeremiah Wright, became a household name, as snippets from his sermons went viral on the World Wide Web and talk-show hosts ranging all over the political spectrum prattled on throughout the twenty-four-hour news cycle about what Wright said. Endlessly replayed, Wright could be heard from his pulpit shouting: "God damn America" for treating Native Americans and black Americans so badly; "God damn America" for its unrighteous "war on terror" and its torturing ways; and "God damn America" for supporting Israel and its mistreatment of Palestinians. Wright justified his political positions by turning to the Bible and invoking ideas from liberation theology: "Jesus was a poor black man," Wright intoned, "who lived in a culture that was controlled by rich white people."[1]

For Wright's large and nearly all-black congregation in Chicago, there was nothing outlandish about his politics or theology. For most other Americans, though, it was bewildering and infuriating. Other Americans were not used to hearing the words "God," "damn," and "America" strung together from a United Church of Christ pastor or a former Marine like

Wright. The claim that Jesus was black and that his killers were white was, to them, downright bizarre. Newspaper reporters and television stations cast about for the genesis of such ideas.[2]

In this maelstrom, black liberation theology rose from its place in academic circles and particular black communities to become a nationwide political discussion. New media outlets hummed with commentary. One blogger ranted that Wright was a "race-monger" who had appointed himself "campaign manager for Jesus." An online newspaper featured Bishop E. W. Jackson, a black pastor in Virginia, for his opposition to Wright. Jackson believed Wright was "deeply and profoundly spiritually confused" and that his black liberation theology was "heretical." Jackson called on Americans to reject his "divisive" rhetoric in favor of Martin Luther King's Christ. This Jesus taught all people to "love each other regardless of race, color or creed." Even outspoken liberals had a difficult time explaining the substance of Wright's message. Jon Stewart, the host of *Comedy Central*'s nightly comedy spoof *The Daily Show*, who often references his own Judaism, turned to therapeutic eating. As he listened to the media spectacle of Wright's wrongs, Stewart had no words. He could only grab a tub of ice cream and let the sugary sweetness dull the pain.[3]

The sacred script had been flipped. Gone were the days when a southern black minister tried to redeem the nation with prophetic dreams of God's children holding hands and a universal Jesus who transcended race leading the way. Now, a northern African American minister served as the demonized example of all that had gone wrong with race in America. The media mob caricatured Wright as a close-minded bigot who taught a colored Christ. In turn, white commentators, politicians, and religious leaders cast themselves as the true followers of Martin Luther King Jr., with their faith in Jesus as both colorless and color-blind.

Barack Obama was torn. He admired Reverend Wright and respected his right to speak. The church was a place of great meaning for Obama. The stories he heard there "of survival, and freedom, and hope—became our story, my story; the blood that had spilled was our blood, the tears our tears." Wright's church brought a "bright day" to Obama's life, and it felt like "a vessel carrying the story of a people into future generations and into a larger world." But when Wright damned the United States or denounced whites as villains, Obama dissented. He depicted Wright as stuck in the 1960s and unable to see how much America had and could "change." When it came to the color of Christ, though, Obama kept silent.[4]

As if the story did not have enough twists and turns, Obama himself was fast becoming a messianic symbol during these years. Statues and paint-ings, beginning in 2006 and then throughout the 2008 presidential elec-tion, made Obama look like Jesus. Some placed thorns or a halo around his forehead; others had him wearing a white robe or riding a donkey, as Christ had done for his "triumphal entry." At the other end of the political and spiritual spectrum, outraged conservatives openly wondered if Obama was the Antichrist, never saying it was because he was black, but that certainly seemed to be a subtext. Despite the fulminations of conservative commen-tators and the Wright scandal, in January 2009, the child of an African immigrant and of an interracial marriage whose pastor had preached that Jesus was a black man crucified by white people became president of the United States.[5]

How did it come to pass that by 2008 the race of Jesus could be a pro-found media spectacle and the presidential victor could be spiritually asso-ciated with a minister known for pronouncing the blackness of Jesus? Why were Wright's sermons so baffling to so many, and how did whites so easily portray themselves as the spokespeople of racial harmony and equality?

Obama, it turned out, was right. The United States had changed pro-foundly since the 1960s. Most white Christians joined Martin Luther King Jr. in explicitly denouncing the concept of Jesus as white and distanced themselves rhetorically from this claim and its history. They no longer heralded with their words his holy whiteness or held up Christ's supposed white face as a rationale for racial segregation. Many new churches, in fact, were so committed to avoiding any offenses to potential members that they removed all images of Jesus from their places of worship.

Christ's absence in new sanctuaries and the rhetorical move away from his whiteness, however, did not stop the production, dissemination, or mass consumption of white Christ images. As displayed on books, post-ers, air balloons, T-shirts, and movies, the white Jesus became younger, more muscular, and bloodier. Divorcing word from image, white Christians gained the power to present themselves as egalitarian heirs of the civil rights movement and to continue as producers of racial sacred imagery that tied whiteness to godliness. In essence, they could sanctify whiteness without saying a word.

All of this happened while the racial demographics of the nation shifted dramatically. Massive population movements reshaped the face of the na-tion, and the black liberation theology that rang radical and full of racial pride in the 1960s started to sound parochially race-bound by the pluralist standards of the twenty-first century. Immigration reform in 1965 opened wide America's doors once again. Millions of immigrants from Central and South America, the Caribbean, and Asia flocked to the United States. The numbers were staggering. In 1960, African Americans accounted for 10.5 percent of the nation's population; Hispanic Americans were under 5 percent; and Asian Americans were less than 1 percent. By 2005, Asian Americans had become more than 4 percent of the population, and Hispanic Americans numbered more than 12 percent. Overall, the number of Asian Americans and Hispanic Americans had risen from about 10 million in 1960 to more than 45 million by 2005.[6]

When it came to renderings of Jesus, new immigrants benefited from the long and bloody religious histories of African Americans and Native Americans and the more recent gains of the civil rights era. When these new groups represented Jesus with their own distinct images or debated how best to relate to him given their status in America, they experienced little opposition. Jesus could be made "Asian," "Jamaican," or "Eskimo" and placed visually in churches or on websites. Black and red Americans had done the heavy lifting and bore the burdens of making it acceptable to render Jesus beyond the parameters of whiteness.

Immigration was matched by the rapid growth of the American news media and its attention to global affairs. The advent of twenty-four-hour news television in the late 1980s and then the digital explosion of blogs, Twitter accounts, and YouTube videos altered the entirety of news making and news consuming. Production shifted from the domain of a small group of writers, reporters, and producers to an almost unlimited number of individuals. In the process, the visual production and dissemination of Jesus imagery hit unparalleled heights. He became a deity remade and displayed numberless times in the digital age.

All these changes worked together to make Wright's sound bites sound out of place. His world of good blacks and bad whites in both the American present and the Middle Eastern past made little sense. Americans had been attacked on September 11, 2001, and seemingly without provocation. Moreover, from television, newspapers, blogs, and internet videos, Americans knew that the Middle East—now and in the biblical past—was not a land of evil whites and sacred blacks. The people staring back at them from televisions, computer screens, and magazine pages looked neither white nor black. On the American home front, black liberation theology taught that Christ affiliated with those who suffered, but why would he then be "black" if "red" Americans and "yellow" Americans and "brown" Americans were oppressed too? The result was Jesus shape-shifting frantically into a variety of guises, taking on new face after new face. The past continued to have power, though. When it came time to represent him nationally and globally, he remained white. He had achieved so much historical and visual authority that he could be white without words.

The Chaos of Liberation Theologies

After its modern birth in the late 1960s, black liberation theology grew, expanded, and found itself trapped. Just as political liberalism seemed to spin out of control in the late 1960s as it tried to juggle the many, varied, and oftentimes conflicting agendas of the disempowered, liberation theology too found it difficult to be all things to all people. It ran into particular trouble as its distinct forms met one another, and it became stuck between the twin forces of globalism and localism.[7]

South of the U.S. border and at the same time that James Cone and his theological comrades were seeking to mesh their black spiritual pasts, seminary training, and black power sensibilities into a new brand of Christianity, Gustavo Gutiérrez in Peru was rising from childhood illness and a social context of rampant poverty to reshape Catholic beliefs about the relationship between God and the poor. His theology of liberation was profoundly different and remarkably similar to Cone's. It too came from marginalized peoples who were trying to understand Christ's role and presence among the oppressed, and it too emerged from an embrace and rejection of Western theological traditions. But unlike black liberation theology, Gutiérrez's theology had Catholic, agrarian, and Latin American roots.

Catholic liberation theology was born following the Second Vatican Council (1962–65) and the explosion of social protests throughout Central and South America. Gutiérrez and his colleagues admired the activity of Vatican II and its congregation-friendly changes to church life. But they were disappointed that Pope John Paul sounded so optimistic and hopeful, as if the world was getting better for everyone. Priests in South America knew that if the church did not get right with the people, it could lose them. A vast team of priests, theologians, social workers, academics, and teachers brought their global educations to their local communities of suffering. In the process, they revamped Catholic theology.[8]

According to Gutiérrez and his fellows, the "human face of God" was being revealed every day, and it could be seen in the "scars of the poor." And when Gutiérrez referenced the poor in the late 1960s and early 1970s, he meant the South American poor. Latin America was special, he claimed, because it was "the only continent among the exploited and oppressed peoples where Christians are in the majority."⁹

Before black theologians would grapple with Gutiérrez's theology, Hispanic Americans in the United States were already struggling with their Catholicism and their status as agrarian and migrant laborers in the Southwest. Their most vocal and powerful leader was César Chávez. Born in Arizona and working as a migrant since childhood, Chávez grew to prominence as a labor leader in the 1960s and 1970s. As he reached out to migrant agrarian workers—mostly of Mexican heritage—he wondered about Jesus and particularly the Beatitudes. Like Gutiérrez, Chávez wanted to understand Christianity from the perspective of the poor. But unlike Gutiérrez, he did not approach Jesus "the way scholars do." For Chávez, it was a feeling of comradeship. Jesus "spent his life with the poor, the sick, the outcasts, the powerless people. He attacked the wealthy and the powerful. He is with us! We feel that he is our friend, our advocate, our leader. . . . It may be too simple to say that Jesus is on our side: but we tend to feel that way."¹⁰

A variety of Latino Americans followed Chávez and Gutiérrez to rethink their relationship to the church and to Christ. In Texas, several Mexican American priests formed the Padres Asociados para Derechos Religiosos, Educativos y Sociales (Priests Associated for Religious, Educational, and Social Rights) to push for recognition within both the Catholic Church and the United States. One of their leaders was Virgilio Elizondo. His experiences growing up as the son of Mexican immigrants to southern Texas informed his reading of the Bible, and Elizondo crafted another form of liberation theology: a mestizo form. Jesus was not just from the Middle East, Elizondo discovered, and he was not just from Israel. He was from Galilee, a small cultural crossroads in Israel, and Jesus was a child of biological and social intermingling. "By growing up in Galilee, Jesus was a cultural *mestizo*," Elizondo insisted. "Culturally and linguistically speaking, Jesus was a *mestizo*. And we dare say that to those of his time, he must have even appeared to be a biological *mestizo*—the child of a Jewish girl and a Roman father. . . . He appeared to be a half-breed." This gave Mexican Americans a special relationship to Christ: "Being a Jew in Galilee was very much like being a Mexican-American in Texas." Elizondo was a success—he was eventually hired as a professor at Notre Dame University in Indiana.¹¹

Catholic theologians, poets, and novelists began invoking a "Chicano Christ," who struggled with them in the barrio, tried to learn English among a white population that bastardized Spanish, and went to prison with them. The Anglo Jesus, one Chicano theologian explained, "is clean and His wounds shine." The Chicano Christ "grotesquely bleeds and gri-maces on the cross." This Jesus and his mother, Mary, were sometimes given brown faces when literally tattooed onto Chicano flesh. Sometimes with a crown and sometimes without, bleeding or not, the ink-on-skin Christ figures place older sacred imagery onto new bodies to bring Jesus directly to the lives of Hispanic men and women. In a novel by Genaro González, the people long for "a Chicano Christ, the macho Christ tattooed on ex-cons who sweated blood for his image and identified with his mas-ochistic machismo."[12]

Buddhist, Hindu, and new Muslim Americans, many of whom were from Asia or the Middle East, were compelled to interact with Jesus, but they did so in very different ways. For Muslims, Jesus was recognized as a messenger of God but not as a holy incarnation. Pictures of him, thus, were irrelevant. Allah had no body or physical form, and Muslims were far more concerned with debates about how to respond to representations of their Muhammad than they were with images of Jesus. Hindu Americans, on the other hand, brought Jesus into their wide panoply of divine incarnations. Christ as Yogi became a staple material image for Americans who joined him by crossing their legs, shutting their eyes, and meditating to find the divine within. These darkened "Oriental" Christ figures could be seen in Hindu temples and even on refrigerator magnets.[13]

Asian American Christians came later to liberation theology. But in in-creasing numbers in the 1980s and 1990s, they too looked to understand Jesus in the context of their traditions, experiences, and encounters with white Christianity. They linked Christ to poverty and mobility, but with dis-tinct national and religious affiliations. Aloysius Pieris was born and raised in Sri Lanka. He became a Jesuit priest, earned a doctorate in Buddhism, and found Jesus to be a poor monk in the tradition of the Buddha. Jung Young Lee was born in Korea, but while teaching at Drew University in New Jersey, he used Taoist philosophy to see Jesus as both light and dark-ness, insider and outsider. Just as immigrant groups sat on the margins of society and were designated as distinct with hyphens between their ethnic identity and their American presence, Jesus was also a hyphenated human. For Lee, he was "Jesus-Christ," for he was both man and God, "just as 'Asian-American' means an Asian and an American." Other Asian Ameri-can theologians have defined Jesus as an "eldest son," an "ancestor," and even the "flat-nosed one." In popular culture, some Americans after 2008 purchased a new comic-book Bible in which Jesus is depicted as a "Samurai stranger."[14]

In the 1970s and 1980s, the various liberation theologies became aware of one another, and their leaders felt a tremendous burden. Not only did they have to fight back hundreds of years of racial oppression and the theological traditions made to reinforce the abuse, they now had to reconcile their divergent approaches to God, the Bible, history, the church, and Jesus. How could Jesus be black, Latin American, and Asian all at the same time? How could he be in and among exploited migrant workers, unemployed welfare sufferers, and model minority citizens all at once? What did it mean for his spirit to be outside crack houses in Chicago and in orange groves in southern California and for him to speak to the children of Baptists with a black southern dialect or to Catholic kids in Spanish or in broken English?

In 1975, liberation theologians convened their first hemispheric conference to address one central question: "What would constitute a 'theology in the Americas'"? It was a who's who of the new theologies. James Cone was there. So were Gustavo Gutiérrez and Rosemary Ruether, a mother of feminist theology. Cone took his experience back to New York and wrote in 1977 that the new frontier of black liberation theology was the globe. Black theologians "must enlarge our vision by connecting it with that of other oppressed peoples so that together all the victims of the world might take charge of their history for the creation of a new humanity."[15]

The goal was grand, and the intellectual expansion of liberation theology was striking. The movement developed its own publishing house—Orbis Books from Catholic Maryknoll Fathers and Brothers of New York. Started in 1970, Orbis did more than any other publisher to present liberation theology texts from a variety of religious positions and racial affiliations.[16]

One of the most innovative theologies to benefit from Cone's mentoring, the new publishing house, and the confluence of local and global concerns was womanism. These scholars and ministers took the brilliance and blind spots of feminism (which highlighted gender but tended to ignore race) and black liberation theology (which highlighted race but tended to ignore gender) to characterize Jesus as against any and all forms of oppression, especially racism, sexism, classism, heterosexism, and Western cultural chauvinism. Jacquelyn Grant's *White Women's Christ and Black Women's Jesus* became the movement's iconic text for its effort to liberate all people—men and women—through black women's approaches to Jesus.[17]

Just as womanist theology exemplified the creative expansion of liberation theology, it also featured its limitations and trends toward chaos. Liberation theologies moved in too narrow or too expansive a fashion.

Some so particularized Christ that he seemed attached solely to a distinct category or person or experience. This approach seemed parochial when confronted with other groups. Other scholars universalized the notion of marginal status so much that it seemed Christ was among everyone except for a few white male capitalists. In 1985, for instance, Christian Duquoc congratulated Gutiérrez for teaching the world to encounter Christ as a "crucified slave" and "to think the faith from the standpoint of a humiliated race—the Amerindians, the marginalized, women, the hopeless."[18] The liberation theologies seemed in the aggregate to reduce a relationship with Jesus to any and all marginal positions.

The result was frustration, fragmentation, and an inability to account for changes in status. Gutiérrez was one of the first to raise his voice in disgust. Every particular group claimed a distinct approach, and all of it together added up to nothing. "You are Black, you have your point of view; you are Hispanic, you have your point of view; you are Asian, you have your point of view; you are a woman, you have your point of view; you are White, nice White people, you have your point of view. But enough is enough! With this tool, it is impossible to struggle for liberation." No one was really sure who was the most oppressed. Twenty years after Cone's and Gutiérrez's first published insights, Jacquelyn Grant asked the question that at first inspired, and then vexed, liberation theologians: "If Christ is among 'the least' then who are they?" And finally, what was to be made of the "least of these" who had risen in status? Harvard ethicist Jonathan Walton went to graduate school "armed with James Cone's *God of the Oppressed*." He left convinced that this did not "jibe with the Jesus that black people in suburban Atlanta desired to know firsthand." There was too much socioeconomic diversity among African Americans, Walton pointed out, for theology or Christ to be reduced to racial categories.[19]

Liberation theologies were never strictly academic affairs. Their concepts influenced and were influenced by novelists, songwriters, and artists who struggled with their creative might to render Jesus as a sacred image tied to the experiences and encounters of themselves and their communities. When depicting Jesus on stained-glass windows, canvases, or movie screens, artists could not depict a universal Jesus who sided with all the suffering. When made into an object, Jesus necessitated a particular face and race. With each new liberation theology, a new racialized Jesus was born.

In Detroit, only a few years before the international "theologies in America" conference, a black Jesus with short curly hair was painted on the dome of St. Cecelia Church. He came after the city had erupted in street riots, during which blacks and whites had gone back and forth, painting and repainting statues of Jesus black and then white. The new Jesus in St. Cecelia's was twenty-four-feet-long and had a black face. The sacred canopy surrounding him was racially redefined with black, white, Native American, and Chinese American angels. According to the church, the unveiling of this Jesus was "the biggest and most joyful event ever to take place" at the church.[20]

Black Christ figures appeared frequently in the 1970s and 1980s but were different from those of the Harlem Renaissance and Great Depression, when Jesus was a lynched black southerner. In the 1970s, he was made more African (or at least how Americans thought native Africans looked) with large, bushy Afros and dressed in dashikis. From Philadelphia to Los Angeles, from Washington, D.C., to Houston, Texas, new Jesus figures started to replace the white Christs of African American churches. When Sixteenth Street Baptist Church in Birmingham replaced its white Jesus, which had been dynamited to destruction, its new Christ was a black man. Philadelphia's *Wall of Consciousness* (1972) had a black Jesus sitting with Malcolm X and Jesse Jackson, and in 1993 a Los Angeles church had its white stained-glass Christ figures blackened. By the 1990s, it was common for exhibits of black art to include black Jesus paintings and sculptures.[21]

The black Jesus was further reshaped by the lyrical brilliance of a new form of music: rap. These Shakespeares of the streets took Christ down from church windows and placed him in the tough spaces of urban America. As hip-hop rocketed to international heights in the 1990s, the black Jesus went with it as part of its soul. Hip-hop artist Kool Moe Dee explained in words that could have come directly from Jeremiah Wright: "Once you start to develop your African mind . . . you will see, you will understand that you can't just know the story of Jesus, you have to understand the fact that he was black. The fact that it was a white society that killed him." Poor Righteous Teachers, a hip-hop group from New Jersey, rapped about the visual dissonance between white Christ imagery and black Christ reality: "Pictures you show of the Son of God is like that of the slave masters. . . . These just ain't the fact. Why, God is true and livin.' Listen, Jesus Christ was Black!"

Rapper Tupac Shakur testified to the place of the black Jesus in hip-hop culture and to Christ's role in the violence of "thug life." Two weeks before his death, Shakur explained: "I feel like Black Jesus is controlling me. He's our saint that we pray to; that we look up to." Shakur believed that the black Jesus protected him for a greater purpose: "How I got shot five times—only a saint, only Black Jesus, only a nigga that know where I'm coming from, could be, like, 'You know what? He gonna end up doing some good.'"[22]

Black liberation theology reached a new technological peak in 2006. Jean-Claude La Marre, a native of Harlem and born of Haitian immigrants, directed and starred in the first feature-length movie featuring a black Jesus. *The Color of the Cross* was filmed in southern California and followed Christ's life from arrest to crucifixion. The film brought contemporary conversations about race and civil rights to the biblical past. Christ's mother, for instance, explains that she was originally denied a room at the inn when pregnant with Jesus not because there were not any spaces but because she is "different." Now, thirty years later, she wonders if Jesus was crucified "because he is black." Jesus was a "dark-skinned Nazarene," a point the characters never tire of mentioning. His disciples were an interracial bunch, "a genuine rainbow coalition," as one reviewer teased. White and black, they played together and struggled to understand Christ's teachings about God and human difference. Like African Americans in the second half of the twentieth century and beyond, they were trying to determine how to be included with others without having to conform to their standards. Asked, "How does it feel to be different?" Jesus offers a post–civil rights answer: "In my father's eyes, we are all different and the same."[23]

The Color of the Cross was a high point of black liberation theology that revealed just how limited its appeal was. The film cost more than $2.5 million to create, which made it a low-budget production but nonetheless the most expensive visual representation of a black Jesus ever made. It was released in Atlanta, Baltimore, Detroit, Memphis, St. Louis, and Washington, D.C., reviewed in newspapers and magazines throughout the nation, and discussed on websites and blogs. Whites did not scream "blasphemy," as they had when Vernon Jordan had performed as Christ at DePauw University. Black leaders did not rush to distance themselves from the film or stop its production like the school superintendent did in "The Boy Who Painted Christ Black." La Marre, his producers, and his friends had high hopes. "The world will finally know," they exclaimed, that "Jesus was black." La Marre expected to "create an amazing amount of controversy" with the film and hoped it would be "tantamount to *Roots*."[24]

He did not, and it was not. The film was a flop. It earned less than $100,000 at the box office, which meant that neither whites, nor blacks, nor any community found it interesting enough to watch. The film was so overbearing in its racial emphasis that Christ's life and death were boiled down to racial morality tales that said everything about the United States and little about Christ. The blackness of Jesus was verbalized and visualized so often that it became irritating. Time and again, race or racism explained complicated dilemmas. What theologians and philosophers had debated for thousands of years—the reason for and meaning of Christ's death—was transformed into a simple act of racial violence. On gender, *Color of the Cross* continued the misogynistic biblical interpretation (which is nowhere in the Bible) that Mary Magdalene was a prostitute. Reviewers found the film boring. It contains "nothing really incendiary, or even thought-provoking," one yawned. Another mentioned that La Marre thought the film was "controversial." But this viewer responded, "It's really not."[25]

By the time of the film's release, black liberation theology had slowly crept into the lives and imaginations of many African Americans. A survey from 1993 asked more than 1,200 African Americans about race and religion in their lives. It showed that their conceptions of Christ had changed remarkably since the days of E. Franklin Frazier and Prophet Cherry. Two-thirds of the respondents in 1993 knew that there was a debate over the race of Jesus, but less than half of the group believed it was important for their churches to have depictions of black Christ figures in their churches. Of those who knew about the debate, less than one-third claimed to imagine Jesus as black. The vast majority of the respondents asserted that Jesus was "nonracial." And buried at the bottom of the survey was perhaps the most telling statistic. Only 7 percent believed Jesus was white.[26]

By the twenty-first century, the idea that Jesus was black was subversive enough to draw media attention but not remarkable enough to make or break a career. Entertainer Kanye West rapped about Jesus and was photographed with a crown of thorns for a provocative cover of *Rolling Stone* magazine, but it did little more than briefly grab headlines.[27] The civil rights crusades and liberation theologies of the twentieth century had created spaces for black Americans to proclaim the nonwhiteness of Jesus and perhaps his blackness, but the massive diversification in media and news outlets allowed Americans to self-segregate their choice of media outlets with particular ideological dispositions.

Other liberation theologies also spawned new artistic creations, and the number of Jesus guises grew by leaps and bounds. At Seattle University, a Catholic university, artist J. Michael Walker's *The Seven Social Sacraments* featured the Virgin of Guadalupe, Martin Luther King Jr., and a distinctive

Janet McKenzie, *Jesus of the People* (1999). © 1999 Janet McKenzie, www.janetmckenzie.com.

Jesus. He had short and thin hair that fell to his shoulders, a slight beard, and dark and wide facial features. He was specifically made to look like a member of the Coast Salish peoples, an indigenous population in the Pacific Northwest. In 2000, the *National Catholic Reporter* went looking for a new Jesus image for the new millennium. It gave the award to Janet McKenzie, a white New Yorker, for her *Jesus of the People* (1999). Believing that Jesus was linked especially to African Americans, Native Americans, and women, McKenzie's Christ was dark-skinned and had thick lips and hair that was dark, thick, and matted. This Jesus looked nothing like Warner Sallman's. According to one art historian, it was "a haunting image of a peasant Jesus" who looked at the observer with "ineffable dignity." McKenzie followed this painting with a series of works dedicated to African American women, and *Jesus of the People* was shown as part of the exhibit.[28]

Although Native Americans have figured prominently in South American and Catholic liberation theologies, the association of Jesus with them in the modern United States has caused little stir. There have been no prominent media explosions over Indians declaring the redness of Christ. Compared to Christ's blackness, his redness seems almost irrelevant.

None of this means, though, that Jesus has not been vital to contemporary Native Americans. In fact, Jesus may be far more important among native communities in the present than in the colonial past, and statistics indicate that the Son of God will continue to be a powerful influence. A 1990 poll of Native American high school seniors, for instance, showed that two of every three claimed they were Christians (47 percent were Protestants and 21 percent were Catholics). Through the course of 400 years, Jesus was transformed from an ignored and confusing figure among natives to one widely, if sometimes ambivalently, embraced.[29]

The relationship between Christ and the colonized was and is complicated, though. Native artwork of the 1960s and 1970s reflected the confusion and the rise of red liberation theologies. Alex Twins's stained-glass piece *The Wounded Healer* and his portraits of Jesus at Our Lady of Seven Sorrows Church near Edmonton, Alberta, portrayed Jesus as a great healer and a persecuted Indian. "To me it is natural, when I pray, to picture Jesus as a loving Native person with long braids, eagle feathers and the sweetgrass," Twins explained.[30]

Perhaps no other Native American artist has thought more about how to represent Jesus than Norval Morrisseau. In *Portrait of Christ in Sacred Robes* (1973), Jesus wears a headdress of an Ojibwa tribal leader, while in *Portrait of the Artist as Jesus Christ* (1966), Morrisseau melds hero stories of the shaman Blue Jay (who had visited heaven in a medicine dream) and Jesus. Alternatively, in *White Man's Curse* (1969), Morrisseau depicts a devilish figure who coughs out smallpox and leads an Indian by the hand. The naive Indian carries a cross at his side.

An Ojibwa who was brought up in a Catholic boarding school in Ontario, Morrisseau felt attracted to and repulsed by Christianity. As an adult he claimed that "Indian beliefs" were far more vital to him than Christianity and that "Christ never enters my mind much anymore. But I do believe he was a good soul. He is up there. I know where he is. I admire Christ. He was a very good man, but I only loved Christ out of part of me. I loved him, and I worshipped him, but I had been brainwashed until I feared him." He painted Christian-themed artwork but "always saw them with the eyes of the Indian. My mind may have been thinking the way the Christians thought in Byzantine times. My mind perceives the richness, the jewellery and so on, but when I translate the thoughts that are in my mind, when I put them down on paper or on canvas, something different comes out."

Morrisseau's assertion that "Christ never enters my mind much any-more" was disingenuous. On other occasions, he had visions that included "imagery about Christ and about the Virgin Mary. In fact, one time I think I actually went into the Astral Heaven, and worked there for twelve hours. I was lying down at the time. It was amazing. In that vision I saw Christ and a room full of people on one side of the room, the people were all dressed in green, flowing robes; on the other side, they were dressed in maroon robes. All at once there were choirs upon choirs upon choirs of angels and saints. They were all singing. It's something you just cannot explain." He felt attracted to religious paintings with a "mystical or supernatural quality to them." They were erotic and exotic to him. Sometimes paintings of saints moved him, but the "Christ figure was always the one that was dominant for me." He finally concluded that "Christ to me is still the greatest shaman, and that is why some religious visions are so complex, and so very hard to explain to people. So whenever you are looking at my pictures, you are looking at my visions, whatever they may be."[31]

Just as in hip-hop, Jesus came to new Indian music. John Trudell's "Bone Days" called upon his listeners to see "hanging from the cross / hanging from the cross / Indians are Jesus." Trudell then railed against white religious chauvinism and its sacred text: "We weren't lost / And we didn't need any book."[32]

Contemporary native believers mixed Indian ways with gospel narra-tives to make Jesus a shaman, a medicine man, and a healer. His ministry began with his vision quest, they contended. From there, Jesus followed a nomadic life and responded to his inner light. All of the characteristics of his life and ministry spoke to native lifeways. Scholar of native religion Abe Hultkrantz met natives "for whom the lodge symbolized the tomb of Jesus from which one rises, at the end of the dance, as a renewed being. Other native people compare the central pole to the cross of Jesus or to Jesus him-self." Catholic priests encountered Indians who came to visions of Christ while dancing "or for whom the poles of the lodge represent Christ and his apostles." The dancers addressed prayers to Christ when facing the central pole and identified the sacred tree with Jesus.[33]

Liberation theologies were trying to bring victory and power to margin-alized peoples. By linking Jesus to "the least of these," they altered Amer-ica's sacred material culture and imbued racial categories beyond whiteness with the links to the divine. They made it possible for Jesus to become a racial shape-shifter, represented in any number of forms and displayed in churches, in music, at the movies, and on the internet. Liberation theologians and artists failed to create a single unifying Christ image, but that was never the point. They were successful in compelling white Americans to distance themselves from claims of Christ's whiteness. What liberation theologies and their visual expressions of Jesus were unable to stop, however, was the new expressions and explosions of white Jesus figures. They brought debate and conflict to any new white Christ but could not thwart his continued unspoken power.

White without Words

In 2003, a new "quiet time" devotional guide offered American teenagers a short scriptural passage, a few paragraphs of commentary, and some thought-provoking questions to consider each day of the year. The entry for January 22 brought them directly to the confluence of race and religion. It asked, "What Color Is Your Jesus?" One of the guide's co-authors, Josh McDowell, was a lion of evangelicalism and had helped the movement rise to national prominence in the 1970s and 1980s. A protégé of Billy Graham, his books, *Evidence That Demands a Verdict* (1972) and *More Than a Carpenter* (1977), had inspired a generation of white evangelicals to defend their faith in debate-team style. Dabbling in history, biblical studies, and logic, McDowell would often preach that there were only three possibilities for Jesus. He was a liar, a lunatic, or the Lord. By 2003, the color of Christ was another important matter, and it could not be ignored.

"Most Americans," the devotional began, "picture Jesus looking something like a young Harrison Ford—brown hair, brown eyes, handsome. Oh yeah—and he's Caucasian. Tan, most likely, but definitely white." This image was anathema. "That's a racist myth," the devotional blasted, and it knew whom to blame. It was "a falsehood spread by people and movements for centuries," such as the "Ku Klux Klan" and "the Nazis." For prayer time, the devotional recommended that the reader look to God and ask "Jesus to help you overcome prejudices of race, class, and sex."[34]

The devotional showed just how much the civil rights movements and liberation theologies had transformed considerations of Christ. The racial implications of sacred imagery had to be reckoned with, and they could only be considered through layers of historical and cultural creation. The color of Christ was inescapable; even white, middle-class evangelicals acknowledged that their preconceived notions of Christ's whiteness clouded their relationships with the Son of God. They were not only willing to address the whiteness of Jesus but to state flatly that it was false and sinful.

But for all the change revealed, the devotional also exposed the limits of how far most whites would go. The devotional attached the historical construction of the white Jesus to extremists: Klan members and German Nazis. It distanced everyday people from the production, dissemination, and consumption of white Jesus figures. It failed to mention that Sunday school teachers, popular preachers, Hollywood directors, and children's authors had done far more than the Klan or Nazis to populate the world with white Jesus images. McDowell did not mention that his friend Billy Graham or artists he knew or books that he bought or churches that he attended or college Christian fellowships that he had helped to form were instrumental in teaching the world to worship a white Jesus.

Even more, the devotional called for no action beyond prayer and a personal change of heart. It made no reference to righting the wrongs of the racist past or battling the racial discrimination of the present. As the leading sociologist of racial segregation in churches, Michael Emerson, has pointed out, the white evangelical emphasis on individualism and emotionalism has severely limited churches' capacity to engage with social and racial problems.[35] Through historical misdirection and by spiritualizing social problems, the devotional gave white evangelicals absolution without any requirement to take action.

McDowell's devotional exemplified what happened to notions of Jesus and race during the last decades of the twentieth century, a move that paralleled the place of race in conservative politics. White Protestants disconnected language from image and in so doing presented themselves as colorblind individualists who believed in universal rights and a universal Jesus (and hence in the tradition of Martin Luther King Jr.). But they retained and even continued to create visual imagery that associated Jesus with whiteness. It was the same kind of conservative work that denounced affirmative action as "reverse racism" and targeted "welfare queens" with commercial advertisements picturing black women but never mentioning race. Civil rights, cultural pluralism, and greater engagement with the world of racial diversity led these whites to change verbally but not materially. The result was that the white Jesus and white privilege were denounced by everyone, but they remained as still-powerful material realities.[36]

By the end of the twentieth century, only extremists on the fringes of

American society continued to claim that whiteness was godliness and that Jesus was white. Billy Graham had used gigantic billboards of Warner Sallman's *Head of Christ* in his massive mid-century revivals, but he later distanced himself from these pictures. In his best-selling autobiography, *Just as I Am* (1999), Graham stated unequivocally: "Jesus was not a white man."[37]

Another popular Protestant writer, Philip Yancey, took this even further. In *The Jesus I Never Knew* (2002), Yancey acknowledged that "reporting" on Jesus was a difficult task because he could not begin by "describing what my subject looked like." The Bible does not describe him, and thus all images were "pure speculation." The Publius Lentulus letter, moreover, was a "forged document" that in America was made into "oil paintings" and put on the "concrete-block walls of my childhood church." To counteract the power of the white Jesus, Yancey showed classes various different paintings of Jesus—some as African, some as Korean, some as overweight. His audience accepted the visual materials intellectually but not emotionally. When asked to imagine Jesus, they continued to view him as "tall, handsome, and, above all, slender."[38]

The movement against white Christ figures found new homes in the "megachurch" phenomenon. These gigantic churches, usually with more than 2,000 and some rising above 10,000 congregants, had to avoid certain controversies if they wanted to have mass appeal. One approach has been to embrace multiculturalism of music and leadership and to avoid sacred imagery that privileges any racial group. The most prominent and popular black preacher of the twenty-first century, for instance, T. D. Jakes, formed a megachurch in Dallas, Texas, that has no crosses or stained-glass windows of Christ. On Jakes's website, one will find numerous pictures of Jakes but none representing Jesus. Two hundred miles south, but just as easily accessible on the internet or cable television or at the bookstore, is Joel Osteen. His even bigger congregation in Houston listens to Osteen's folksy sermons with only a large globe in the background. When Jakes, Osteen, and other megachurch leaders publish books, they do not have Christ figures on the covers. Instead, a picture of the minister himself looks out at the reader. This cult of personality revolves not around the body of Christ but around the face of the religious franchise.[39]

Declarations of Christ's nonwhiteness and the megachurch removal of Jesus imagery, however, have not stopped the wide production and dissemination of white Jesus images. In fact, throughout these decades, the white Jesus has been continually made and remade to appeal to shifts in American popular culture. In posters, on T-shirts, and at the movies, he is continually born again as younger, sexier, tougher, and bloodier.

It was a great game of misdirection, and Protestants and Mormons played it remarkably well (if not consciously). Philip Yancey, for instance, attacked visual representations of Jesus as white, but the cover of his book featured a white, brown-haired Jesus. In the 1980s, the children of Billy Graham's born-again evangelicals brought Jesus to the new emphasis on health and fitness. Developed for junior high and high school students, Lord's Gym T-shirts were modeled after those of the popular fitness centers World's Gym and Gold's Gym. The most striking Lord's Gym shirt featured a white, bloody, and brawny Jesus with a cross at his back. Jesus appeared to be doing a push-up as he carried the "weight of the world." The shirt changed the catchy workout slogan "no pain, no gain" into "His pain, your gain." Jesus could kick your ass just as easily as save it.

For Eric Roundtree, a young white evangelical in the West who grew up in the late 1980s, this Jesus was his ticket to the elusive dream of being both cool and a Christian. His parents were "super conservative" and did not allow him to listen to popular music like Bon Jovi. He was not allowed to have "brand name clothing," because he was to be in the world, but not of it. One Christmas, though, he got a whole "wardrobe" of Living Epistle T-shirts. Proud of his new shirts, he wore them to school after the New Year. The muscular Christ was no match, though, for the school's bully. He pushed Roundtree up against a locker, took his lunch money, and taunted him: "Your pain, my gain."[40]

Images of the white Jesus even invaded struggles with and expressions of sexuality. One treatment center developed to help gay men turn straight had the men shut their eyes and visualize their bodies moving onto Christ's. Merging one's masculinity with a mental picture of Jesus was somehow supposed to activate and invigorate one's heterosexuality. One man in the group kept above his desk a watercolor of Jesus in blue jeans. Christ's biceps bulged from a work shirt, and he epitomized the rugged man. The idea was that this image would help the male viewer become attracted to women, but one wonders how many men found Jesus sexually appealing.[41]

At the esoteric Esalen compound in northern California, where approaches to faith, science, and psychology swirled into an anarchy of spiritualisms, one leader described his "homoerotic relation with the imagined naked body of Jesus." Viewing a Catholic reproduction of a painting of

Christ's death, he would stare at the "voluptuously writhing muscular Jesus, naked save for a wisp of cloth across his penis." Hour after hour, this worshiper would imagine "the pain of the nails in my hands and feet, the pricks of the thorns in my head, the muscular strains in my body." It left him "deliciously aroused."[42]

The sexual nature of Christ's body and image has posed one of the newest problems for theologians. According to humanist theologian Anthony Pinn, "The embodied nature of the Christ Event guarantees that Christ had a penis," and whether art or theology ignores it, the reality must be dealt with. But the meaning is vexing—how should living bodies today interact with perceptions of his holy body of yesterday? "This issue," Pinn claimed, could not be resolved with a heterosexual masculinity that shouts, "Jesus had a penis!" Christ's penis, in fact, was a problem. What did he do with it? "Was it erect? Did it serve as an outlet of personal pleasure, or pleasure for either men or women, or both?" Just as Americans of the ages of slavery or segregation struggled with the body of Christ and his relationship to those systems, they now begin in the twenty-first century to tussle with Christ's body as it relates to issues of sexuality and marriage.[43]

For decades and centuries, children have often been shown white images of Jesus as part of their religious education. *Let's Thank God for Freedom* (2004), a book for two-to-three-year-olds produced by an evangelical publisher, highlights how far evangelicals had moved in their approaches to race. The story is a celebration of freedom and integration. The first page features black and white children honoring Martin Luther King Jr. as a man who "spoke out for freedom." The rest of the book teaches children to praise those who had lived and died for freedom in America (including black veterans), to participate in civic ceremonies like the Fourth of July, to carry the American flag with joy and reverence, and to embrace people of all shapes and sizes, colors and constitutions. The center of the book features an interracial group of children—white, black, and Asian—at church, where "every Sunday we celebrate Jesus, who was born to set us free." In the background, a white Jesus with long brown hair and rosy cheeks looks down and smiles. God made freedom; he made integration; but when he made himself, he did so with white skin.[44]

No group performs the rhetoric-versus-image magic better than the Latter-day Saints. In 1978, they finally bowed to civil rights demands to desegregate the church and opened the priesthood to blacks. Ostensibly, this meant that blacks could become members of the church and hold positions

And every Sunday we celebrate Jesus, who was born to set us free.

"For God so loved the world that he gave his only Son."
John 3:16

"Every Sunday we celebrate Jesus," in *Let's Thank God for Freedom* by Amy Beveridge. © 2004 Standard Publishing. Used with permission.

of authority. But as it gave with one hand, the Mormon leadership took with another. In 1969, John Scott painted his *Jesus Christ Visits the Americas*. It was an instant hit and features Jesus with blond hair and fair skin. He shows his wounded hands to Anglo-looking Native Americans, who bow, weep, and marvel at his power. The women wear skirts and dresses that come straight from the 1960s, while the men display their muscular physiques. This presentation of the white Jesus and his relationship to white Native Americans became so popular that Mormon leadership had it featured in *The Book of Mormon* they put in hotel room dresser drawers.[45]

Also at the end of the 1960s, Mormons resurrected an old Danish statue to affirm their commitment to Jesus, whiteness, and power. *Christus* was created in 1821 by Danish sculptor Bertel Thorvaldsen. In 1966, a white marble replica of it was placed at Temple Square in Salt Lake City, and since then it has become a staple of Mormon iconography. The first one that Mormons placed in Salt Lake City was gigantic and muscular—over eleven feet tall with an exposed chest that showed a powerful physique. Replicas of *Christus* were then placed primarily in welcome centers throughout the nation. Blacks were technically welcome, but they first had to pass by the powerful white *Christus*.[46]

By the 1990s, Jesus art was a vital part of Mormon culture and everyday experience. One student voiced this beautifully. He wrote of the picture of the white Jesus hanging in his room: "When I awake in the morning, I look at that picture. Because of my testimony of the Savior, I consciously make a decision to honor his name during the day. Of course when I make mistakes, I look at that picture and wonder how I could have let him down."[47]

So much had changed since the age of the Puritans. Through film, television, T-shirts, and prints at home and in church, the white Jesus pushed so deeply into the psyches of everyday people that when individuals had visions of Jesus, they saw the artwork. In the 1980s and 1990s, a social psychologist interviewed thirty individuals who claimed to see Jesus literally. Unlike the handful of Puritans who had seen Jesus in their dreams as hidden or blinding, and unlike African Americans who had seen Jesus as a little man, most who beheld Jesus now saw the man represented in popular artwork. In 1977, for instance, Jim Link saw Jesus one night after a Bible study. Link told an interviewer that Jesus "had a beard and brown shoulder-length hair, and looked like the popular images of Jesus in pictures."

John Vasse, a Catholic man from Connecticut educated at a Jesuit school, was angry with Jesus as a young man. He would enter his church at night, "scream at and curse the figure on the crucifix, daring Jesus to come off the cross." Then, in 1984, he did. Jesus appeared, but all Vasse could see was "the outline of a head, neck, and shoulders." He explained to the interviewer that he saw "a cameo." Another woman saw a Jesus who was "about six feet tall." In Palm Springs, California, in the late 1980s, Rose Fairs was stunned when she saw Jesus—not because she was literally viewing the divine but because he did not look very Jewish. She described him as having "brown curly hair, and a beard to match his hair, and . . . his eyes were blue." According to the interviewer, this "point puzzled her then and still does, for she doesn't think that a Jewish person would have blue eyes."[48]

Blue eyes in Christ's face confused Rose Fairs. She was smart enough to know that Jesus was a Jewish man who had lived in the Middle East, but her vision told her that he had blue eyes, and this did not fit with her conception of Jews. The disconnect between art that represented Jesus as white with blue eyes and rhetoric that distanced him from it left her disoriented. Most white Christians never confronted the disjunction, and media productions made sure they did not have to. New movies and television shows rendered Jesus as white without proclaiming or defending it. They allowed Americans to adore and cheer a savior in white skin as they professed to believe in a God that did not discriminate.

A Cinematic Savior

Even though fewer and fewer white Americans defended the whiteness of Jesus, his image was mass-produced with renewed vigor in the final decades of the twentieth century. Big-budget and blockbuster films continued to present him as white, and in the first years of the twenty-first century, Jesus became one of the biggest stars in cinematic history. The civil rights movement, liberation theologies, and demographic changes brought controversy to his white appearances but never enough resistance to stop millions of Americans from loving them at the box office and shipping the image throughout the world.

Warner Sallman's *Head of Christ* inspired a variety of Christ representations on both the small and the silver screens. When the made-for-television miniseries *Jesus of Nazareth* debuted in 1977, it put Sallman's holy imagination in motion. The miniseries had an all-star cast. Anne Bancroft was Mary Magdalene. Ernest Borgnine played a Roman soldier. Michael York was John the Baptist. Laurence Olivier was Nicodemus, and James Earl Jones suited up as one of the Magi.[49]

Selecting the actor to play Jesus was tricky. A star would draw more viewers, but his popular appearance might conflict with how Americans imagined Jesus. Visual dissonance might lead viewers to reject him and the series. The filmmakers first considered Dustin Hoffman, who had just starred in *All the President's Men* (1976), and then Al Pacino, who had electrified audiences in *The Godfather* (1972) and *The Godfather: Part II* (1974). They went in another direction, though, and cast a relatively obscure English actor, Robert Powell, who at thirty-three was about the age Jesus allegedly died and was considerably younger than cinematic performers of Jesus from the earlier twentieth century. For film writer Franco Zeffirelli, Powell emitted a spiritual power that other actors did not have. He had an "aura not his own," Zeffirelli gushed. On the set, a seamstress looked into his eyes and exclaimed, "He is Jesus!"

Throughout the film, Powell exuded tenderness, love, and humanity. His small frame and gaunt body portrayed Jesus as more human than divine. His eyes, made even bluer by dark blue eyeliner, captivated audiences. The visual cues, however, disappointed one reviewer for the *Chicago Sun-Times*, who complained that "Robert Powell as Jesus looked too much like every Jesus picture I'd ever seen on Sunday School walls."[50]

Early twentieth-century Fundamentalists had denounced movies, but their evangelical children and grandchildren vigorously embraced movies as a vehicle to spread the word of the Son of God. Missionary boards sent Jesus films throughout the world, sometimes as movies and other times as filmstrips. Campus Crusade for Christ, led by Billy Graham's mentee Bill Bright, created its own Christ film, simply titled *Jesus* (1979), basing it on Luke's gospel. According to Campus Crusade leadership, the film helped them get closer to Catholics both within the United States and beyond its national borders. It starred Brian Deacon, a British actor in his thirties, and was made primarily for church and mission work. Deacon as Jesus was remarkably white—with blue eyes and long brown hair that was so smooth and shiny that he was clearly using either hair conditioner or a straightener.[51]

Unlike *Jesus of Nazareth*, Campus Crusade's *Jesus* had no stars. It featured no cameo appearances, and mainstream media outlets panned it as dull. But because of Campus Crusade's energetic missionaries, its focus on translations into indigenous languages, and its willingness to move with technological advances, *Jesus* has been viewed by far more people than any other movie about Jesus. By 2010, it had its own website at which the film could be watched for free. It has been translated into more than 1,000 languages, and it claims to have been viewed by more than 6 billion people. This would make it the most-watched film in world history.[52]

As for all visual displays of Jesus after the 1960s, the racial representations within *Jesus* have elicited debate. The film's website tries to deflect racial questions by explaining how and why certain characters were portrayed, especially Jesus. Just as was the case with Puritan John Eliot's fictional question-and-answer writings from the seventeenth century, there is a pronounced disconnect between the directness of the questions and the obliqueness of the answers. One "Frequently Asked Question," for instance, is "Why was Jesus depicted with light skin?" The answer claims that the director wanted an actor who spoke "English without an accent" (even though translations dubbed out his voice) and could portray Jesus as the Gospel of Luke rendered him, as if Luke described Jesus physically at all, let alone as an Englishman. To the question, "Why was Jesus depicted with long hair," the website answers, "[This is] the most familiar depiction of Jesus." Biblical or geographical accuracy, it appeared, was less vital than familiarity.[53]

Even when Jesus is not the lead character, his cinematic presence has often been powerful. Perhaps no film better showed the role of Jesus in southern society after the civil rights era than *The Apostle* (1997). In it, Jesus as an idea, a word, and an image has the ability to knit together a

South fractured by sin and salvation, hate and love, violence and sensuality. In it, a Holiness minister named Sonny (played by Robert Duvall) exudes charisma. At his biracial church in southeastern Texas, he rolls in "Holy Ghost Power" and raw sexuality. His life falls apart, though, when his wife (played by the late Farah Fawcett) leaves him for a younger man, a "puny-assed youth minister," as Sonny spits. Aligned with his estranged wife, some members of the church stage a successful coup. They oust Sonny from his Pentecostal pulpit and his wife rips him from his children. Sonny visits the church one last time. In an apparent act of forgiveness, blessing, and judgment, he hugs the minister and some members after parading cash around the sanctuary to signify the greedy hypocrisy of his opponents. A raucous biracial choir screams out a Pentecostal praise anthem of Jesus, "He's All Right."

But very little is all right. Forgiveness turns into fight, and fight becomes flight. A short time later, at his son's baseball game, Sonny downs a healthy gulp of liquor from his flask. The spirits let loose the demons inside. He storms across the field and smacks his wife's new lover with an aluminum baseball bat. The youth pastor experiences a southern brand of mercy and justice. Hugged on one day and beaten on another, the youth minister feels the full force of Sonny's love and wrath. Helped by an ex-convict whom Sonny had converted to Christianity, he escapes town. He ditches his car in a creek and walks across bayou country. Eventually, he ingratiates himself in a rural Louisiana town. His identity always in preaching and teaching, Sonny appears at the doorstep of a retired African American minister. He explains his call simply. God wants them to start a new church together. The retired preacher protests, "I don't preach no more," but Sonny coaxes the pastor to inspect a decrepit church building. With a group of mostly black young people, they rebuild the church and rejuvenate an old junker into a church bus. Sonny shouts sermons over the local AM airwaves and falls in love. His church services attract a reasonable crowd of mostly African American women. The church also draws the ire of a stereotypical redneck local (played by Billy Bob Thornton). He threatens to bulldoze the new church, but even belligerent "white trash" proves no match for Holy Ghost Power. The local radio station carries Billy Bob's conversion live on the airwaves.

Calling himself just "The Apostle," or "E. F.," and evading all questions about his background, Sonny seeks to redeem his life before the lawmen catch up to him. They do and take him away. But they allow him one more sermon, and the Apostle E. F. leaves his parishioners with passion and pathos. He ends by asking the Lord to "give me peace." He needs Jesus to somehow reconcile his world of faith and fighting, spirit and spirits, angels and adulterers.

Jesus braids this tattered southern society together. Christ imagery suffuses *The Apostle*, and the white Jesus of American art transcends all racial barriers in this cinematic South. As a little boy, Sonny went to an all-black church with an African American woman. The church had barren walls and a black preacher. A white Jesus, however, flutters on the back of a woman's fan. He helps cool her amid the fires of the spirit. The aged Sonny hits the revival circuit and Jesus is there. Preaching to a group of Hispanic men and women, a large painting of Jesus rests behind him. This Jesus has white skin and huge blue eyes. Sonny and a Spanish interpreter preach side by side to put faith in this white Jesus. Later, at a Holiness ministerial convention, Sonny and a black compatriot shout questions to the crowd: "Who's the King of Kings? Who's the everlasting one?" The biracial audience rhythmically replies: "Jesus!" When Sonny rebuilds the church in the bayou, he installs Warner Sallman's *Head of Christ* directly behind the pulpit. In his new congregation, the white savior looks down upon the members of the congregation as they dance, sing, and praise. Even at the end, Sonny still loves and preaches Jesus. As the credits roll, he leads his fellow inmates working in the field with chants of "Jesus." His call and their responses mark time as they perform convict labor, while they bridge geographical divides of space and place. He asks, "If I got to New York City who will I encounter in the middle of Times Square?" The men shout back in unison, just as the congregation had, just as the ministers had: "Jesus!"[54]

The Apostle was a modest project with a redemptive message. *The Passion of the Christ*, by contrast, was a bold move by a brash innovator. *The Passion* vaulted the body and the blood of Christ into national debate and consciousness. The film served as a vehicle by which Christ's body became a visual and ideological literal whipping post for Americans to hash out their political, social, cultural, international, and religious conflicts.

The Passion also arrived just as Jesus and his body entered a new era of attention, both in popular culture and in more formal academic study. In the 1990s, American teenagers resurrected a question from a late-nineteenth-century novel, "What Would Jesus Do?" with a new series of wristbands and bumper stickers. Presidential candidate George W. Bush claimed that Jesus was his favorite "philosopher," and new histories of "Jesus in America" chronicled his story throughout the nation's past.[55]

Jesus adoration was matched by visual questions of sacred representations in Dan Brown's blockbuster novel *The Da Vinci Code* (2003). Seeming to cross the line between fiction and nonfiction, *The Da Vinci Code* was based upon the idea that a long historical conspiracy had covered up the feminine elements of the divine. A secret society of geniuses and artists, however, had encoded the truth in art. Through small visual cues (hand motions or soft facial features) European artwork held the key to the "divine feminine" that the Catholic Church had tried to destroy. Although Brown was so compelling in his interpretations of gender and sexuality in the artwork that he led readers and academics to debate the truth of his fiction, he never even broached the subject of race. Neither he nor his critics wondered what kinds of racial secrets those paintings may have held. The white face of Jesus and his brown hair and brown or blue eyes had become so widely accepted that in a novel questioning the deepest recesses and longest histories of religious and political power—power that was mapped onto and hidden within portrayals of Christ—the racial implications of it all were completely ignored.[56]

Scientific advancements in archeology and visual technologies and the American response to the terrorist attacks of September 11, 2001, gave Americans new opportunities to visualize Jesus as an ancient man from the Middle East. The United States had interests in the Middle East from the eighteenth-century encounters with the Barbary pirates to the colonial struggles and contests for oil and Israel in the twentieth century. In the twenty-first century, however, twenty-four-hour cable and internet news allowed for the widespread dissemination of a particular kind of Middle Eastern imagery. Americans had to reconcile the physical appearance of Middle Easterners with that of the Christ they had been shown for the past 200 years.[57]

In 2002, science and computers offered a new "face of Jesus" that linked up with the new attention to the Middle East. First pictured on the cover of *Popular Mechanics* in 2002, Jesus appears with short curly hair, dark olive skin, and a broad nose. The article claimed that he was most likely short— just a tad over five feet tall—and that he weighed about 110 pounds. The image was based upon a new academic field: forensic anthropology, the kind of science popular television shows use to fascinate viewers with cold cases that are finally cracked. Jesus researchers took an Israeli skull from the first century, used computers to simulate skin, and looked to the Bible for any clues about Christ's appearance (such as the Pauline declaration against long hair in his letters to the Corinthians). Beginning in 2002, CNN began displaying this Jesus each Christmas and Easter season. Interviews with everyday Americans show them laughing at the image, although acknowledging that it probably looks more like Jesus than most artwork or saying that he looks like a "terrorist." Although a media fascination, the image has not and probably will not become an icon of American churches or homes.[58]

Into the mix came Mel Gibson's *The Passion of the Christ*. It generated so much fuss and fury that the hundreds of years of conflict in America over if and how Jesus should be visualized were mostly overlooked. Based largely on the vision of a nineteenth-century Catholic woman, Gibson's film spends two hours showcasing the bloodshed of Christ's final days. Whipped and beaten over and over, Jesus in the film suffers until neither he nor the audience can take anymore. Two moviegoers allegedly died from watching it.

The Passion was filmed in Italy, and the dialogue was in Latin and Aramaic. Trying to present the events "just the way it happened," in an unconscious imitation of Leopold Van Ranke's admonition to write history "as it actually happened," Gibson made Christ's world strange for moderns to hear (except perhaps for older Catholics accustomed to Latin) but familiar and modern in other ways. As a craftsman, Jesus had a terrific physique, with bulging biceps and chiseled pectorals. He was innovative and entrepreneurial, building a new tall table so that individuals could sit in chairs rather than on the ground to eat. The buff yet bright Jesus seemed to symbolize America. The violence committed against him appeared to play into the visual appetites of Americans, who by 2004 were keyed to suffering, torture, and violence by militant terrorism, the wars in Afghanistan and Iraq, and discussions of torture.[59]

For Jesus, Gibson turned to James Caviezel, an up-and-coming actor in his early thirties. He had starred in big films before, including *Frequency* (2000) and *The Count of Monte Cristo* (2002), but never in anything this big. Caviezel spent more than two hours on camera, brutalized, battered, and bleeding through it all. To make Caviezel appear more Jewish and less feminine, Gibson digitally altered his blue eyes to be brown, gave him a prosthetic nose, and had him bulk up. Gibson was so dedicated to visual presentation that almost 200 scenes were digitally altered to transform Caviezel's eyes, because color-altering contacts would have been visible in the numerous close-up scenes of his face. The special effects and make-up crews acknowledged that Caviezel's image was by far the "most difficult" task of the film. The viewing audience had an image in their minds of what Christ looked like, and they wanted to "satisfy that image."[60]

Whatever Gibson's intent and in spite of the tireless work of make-up artists and computer-graphics experts, many Americans saw Caviezel as far more American than Middle Eastern. As one reviewer put it, "This is a strong, good-looking American white guy. In the Hollywood visual lexicon, good-looking, American and white usually code 'morally good.'" The film's finale was powerful. Jesus came back from the tomb powerful and upright. He walked off the screen with confidence in his gait, and the musical background featured a drumbeat that was a clear "call to arms." Gibson asked audiences if they too would endure their pain to join Christ with strength.[61]

The promotion of Gibson's film demonstrated a genius of niche marketing. He reached out to Protestant and Catholic churches and brought in Outreach, Incorporated, an organization dedicated to equipping evangelical Christians with tools to extend their faith. Gibson offered prescreenings to Protestants and sold booklets to churches with pictures of the film. Gibson, his team, and Protestant marketers tried to brand Caviezel's face as the new face of Christ. Passion calendars showed Caviezel's Christ throughout the year, and some even included larger posters for walls or lockers. Gibson published a book of images from film photographs and placed Caviezel's image on a tidal wave of advertising. Churches exploited the film as an incredible opportunity to energize their faithful and to show Christ's sacrificial love to unbelievers.[62]

The Passion was amazingly popular. Billy Graham was "moved to tears," and reports claimed that Pope John Paul II watched it privately and remarked, "It is as it was." Writing for *Time* magazine, Jerry Jenkins (one of the co-authors of the popular apocalyptic *Left Behind* novels) applauded Gibson for his courage. "I cannot imagine a more courageous insider than Gibson," Jenkins exalted. "He is the courage we need to follow." *The Passion* came from the gut, Jenkins concluded, and Christians needed to follow in this aggressive manner. "From Gibson we have learned that we should not be afraid, should not run from controversy and should be willing to employ a work ethic and invest the dollars necessary to compete in the marketplace of ideas."[63]

At the box office and through rentals and DVD sales, *The Passion* made close to a billion dollars. In its opening weekend, the film grossed more than $80 million. In the United States alone, it earned more than $370 million at theaters. Internationally, *The Passion* took in another $240 million. It did extremely well in nations with large Catholic and evangelical populations, especially Italy, Mexico, Poland, and South Korea.[64]

Part of the appeal was that digital technologies allowed countless Americans to comment upon the film, creating and consuming controversy.

Moviegoers not only watched it through their own social, spiritual, and political prisms but also had so many digital outlets to speak their minds publicly. Reviewers damned the movie as anti-Semitic, as a "pornographic gore fest," as evangelical conservative politics masquerading as a story of a savior, and as an expression of Gibson's own sadistic personal fetishes. A small college in Florida banned the film, which led Christian students to scream that they were being oppressed. One blogger was concerned that conservative Christians would take their fascination with violence and wield it against proponents of same-sex marriage: "So much of the opposition to same-sex unions is intrinsically tied to religious belief held by many Christian evangelical heterosexuals," wrote this concerned blogger. "They will by any means possible—and violence is not excluded—oppose any bill sanctioning such a union, because their fight is not only just, but it is also redemptive."

Race and imperialism came up again and again in criticisms of the film. One letter to the editor of *Christian Century* was upset that instead "of a story in which a powerful European emperor kills a peasant rebel, Gibson shows an angry dark-skinned crowd forcing a benevolent imperial ambassador to kill a white American saint. . . . The anti-Semitism of the film has been matched by Gibson's personal anti-Semitic rants. Gibson's film ends up being an apologetic for imperial privilege and power which deviates sharply from the good news of Jesus Christ." But for every letter like this one, there were others praising the film. "Gibson says he . . . wanted to impress upon viewers the tremendous cost of humankind's redemption," wrote another individual to *Christian Century*. "From what I hear from many, he succeeded."[65]

African Americans, Native Americans, and Hispanic Americans flocked to *The Passion* too, many experiencing it in distinct spiritual registers because of their racial experiences and histories. Charity Dell, a librarian, went to the film in Newark, New Jersey. She found it more like a church service than a cinematic spectacle. As Jesus was caned and whipped, audience members cried, "Lord, have mercy!" and "Lord Jesus!" The physically brutalized Christ, she continued, resonated with African Americans because they knew such pain. They knew scourging, flogging, and crucifixion. Blacks recognized this Jesus because he was like them. "Those of us deemed marginal by media elites," she continued, "are *not* the ones complaining there's just too much graphic, gratuitous violence." Blacks embraced the film, Dell concluded, because they too "have suffered and can recognize the crushed Son of God who was mistreated, and yet triumphed through it all." Womanist theologian Joanne Terrell considered this reasoning repugnant. Although marveling at how popular the film was with black Americans, especially the elderly, Terrell was "unashamedly bored." She saw the movie as an exercise in exorcising past and present demons of whiteness: "I saw the movie as yet another attempt to pass Jesus off as a white man, an image that many people of all races take for granted is the 'correct' one. It is, of course, the image with which I grew up and that I now find I must resist, since it continues both to live in and limit my imagination."[66]

Writing for *Indian Life*, Viola Fehr invoked a host of liberal and conservative political positions to offer a mixed review of the film. She brushed off the anti-Semitic charge by asserting, "I grew up watching television and movies that portrayed the Germans during World War 2 or the Russian KGB as terrible villains. Has that made me hate Germans or Russians? No." Fehr then brushed aside concerns about Christ's appearance and focused on his universality. "If He had come to earth as a Norwegian or Polynesian, He would also have been put to death because all of our sins put Him on the cross." She then juxtaposed the brutal imagery of *The Passion* with the kinds of pictures used in Indian schools and missions—"sanitized Sunday School pictures where Jesus is calmly hanging on the cross with only a few artistic drops of blood." The subdued imagery may be fine for children, but adults needed "to understand the depth of suffering that was the payment for our sin." She viewed sin, however, as far more expansive than did Gibson or his conservative allies. To her, sin "includes genocide, racism, sexual abuse, murder, lies. . . . Any employee who is not paid fairly for his or her work is wronged by sinful action." At the end of the day, the film was a godsend. "This is not entertainment but an experience—for many a life-changing experience."[67]

VIOLA FEHR WAS RIGHT. Watching Jesus has been both entertaining and life changing for modern Americans. His body was made to bear so many burdens, and it took a continuous succession of new vessels to do so. According to liberation theologians, his skin certainly was not white, and he somehow had the power to free all marginalized peoples of the world. No one could agree exactly who the "least of these" were or how to represent Jesus as black, red, brown, yellow, female, and gay all at the same time. According to white Christians, the image of Jesus was supposed to circle the globe, speak with clarity and certainty, and draw all women and men to himself. He was to bring peace to a world of strife; he was to embolden the powerful to accept their suffering in the face of terrorism. For novel readers, he was the key to the "divine feminine"; for southern evangelicals, he was a means for them to have interracial connections after segregation, peace after infidelity, and redemption after murder.

To the tears, angry stares, and adoring looks that the body of Jesus and claims about it have elicited in modern America, something else has joined the crowd: laughter. Beginning as a trickle in the 1970s, jokes about Christ's physicality and assumptions about his racial identity have emerged as a new way for Americans to sort through their pasts and presents. Unable to resolve the racial tensions of hundreds of years of discrimination, of civil rights victories half-won and half-avoided, and of dynamic changes to the demography of the nation, Americans turned to jokes. Laughter at the Lord was a sign not of less faith in God but of a dwindling trust that the people could right the nation's social wrongs—with or without Christ's aid.

JESUS JOKES

When Jesus and the devil fought the battle of Armageddon, it happened in the American West. The day starts simply when a new third-grade student named Damien arrives at South Park Elementary School in Colorado. Asked to tell the class about himself, Damien explains that he came from the "seventh layer of hell." His teacher assumes Damien is speaking metaphorically and responds warmly, "Oooh, that's exciting, my mother was from Alabama." Damien really is from hell, though, and has come to announce the apocalypse. "Bring me Jesus!" Damien demands as he tears up the school's cafeteria by using his superhuman mental powers to smash lunch trays and textbooks against the walls.

Jesus is in South Park too. He has been there the entire time as the host of a rarely watched public television show called *Jesus and Pals*. He has white skin, brown eyes, and straight brown hair that falls beneath his shoulders. He embodies the Publius Lentulus description. Thin-framed, Jesus wears a simple white robe and cannot get through a sentence without using King James biblical words like "thou" and "thee." Damien damns Christ as the "son of stench" and the "cursed ruler of the weak" and then challenges Jesus to fight his father, the devil. Jesus accepts, and the people of South Park rally to his side.

Everyone believes in Jesus, even one little Jewish boy who off-handedly asks Jesus for a favor "if" he wins. "What the hell do you mean, if I win the fight?" Jesus reacts. With a southern accent, the local Catholic priest shores up Christ's courage: "You're gonna kick his ass, Jesus."

The mood changes when Satan appears. He sports red skin, yellow horns, and a buffed physique. "Holy crap," one little boy exclaims, "Satan is huge." The frightened Jesus shakes in his sandals, while South Parkers wonder if they have backed the wrong superpower.

Jesus and Satan fight to decide humanity's fate in a boxing ring. It is aired on pay-per-view television for only $49.95, and fight advertisements digitally alter Christ's appearance to make it look like he has a chance. In place of his holy gauntness, he is now a superpower savior with a chiseled chest and washboard stomach. The scales cannot lie, though. Satan weighs in at 326 pounds—Jesus at a paltry 135. The people of South Park are devastated. They shift their bets from Jesus to Satan, and when Jesus learns of this, he complains at the local bar: "I have been forsaken." One drunk overhears Christ's complaint and whispers to his neighbor, "He's so gay."

The children come to Jesus. They help him train and convince the school's overweight African American chef to spar with him. "I can't," the chef refuses, and references his mother in ways reminiscent of James Cone's desire to reconcile black power with his mother's faith. "I can't hit Jesus Christ. My mother would never speak to me again." Persuaded that Christ needs his help, the chef knocks Jesus down with one punch. It does not look good for the Son of God.

On the day of the fight, it appears that Satan will crush the Christ. The announcer introduces Jesus as "Hay-zeus Savior-r-r-r-r-r Christ," rolling the "r" in "Savior" to present Jesus as Hispanic. Then introducing the red devil, the announcer's voice booms: "In the black corner, wearing very black trunks, the king of all that is evil, Beeeeelzebub!" Satan pummels Christ in the opening rounds, and the crowd cheers thunderously. Jesus withstands blow after blow, and Satan mocks, "C'mon you little wuss. Fight! Throw a punch!" The prince of peace just cannot do it. He won't hit back. Perhaps he really is a nonviolent resister like the civil rights crusaders of the 1950s and 1960s had said he is.

In a twist, Satan grows angrier and angrier that Jesus refuses to punch. "Fight, dammit!" the devil sneers. Between rounds, a local boy offers words of courage to Jesus, who is now bathed in blood: "Don't try to be a great man, just be a man." Liking this motto, Jesus asks, "Who said that?" "You did," the boy responds, as if the words come from the Bible (they do not). Inspired by his own supposed scripture, Jesus lands a weak blow on Satan's midsection. The devil falls to the mat and is counted out. "Hay-zeus Savior-r-r-r-r-r-r Christ" prevails, but Satan has the last laugh. He has thrown the fight and has outwitted everyone by being the only one to bet on Jesus to win. Satan returns to hell a far richer devil.

When Comedy Central aired this farcical animated apocalypse in 1998 as part of the cartoon *South Park*, it showcased a new approach to Jesus and race. From the 1970s to the present, jokes about Jesus and his body have entered the culture of comedy. The jokes rely upon a host of other references to race, gender, sexuality, geography, ethnicity, the media, and technology, and they are layered over centuries of creations of and conflicts over visual representations of Jesus. The punch lines also show how powerfully Christ's whiteness has lodged itself in various American cultures.

South Park showed his image and body as malleable. Small and white in real life, television advertising altered him to look more muscular. The boxing announcer rhetorically rendered him Hispanic when pronouncing his name and then associated blackness with the red devil. Cheered as a tough guy by the townspeople, Jesus was then called "gay" in whispers to criticize his masculinity. Geographically, Jesus lived in the American West, and hell was located in the American South. The black chef worried about his mother's love for the white Jesus while trying to save him for the mostly white community.[1]

Beginning as a trickle in the 1970s and then flooding American comedy in the twenty-first century, jokes about Jesus and his body have become another way for Americans to handle their past and present. Unable to resolve racial tensions from hundreds of years of discrimination and from a civil rights era that left much changed and much unchanged and coupled with significant shifts in the nation's demography, a rise in self-professed atheism, and leading comedians targeting religion as a new and fertile frontier, Americans looked to laughter. Many have chuckled at sacrilegious shows like *South Park* because Christ had failed in many ways to solve the nation's racial problems.[2]

Some of the first jokes about Christ's racial identity came from the 1970s, as the fires of the civil rights era died down and the affluence of the prior two decades gave way to stagflation. *All in the Family* was the most popular television show of the decade, and the fictional Archie Bunker was the white racist you loved to hate and hated to love. Hippies, Black Panthers, feminists, and war protesters could all go to hell, in Bunker's malapropfilled tirades. Most often, Jesus was a swear word for Archie to express his limitless frustrations, but he also invoked the race of Jesus in his aggressive humor. "Jesus was white and so is Santa Claus," he shouts at one point, and on another occasion it is a means to lessen Christ's Jewishness. When Bunker's son-in-law challenges his rampant anti-Semitism with the claim, "Jesus was Jewish," Bunker only has to think for an instant before he shoots back: "Only on his mother's side." This is as far as Bunker would go. He accepts that Jesus was Jewish, since Mary—his mother—was Jewish. But the holy half of Jesus is not.[3]

Another popular show of the decade, which was developed by the same creative minds behind *All in the Family*, was *Good Times*. It features a black family that lives in an inner-city housing project, probably Chicago's infamous Cabrini Green. The family's zany adventures and family dynamics left audiences doubled over with laughter as the parents, Florida and James Evans, try to comprehend their children's attitudes and choices. The most popular character was James Jr., known as J. J. and famous for his tagline "dyno-mite!" On the show's second episode, J. J. astounds the family with a new painting: a black Jesus.

J. J.'s Jesus has black skin and wears a yellow robe with a red tunic. His hair and beard are short, black, and salted with gray. The inspiration for the painting was "Ned the Wino," a local drunk and street preacher who is known for prophesying the end-times. Since Ned spends most of his time passed out, he is the only one who sits still long enough to serve as a model. As the family debates whether this black Jesus should be hung on the wall in place of a white Jesus painting and as they discuss what the Bible says about Christ's color, they are surprised to receive $140 back from the Internal Revenue Service. It is a miracle, but is it a real miracle? Did the black Jesus bless them? After some twists and turns, the show ends with the family agreeing to place the painting on the living room wall. The thrilled J. J. shouts out, "Dyno-mite!"[4]

As the United States continued to struggle with its racial and religious identity in the decades to come, the jokes in the 1990s and then in twenty-first century joined the political culture wars. They became more biting, sometimes more subtle, and definitely more numerous. Jokes based on Christ's whiteness came from several different angles and attested to his continuing power as a sacred figure. First were those used strategically to mock political and social conservatives, the so-called moral majority, which wanted to bring the worship of Christ to American politics. These jokes were not the kind of "equal-opportunity-offender" comedy usually seen on the major networks but were rather visceral and partisan reactions to the political right. They mocked those who wept at the digitally adjusted Jesus of *The Passion of the Christ*. As a cartoon figure, for instance, he has been a regular figure on Comedy Central's *Colbert Report*. A satirical newscast that parodies the conservative polemics of televised bombasts like Bill O'Reilly, the *Colbert Report* pictured an animated Jesus emerging from behind his tomb and firing bullets from his pistol at the camera in its 2006 commentary on the liberal "War on Easter." In these bits, the animated white Jesus uses his Second Amendment rights to protect his holiday from liberal and progressive encroachment.[5]

The naïveté of the conservative "NASCAR South" was mocked with Jesus references in Will Ferrell's comedy *Talladega Nights*. Before dinner, the racecar driver with two first names, "Ricky Bobby," begins his prayer by addressing the "tiny infant Jesus." Irritated, his wife interrupts and explains that it is "off putting" to always pray to "baby Jesus." Ricky Bobby retorts that she can pray to whichever Jesus she wants—"grownup Jesus, or teenage Jesus, or bearded Jesus"—but when he says grace, he is speaking to the "tiny Jesus, in your golden-fleece diapers, with your tiny, little, fat, balled-up fists." His father-in-law protests that Jesus "was a man! He had a beard!" Ricky Bobby's best friend then explains that he likes to "picture Jesus like a ninja, fightin' off evil samurai." Undeterred by the commotion, Ricky Bobby continues his prayer: "Dear 8 pound, 6 ounce newborn infant Jesus, don't even know a word yet, just a little infant and so cuddly, but still omnipotent, we just thank you for all the races I've won and the 21.2 million dollars." Although never specifically rendered white, the jokes hinge on conceptions of what Jesus looked like as a baby and as a man.[6]

Another type of white Christ humor relies on assumptions of his whiteness for the punch lines. In one episode of *The Office*, a popular NBC comedy about a bungling paper supply manager in Pennsylvania, the characters learn that a new black employee had been in prison. Attempting to convince his employees to accept their colleague, manager Michael Scott insists that for any white person the office members can name, he can name a black person more trustworthy. The secretary offers: "My dad." Scott fires back with the name of a black actor: "Danny Glover." A young salesman jokingly replies with a popular white singer and entertainer: "Justin Timberlake." Michael names the decorated general and then secretary of state, "Colin Powell." Another employee thinks she has the ticket: "Hey, I got one . . . Jesus." Michael takes a moment to think and then counters with "Apollo Creed," the fictional black boxer who battled and then befriended the cinematic star Rocky Balboa in the popular 1970s and 1980s films. The joke hinges not just on ridiculous conceptions of trust but also on Christ's assumed whiteness.[7]

Samantha Bee, a "reporter" for Comedy Central's *Daily Show*, brought Jesus into the realm of humor, sexuality, race, and Catholic adolescence with her fascinating autobiography, *I Know I Am, but What Are You?* (2010).

"I come from a long, magnificent tradition of divorce," Bee explains to readers early in the narrative to point to the bittersweet comic features of her life.

She dealt with family rupture by turning to Jesus. At her Catholic school, "Jesus was everywhere." He was on the walls, in her books, overlooking the sink, and always watching. Bee liked his omnipresence. As a little girl, "Jesus was totally my boyfriend." She spoke to him and he sang to her. She imagined stroking his "lustrous but well-maintained chestful of hair" and looking into his "penetrating blue eyes." Her Jesus was strong and tender. He had "nice big, rough hands with clean fingernails, so you knew that He could chop down a tree if He had to, but that He could handle a kitten with tenderness."

"My Jesus was cool," Bee remembered. He looked like the actor Kris Kristofferson and had "sexual magnetism." The lion of Judah was a sexy beast: "You knew He had a great ass and could have pulled off a pair of jeans and worn-out cowboy boots, even if you weren't sure why you would want that." Bee's mother put a damper on her love affair, though, suggesting that perhaps Jesus was "swarthy (maybe even a little bit black!)" and did not speak English. The reality of Christ's teachings and experiences with real bodies curbed the relationship too. Was Jesus corporally present with and in the poor, even the "panhandlers" wearing "poo stained tracksuits"? His physicality was defined by excrement. How was Bee to reconcile the poo with her beau? She resolved it in fantasy and farce. Bee longed for her future, when she would have a new identity as the bride of Christ. What name would she choose: "Samantha Christ. Mrs. Jesus Christ, Lamb of God. Mrs. Samantha H. Christ."[8]

Because of the long struggle of African Americans and Native Americans with the figure of Jesus in America, jokes about Christ's body could also engage divisions within these communities and cut directly against white supremacy. When twenty-first-century black Americans deployed jokes that reference Jesus as white among black communities, they often turned to concepts of generational differences.

Known at one time as the "angriest black man in America," Aaron Mc-Gruder gained notoriety for his cartoon series *Boondocks*, about the raucous adventures of two inner-city African American boys who move to the suburbs. In one episode, the main character, named Huey Freeman after the famous Black Panther Huey Newton, brought liberation theology to his anticonservative politics: "Jesus was black, Ronald Reagan was the devil, and the government is lying about 9/11." Just as he stabbed at white racial conceptions, McGruder also poked fun at black communities for their religious cultures. In his little-known graphic novel, *Birth of a Nation*, he and co-author Reginald Hudlin link the white Jesus to a new secession scenario for the United States. This time it does not come from Dixie; and it also does not come from whites. African Americans in East St. Louis have had enough. They are tired of police forces that keep them from voting at the polls, and they are fed up with conservative politicians who ignore their needs. It is time to form their own nation: "Blackland."[9]

The leaders of Blackland establish a "Nation Time" committee to create new national symbols. The debates are ferocious; one in particular rages over whether the musically brilliant, but misogynistic and violent, Ike Turner should be placed on the new five-dollar bill. Designing a suitable flag is the hardest part. The committee eventually settles on one that shocks the younger population of Blackland.

A white Jesus is the focal point of the new flag. Blackland's new flag has a tri-colored background of red, black, and green rectangles—the colors "back-to-Africa" proponent Marcus Garvey had hoped would unite Africans and their descendants. In the center is a white-skinned, blue-eyed, and bearded Jesus. "The most creative people in the world, and they came up with that?" a young female character wonders in amazement. "Hey, it was mostly old people at the Nation Time meetings," her boyfriend responds. "You know how old black people feel about Jesus."[10]

Throughout the rest of the novel, the white Jesus with the pan-African background figures in every critical aspect of Blackland's story. He is in their economics, raised outside the First Bank of Blackland. He is in their education, flying outside of Martin Luther King Jr. Elementary School. He is even there to defend the nation diplomatically, politically, and economically. On a television news program to debate an accusation from white Americans that the Blacklanders are Communists, an elderly spokeswoman for Blackland holds up the flag and explains: "Communists? Oh, no. . . . Look, baby, we got Jesus on our flag, and He wasn't no communist." The white reporter—modeled after conservative talk-show host Rush Limbaugh—immediately gives way: "Well, that sure is Jesus and he sure wasn't a communist."[11]

The presence of "white Jesus" is also part of the offbeat comedy *First Sunday* (2008), starring Ice Cube and Tracy Morgan. In this misadventure film, the two play inept criminals who are given one week to get $17,000 or else the mother of Ice Cube's son is going to take him to Atlanta. Their ingenious plan is to rob a church that had recently raised $200,000 in revival services. When they realize that someone else has already robbed the church—with Morgan's character complaining hypocritically, "Who would rob a church?"—they set out to find the real bad guys. At one point in the dark of the night as they search the church for the cash, Morgan's character is shocked when his flashlight illuminates a framed white Sacred Heart Jesus. It watches and terrifies him. The eyes seem to follow Morgan. "The white Jesus keeps staring at me," Morgan's character complains in a bit so funny it is featured on the film's trailer. Once and still an object of reverence, frustration, and conflict, the white Jesus for African Americans is now rendered a joke within other jokes.

While jokes relying on Christ's whiteness are typically used to mock conservative naïveté (of either the social or the political brand) or generational differences, references to Christ's blackness in comedies are often deployed for shock value. They depend upon audience assumptions that Jesus was white and in so doing try to expose the limits of the civil rights revolution and how much has failed to change. Kevin Smith is best known for writing and directing raunchy New Jersey–based comedies, such as *Clerks*, *Mall Rats*, and *Chasing Amy*, in which characters spend their time griping about work, smoking dope, and pursuing sex. His film *Dogma*, released in 1999, had much more to offer. It featured an all-star cast that included Matt Damon, Ben Affleck, Jason Lee, George Carlin, Salma Hayek, and Chris Rock. It challenged a bevy of religious dogmas by presenting God as a white woman who loves to play skee ball, by depicting fallen angels as funny and sexy, and by referencing Jesus as black.

Dogma's jokes about the color of Christ brought violence and sarcasm into the mix. Caustic black comedian Chris Rock plays Rufus, one of Christ's original apostles (the thirteenth apostle, who was written out of the gospels). He drops from heaven into the present to help guide the forces of good trying to stop the demonic destruction of the universe. He explains to several characters, "Jesus wasn't white. Jesus was black." "Bullshit," one white figure replies, "I've seen pictures of Jesus, and He's white." Rufus then chronicles a history of "Eurocentric" whitening that puts a "spin on His ethnicity." Rufus even had been martyred 2,000 years ago—"bludgeoned to shit by big fucking rocks," as he puts it—for mentioning that Jesus "was black." Rufus concludes by connecting racism against him in the past with it in the American present. Just as William Apess and David Walker had generations earlier hammered away at religious hypocrisy in the form of racial hierarchies, Rufus declares: "White folks only want to hear the good shit: life eternal, a place in God's Heaven. But as soon as

273

they hear they're getting this good shit from a black Jesus, they freak. And that—my friends—is called Hypocrisy. A black man can steal your stereo, but he can't be your Savior."[12]

Only occasionally do jokes about Jesus reference his Middle Eastern or Jewish identity. When Ben Stiller's character meets his girlfriend's old lover in the quirky comedy *Meet the Parents*, the skeptical family introduces him suspiciously as "Jewish." The former boyfriend, played by Owen Wilson, embraces Stiller and his Judaism through Jesus. "So was J. C.," Wilson's character says with a smile.[13]

Anti-Semitism often subtly surrounds many of the Jesus jokes. On an episode of *South Park*, the white animated Jesus has but one supernatural strength: "resurrection power." If killed, he can raise himself from the dead wherever he wants. Finding himself imprisoned, Jesus must be "saved" by being killed, and only one character can do it: the lone Jewish boy of the cast. The joke, of course, is that to save Jesus, a Jew must kill him. On the animated show *Family Guy*, a white family discovers the white Jesus working at a music store. They bring him to dinner. He swaps stories with the family's father, Peter Griffin, who responds to Christ's tale of betrayal, execution, and resurrection with a narrative of drunkenness and movie watching. At this point, Mrs. Griffin begs Jesus to talk to her friend "Muriel Goldman" on her cell phone. "I really just want to rub her Jewish nose in this," Mrs. Griffin exclaims.[14]

Even fewer jokes address Jesus as Middle Eastern. Paul Mooney gained comedic fame writing for Richard Pryor in the 1970s and 1980s, writing for *In Living Color* in the 1990s, and writing for the *Chappelle Show* in the 2000s. His 2007 stand-up routine *Know Your History: Jesus Was Black . . . So Was Cleopatra* featured Mooney on the cover as Jesus. He had long black hair and a full beard. He was dressed in a white robe and was wading in a pool of water with a look of peaceful mischief on his face. In another stand-up routine, *Analyzing White America*, Mooney shifted the references from Jesus as black to Jesus as Middle Eastern. Mooney developed this material shortly after the September 11, 2001, terrorist attacks on New York City and Washington, D.C. He mocked whites for being so frightened of terrorism and portrayed black Americans as so used to it that they hummed "Amazing Grace" and sang "I got shoes, you got shoes, all God's children got shoes" as the Twin Towers collapsed. When it came to Jesus, Mooney linked him, conservative fears, and widespread television news replays of the chief symbol of Islamic terrorism for most Americans: Osama bin

Laden. Republicans, Mooney chided, "done made Bin Laden more popular than Jesus. Cause when I first saw him he looked like an old Jesus that went postal."[15]

Jesus envisioned alternatively as an "Arab" and as a Native American was also a comedic part of Rayne Green's short story "High Cotton," in which Jesus appeared during an alcohol-induced vision. In the story, Will, an alcoholic white man married to an Indian woman, finally goes too far when he takes a drunken joy ride on his tractor. After tearing up his property, he is tied to his bedpost by his family, where he soils himself. Aunt Rose enters his room: "Will, crazy with having the whiskey took from him, thought it was Jesus to come to take him away. . . . Guilty through all the whiskey boldness, he called out to Jesus and begged Him not to take him now." Aunt Rose impersonates the savior: "[She] made out to him like she was Jesus. Well, if he could give up his sins, she reasoned, why couldn't she take some up since there'd be room left in the emptiness." She explains to Will: "I want you to come out of that piss and shit, out of the hog wallow you've fallen in, and I want you to preach my word." Will promises to "preach Jesus' word until he died." Ironically, Will's wife is not very happy. The family is "in the whiskey business not the salvation business," and she wants nothing to do with that savior who "looked like an Arab and dressed like a woman and that ain't what we're about."[16]

Absent from televised and film humor about Christ's race have been claims that he was Native American. Jake Jacoby's *Biggest Joke Book Ever*, for instance, had jokes to reference Jesus as black, Jewish, Italian, Californian, Irish, and Puerto Rican. But there are no joking "proofs" given that Jesus was Native American.[17] The whiteness, blackness, or ethnic-ness of Jesus has been used to tease the naive, mock the traditional, or shock the conservative, but Christ's redness has not—as of 2010—entered American humor culture. Even Rolando Merullo's somewhat funny novel *American Savior*, in which a returned Jesus runs for president in 2008 and selects his mother—a Native American—as his vice presidential partner, pays respect for her Indian traditions. Although throughout the novel Jesus jokes about his interracial heritage (he is "part-Indian, maybe part-Mexican" and from "Texas"), neither his mother's Native American heritage nor her teachings are ever joked about. Jesus can be mocked as white, black, or Mexican in various contexts, but with the exception of some Indians, the vast majority of other Americans never consider what it would mean for him to be red, let alone why or how that would be funny.[18]

POET LANGSTON HUGHES once wrote that black Americans "laugh to keep from crying." This may be the case for many modern Americans when it comes to issues of race, religion, power, and Jesus. Laughter stops the tears, but only for a moment. It is possible that the jokes about Jesus' race may be on us, for the laughter may mask more pain than it heals. No matter how much we laugh about Jesus in the racial sagas of America, the imagery and the histories are still with us. At churches, in movies, on television, within websites, in school art contests, and at Easter passion plays, Jesus continues to be represented in a variety of forms, but few Americans can explain where they came from, how they got there, what they mean, or why most of them are white. We laugh not just to keep from crying but also to keep from comprehending. The white Jesus and his opponents did not emerge from nowhere in the United States. They came from contact and conflict, violence and vision, creativity and destruction.

The crying amid the laughing and the effort to both accept and transcend these pasts can be witnessed in the political and spiritual burdens of Barack Obama. In 2006, when setting himself up for a run at the presidency in 2008, he published his views on politics, race, family, community, and faith in a book that took its title from a Jeremiah Wright sermon: *The Audacity of Hope*. In it, Obama called himself "a Christian and a skeptic" and claimed that he was "absolutely sure" about "the Golden Rule, the need to battle cruelty in all forms, the value of love and charity, humility and grace."

These points were "driven home" for him during a trip to Birmingham, Alabama. There he encountered Jesus at Sixteenth Street Baptist Church. Before a speech at the city's Civil Rights Institute, Obama toured the church and saw the "still-visible scar along the wall where the bomb went off." He saw the "clock at the back of the church, still frozen at 10:22 A.M." He saw the portraits of the four young martyrs: Addie Mae Collins, Carole Robertson, Cynthia Wesley, and Denise McNair. Obama prayed with the pastor and deacons, and then he was left to himself. He sat in a pew to pray. Above him, the black Jesus who had replaced the bombed-out white one looked down.

It was a sacred place and moment that moved Obama's spirit backward and forward in time. He imagined the parents of forty years earlier and marveled at their faith that the nation could be made better. He wondered, "How could they endure the anguish unless . . . some meaning could be found in immeasurable loss?" Was the civil rights movement enough? Would all the changes "be enough to console your grief, to keep you from madness and eternal rage—unless you also knew that your child had gone on to a better place?"

That night, Obama was back in Chicago with his wife and two young daughters. Only a few years later, these girls would call the White House home at the same age that the Birmingham girls died. Obama listened to his daughters laugh and bicker and then imagined them growing up. He thought of a conversation in which his younger daughter had asked what happened when we die. Obama assured her, "You've got a long, long way before you have to worry about that." But this was not necessarily true, and Obama knew it spiritually and historically. "I wondered whether I should have told her the truth, that I wasn't sure what happens when we die." Obama also knew, but would not say, that black fathers have not always been able to guarantee that their daughters would live to ripe old ages. At Birmingham in 1963, as Obama knew but would not say, neither Jesus nor their fathers or mothers had been able to save them.[19]

Sixteenth Street Baptist Church was but one of the many places where the face of Jesus had stories to tell about racial sagas in America. From slave ships of the Atlantic Ocean to Hollywood sets along the Golden Coast, from visions in Indian country to children's artwork, from the firing of bullets to the construction of billboards, Jesus has been born, crucified, and resurrected as a physical symbol to address the racial sagas of the land. He is still here—still worshiped, seen, painted, bought, sold, played, despised, ridiculed, and parodied. He was made by men and women, transformed by them, and given powers he could not control. Jesus will probably remain white for most Americans, because that Christ is but a symbol and a symptom of racial power yet to be put fully to death. But because of the nation's racial and religious histories, Jesus will continue to be a complicated savior made and remade in red, white, and black.

Our gratitude list grows longer each day. Those who helped did so as friends, mentors, and cynics, but all made this a much better book. Our blog communities, including those at Religion in American History, Immanent Frame, Juvenile Instructor, Patheos, History News Network, and Religion Dispatches, allowed us to trot out ideas and gain new insights. Everyone involved with the Young Scholars in American Religion program played a role as well. Matt Sutton carefully read multiple revisions of the manuscript and provided rigorous criticisms. Randall Stephens gave good humor and a constant flow of ideas. Kate Carte Engel, Spencer Fluhman, and Kathryn Lofton were particularly helpful with images. Rebecca Goetz helped us navigate through colonial America materials, while Charles Irons offered much about the antebellum era. Amanda Porterfield was kind, generous, and thoughtful, as she always is.

There are too many places and people to thank, but several were particularly supportive. Stephen Prothero supported the initial proposal with terrific suggestions. Our colleagues at the University of Colorado at Colorado Springs and San Diego State University brought good cheer to the daily grind, while the authors for our edited volume *The Columbia Guide to Religion in American History* helped us arc the book from the sixteenth century to the present day. Other colleagues helped far and wide, including Robert Abzug, Michael Alexander, Jackie Bacon, Richard Bailey, Kelly Baker, Ed Beasley, Matthew Bowman, Daphne Brooks, Joanna Brooks, Allen Callahan, Jane Dailey, Jacob Dorman, Jodi Eichler-Levine, Curtis Evans, Tracy Fessenden, Craig Friend, John Giggie, Eddie Glaude, Brian Goodwyn, Matthew Grow, Michelle Hamilton, Luke Harlow, Peter Heltzel, Jennifer Hughes, Max Hunter, John Jackson, Randal Jelks, Gale Kenny, Michelle Kuhl, Jennifer Lindell, Ashley Makar, Waldo Martin, Martin

Marty, Aundrea Matthews, Bethany Moreton, David Morgan, Mark Noll, June O'Connor, Joshua Paddison, Josh Probert, Paul Reeve, Sonnet Retman, David Sehat, Jeffrey Siker, Phil Sinitiere, Peter Slade, Ivan Strenski, Patricia Sullivan, Lisa Szefel, Zoe Trodd, John Turner, Kirsten Twelbeck, and Jonathan Walton. We are also grateful to James Cone, not only for his long and brilliant career but also for sharing his work-in-progress on Christianity and lynching.

Paul would like to thank especially his longtime colleague and partner-in-crime Philip Goff, director of the Center for the Study of Religion and American Culture in Indianapolis, and Charles Reagan Wilson, whose support since a 1992 National Endowment for the Humanities Seminar on Religion in the South has been instrumental and who provided tremendous insight for this manuscript. Linford Fisher and Rachel Wheeler helped him work through Indian and Moravian topics, and his longtime editor, Elaine Maisner, was a joy to work with once again.

Ed would like to thank his many wonderful students, mentors, and friends. Several students read and discussed drafts of this work, including Ross Bruce, Matthew Cromwell, Michael Diaz, Ryan Forbes, Stacy Kiser, Joseph Riggs, Samantha Sneen, Denise Swyor, Byron Winick, and Kevin Witt. The History Department, Sociology Department, and Department of Religious Studies at Rice University were tremendously supportive. Michael Emerson's class on race and religion was a delight, and the time spent with his seminar on the Power of Race at Calvin College helped articulate the theoretical points of this book. Anthony Pinn's seminar on liberation theology and his African American Religious Studies Forum offered too many good ideas for them all to be included.

At Columbia University, Randall Balmer's Seminar in American Religion provided a wonderful venue to share work, meet new friends, and bat around new ideas, and Randall Stephens's crew at Eastern Nazarene College laughed at just the right moments in Ed's talk on race and religion in modern comedic culture. Skip Stout's seminar on Religion and War at Calvin College, and especially colleagues Kyle Crews, Jonathan Ebel, Thomas Kidd, Ben Miller, John Pinheiro, and Andrew Polk, provided encouragement for thinking broadly and deeply about the links to war. A joint symposium held by the Harvard Divinity School and the Episcopal Divinity School on the film *The Color of the Cross* helped kick off this project. Loyola Marymount University was kind enough to invite Ed to share research along the way. And finally, Cornel West continues to be an inspiration. Whether through his writings or phone calls of cheer, his encouragement to think, love, and hope motivated this book in ways he would have never imagined.

The saga of this book's completion coincided with another saga, the life and journey of Elijah James Blum. You and your struggle gave so much. You were a good friend who swayed happily in your swing at Dad's office (sometimes at 4:00 A.M.) so this book could be revised. As cataracts dimmed your vision, we longed for new ways to see this world and ones beyond. As your oral muscles degenerated and as you fought to eat and to breathe, we contemplated with greater depth the "bread of life" and the spirit moving in the wind. And as you giggled with your mom while playing peek-a-boo, you offered a vision of what it meant to laugh amid terrible loss. Elijah, you endured everything we asked, and we're so proud of you. When the lights went out, we were grateful to have you in our arms. This book is for you.

PROLOGUE

1 For more on Birmingham and the Sixteenth Street Baptist Church, see Christopher Hamlin, *Behind the Stained Glass: A History of Sixteenth Street Baptist Church* (Birmingham, Ala.: Crane Hill, 1998); Diane McWhorter, *Carry Me Home: Birmingham, Alabama: The Climactic Battle of the Civil Rights Revolution* (New York: Simon and Schuster, 2002); and Glenn T. Eskew, *But for Birmingham: The Local and National Movements in the Civil Rights Struggle* (Chapel Hill: University of North Carolina Press, 1997).

2 Anne Moody, *Coming of Age in Mississippi* (New York: Dell, 1968), 317–18.

3 James M. Washington, ed., *Testament of Hope: The Essential Writings and Speeches of Martin Luther King, Jr.* (New York: HarperCollins, 1991), 217–23.

4 Langston Hughes, *The Panther and the Lash: Poems of Our Times* (New York: Knopf, 1967), 46; Pete Seeger and Rob Reiser, *Everybody Says Freedom* (New York: W. W. Norton, 1989), 117–18; "Joan Baez—Folk Singing: Sybil with Guitar," *Time*, November 23, 1962; Bill Cole, *John Coltrane* (Cambridge, Mass.: Da Capo, 2001), 150.

5 Ronald H. Stone, *Professor Reinhold Niebuhr: A Mentor to the Twentieth Century* (Louisville: Westminster John Knox Press, 1992), 236; Elisabeth Sifton, *The Serenity Prayer: Faith and Politics in Times of Peace and War* (New York: W. W. Norton, 2005); "The Meaning of the Birmingham Tragedy," Conversation with Reinhold Niebuhr and James Baldwin, http://speakingoffaith.publicradio.org/programs/niebuhr/sermons.shtml (October 6, 2011); James H. Cone, *The Cross and the Lynching Tree* (Maryknoll, N.Y.: Orbis Books, 2011), 53–54.

INTRODUCTION

1 The literature on whiteness is rich but tends to neglect religion. See Matthew Frye Jacobson, *Whiteness of a Different Color: European Immigrants and the Alchemy of Race* (Cambridge: Harvard University Press, 1998); David R. Roediger, *The Wages of Whiteness: Race and the Making of the American Working Class* (London: Verso, 1991); David R. Roediger, *Working toward Whiteness: How America's Immigrants Became White, the Strange Journey from Ellis Island*

to the Suburbs (New York: Basic Books, 2005); George Lipsitz, *The Possessive Investment in Whiteness: How White People Profit from Identity Politics* (Philadelphia: Temple University Press, 1998); and Nell Irvin Painter, *The History of White People* (New York: W. W. Norton, 2010). For more on religion and whiteness, see "Forum," *Religion and American Culture: A Journal of Interpretation* 19, no. 1 (Winter 2009): 1–35; James W. Perkinson, *White Theology: Outing Supremacy in Modernity* (New York: Palgrave Macmillan, 2004); Daniel B. Lee, "A Great Racial Commission: Religion and the Construction of White America," in *Race, Nation, and Religion in the Americas*, ed. Henry Goldschmidt and Elizabeth McAlister (New York: Oxford University Press, 2004), 85–110; Edward J. Blum, *Reforging the White Republic: Race, Religion, and American Nationalism, 1865–1898* (Baton Rouge: Louisiana State University Press, 2005); and Edward J. Blum, *W. E. B. Du Bois, American Prophet* (Philadelphia: University of Pennsylvania Press, 2007).

2 Our thinking on the religious meaning of the white Jesus in American history is based on Emile Durkheim's theories on totems and societies in *The Elementary Forms of Religious Life*, trans. Karen E. Fields (New York: Free Press, 1995); and on Mircea Eliade's theories on hierophanies in Mircea Eliade, *The Sacred and the Profane: The Nature of Religion* (San Diego: Harcourt, Brace, 1987). Along with these classics, we have also been influenced by more recent literature about the "embodiment" and "materiality" of works that try to balance current academic theories of the social construction of religious realities alongside the real physical aspects of religious experience as felt, seen, and envisioned by biological bodies. For that, see Anthony B. Pinn, *Embodiment and the New Shape of Black Theological Thought* (New York: New York University Press, 2010); and Manuel A. Vasquez, *More Than Belief: A Materialist Theory of Religion* (New York: Oxford University Press, 2010).

3 Stephen Prothero, *American Jesus: How the Son of God Became a National Icon* (New York: Farrar, Straus and Giroux, 2003); Richard Wightman Fox, *Jesus in America: Personal Savior, Cultural Hero, National Obsession* (San Francisco: HarperSanFrancisco, 2004); Kelly Brown Douglas, *The Black Christ* (Maryknoll, N.Y.: Orbis Books, 1994); Stephen J. Nichols, *Jesus Made in America: A Cultural History from the Puritans to* The Passion of the Christ (Westmont, Ill.: Intervarsity Press, 2008); Craig R. Prentiss, "Coloring Jesus: Racial Calculus and the Search for Identity in Twentieth-Century America," *Nova Religio* 11, no. 3 (February 2008): 64–82.

4 Beverly Daniel Tatum, *"Why Are All the Black Kids Sitting Together in the Cafeteria?" and Other Conversations about Race* (New York: Basic Books, 1997); Jason Marsh, Rodolfo Mendoza-Denton, and Jeremy Adam Smith, eds., *Are We Born Racist? New Insights from Neuroscience and Positive Psychology* (Boston: Beacon Press, 2010); Georgene L. Troseth, Sophia L. Pierroutsakos, and Judy S. DeLoache, "From the Innocent to the Intelligent Eye: The Early Development of Pictorial Competence," *Advances in Child Development and Behavior* 32 (2004): 1–38.

5 Our thinking on the confluence of race and religion has been most influenced

by Cornel West, *Prophesy Deliverance! An Afro-American Revolutionary Christianity* (Louisville: Westminster John Knox Press, 2002); Anthony B. Pinn, *Terror and Triumph: The Nature of Black Religion* (Minneapolis: Fortress Press, 2003); Colin Kidd, *The Forging of the Races: Race and Scripture in the Protestant Atlantic World, 1600–2000* (Cambridge: Cambridge University Press, 2006); Alan Davies, *Infected Christianity: A Study of Modern Racism* (Kingston: McGill-Queen's University Press, 1988); Allen Dwight Callahan, *The Talking Book: African Americans and the Bible* (New Haven: Yale University Press, 2006); Joel W. Martin, *Sacred Revolt: The Muskogees' Struggle for a New World* (Boston: Beacon Press, 1991); Joanna Brooks, *American Lazarus: Religion and the Rise of African-American and Native American Literatures* (New York: Oxford University Press, 2003); Eddie Glaude, *Exodus! Religion, Race, and Nation in Early Nineteenth-Century Black America* (Chicago: University of Chicago Press, 2000); and Gayraud S. Wilmore, *Black Religion and Black Radicalism: An Interpretation of the Religious History of Afro-American People* (Maryknoll, N.Y.: Orbis Books, 1994).

6 Richard Wright, introduction to St. Clair Drake and Horace Roscoe Cayton, *Black Metropolis: A Study of Negro Life in a Northern City* (1945; Chicago: University of Chicago Press, 1993), xxi.

7 Prothero, *American Jesus*, chaps. 2, 3.

8 Pinn, *Embodiment and the New Shape of Black Theological Thought*, chap. 4; Fay Botham, *Almighty God Created the Races: Christianity, Interracial Marriage, and American Law* (Chapel Hill: University of North Carolina Press, 2009).

9 Our thinking on these forces has been most influenced by David Morgan, *The Lure of Images: A History of Religion and Visual Media in America* (London: Routledge, 2007); David Morgan and Sally M. Promey, *The Visual Culture of American Religions* (Berkeley: University of California Press, 2001); Colleen McDannell, *Material Christianity: Religion and Popular Culture in America* (New Haven: Yale University Press, 1995); John Dillenberger, *Images and Relics: Theological Perceptions and Visual Images in Sixteenth-Century Europe* (New York: Oxford University Press, 1999); and Robin Margaret Jensen, *Face to Face: Portraits of the Divine in Early Christianity* (Minneapolis: Fortress Press, 2005).

10 E. Franklin Frazier, *Negro Youth at the Crossways: Their Personality Development in the Middle States* (1940; New York: Schocken Books, 1967), 116.

11 Our thinking on geographies and space is most influenced by Eliade, *The Sacred and the Profane*; and Thomas A. Tweed, *Crossing and Dwelling: A Theory of Religion* (Cambridge: Harvard University Press, 2006).

12 Frederick Buechner and Lee Boltin, *The Faces of Jesus* (New York: Riverwood/Simon and Schuster, 1974).

13 "The whole Jesus scheme" is from an Indian character in N. Scott Momaday's classic novel *House Made of Dawn* (New York: Perennial Classics, 1999), 132.

14 *The Crucifixion, by an Eye-Witness* (Chicago: Indo-American Book, 1913).

15 "Black Liberation Theology, in Its Founders' Words," *NPR Books*, March 31, 2008, http://www.npr.org/templates/story/story.php?storyID=89236116 (October 6, 2011).

16 Prothero, *American Jesus*, 298; Fox, *Jesus in America*.
17 Hamlin, *Behind the Stained Glass*, 62–66.

CHAPTER ONE

1 Frances Hill, ed., *The Salem Witch Trials Reader* (Da Capo Press, 2000), 121–31.
2 Ibid., 229.
3 Mary Beth Norton, *In the Devil's Snare: The Salem Witchcraft Crisis of 1692* (New York: Vintage Books, 2002); Carol F. Karlsen, *The Devil in the Shape of a Woman: Witchcraft in Colonial New England* (New York: Norton, 1987); John Demos, *Entertaining Satan: Witchcraft and the Culture of Early New England* (New York: Oxford University Press, 2004).
4 Hill, *Salem Witch Trials Reader*, 191–99; Elizabeth Reis, *Damned Women: Sinners and Witches in Puritan New England* (Ithaca: Cornell University Press, 1997), 55; David D. Hall, *Worlds of Wonder, Days of Judgment: Popular Religious Belief in Early New England* (New York: Alfred A. Knopf, 1989), 16, 25–26, 74, 133; Norton, *In the Devil's Snare*, 65, 80–81, 136, 148, 180, 217, 234.
5 Paul Boyer and Stephen Nissenbaum, eds., *Salem-Village Witchcraft: A Documentary Record of Local Conflict in Colonial New England* (Boston: Northeastern University Press, 1970), 18–19.
6 Reis, *Damned Women*, 80; W. Scott Poole, *Satan in America: The Devil We Know* (Lanham, Md.: Rowman and Littlefield, 2009), chap. 1.
7 Richard Wightman Fox, *Jesus in America: Personal Savior, Cultural Hero, National Obsession* (San Francisco: HarperSanFrancisco, 2004), chaps. 1, 2.
8 Edmund S. Morgan, *American Slavery, American Freedom: The Ordeal of Colonial Virginia* (New York: W. W. Norton, 1975); Kenan Malik, *The Meaning of Race: Race, History, and Culture in Western Society* (New York: New York University Press, 1996), chap. 2; Roxann Wheeler, *The Complexion of Race: Categories of Difference in Eighteenth-Century British Culture* (Philadelphia: University of Pennsylvania Press, 2000); Audrey Smedley, *Race in North America: Origin and Evolution of a Worldview* (Boulder: Westview Press, 1993); Winthrop Jordan, *White over Black: American Attitudes toward the Negro, 1550–1812* (Chapel Hill: University of North Carolina Press, 1969), part I; Nell Irvin Painter, *The History of the White Race* (New York: W. W. Norton, 2010), 40–42.
9 Pauline Moffitt Watts, "Prophecy and Discovery: On the Spiritual Origins of Christopher Columbus's 'Enterprise of the Indies,'" *American Historical Review* 90, no. 1 (February 1985): 73–102; Jennifer Scheper Hughes, *Biography of a Mexican Crucifix: Lived Religion and Local Faith from the Conquest to the Present* (New York: Oxford University Press, 2010); Fox, *Jesus in America*, 29; Carolyn Dean, *Inka Bodies and the Body of Christ: Corpus Christi in Colonial Cuzco, Peru* (Durham: Duke University Press, 1999).
10 Fox, *Jesus in America*, 33.
11 Ibid., 59.
12 Carole Blackburn, *Harvest of Souls: The Jesuit Missions and Colonialism in North America, 1632–1650* (McGill-Queen's University Press), 111–12; Reuben

Gold Thwaites, ed., *Jesuit Relations and Allied Documents*, 73 vols. (Cleveland: Burrow Brothers, 1901), 15:19.

13 Kenneth Morrison, *The Solidarity of Kin* (Albany: State University of New York Press, 2002), 127.

14 Nicholas Griffiths, "Introduction," in *Spiritual Encounters: Interactions between Christianity and Native Religions in Colonial America*, ed. Nicholas Griffiths and Fernando Cervantes (Lincoln: University of Nebraska Press, 1999), 1–41; Richard White, *The Middle Ground: Indians, Empires, and Republics in the Great Lakes Region, 1660–1815* (New York: Cambridge University Press, 1991), 26–27.

15 Thwaites, *Jesuit Relations*, 38:115, 61:128.

16 Ibid., 60:137; James Axtell, *The Invasion Within: The Contest of Cultures in Colonial North America* (New York: Oxford University Press, 1985), 114–15.

17 Thwaites, *Jesuit Relations*, 55:221.

18 Ibid., 57:93–95, 66:149.

19 Tracy Neal Leavelle, "'Bad Things' and 'Good Hearts': Mediation, Meaning, and the Language of Illinois Christianity," *Church History* (June 2007): 379.

20 John Steckley, "The Warrior and the Lineage: Jesuit Use of Iroquoian Images to Communicate Christianity," *Ethnohistory* 39 (1992): 486–88.

21 Thwaites, *Jesuit Relations*, 66:262–63.

22 Charles Hackett Wilson, ed., *Revolt of the Pueblo Indians of New Mexico and Otermín's Attempted Reconquest, 1680–1682*, 2 vols. (Albuquerque: University of New Mexico Press, 1942), 1:26, 2:225; Letter of the governor of El Parral, Don Bartolome de Estrada, to the viceroy, El Parral, July 22, 1680, ibid., 1:45.

23 Ibid., 2:204–7.

24 Edmund Morgan, *Visible Saints: The History of a Puritan Idea* (Ithaca: Cornell University Press, 1965); Harry S. Stout, *The New England Soul: Preaching and Religious Culture in Colonial New England* (New York: Oxford University Press, 1988); Richard A. Bailey, *Race and Redemption in Puritan New England* (New York: Oxford University Press, 2011); Fox, *Jesus in America*, chap. 2.

25 John Dillenberger, *Images and Relics: Theological Perceptions and Visual Images in Sixteenth-Century Europe* (New York: Oxford University Press, 1999), 178, 183–84; see also Terry Lindvall, *Sanctuary Cinema: Origins of the Christian Film Industry* (New York: New York University Press, 2007), 27.

26 Ralph Adams Cram, *The Ministry of Art* (1914; Freeport, N.Y.: Books for Libraries Press, 1967), 227–28, 230, 244. For more on colonial church architecture, see Harold Wickliffe Rose, *The Colonial Houses of Worship in America* (New York: Hastings House, 1963); Marian Card Donnelly, *The New England Meeting Houses of the Seventeenth Century* (Middletown, Conn.: Wesleyan University Press, 1968); and Peter W. Williams, *Houses of God: Region, Religion, and Architecture in the United States* (Urbana: University of Illinois Press, 1997). For more on Puritans and seeing God, see Tom Schwanda, "Gazing at God: Some Preliminary Observations on Contemplative Reformed Spirituality," *Reformed Review* 56, no. 2 (2003): 101–21; and John K. La Shell, "Imagination and Idol: A Puritan Tension," *Westminster Theological Journal* 49, no. 2 (1987): 305–34.

27 Hall, *Worlds of Wonder, Days of Judgment*, 10, 40; Tracy Fessenden, *Culture and Redemption: Religion, the Secular, and American Literature* (Princeton: Princeton University Press, 2007), 21–58; Paul Leicester Ford, ed., *The New-England Primer: A History of Its Origin and Development* (1897; New York: Columbia University Press, 1962), 58–59, 68, 126; Thomas Morton, *New England Canaan* (1637; New York: Da Capo Press, 1969), 153.

28 Reis, *Damned Women*, 1; Norton, *In the Devil's Snare*, 252.

29 Hall, *Worlds of Wonder*, 227; Schwanda, "Gazing at God."

30 Quoted in Michael Bath, *Speaking Pictures: English Emblem Books and Renaissance Culture* (London: Longman, 1994), 226.

31 Ford, *New-England Primer*, 158.

32 Michael Wigglesworth, *The Day of Doom: Or, a Description of the Great and Last Judgment* (London: Printed by W. G. for John Sims, 1673), 8.

33 Basil Davidson, *The African Slave Trade* (Boston: BackBay Books, 1980), 28.

34 Nick Hazlewood, *The Queen's Slave Trader: John Hawkyns, Elizabeth I, and the Trafficking in Human Souls* (New York: William Morrow, 2004), 193–95; Harry Kelsey, *Sir John Hawkins: Queen Elizabeth's Slave Trader* (New Haven: Yale University Press, 2003).

35 Albert J. Raboteau, *Slave Religion: The "Invisible Institution" in the Antebellum South* (New York: Oxford University Press, 1978), chap. 1; Sylvia R. Frey and Betty Wood, *Come Shouting to Zion: African American Protestantism in the American South and British Caribbean to 1830* (Chapel Hill: University of North Carolina Press, 1998), chap. 1; John Thornton, "The Development of an African Catholic Church in the Kingdom of Kongo, 1491–1750," *Journal of African History* 25, no. 2 (1984): 147–67.

36 John S. Mbiti, *Concepts of God in Africa* (New York: Praeger, 1970), 7, 16, 23, 41, 155; Dwight N. Hopkins and George C. L. Cummings, eds., *Cut Loose Your Stammering Tongue: Black Theology in the Slave Narratives* (Maryknoll, N.Y.: Orbis Books, 1991), 5–7.

37 Ira Berlin, *The Making of African America* (New York: Penguin, 2010), chap. 1; Philip D. Curtin, *The Atlantic Slave Trade: A Census* (Madison: University of Wisconsin Press, 1969), 268; Mechal Sobel, *Trabelin' On: The Slave Journey to an Afro-Baptist Faith* (Westport, Conn.: Greenwood Press, 1979), 21–23; Daniel P. Mannix (in collaboration with Malcolm Cowley), *Black Cargoes: A History of the Atlantic Slave Trade, 1518–1865* (New York: Viking, 1962), introduction; Michael Gomez, *Exchanging Our Country Marks: The Transformation of African Identities in the Colonial and Antebellum South* (Chapel Hill: University of North Carolina Press, 1998), chap. 2; "Assessing the Slave Trade: Estimates," *The Trans-Atlantic Slave Trade Database*, http://slavevoyages.org/tast/assessment/estimates.faces (October 6, 2011).

38 William D. Piersen, "White Cannibals, Black Martyrs: Fear, Depression, and Religious Faith as Causes of Suicide among New Slaves," *Journal of Negro History* 62, no. 2 (April 1977): 147–59; John Thornton, "Cannibals, Witches, and Slave Traders in the Atlantic World," *William and Mary Quarterly* 60, no. 2 (April 2003): 273–94.

39 Raboteau, *Slave Religion*, chap. 3; Carter Godwin Woodson, *The History of the Negro Church* (Washington, D.C.: Associated Press, 1921), 7.

40 For more on the seals, see Kristina Bross, *Dry Bones and Indian Sermons: Praying Indians in Colonial America* (Ithaca: Cornell University Press, 2004), 4–5; Benson J. Lossing, *Harper's Popular Cyclopaedia of United States History* (New York: Harper, 1892), 2:1457.

41 Axtell, *Invasion Within*; Alden T. Vaughan, *New England Frontier: Puritans and Indians, 1620–1675* (Norman: University of Oklahoma Press, 1995); Bailey, *Race and Redemption in Puritan New England*.

42 Richard W. Cogley, *John Eliot's Mission to the Indians before King Philip's War* (Cambridge: Harvard University Press, 1999).

43 Richard Pointer, *Encounters of the Spirit: Native Americans and European Colonial Religion* (Bloomington: Indiana University Press, 2007), 62.

44 John Eliot and Thomas Mayhew, *Tears of Repentance: Or, A Further Narrative of the Progress of the Gospel amongst the Indians in New England*, in *Collections of the Massachusetts Historical Society*, 3rd series, 4 (1834): 231. See also Kenneth Morrison, "'That Art of Coyning Christians': John Eliot and the Praying Indians of Massachusetts," *Ethnohistory* 21, no. 1 (Winter 1974): 86. Eliot's theory of the soul as the eye of faith is explored in Sarah Rivett, "Empirical Desire: Conversion, Ethnography, and the New Science of the Praying Indian," *Early American Studies* (Spring 2006): 16–45.

45 Bross, *Dry Bones and Indian Sermons*; Eliot and Thomas, *Tears of Repentance*; Henry W. Bowden and James P. Ronda, eds., *John Eliot's Indian Dialogues: A Study in Cultural Interaction* (Westport, Conn.: Greenwood Press, 1980).

46 Michael P. Clark, ed., *The Eliot Tracts: With Letters from John Eliot to Thomas Thorowgood and Richard Baxter* (Westport, Conn.: Praeger, 2003), 85.

47 Pointer, *Encounters of the Spirit*, 52, 58; Jill Lepore, "Dead Men Tell No Tales: John Sassamon and the Fatal Consequences of Literacy," *American Quarterly* 46 (December 1994): 479–512; Bowden and Ronda, *John Eliot's Indian Dialogues*, 71.

48 Bross, *Dry Bones and Indian Sermons*, 96.

49 Bowden and Ronda, *John Eliot's Indian Dialogues*, 71.

50 Daniel K. Richter, *Facing East from Indian Country: A Native History of Early America* (Cambridge: Harvard University Press, 2003), 128.

51 Cotton Mather, *Magnalia Christi Americana* (Hartford, Conn.: S. Andrus, 1853), 565.

52 Ibid.

53 Rebecca Anne Goetz, "From Potential Christians to Hereditary Heathens: Religion and Race in the Early Chesapeake, 1590–1740" (Ph.D. diss., Harvard University, 2006), 55–56; William S. Simmons, "Cultural Bias in the New England Puritans' Perception of Indians," *William and Mary Quarterly* 3, no. 38 (1981): 56–72; Bross, *Dry Bones and Indian Sermons*; Jill Lepore, *The Name of War: King Philip's War and the Origins of American Identity* (New York: Vintage, 1999).

54 Nathaniel Salstonall, *The Present State of New England, with Regard to the Indian War* (London, 1675), 37.

55 James Axtell, *Natives and Newcomers: The Cultural Origins of North America* (New York: Oxford University Press, 2001), 146, 157, 160, 180.

56 David Brion Davis, *The Problem of Slavery in Western Culture* (New York: Oxford University Press, 1988), 99–104; David Brion Davis, *Inhuman Bondage: The Rise and Fall of Slavery in the New World* (New York: Oxford University Press, 2006), 128.

57 Goetz, "From Potential Christians to Hereditary Heathens"; Barbara L. Solow, *Slavery and the Rise of the Atlantic System* (Cambridge: Cambridge University Press, 1991), 271; Reis, *Damned Women*, xiii; Fay Botham, *Almighty God Created the Races: Christianity, Interracial Marriage, and American Law* (Chapel Hill: University of North Carolina Press, 2009), 54–55; Werner Sollors, *Interracialism: Black-White Intermarriage in American History, Literature, and Law* (New York: Oxford University Press), 45.

58 William H. Robinson, ed., *Phillis Wheatley and Her Writings* (New York: Garland, 1984), 160.

59 Phillis Wheatley, *An Elegiac Poem, on the Death of That Celebrated Divine, and Eminent Servant of Jesus Christ, the Late Reverend, and Pious George Whitefield* (Boston: Russell and Boyles, 1770).

CHAPTER TWO

1 Martin Marty, *Pilgrims in Their Own Land: 500 Years of Religion in America* (New York: Penguin), chaps. 5–9.

2 John Galt, *The Life, Studies, and Works of Benjamin West* (London: T. Cadell and W. Davies, Strand, 1820); Jerry D. Meyer, "Benjamin West's 'St. Stephen Altar-Piece': A Study in Late Eighteenth-Century Protestant Church Patronage and English History Painting," *Burlington Magazine* 118, no. 882 (September 1976): 634–43; Jerry D. Meyer, "Benjamin West's Window Designs for St. George's Chapel, Windsor," *American Art Journal* 11, no. 3 (July 1979): 53–65; "Staley/von Erffa Benjamin West Archive, 1940–2000," *The Historical Society of Pennsylvania,* http://www2.hsp.org/collections/manuscripts/s/staley3000 .xml (October 6, 2011).

3 Alan Taylor, *American Colonies: The Settling of North America* (New York: Penguin, 2002), part 3; Daniel Vickers, ed., *A Companion to Colonial America* (Malden, Mass.: Blackwell, 2006).

4 Gary B. Nash, *The Unknown Revolution: The Unruly Birth of Democracy and the Struggle to Create America* (New York: Penguin, 2006); Joanne Pope Melish, *Disowning Slavery: Gradual Emancipation and Race in New England, 1780–1860* (Ithaca: Cornell University Press, 2000); Duncan J. MacLeod, *Slavery, Race, and the American Revolution* (Cambridge: Cambridge University Press, 1975).

5 Thomas S. Kidd, *The Great Awakening: The Roots of Evangelical Christianity in Colonial America* (New Haven: Yale University Press, 2007); Frank Lambert, *Inventing the "Great Awakening"* (Princeton: Princeton University Press, 2001); Harry S. Stout, "Religion, Communications, and the Ideological Origins of the

American Revolution," *William and Mary Quarterly* 34, no. 4 (October 1977): 519–41.

6 Susan Juster, *Doomsayers: Anglo-American Prophecy in the Age of Revolution* (Philadelphia: University of Pennsylvania Press, 2003), 124–25; Stephen J. Stein, *The Shaker Experience in America: A History of the United Society of Believers* (New Haven: Yale University Press, 1994); Herbert A. Wisbey Jr., *Pioneer Prophetess: Jemima Wilkinson, the Publick Universal Friend* (Ithaca: Cornell University Press, 1965).

7 William G. McLoughlin, ed., *The Diary of Isaac Backus: Volume I: 1741–1764* (Providence: Brown University Press, 1979), 5, 49, 74, 111, 140, 163, 202.

8 David Morgan, *Visual Piety: A History and Theory of Popular Religious Images* (Berkeley: University of California Press, 1998), 74–75; Leigh Eric Schmidt, *Holy Fairs: Scotland and the Making of American Revivalism* (1989; 2nd edition, Grand Rapids, Mich.: Eerdmans, 2001), 149. See also quote from John Wesley in Ann Taves, *Fits, Trances, and Visions: Experiencing Religion and Explaining Experience from Wesley to James* (Princeton: Princeton University Press, 1999), 53.

9 Amanda Porterfield, *Conceived in Doubt: Religion and Politics in the New American Nation* (Chicago: University of Chicago Press, 2012); Schmidt, *Holy Fairs*, 149.

10 Quoted in Taves, *Fits, Trances, and Visions*, 62.

11 John L. Brooke, *The Refiner's Fire: The Making of Mormon Cosmology, 1644–1844* (New York: Cambridge University Press, 1994), 63. See also Mechal Sobel, *Teach Me Dreams: The Search for Self in the Revolutionary Era* (Princeton: Princeton University Press, 2000), 49; Daniel B. Shea Jr., *Spiritual Autobiography in Early America* (Princeton: Princeton University Press, 1968); and David Ferris, *Memoirs of the Life of David Ferris: An Approved Minister of the Society of Friends; Late of Wilmington, in the State of Delaware* (Philadelphia: Merrihew and Thompson's Steam Power Press, 1855), 27.

12 Sobel, *Teach Me Dreams*, 40; Stephen J. Stein, ed., *Jonathan Edwards: Apocalyptic Works* (New Haven: Yale University Press, 1977), 99.

13 John Churchman, *An Account of the Gospel Labours, and Christian Experiences of a Faithful Minister of Christ, John Churchman* (Philadelphia: Printed by Joseph Crukshank, 1779), 185–86.

14 Linford Fisher, "The Indian Great Awakening: Rethinking Native Christianization in Early America" (book manuscript draft), 170.

15 Fisher, "The Indian Great Awakening," 263, 253; Joseph Johnson, diary entry for December 20, 1772, in Laura J. Murray, ed., *To Do Good to My Indian Brethren: The Writings of Joseph Johnson* (Amherst: University of Massachusetts Press, 1998), 162.

16 Joanna Brooks, ed., *The Collected Writings of Samson Occom, Mohegan: Leadership and Literature in Eighteenth-Century Native America* (New York: Oxford University Press, 2008), 53.

17 Ibid., 98–99, 206–7.

18 Ibid., 94; Joanna Brooks, *American Lazarus: Religion and the Rise of African-*

American and Native American Literatures (New York: Oxford University Press, 2003), 68, 71.

19 Brooks, *Collected Writings of Samson Occom*, 306, 234–37; Brooks, *American Lazarus*, 77, 84.

20 Rachel Wheeler, *To Live upon Hope: Mohicans and Missionaries in the Eighteenth-Century Northeast* (Ithaca: Cornell University Press, 2008), 99.

21 Ibid., 73.

22 Linford D. Fisher, "'I Believe They Are Papists!' Natives, Moravians, and the Politics of Conversion in Eighteenth-Century Connecticut," *New England Quarterly* 81, no. 3 (September 2008): 430–31.

23 Wheeler, *To Live upon Hope*, 137, 144.

24 Jane T. Merritt, "Dreaming of the Savior's Blood: Moravians and the Indian Great Awakening in Pennsylvania," *William and Mary Quarterly* 54 (October 1997): 743; Wheeler, *To Live upon Hope*, 151, 111, 107.

25 Merritt, "Dreaming of the Savior's Blood," 723–46.

26 James A. Sandos, "Between Crucifix and Lance: Indian-White Relations in California, 1769–1848," in *Contested Eden: California before the Gold Rush*, ed. Ramón A. Gutiérrez and Richard J. Orsi (Berkeley: University of California Press, 1998), 196–229.

27 Ibid., 205.

28 Francis Guest, "An Inquiry into the Role of the Discipline in California Mission Life," *Southern California Quarterly* 71 (1989): 1–77.

29 Ibid.; Steven W. Hackel, *Children of Coyote, Missionaries of Saint Francis: Indian-Spanish Relations in Colonial California, 1769–1850* (Chapel Hill: University of North Carolina Press, 2005), 150–53, 163.

30 Quoted in Thomas J. Steele, *Folk and Church in New Mexico* (Colorado Springs: Hulbert Center for Southwestern Studies, Colorado College, 1993), 7.

31 John Heckewelder, *History, Manner, and Customs of the Indian Nations: Who Once Inhabited Pennsylvania and the Neighboring States* (1819; Westminster, Md.: Heritage Books, 2007), 294; Alfred A. Cave, "The Delaware Prophet Neolin: A Reappraisal," *Ethnohistory* 46 (Spring 1999): 269; Merritt, "Dreaming of the Saviors' Blood," 735.

32 Quoted in Brooks, *American Lazarus*, 23.

33 Albert J. Raboteau, *Slave Religion: The 'Invisible Institution' in the Antebellum South* (New York: Oxford University Press, 1978), chap. 3; Sylvia R. Frey and Betty Wood, *Come Shouting to Zion: African American Protestantism in the American South and British Caribbean to 1830* (Chapel Hill: University of North Carolina Press, 1998), chap. 4.

34 Frey and Wood, *Come Shouting to Zion*, 87–90.

35 Rt. Rev. Richard Allen, *The Life Experience and Gospel Labors of the Rt. Rev. Richard Allen, to Which Is Annexed the Rise and Progress of the African Methodist Episcopal Church in the United States of America* (Nashville: Abingdon Press, 1983); Richard S. Newman, *Freedom's Prophet: Bishop Richard Allen, the AME Church, and the Black Founding Fathers* (New York: New York University Press, 2008).

36 Jon F. Sensbach, *Rebecca's Revival: Creating Black Christianity in the Atlantic World* (Cambridge: Harvard University Press, 2005).

37 See, for instance, Johann Jakob Bossart's painting *Baptism of the Negroes* (1757) for the lack of church art. See also Sensbach, *Rebecca's Revival*, 97.

38 William H. Robinson, ed., *Phillis Wheatley and Her Writings* (New York: Garland, 1984), 133.

39 *Memoir of Old Elizabeth, a Coloured Woman* (Philadelphia: Collins, Printer, 1863), in *Six Women's Slave Narratives*, ed. William L. Andrews (New York: Oxford University Press, 1988), 6–7.

40 Kenneth L. Carroll, *John Perrot: Early Quaker Schismatic* (London: Friends' Historical Society, 1971), 60; Benjamin Whichcote, "The Glorious Evidence and Power of Divine Truth," in *The Cambridge Platonists: Being Selections from the Writings of Benjamin Whichcote, John Smith, and Nathanael Culverwel*, ed. E. T. Campagnac (Oxford: Clarendon Press, 1901), 8; Joseph Smith, ed., *A Descriptive Catalogue of Friends' Books, or Books Written by Members of the Society of Friends, Commonly Called Quakers*, vol. 1 (London: R. Barrett, 1867).

41 *The Literary Diary of Ezra Stiles, Volume 1* (New York: Charles Scribner's, 1901), 269; Nicholas Guyatt, *Providence and the Invention of the United States, 1607–1876* (Cambridge: Cambridge University Press, 2007), 132.

42 Schmidt, *Holy Fairs*, 145; "The Narrow Gate: Das Neue Jerusalem," *Religion and the Founding of the American Republic*, http://www.loc.gov/exhibits/religion/rel01–2.html (October 6, 2011). According to historian Susan Juster, a certain disgust with the body led many spiritual seekers to identify with Christ's "Ethereal Body" as a way to rid themselves of their physicality. Juster, *Doomsayers*, 100, 120.

43 Jane Dillenberger and Joshua C. Taylor, *The Hand and the Spirit: Religious Art in America, 1700–1900* (Berkeley: University Art Museum, 1972), 40; Sensbach, *Rebecca's Revival*, 189–90.

44 Robert Henkes, *The Crucifixion in American Art* (Jefferson, N.C.: McFarland, 2003), 1–14; John Hagerty, *The Tree of Life* (1791), hand-colored engraving (Baltimore: Maryland Historical Society Library); Dillenberger and Taylor, *Hand and the Spirit*, 63.

45 Fisher, "I Believe They Are Papists," 410, 412, 429.

46 Thomas S. Kidd, *God of Liberty: A Religious History of the American Revolution* (New York: Basic Books, 2010), 78.

47 Ibid., 33, 90, 116; Mark A. Noll, *America's God: From Jonathan Edwards to Abraham Lincoln* (New York: Oxford University Press, 2002), 64–73.

48 Stephen Prothero, *American Jesus: How the Son of God Became a National Icon* (New York: Farrar, Straus and Giroux, 2003), chap. 1; Kidd, *God of Liberty*, 114.

49 Ruth H. Bloch, *Visionary Republic: Millennial Themes in American Thought, 1756–1800* (Cambridge: Cambridge University Press, 1985), 30, 39, 57–59; Nathan O. Hatch, *The Sacred Cause of Liberty* (New Haven: Yale University Press, 1977); Kidd, *God of Liberty*, 17–18, 92.

50 For the transcripts of presidential addresses, see "Annual Messages of the Pres-

idents," *The Avalon Project: Documents in Law, History, and Diplomacy*, http://avalon.law.yale.edu/subject_menus/sou.asp (October 6, 2011).

51 David Sehat, *The Myth of American Religious Freedom* (New York: Oxford University Press, 2011); Kidd, *God of Liberty*, 217. For the treaties, see "The Barbary Treaties, 1786–1816," *The Avalon Project: Documents in Law, History, and Diplomacy*, http://avalon.law.yale.edu/18th_century/bar1796t.asp (October 6, 2011).

52 John P. Kaminiski and Richard Leffler, eds., *A Necessary Evil? Slavery and Debate over the Constitution* (Madison, Wis.: Madison House, 1992), 12.

53 Barbara J. Mitnick, "Parallel Visions: The Literary and Visual Image of George Washington," in *George Washington: American Symbol*, ed. Barbara J. Mitnick (New York: Hudson Hills Press, 1999), 59; Catherine L. Albanese, *Sons of the Fathers: The Civil Religion of the American Revolution* (Philadelphia: Temple University Press, 1976), 159.

CHAPTER THREE

1 Joseph Smith and B. H. Roberts, *History of the Church of Jesus Christ of Latter-day Saints* (Whitefish, Mont.: Kessinger Publications, 2004), 3–6; Richard Abanes, *One Nation under Gods: A History of the Mormon Church* (New York: Thunder's Mouth Press, 2003), 12, 17, 47–57, 47–48nn, 484–85; Richard Lyman Bushman, *Joseph Smith: Rough Stone Rolling* (New York: Alfred A. Knopf, 2005), 39–43.

2 David Waldstreicher, *Slavery's Constitution: From Revolution to Ratification* (New York: Hill and Wang, 2010); Matthew Frye Jacobson, *Whiteness of a Different Color: European Immigrants and the Alchemy of Race* (Cambridge: Harvard University Press, 1998), chap. 1.

3 David Sehat, *The Myth of American Religious Freedom* (New York: Oxford University Press, 2011); Nathan O. Hatch, *The Democratization of American Christianity* (New Haven: Yale University Press, 1991); Amanda Porterfield, *Conceived in Doubt: Religion and Politics in the New American Nation* (Chicago: University of Chicago Press, 2012); David R. Roediger, *The Wages of Whiteness: Race and the Making of the American Working Class* (London: Verso, 1991), chap. 7.

4 *Colporteur Reports to the American Tract Society, 1841–1846* (Newark: Historical Records Survey, 1940), 4; Catherine L. Albanese, *Sons of the Fathers: The Civil Religion of the American Revolution* (Philadelphia: Temple University Press, 1976), 159.

5 Daniel Walker Howe, *What Hath God Wrought: The Transformation of America, 1815–1848* (New York: Oxford University Press, 2007); Charles Sellers, *The Market Revolution: Jacksonian America, 1815–1846* (New York: Oxford University Press, 1991).

6 David Paul Nord, *Faith in Reading: Religious Publishing and the Birth of Mass Media in America* (New York: Oxford University Press, 2004); Candy Gunther Brown, *The Word in the World: Evangelical Writing, Publishing, and Reading in America, 1789–1880* (Chapel Hill: University of North Carolina Press, 2004); R. Laurence Moore, *Selling God: American Religion in the Marketplace of Culture*

(New York: Oxford University Press, 1994), chap. 1; *The Centennial Report of the American Tract Society* (New York: American Tract Society, 1925), 10–11.

7 Mark Twain, *Life on the Mississippi* (1883; Mineola, N.Y.: Dover Publications, 2000), 50–51.

8 "Tenth Report," in *Proceedings of the First Ten Years of the American Tract Society* (Boston: American Tract Society, 1824), 123.

9 *Proceedings of the First Ten Years of the American Tract Society*, 24; *Sketch of the Origin and Character of the Principal Series of Tracts* (New York: American Tract Society, 1859), 2; Rev. Dr. W. Newman, *Sin, No Trifle* (New York: American Tract Society, 1824), cover; J. Drummond, *Mary at the Feet of Jesus* (New York: American Tract Society, 18—?); *My First Sunday-School* (New York: Carlton and Porter, 1861).

10 Jane Dillenberger and Joshua C. Taylor, *The Hand and the Spirit: Religious Art in America, 1700–1900* (Berkeley: University Art Museum, 1972), 29, 74, 78.

11 *Proceedings of the First Ten Years of the American Tract Society*, 10; *Instructions of the Executive Committee of the American Tract Society, to Colporteurs and Agents: With Statements of the History, Character, and Object of the Society* (New York: American Tract Society, 1868), 39.

12 *A Pretty Picture-Book* (New York: American Tract Society, 1830), 12, 13. For another example, see Rev. John P. Carter, *My Own Primer, or First Lessons in Spelling and Reading* (Philadelphia: Presbyterian Board of Publication, 1857), 22, 26.

13 Brown, *Word in the World*, 76–77; Stephen Prothero, *American Jesus: How the Son of God Became a National Icon* (New York: Farrar, Straus and Giroux, 2003), 65; "The Book Trade," *Hunt's Merchant's Magazine* (April 1844), in *The Merchant's Magazine and Commercial Review* 10 (January–June 1844 [New York, 1844]): 391; William Andrew Chatto, John Jackson, and Henry George Bohn, *A Treatise on Wood-Engraving* (London: Henry G. Bohn, 1861); *Sights and Wonders in New York* (1849), quoted in James W. Cook, ed., *The Colossal P. T. Barnum Reader* (Urbana: University of Illinois Press, 2005), 123–25.

14 E. D. Clarke, *Travels in Various Countries of Europe, Asia, and Africa, Part the Second: Greece, Egypt, and the Holy Land* (London: T. Cadell and W. Davies, 1817), 177n1. See also "Letters of Lucius M. Piso, from Rome, to Fausta, the Daughter of Gracchus, at Palymra," *Knickerbocker* 11, no. 3 (March 1838): 248–62.

15 John Colby, *John Colby, Preacher of the Gospel* (Lowell, Mass.: N. Thurston and A. Watson, 1838), 216–17.

16 Rembrandt Peale, *Portfolio of an Artist* (Philadelphia: Henry Perkins, 1839), 181–82; Oliver Alden Taylor, *Catalogue of the Library of the Theological Seminary in Andover, Massachusetts* (Andover, Mass.: Gould and Newman, 1838), 381; *The Christian Almanac for Kentucky* (Louisville: American Tract Society, 1838), cover; Mary Byfield, *Suffer the Little Children*, wood engraving, from *Address to a Child* (New York: American Tract Society, n.d.); David Morgan, *Visual Piety: A History and Theory of Popular Religious Images* (Berkeley: University of California Press, 1998), 82–83.

17 Alexis de Tocqueville, *Democracy in America*, trans. George Lawrence and ed. J. P. Mayer (New York: Perennial Classics, 2000), 287–88; Roger Finke and Rodney Stark, *The Churching of America, 1776–1990* (New Brunswick, N.J.: Rutgers University Press, 1997), 110.

18 See Richard Wightman Fox, *Jesus in America: Personal Savior, Cultural Hero, National Obsession* (San Francisco: HarperSanFrancisco, 2004), fig. 11.

19 "Mr. Miller's Reply . . . ," *Signs of the Times* 1, no. 1 (March 20, 1840): 2; Ellen G. White, *Spiritual Gifts: Volumes I and II* (Battle Creek, Mich.: Steam Press of the Review and Herald Office, 1945), 160; Ronald L. Numbers and Jonathan M. Butler, eds., *The Disappointed: Millerism and Millenarianism in the Nineteenth Century* (Knoxville: University of Tennessee Press, 1993).

20 Bushman, *Joseph Smith: Rough Stone Rolling*.

21 Klaus J. Hansen, *Mormonism and the American Experience* (Chicago: University of Chicago Press, 1981), 181–85, 195–98; Jan Shipps, *Mormonism: The Story of a New Religious Tradition* (Urbana: University of Illinois Press, 1985); Abanes, *One Nation under Gods*, 63–73, 355–62.

22 Leon F. Litwack, *North of Slavery: The Negro in the Free States, 1790–1860* (Chicago: University of Chicago Press, 1961), chap. 3; Noel A. Carmack, "Images of Christ in Latter-day Saint Visual Culture, 1900–1999," *BYU Studies* 39, no. 3 (2000): 18–76; 1 Nephi 13:15 and 11:13.

23 Paul E. Johnson and Sean Wilentz, *The Kingdom of Matthias: A Story of Sex and Salvation in 19th-Century America* (New York: Oxford University Press, 1994); Nell Irvin Painter, *Sojourner Truth: A Life, a Symbol* (New York: W. W. Norton, 1996).

24 *Narrative of Sojourner Truth* (1878; New York: Arno Press, 1968), 67.

25 Gilbert Vale, *Fanaticism; Its Source and Influence, Illustrated by the Simple Narrative of Isabella, in the Case of Matthias, Mr. and Mrs. B. Folger, Mr. Pierson, Mr. Mills, Catherine, Isabella, &c. &c. A Reply to W. L. Stone, with the Descriptive Portraits of All the Parties, While at Sing-Sing and at Third Street.—Containing the Whole Truth—and Nothing but the Truth* (New York: G. Vale, 1835), 17–18, 37–40.

26 William L. Stone, *Matthias and His Impostures* (New York: Harper, 1835), 125.

27 James A. Sandos, "Between Crucifix and Lance: Indian-White Relations in California, 1769–1848," in *Contested Eden: California before the Gold Rush*, ed. Ramón A. Gutiérrez and Richard J. Orsi (Berkeley: University of California Press, 1998), 202–3.

28 James S. Griffith, "The Black Christ of Imuris: A Study in Cultural Fit," in *A Shared Space: Folklife in the Arizona-Sonora Borderlands* (Logan: Utah State University Press, 1995), 93.

29 William Wroth, *Images of Penance, Images of Mercy: Southwestern Santos in the Late Nineteenth Century* (Norman: University of Oklahoma Press, 1991); Larry Frank, *New Kingdom of the Saints: Religious Art of New Mexico, 1780–1907* (Santa Fe: Red Crane Books, 1992), xii; Thomas J. Steele, *Folk and Church in New Mexico* (Colorado Springs: Hulbert Center for Southwestern Studies, Colorado College, 1993), 7.

30 Gregory Dowd, *A Spirited Resistance: The North American Indian Struggle for Unity, 1745–1815* (Baltimore: Johns Hopkins University Press, 1992), 174–75.

31 Gregory Dowd, "Thinking and Believing: Nativism and Unity in the Ages of Pontiac and Tecumseh," *American Indian Quarterly* 16 (Summer 1992): 309–35.

32 William L. Stone, *Life and Times of Red-Jacket, or Sa-go-ye-watha* (New York: Wiley and Putnam, 1841), 346.

33 Dowd, *Spirited Resistance*, 128, 142, 201, 272–73.

34 Anthony F. C. Wallace, *The Death and Rebirth of the Seneca* (New York: Viking, 1972), 268, 244, 247–48, 279.

35 Joel Martin, *The Land Looks After Us: A History of Native American Religion* (New York: Oxford University Press, 1999), 70–72.

36 Theda Perdue and Michael D. Green, *The Cherokee Removal: A Brief History with Documents* (Boston: Bedford/St. Martin's, 2004), 107, 109, 120.

37 *Cherokee Phoenix and Indians' Advocate*, February 11, 1829, p. 1; *Cherokee Phoenix*, June 11, 1828, p. 2; *Cherokee Phoenix and Indians' Advocate*, August 26, 1829, p. 2; *Cherokee Phoenix*, January 28, 1829, p. 2. Copies of the *Cherokee Phoenix* are available online at "The Cherokee Phoenix from Hunter Library," http://www.wcu.edu/library/cherokeephoenix (October 6, 2011).

38 Perdue and Green, *Cherokee Removal*, 125, 137.

39 Artemis Ehnamani Sermons, Minnesota Historical Society, quoted in Bonnie Sue Lewis, *Creating Christian Indians: Native Clergy in the Presbyterian Church* (Norman: University of Oklahoma Press, 2003), 34, 39; Rev. P. J. deSmet, *New Indian Sketches* (New York: D and J Sadlar, 1865), 34.

40 Allen Dwight Callahan, *The Talking Book: African Americans and the Bible* (New Haven: Yale University Press, 2006), 186; Edward J. Blum, "'Look, Baby, We Got Jesus on Our Flag': Robust Democracy and Religious Debate from the Era of Slavery to the Age of Obama," *Annals of the American Academy of Political and Social Science* 637, no. 1 (September 2011): 17–37.

41 Callahan, *Talking Book*, 192.

42 Historian Lawrence Levine and theologian Riggins R. Earl claim that biblical characters were not tricksters for African Americans. Lawrence W. Levine, *Black Culture and Black Consciousness: Afro-American Folk Thought from Slavery to Freedom* (New York: Oxford University Press, 1977), 385; Riggins R. Earl Jr., *Dark Symbols, Obscure Signs: God, Self, and Community in the Slave Mind* (Maryknoll, N.Y.: Orbis Books, 1993), 158.

43 Erskine Clarke, *Dwelling Place: A Plantation Epic* (New Haven: Yale University Press, 2005), 127; Charles Colcock Jones, "The Religious Instruction of the Negroes," in *God Ordained This War: Sermons on the Sectional Crisis, 1830–1865*, ed. David B. Chesebrough (Columbia: University of South Carolina Press, 1991), 171; Charles C. Jones, *The Religious Instruction of the Negroes in the United States* (Savannah: Thomas Purse, 1842), 168.

44 William Meade, *Pastoral Letter of the Right Rev. William Meade, Assistant Bishop of Virginia, to the Ministers, Members, and Friends, of the Protestant Episcopal Church in the Diocese of Virginia, of the Duty of Affording Religious Instruction to Those in Bondage* (Richmond: H. K. Ellyson, 1853), 8–12.

45 Henry Brown, *Narrative of Henry Box Brown, Who Escaped from Slavery Enclosed in a Box 3 Feet Long and 2 Wide. Written from a Statement of Facts Made by Himself. With Remarks upon the Remedy for Slavery* (Boston: Charles Stearns, 1849), 16–17.

46 Levine, *Black Culture and Black Consciousness*, 54.

47 Kelly Brown Douglas, *The Black Christ* (Maryknoll, N.Y.: Orbis Books, 1994), 21; Levine, *Black Culture and Black Consciousness*, 43; Dwight Hopkins, "Slave Theology in the 'Invisible Institution,'" reprinted in *African American Religious Thought: An Anthology* (Louisville: Westminster John Knox Press, 2003), 813; Callahan, *Talking Book*, 236.

48 Eddie Glaude, *Exodus! Religion, Race, and Nation in Early Nineteenth-Century Black America* (Chicago: University of Chicago Press, 2000), 20; Levine, *Black Culture and Black Consciousness*, 36.

49 Callahan, *Talking Book*, 189–90; Earl, *Dark Symbols, Obscure Signs*, 90.

50 Earl, *Dark Symbols, Obscure Signs*, 99; George White, *A Brief Account of the Life, Experience, Travels, and Gospel Labours of George White, an African* (New York: John C. Totten, 1810), in *Black Itinerants of the Gospel: The Narratives of John Jea and George White*, ed. Graham Russell Hodges (Madison, Wis.: Madison House, 1993), 58; Dwight Hopkins, "Slave Theology in the 'Invisible Institution,'" in *Cut Loose Your Stammering Tongue: Black Theology in the Slave Narratives*, ed. Dwight N. Hopkins and George C. L. Cummings (Maryknoll, N.Y.: Orbis Books, 1991), 7.

51 Glaude, *Exodus*, 4; Earl, *Dark Symbols, Obscure Signs*, 79, 82.

52 Peter Randolph, *Sketches of Slave Life: Or, Illustrations of the Peculiar Institution* (Published for author, 1855), 25–26, 34.

53 Octavia V. Rogers Albert, *The House of Bondage: Or, Charlotte Brooks and Other Slaves* (New York: Oxford University Press, 1988), 32–34.

54 Martha Griffith Browne, *Autobiography of a Female Slave* (New York: Redfield, 1857), 46–48.

55 Clifton H. Johnson, ed., *God Struck Me Dead: Voices of Ex-Slaves* (1969; Cleveland: Pilgrim Press, 1993), 74–75, 109, 168; George P. Rawick, ed., *The American Slave: A Composite Autobiography*, vol. 19 (Westport, Conn.: Greenwood Press, 1974). For other analyses of the interviews in *God Struck Me Dead* or uses of their narratives, see Jean E. Friedman, *The Enclosed Garden: Women and Community in the Evangelical South, 1830–1900* (Chapel Hill: University of North Carolina Press, 1985), 72–80; Alonzo Johnson, "'Pray's House Spirit': The Institutional Structure and Spiritual Core of an African American Folk Tradition," in *"Ain't Gonna Lay My 'Ligion Down": African American Religion in the South*, ed. Alonzo Johnson and Paul T. Jersild (Columbia: University of South Carolina Press, 1996), 8–38; Jocelynn Moody, *Sentimental Confessions: Spiritual Narratives of Nineteenth-Century African American Women* (Athens: University of Georgia Press, 2001), 153–70; and Edward J. Blum, "A Subversive Savior: Manhood and African American Images of Christ in the Early Twentieth-Century South," in *Southern Masculinity: Perspectives on Manhood*

in the South since Reconstruction, ed. Craig Friend (Athens: University of Georgia Press, 2009), 150–73.

56 Johnson, *God Struck Me Dead*, 63, 91, 143, 148; Randolph, *Sketches of Slave Life*, 25–26, 34.

57 Johnson, *God Struck Me Dead*, 16, 83.

58 Levine, *Black Culture and Black Consciousness*; William Courtland Johnson, "Trickster on Trial: The Morality of the Brer Rabbit Tales," in *"Ain't Gonna Lay My 'Ligion Down": African American Religion in the South*, ed. Alonzo Johnson and Paul T. Jersild (Columbia: University of South Carolina Press, 1996), 52–71; Mechal Sobel, *Trabelin' On: The Slave Journey to an Afro-Baptist Faith* (Westport, Conn.: Greenwood Press, 1979), xix–xx.

CHAPTER FOUR

1 Barry O'Connell, ed., *On Our Own Ground: The Complete Writings of William Apess, a Pequot* (Amherst: University of Massachusetts Press, 1992), 8, 19, 130, 158–59.

2 Mark A. Noll, *America's God: From Jonathan Edwards to Abraham Lincoln* (New York: Oxford University Press, 2002), 393.

3 Elizabeth Fox-Genovese and Eugene D. Genovese, *The Mind of the Master Class: History and Faith in the Southern Slaveholders' Worldview* (Cambridge: Cambridge University Press, 2005), 76, 492, 497, 627.

4 *Anti-Abolition Tracts—No. 6: Soliloquies* (New York: Van Evrie, Horton, 1866), 11–12. See also Dr. P. B. Barringer, *"The Sacrifice of a Race"* (Raleigh: Edwards and Broughton, 1900), 8–9, in *The Benefits of Slavery*, vol. 4 of *Anti-black Thought, 1863–1925: "The Negro Problem,"* ed. John David Smith (New York: Garland, 1993).

5 J. H. Van Evrie, *White Supremacy and Negro Subordination: Or, Negroes a Subordinate Race, and (So-Called) Slavery Its Normal Condition* (New York: Van Evrie, Horton, 1868), 181–82, in *Van Evrie's White Supremacy and Negro Subordination*, vol. 3 of *Anti-black Thought, 1863–1925: "The Negro Problem,"* ed. John David Smith (New York: Garland, 1993); James Thornwell, "The Rights and Duties of Masters," in *God Ordained This War: Sermons on the Sectional Crisis, 1830–1865*, ed. David B. Chesebrough (Columbia: University of South Carolina Press, 1991), 188; Edward J. Blum and W. Scott Pole, eds., *Vale of Tears: New Essays on Religion and Reconstruction* (Macon, Ga.: Mercer University Press, 2005), 1.

6 Mason Lowance, ed., *Against Slavery: An Abolitionist Reader* (New York: Penguin, 2000), 12, 33–34, 37, 198.

7 Jacquelyn Bacon, *Freedom's Journal: The First African-American Newspaper* (Lanham, Md.: Lexington Books, 2007), 225–26.

8 *Liberator*, March 9, 1855; Albert J. Von Frank, *The Trials of Anthony Burns: Freedom and Slavery in Emerson's Boston* (Cambridge: Harvard University Press, 1999); Frederick Douglass, *My Bondage and My Freedom* (1855; New York: Arno Press and the New York Times, 1968), appendix.

9 Gayraud S. Wilmore, *Black Religion and Black Radicalism: An Interpretation of the Religious History of Afro-American People* (Maryknoll, N.Y.: Orbis Books, 1994), 36–37; Robert Alexander Young, *The Ethiopian Manifesto: Issued in Defence of the Black Man's Rights in the Scale of Universal Freedom* (New York: Robert Alexander Young, 1829).

10 Peter P. Hinks, ed., *David Walker's Appeal to the Coloured Citizens of the World* (1829; University Park: Pennsylvania State University Press, 2000); Cornel West, *Prophesy Deliverance! An Afro-American Revolutionary Christianity* (Louisville: Westminster John Knox Press, 2002), 102.

11 Rt. Rev. Richard Allen, *The Life Experience and Gospel Labors of the Rt. Rev. Richard Allen, to Which Is Annexed the Rise and Progress of the African Methodist Episcopal Church in the United States of America* (Nashville: Abingdon Press, 1983), 71, 81. For another example, see Leonard Black, *The Life and Sufferings of Leonard Black, a Fugitive from Slavery* (New Bedford: Benjamin Lindsey, 1847), 52–54.

12 Terrie Dopp Aarmodt, *Righteous Armies, Holy Cause: Apocalyptic Imagery and the Civil War* (Macon, Ga.: Mercer University Press, 2002), 41–43.

13 Harriet Beecher Stowe, *The Key to Uncle Tom's Cabin* (1854; New York: Arno Press, 1968), 41, 45–46, 47–49, 53, 503–4.

14 George Fredrickson, *The Black Image in the White Mind: The Debate on Afro-American Character and Destiny, 1817–1914* (New York: Harper and Row, 1971), chap. 4; Curtis J. Evans, *The Burden of Black Religion* (New York: Oxford University Press, 2008), chap. 1.

15 Allen Dwight Callahan, *The Talking Book: African Americans and the Bible* (New Haven: Yale University Press, 2006), 224; Wesley John Gaines, *The Negro and the White Man* (Philadelphia, A.M.E. Publishing House, 1897), 65.

16 Samuel Johnson, "The New Birth of the Nation," *Liberator*, May 8, 1863; "The American War versus the European War," *Douglass' Monthly*, July 1859; M. Waterbury, *Seven Years among the Freedmen* (Chicago: T. B. Arnold, 1891), 7.

17 John Fletcher, *Studies on Slavery, in Easy Lessons* (Natchez, Miss., 1852), 171.

18 "Letters of Lucius M. Piso, from Rome, to Fausta, the Daughter of Gracchus, at Palymra," *Knickerbocker* 11, no. 3 (March 1838): 248–62; L. L. Hamline, "Works of Taste," *Ladies' Repository* 1, no. 2 (February 1841): 33–37.

19 Susan L. Roberson, *Emerson in His Sermons: A Man-Made Self* (Columbia: University of Missouri Press, 1995), 169, 179–80; Nell Irvin Painter, *The History of White People* (New York: W. W. Norton, 2010), 151.

20 Leonard Dinnerstein, *Antisemitism in America* (New York: Oxford University Press, 1994), 16.

21 Tracy Fessenden, *Culture and Redemption: Religion, the Secular, and American Literature* (Princeton: Princeton University Press, 2007), chap. 3.

22 *Awful Disclosures* (New York: Maria Monk, 1836), 53, 57; Lewis Leonidas Allen, *Pencillings of Scenes upon the Rio Grande* (New York, 1848), 8, 9, 11, 17. Our thanks to John Pinheiro for this source.

23 "A Sermon on the Festival of St. Patrick," in *Complete Works of the Most Rev.*

John Hughes, D.D., Archbishop of New York, ed. Lawrence Kehoe (New York: Lawrence Kehoe, 1866), 2:163.

24 Jenny Franchot, *Roads to Rome: The Antebellum Protestant Encounter with Catholicism* (Berkeley: University of California Press, 1994).

25 Horace Bushnell, *Views of Christian Nurture* (Hartford, Conn.: Edwin Hunt, 1847), 220; David Morgan, *The Lure of Images: A History of Religion and Visual Media in America* (London: Routledge, 2007), chap. 4; Kenneth Ames, *Death in the Dining Room and Other Tales of Victorian Culture* (Philadelphia: Temple University Press, 1992); Edward Hale, *The Ingham Papers* (Fields, Osgood, 1869), 111.

26 Emma S. Babcock, *Dutch Tiles: Or, Loving Words about the Saviour* (Philadelphia: Presbyterian Board of Publication, c. 1866), in Special Collections, Presbyterian Historical Society, Philadelphia. See also William M. Blackburn, *The Holy Child: Or, The Early Years of Our Lord Jesus Christ* (Philadelphia: Presbyterian Board of Publication, c. 1860), 3, ibid.

27 II Nephi 30:5–6; Grant Underwood, *The Millenarian World of Early Mormonism* (Urbana: University of Illinois Press, 1999), 66.

28 James S. Brown, *Life of a Pioneer: Being the Autobiography of James S. Brown* (Salt Lake City: George Q. Cannon, 1900), 354–56. Our thanks to Jennifer Lindell for this source.

29 A. Karl Larson and Katharine Miles Larson, eds., *Diary of Charles Lowell Walker* (Logan: Utah State University Press, 1980), 154–55; Armand Mauss, *All Abraham's Children: Changing Mormon Perceptions of Race* (Urbana: University of Illinois Press, 2003), chaps. 8, 9; Klaus J. Hansen, *Mormonism and the American Experience* (Chicago: University of Chicago Press, 1981); Jan Shipps, *Mormonism: The Story of a New Religious Tradition* (Urbana: University of Illinois Press, 1985); Newell G. Bringhurst, *Saints, Slaves, and Blacks: The Changing Place of Black People within Mormonism* (Westport, Conn.: Greenwood Press, 1981); Sarah Barringer Gordon, *The Mormon Question: Polygamy and Constitutional Conflict in Nineteenth-Century America* (Chapel Hill: University of North Carolina Press, 2001).

30 "The Indian Convert," *The Ladies' Repository: A Monthly Periodical, Devoted to Literature, Arts, and Religion* 2 (December 1842): 361–63. See also John Pitezel, *Lights and Shades of Missionary Life* (Cincinnati: Western Book Concern, 1861), 356.

31 Rev. Henry J. Whipple, *Lights and Shadows of a Long Episcopate, by Rev. Henry J. Whipple, Bishop of Minnesota* (New York: Macmillan, 1899), 64–65.

32 Headpiece illustration by Hammat Billings, in Harriet Beecher Stowe, *Uncle Tom's Cabin: Or, Life among the Lowly* (ill. ed.; Boston: John P. Jewett, 1853), chaps. 38, 40, p. 517; Morgan, *Lure of Images*, 56.

33 James F. O'Gorman, *Accomplished in All Departments of Art: Hammatt Billings of Boston, 1818–1874* (Amherst: University of Massachusetts Press, 1998), 48.

34 Kirk Savage, *Standing Soldiers, Kneeling Slaves: Race, War, and Monument in Nineteenth-Century America* (Princeton: Princeton University Press, 1997).

CHAPTER FIVE

1 George F. Kelly to Abraham Lincoln, February 24, 25, 1863, and George F. Kelly to William H. Seward, October 26, 1863, in Abraham Lincoln Papers, Library of Congress; George C. Rable, *God's Almost Chosen Peoples: A Religious History of the American Civil War* (Chapel Hill: University of North Carolina Press, 2010), 194. For more on Lincoln and religion, see Allen C. Guelzo, *Abraham Lincoln, Redeemer President* (Grand Rapids, Mich.: Eerdmans, 2003); Ronald C. White, *Lincoln's Greatest Speech: The Second Inaugural* (New York: Simon and Schuster, 2006); and Mark A. Noll, *America's God: From Jonathan Edwards to Abraham Lincoln* (New York: Oxford University Press, 2002), 425–38.

2 For more on religion in the Civil War and Reconstruction, see Harry S. Stout, *Upon the Altar of the Nation: A Moral History of the American Civil War* (New York: Viking, 2006); Paul Harvey, *Redeeming the South: Religious Cultures and Racial Identities among Southern Baptists, 1865–1925* (Chapel Hill: University of North Carolina Press, 1997); Daniel Stowell, *Rebuilding Zion: The Religious Reconstruction of the South, 1863–1877* (New York: Oxford University Press, 1998); Steven E. Woodworth, *While God Is Marching On: The Religious World of Civil War Soldiers* (Lawrence: University Press of Kansas, 2001); Edward J. Blum, *Reforging the White Republic: Race, Religion, and American Nationalism, 1865–1898* (Baton Rouge: Louisiana State University Press, 2005); James B. Bennett, *Religion and the Rise of Jim Crow in New Orleans* (Princeton: Princeton University Press, 2005); and Derek Chang, *Citizens of a Christian Nation: Evangelical Missions and the Problem of Race in the Nineteenth Century* (Philadelphia: University of Pennsylvania Press, 2010).

3 Robert J. Morgan, *Then Sings My Soul: 150 of the World's Greatest Hymn Stories* (Nashville: Thomas Nelson, 2003), 135.

4 Kenneth S. Greenberg, ed., *The Confessions of Nat Turner and Related Documents* (Boston: Bedford/St. Martin's, 1996), 45–47.

5 Ibid., 48, 57.

6 Joseph Smith, *The Doctrine and Covenants of the Church of Jesus Christ of Latter-day Saints* (Bedford, Mass.: Applewood, 2009), 304.

7 Quoted in Zoe Trodd and John Stauffer, eds., *Meteor of War: The John Brown Story* (Maplecrest, N.Y.: Brandywine, 2004), 150, 137–39, 140–42.

8 Terrie Dopp Aarmodt, *Righteous Armies, Holy Cause: Apocalyptic Imagery and the Civil War* (Macon, Ga.: Mercer University Press, 2002), 28; *Anti-Abolition Tracts—No. 3: The Abolition Conspiracy to Destroy the Union: Or, A Ten Years' Record of the "Republican" Party* (New York: Van Evrie, Horton, 1863), 23–24, 27, in *Anti-abolition Tracts and Anti-black Stereotypes*, vol. 1 of *Anti-black Thought, 1863–1925: "The Negro Problem,"* ed. John David Smith (New York: Garland, 1993).

9 Rable, *God's Almost Chosen Peoples*, 62–63.

10 Ibid., 164, 171; Charles Irons, *The Origins of Proslavery Christianity: White and Black Evangelicals in Colonial and Antebellum Virginia* (Chapel Hill: University of North Carolina Press, 2007), 260.

11 Rable, *God's Almost Chosen Peoples*, 234; Elizabeth Fox-Genovese and Eugene D. Genovese, *The Mind of the Master Class: History and Faith in the Southern Slave-holders' Worldview* (Cambridge: Cambridge University Press, 2005), 403.

12 Virginia Burr, ed., *The Secret Eye: The Journal of Ella Gertrude Clanton Thomas* (Chapel Hill: University of North Carolina Press, 1990), 276.

13 Quoted in Chandra Manning, *What This Cruel War Was Over: Soldiers, Slavery, and the Civil War* (New York: Vintage Books, 2007), 171. See also John Townsend Trowbridge, *The South: A Tour of Its Battle-Fields and Ruined Cities* (Hartford, Conn.: L. Stebbins, 1866), 291.

14 Rable, *God's Almost Chosen Peoples*, 297.

15 Cyrus Bartol, *The Remission by Blood: A Tribute to Our Soldiers and the Sword* (Boston: Walker, Wise, 1862); Gardiner H. Shattuck Jr., *A Shield and Hiding Place: The Religious Life of the Civil War Armies* (Macon, Ga.: Mercer University Press, 1987), 17; James M. McPherson, *For Cause and Comrade: Why Men Fought in the Civil War* (New York: Oxford University Press, 1998), 76.

16 Edward D. Snyder, "The Biblical Background of the 'Battle Hymn of the Republic,'" *New England Quarterly* 24, no. 2 (June 1951): 231–38; Julia Ward Howe, *Reminiscences, 1819–1899* (1899; New York: New American Library, 1969), 274–75; Noah Andre Trudeau, *Like Men of War: Black Troops in the Civil War, 1862–1865* (Boston: Little, Brown, 1998), 263.

17 Rable, *God's Almost Chosen Peoples*, 145; Thomas F. Curran, *Soldiers of Peace: Civil War Pacifism and the Postwar Radical Peace Movement* (New York: Fordham University Press, 2003).

18 Rable, *God's Almost Chosen Peoples*, 337.

19 Elias Gove to Abraham Lincoln, January 2, 1865; Lydia Smith to Abraham Lincoln, October 4, 1862; Charles P. McIlvaine to Abraham Lincoln, March 27, 1862; and Benjamin Talbot to Abraham Lincoln, December 21, 1864; all Abraham Lincoln Papers, Library of Congress.

20 Beaufort South Carolina Baptist Church to Abraham Lincoln, January 1, 1863; J. K. W. Levane and A. M. Milligan to Abraham Lincoln, September–December 1862; and Congregational Church at Paterson, New Jersey, to Abraham Lincoln, July 4, 1864; all Abraham Lincoln Papers, Library of Congress; Rable, *God's Almost Chosen Peoples*, 196.

21 A. Karl Larson and Katharine Miles Larson, eds., *Diary of Charles Lowell Walker* (Logan: Utah State University Press, 1980), 147, 242; Robert Glass Cleland and Juanita Brooks, eds., *A Mormon Chronicle: The Diaries of John D. Lee* (San Marino, Calif.: Huntington Library, 1955), 283–84, 295.

22 Allen Dwight Callahan, *The Talking Book: African Americans and the Bible* (New Haven: Yale University Press, 2006), 201; James West Davidson and Mark Hamilton Lytle, *After the Fact: The Art of Historical Detection* (New York: McGraw Hill, 1999), 149; Charlotte Forten, "Life on the Sea Islands," *Atlantic Monthly*, May 1864, 253.

23 Thomas Wentworth Higginson, *Army Life in a Black Regiment* (New York: Norton, 1984), 192, 202, 209.

24 "The Ideas of a South Carolinian," *Liberator*, June 23, 1865.

25 Blum, *Reforging the White Republic*, 21–22, 30; Herman Melville, *Poems Containing Battle-Pieces, John Marr and Other Sailors, Timoleon, and Miscellaneous Poems* (New York: Harper, 1866), 141–42; Rable, *God's Almost Chosen Peoples*, 385.

26 Katharine L. Dvorak, *An African-American Exodus: The Segregation of the Southern Churches* (New York: Carlson, 1991); Clarence E. Walker, *A Rock in a Weary Land: The African Methodist Episcopal Church during the Civil War and Reconstruction* (Baton Rouge: Louisiana State University Press, 1982); Reginald F. Hildebrand, *The Times Were Strange and Stirring: Methodist Preachers and the Crisis of Emancipation* (Durham: Duke University Press, 1995).

27 T. Morris Chester, "Negro Self-Respect and Pride of Race," in *Pamphlets of Protest: An Anthology of Early African-American Protest Literature, 1790–1860*, ed. Richard Newman, Patrick Rael, and Philip Lapsansky (New York: Routledge, 2001), 304–10.

28 "Reconstruction," in *American Political Prints, 1766–1876: A Catalog of the Collections in the Library of Congress*, ed. Bernard F. Reilly Jr. (Boston: G. K. Hall, 1991), 572; Horatio Bateman, *Explanation of Bateman's National Picture of Reconstruction* (New York: Bateman, 1867); Mark Elliott, *Color-Blind Justice: Albion Tourgée and the Quest for Racial Equality from the Civil War to* Plessy v. Ferguson (New York: Oxford University Press, 2006), 26; Blum, *Reforging the White Republic*, 1–2.

29 Earl Schenck Miers, ed., *When the World Ended: The Diary of Emma LeConte* (New York: Oxford University Press, 1957), 85, 91–92.

30 Charles Reagan Wilson, *Baptized in Blood: The Religion of the Lost Cause, 1865–1920* (Athens: University of Georgia Press, 1980), 25, 31, 45, 75; J. W. Tucker, "God's Providence in War," in *"God Ordained This War": Sermons on the Sectional Crisis, 1830–1865*, ed. David B. Chesebrough (Columbia: University of South Carolina Press), 236; Charles Reagan Wilson, "The Religion of the Lost Cause: Ritual and Organization of the Southern Civil Religion," *Journal of Southern History* 46 (May 1980): 223.

31 Lloyd Hunter, "The Immortal Confederacy: Another Look at Lost Cause Religion," in *The Myth of the Lost Cause and Civil War Memory*, ed. Gary Gallagher and Alan T. Nolan (Bloomington: Indiana University Press, 2000), 204.

32 John William Jones, *Christ in the Camp: Or, Religion in Lee's Army* (Richmond: B. F. Johnson, 1887), 326, 344, 373, 430, 206–7.

33 Hunter, "The Immortal Confederacy," 204.

34 Shattuck, *Shield and Hiding Place*, 123–24.

35 Hunter, "The Immortal Confederacy," 190–97.

36 Ibid., 200, 208.

37 Newell G. Bringhurst, *Saints, Slaves, and Blacks: The Changing Place of Black People within Mormonism* (Westport, Conn.: Greenwood Press, 1981), 153, 161n3.

38 Ibid., 128.

39 Mrs. C. V. Waite, *The Mormon Prophet and His Harem: An Authentic History*

of Brigham Young, His Numerous Wives and Children (Cambridge: Riverside Press, 1866), iii–iv.

40 Gaines M. Foster, *Moral Reconstruction: Christian Lobbyists and the Legislation of Morality, 1865–1920* (Chapel Hill: University of North Carolina Press, 2007); Patrick Q. Mason, "Opposition to Polygamy in the Postbellum South," *Journal of Southern History* 76, no. 3 (August 2010): 541–78.

41 Noel A. Carmack, "Images of Christ in Latter-day Saint Visual Culture, 1900–1999," *BYU Studies* 39, no. 3 (2000): 18–76.

42 Blum, *Reforging the White Republic*, chap. 3.

43 David Morgan, *Protestants and Pictures: Religion, Visual Culture, and the Age of American Mass Production* (New York: Oxford University Press, 1999), 9–11.

44 Henry Ward Beecher, *The Life of Jesus, the Christ* (New York: J. B. Ford, 1871), 134–37.

CHAPTER SIX

1 D. W. Griffith, producer and director, *The Birth of a Nation* (film) (1915; Los Angeles: Republic Pictures Home Video, 1991); Edward J. Blum, *Reforging the White Republic: Race, Religion, and American Nationalism, 1865–1898* (Baton Rouge: Louisiana State University Press, 2005), 2; Richard Wightman Fox, *Jesus in America: Personal Savior, Cultural Hero, National Obsession* (San Francisco: HarperSanFrancisco, 2004), 311–13; Melvyn Stokes, *D. W. Griffith's* The Birth of a Nation*: A History of the Most Controversial Motion Picture of All Time* (New York: Oxford University Press, 2008).

2 Nancy K. McLean, *Behind the Mask of Chivalry: The Making of the Second Ku Klux Klan* (New York: Oxford University Press, 1995); Wyn Craig Wade, *The Fiery Cross: The Ku Klux Klan in America* (New York: Oxford University Press, 1998).

3 Matthew Pratt Guterl, *The Color of Race in America, 1900–1940* (Cambridge: Harvard University Press, 2001), 125.

4 D. W. Griffith, director, *Intolerance* (film) 1916; Patricia Erens, *The Jew in American Cinema* (Bloomington: Indiana University Press, 1984), 71–72; Adele Reinhartz, *Jesus of Hollywood* (New York: Oxford University Press, 2007), 204–6.

5 Mark W. Summers, *The Gilded Age, or, the Hazard of New Functions* (Upper Saddle River, N.J.: Prentice Hall, 1997); Alan Dawley, *Struggles of Justice: Social Responsibility and the Liberal State* (Cambridge: Belknap Press of Harvard University Press, 1991); Daniel T. Rodgers, *Atlantic Crossings: Social Politics in the Progressive Era* (Cambridge: Belknap Press of Harvard University Press, 2000); Nell Irvin Painter, *Standing at Armageddon: The United States, 1877–1919* (New York: W. W. Norton, 1987); Rebecca Edwards, *New Spirits: Americans in the Gilded Age, 1865–1905* (New York: Oxford University Press, 2005).

6 Noel A. Carmack, "Images of Christ in Latter-day Saint Visual Culture, 1900–1999," *BYU Studies* 39, no. 3 (2000): 18–76.

7 Joseph Lewis French, *Christ in Art* (Boston: L. C. Page, 1900), 27–32.

8 Cynthia Pearl Maus, *Christ and the Fine Arts: An Anthology of Pictures, Poetry, Music, and Stories Centering in the Life of Christ* (New York: Harper, 1938), 389–90.

9 Roger Finke and Rodney Stark, *The Churching of America, 1776–1990* (New Brunswick, N.J.: Rutgers University Press, 1997), 121–22; Robert Orsi, *The Madonna of 115th Street: Faith and Community in Italian Harlem, 1880–1950* (New Haven: Yale University Press, 1985).

10 Frank Milton Bristol, *The Ministry of Art* (New York: Eaton and Mains, 1897), 54, 58–59, 183. See also Nathalie Dana, *The Story of Jesus: Pictures from Paintings* (Boston: Marshall Jones, 1920).

11 Stephen Prothero, *American Jesus: How the Son of God Became a National Icon* (New York: Farrar, Straus and Giroux, 2003), 65, 87–90; Alan C. Braddock, "Painting the World's Christ: Tanner, Hybridity, and the Blood of the Holy Land," *Nineteenth-Century Art Worldwide: A Journal of Nineteenth-Century Visual Culture* 3, no. 2 (Autumn 2004), http://www.19thc-artworldwide.org/ index.php/autumn04/298-painting-the-worlds-christ-tanner-hybridity-and-the-blood-of-the-holy-land (October 6, 2011).

12 *The Crucifixion, by an Eye-Witness* (5th ed., Chicago: Indo-American Book, 1913); William Evans, *Epochs in the Life of Christ* (New York: Fleming H. Revell, 1916), 128–29; Joe Mitchell Chapple, ed., *Heart Throbs in Prose and Verse: Dear to the American People* (Boston: Chapple, 1905), 468–69. See also John Kenyon Kilbourn, ed., *Faiths of Famous Men in Their Own Words* (Philadelphia: Henry T. Coates, 1900), 221–22.

13 "Westminster Lesson Cards," in Special Collections, Presbyterian Historical Society, Philadelphia; David Morgan, *The Lure of Images: A History of Religion and Visual Media in America* (London: Routledge, 2007), 95–101. See also the cards collected and digitized at "Berean Sunday School Cards," *Material History of American Religion Project*, http://www.materialreligion.org/cards/index.html (October 6, 2011).

14 "Westminster Lesson Cards," in Special Collections, Presbyterian Historical Society, Philadelphia; see especially "Man Made in the Image of God," 14, no. 1 (January 13, 1907); "Jesus and John the Baptist," 15, no. 1 (January 12, 1908); "The Raising of Lazarus," 15, no. 2 (April 12, 1908); "Philip and the Ethiopian," 16, no. 1 (March 7, 1909); and "Putting God's Kingdom First," 41, no. 1 (February 4, 1934).

15 Charles E. Craven, *Jesus and Children* (Philadelphia: Presbyterian Board of Publication and Sabbath-School Work, 1896), 7, in Special Collections, Presbyterian Historical Society, Philadelphia.

16 J. Leo Fairbanks, "Picture Study in the Sunday Schools," *Juvenile Instructor* 48 (January 1913): 3–5; Clyde R. Forsberg Jr., review, "The Mormons," *Journal of American History* 94, no. 3 (December 2007): 1028–30.

17 "The Talking Picture," in Maus, *Christ and the Fine Arts*, 640.

18 Augusta E. Stetson, *Reminiscences, Sermons, and Correspondence* (New York: G. P. Putnam's, 1913), 211, 270–71, 284–85, 329, 581. See also John V. Shoemaker, *Heredity, Health, and Personal Beauty* (Philadelphia: F. A. Davis, 1890), 71.

19 Quotes from Kambiz GhaneaBassiri, *A History of Islam in America: From the New World to the New World Order* (Cambridge: Cambridge University Press, 2010), 154–55; Sarah M. A. Gualtieri, *Between Arab and White: Race and Ethnicity in the Early Syrian American Diaspora* (Berkeley: University of California Press, 2009), 78; Ian F. Haney Lopez, *White by Law: The Legal Construction of Race* (New York: New York University Press, 1997), 74; and Jennifer Snow, "The Civilization of White Men: The Race of the Hindu in *United States v. Bhagat Singh Thind*," in *Race, Nation, and Religion in the Americas*, ed. Henry Goldschmidt and Elizabeth McAlister (New York: Oxford University Press, 2004), 259–82.

20 "Protestant War against Christianity," *Catholic World* 29, no. 171 (June 1879): 325–35; "The Face of Jesus Christ," in David Gregg, *Our Best Moods: Soliloquies and Other Discourses* (New York: E. B. Treat, 1893), 53–79. See also *Sermons by T. De Witt Talmage: Delivered in the Brooklyn Tabernacle* (New York: Funk and Wagnalls, 1885), 32, 112, 125–27.

21 Mark Elliott, *Color-Blind Justice: Albion Tourgée and the Quest for Racial Equality from the Civil War to* Plessy v. Ferguson (New York: Oxford University Press, 2006); Albion W. Tourgée, *Pactolus Prime* (1890; Upper Saddle River, N.J.: Gregg, 1968).

22 Tourgée, *Pactolus Prime*.

23 Ibid., 16–17, 66–67, 72.

24 Ibid., 166, 79–80.

25 "Christ Jesus Not White," *Cleveland Gazette*, December 16, 1893, 1.

26 Gayraud S. Wilmore, *Black Religion and Black Radicalism: An Interpretation of the Religious History of Afro-American People* (Maryknoll, N.Y.: Orbis Books, 1994), 153–54.

27 W. L. Hunter, *Jesus Christ Had Negro Blood in His Veins: The Wonder of the Twentieth Century* (1901; Brooklyn, N.Y.: W. L. Hunter, 1908), 15–16.

28 W. E. B. Du Bois, *The Souls of Black Folk: Authoritative Text, Contents, Criticism*, ed. Henry Louis Gates Jr. and Terri Hume Oliver (1903; New York: W. W. Norton, 1999), 142; Edward J. Blum, *W. E. B. Du Bois, American Prophet* (Philadelphia: University of Pennsylvania Press, 2007), chap. 2.

29 Marcia M. Mathews, *Henry Ossawa Tanner: American Artist* (Chicago: University of Chicago Press, 1969).

30 Braddock, "Painting the World's Christ."

31 Quoted in ibid.; Kristin Schwain, *Signs of Grace: Religion and American Art in the Gilded Age* (Ithaca: Cornell University Press, 2008), chap. 2.

32 *The Art of Henry O. Tanner* (Washington, D.C.: Smithsonian, 1970), 48–49; Schwain, *Signs of Grace*, 65–66.

33 Mathews, *Henry Ossawa Tanner*, 146–47, 201; *Art of Henry O. Tanner*, 12.

34 Prothero, *American Jesus*, 277; John P. Burris, *Exhibiting Religion: Colonialism and Spectacle at International Expositions, 1851–1893* (Charlottesville: University Press of Virginia, 2001).

35 Heather Cox Richardson, *West from Appomattox: The Reconstruction of America after the Civil War* (New Haven: Yale University Press, 2007).

36 Frederick Jackson Turner, *The Frontier in American History* (New York: Henry Holt, 1920), 357.

37 Indian Rights Association, "Statement of Objectives," Merrill E. Gates, "Land and Law as Agents in Educating Indians" (1885), and Merrill E. Gates, "Christianizing the Indians" (1893), selections reprinted in *Americanizing the American Indians: Writings by the "Friends of the Indian," 1880–1900*, ed. Francis Paul Prucha (Cambridge: Harvard University Press, 1973), 43, 46, 288.

38 David Wallace Adams, *Education for Extinction: American Indians and the Boarding School Experience, 1875–1928* (Lawrence: University Press of Kansas, 1995).

39 Quoted in D. A. Grinde, "Learning to Navigate in a Christian World," in *Native American Religious Identity: Unforgotten Gods*, ed. Jace Weaver (Maryknoll, N.Y.: Orbis Books, 1998), 124–33.

40 "I Just Loved That School," Oral History of Henrietta Chief, *History Matters*, http://historymatters.gmu.edu/d/65 (October 6, 2011).

41 Gregory Smoak, *Ghost Dances and Indian Identity: Prophetic Religion and American Indian Ethnogenesis in the Nineteenth Century* (Berkeley: University of California Press, 2006).

42 Don Lynch, ed., *Wovoka and the Ghost Dance* (Lincoln: University of Nebraska Press, 1997), 69, 101.

43 Ibid., 183, 190, 223; James Mooney, *The Ghost Dance Religion and the Sioux Outbreak of 1890*, Fourteenth Annual Report of the Bureau of American Ethnology, part 2 (Washington, D.C.: Government Printing Office, 1896), 764–76.

44 Lynch, *Wovoka and the Ghost Dance*, 232–33, 243; Mooney, *Ghost Dance Religion*, 792, 795; Heather Cox Richardson, *Wounded Knee: Party Politics and the Road to an American Massacre* (New York: Basic Books, 2010), 124; Lynch, *Wovoka and the Ghost Dance*, 170.

45 Mooney, *Ghost Dance Religion*, 795.

46 Lynch, *Wovoka and the Ghost Dance*, 189–90, 298.

47 Karl Markus Kreis, *Lakotas, Black Robes, and Holy Women* (Lincoln: University of Nebraska Press, 2000), 140; Richardson, *Wounded Knee*.

48 Blum, *Reforging the White Republic*, 219; "Christianity and War," *Century* 58, no. 3 (July 1899): 481.

49 Sister Sallie, *The Color Line: Devoted to the Restoration of Good Government, Putting an End to Negro Authority and Misrule, and Establishing a White Man's Government in the White Man's Country, by Organizing the White People of the South* (Memphis: n.p., c. 1875), 7–9, in *The Biblical and "Scientific" Defense of Slavery*, vol. 6 of *Anti-black Thought, 1863–1925: "The Negro Problem,"* ed. John David Smith (New York: Garland, 1993); Rev. G. C. H. Hasskarl, *"The Missing Link": Or, The Negro's Ethnological Status: Is He a Descendant of Adam and Eve? Is He the Progeny of Ham? Has He a Soul? What Is His Relation to the White Race? Is He a Subject of the Church or the State, Which?* (Chambersburg, Pa.: Democratic News, 1898), 10, 122, 173.

50 A. Hoyle Lester, *The Pre-Adamite, or Who Tempted Eve?* (Philadelphia: J. B. Lippincott, 1875), 25, in *The Biblical and "Scientific" Defense of Slavery*, vol. 6

of *Anti-black Thought, 1863–1925: "The Negro Problem,"* ed. John David Smith (New York: Garland, 1993).

51 Ibid., 42–43; Kilbourn, *Faiths of Famous Men in Their Own Words*, 191.

52 Robert J. Morgan, *Then Sings My Soul: 150 of the World's Greatest Hymn Stories* (Nashville: Thomas Nelson, 2003), 236–37.

53 Maus, *Christ and the Fine Arts*, 597–99; Sandy Brewer, "From Darkest England to *The Hope of the World*: Protestant Pedagogy and the Visual Culture of the London Missionary Society," *Material Religion* 1, no. 1 (January 2005): 98–124.

54 Fred Kaplan, *The Singular Mark Twain* (New York: Anchor Books, 2003), 555, 585, 651; Harold K. Bush, *Mark Twain and the Spiritual Crisis of His Age* (Tuscaloosa: University of Alabama Press, 2007).

55 Randall K. Burkett, *Garveyism as a Religious Movement: The Institutionalization of a Black Civil Religion* (Metuchen, N.J.: Scarecrow Press, 1978), 47, 53.

56 *Negro World*, November 6, 1924; Robert A. Hill, ed., *The Marcus Garvey and Universal Negro Improvement Association Papers*, 7 vols. (Berkeley: University of California Press, 1986), 5:832n3.

57 Quoted in Burkett, *Garveyism as a Religious Movement*, 53.

58 Danielle McGuire, *At the Dark End of the Street: Black Women, Race, and Resistance—A New History of the Civil Rights Movement from Rosa Parks to the Rise of Black Power* (New York: Knopf, 2010).

59 Susannah Heschel, *The Aryan Jesus: Christian Theologians and the Bible in Nazi Germany* (Princeton: Princeton University Press, 2008).

60 Matthew Frye Jacobson, *Whiteness of a Different Color: European Immigrants and the Alchemy of Race* (Cambridge: Harvard University Press, 1998), chap. 2.

61 Leonard Dinnerstein, *Antisemitism in America* (New York: Oxford University Press, 1994), 37, 42, 65, 70.

62 Madison Grant, *The Passing of the Great Race or the Racial Basis of European History* (1916; New York: Charles Scribner's, 1921), vii–viii, 227n9, 385–86; Guterl, *Color of Race in America*, 14–67; Colin Kidd, *The Forging of the Races: Race and Scripture in the Protestant Atlantic World, 1600–2000* (Cambridge: Cambridge University Press, 2006), 45–51; Nell Irvin Painter, *The History of White People* (New York: W. W. Norton, 2010), chap. 22.

63 Grant, *Passing of the Great Race*, 230n9, 385–86.

64 Dr. R. Warren Conant, *The Virility of Christ: A New View* (Chicago, 1915), 12–13, 17–19, 93–105, 118–20. For American religion in World War I, see Jonathan F. Ebel, *Faith in the Fight: Religion and the American Soldier in the Great War* (Princeton: Princeton University Press, 2010).

65 Conant, *Virility of Christ*, 118–20.

66 Ibid., 93.

67 Ibid.

68 G. Stanley Hall, *Jesus, the Christ* (Garden City, N.Y.: Doubleday, Page, 1917); G. Stanley Hall, "The Ministry of Pictures," *Perry Magazine* (February 1900): 243–45; G. Stanley Hall, "The Ministry of Pictures," *Perry Magazine* (May 1900): 387–88; George Reynolds, "Personal Appearance of the Savior," *Elder's Journal* 3, no. 6 (November 15, 1905): 86–87.

69 Ebel, *Faith in the Fight*, 33; James H. Moorhead, *World without End: Main-stream American Protestant Visions of the Last Things, 1880–1925* (Bloomington: Indiana University Press, 1999), 167.

70 Prothero, *American Jesus*, chap. 7.

71 Laura J. Veltman, "(Re)producing White Supremacy: Race, the Protestant Church, and the American Family in the Works of Thomas Dixon, Jr.," in *Vale of Tears: New Essays on Religion and Reconstruction*, ed. Edward J. Blum and W. Scott Poole (Macon, Ga.: Mercer University Press, 2005), 248–54; Thomas Dixon, *The Clansman: An Historical Romance of the Ku Klux Klan* (New York: Grosset and Dunlap, 1905), 338.

72 Dixon, *Clansman*, frontispiece, 326a.

73 Kelly J. Baker, "The Gospel According to the Klan: The Ku Klux Klan's Vision of White Protestant America, 1915–1930" (Ph.D. diss., Florida State University, 2007), 40, 44, 46, 58; Lynn S. Neal, "Christianizing the Klan: Alma White, Branford Clarke, and the Art of Religious Intolerance," *Church History* 78, no. 2 (June 2009): 350–78. Baker's book has now been published as Kelly J. Baker, *Gospel According to the Klan: The KKK's Appeal to Protestant America, 1915–1930* (Lawrence: University of Kansas Press, 2011).

74 "A New Conception of Christ," *Federal Council Bulletin* 16 (1933): 14; *Literary Digest* 115 (1933): 20; "Religion: Easter Dawn," *Time*, April 17, 1933, 40; *Christian Leader* 36, part 2 (1933): 1209; *Lutheran* 22, no. 35 (1940): 17; *Minutes of the General Presbyterian Assembly of the Presbyterian Church in the United States of America*, part 1 (1934), 324.

75 Maus, *Christ and the Fine Arts*, 628–31.

76 "A New Conception of Christ," *Rosicrucian Forum* (October 1933): 33.

CHAPTER SEVEN

1 Upton Sinclair, *They Call Me Carpenter: A Tale of the Second Coming* (Chicago: Paine Book, 1922), 3–10, 10–14, 37–37, 65–66, 68–71, 96, 129, 186, 187–88, 196–205, 217–19.

2 Donald Hayne, ed., *The Autobiography of Cecil DeMille* (Englewood Cliffs, N.J.: Prentice Hall, 1959), 276.

3 Bruce Barton, *The Man Nobody Knows: A Discovery of the Real Jesus* (Indianapolis: Bobbs-Merrill, 1924).

4 Noel A. Carmack, "Images of Christ in Latter-day Saint Visual Culture, 1900–1999," *BYU Studies* 39, no. 3 (2000): 27.

5 William D. Mahon, "What Are the Relations of Capital to Labor and to What Extent and in What Manner Should the Church Occupy Itself with This Problem?" *Motorman and Conductor* 5 (January 1899): 1–3; Harry J. Carman, Henry David, and Paul N. Guthrie, eds., *The Path I Trod: The Autobiography of Terence V. Powderly* (New York: Columbia University Press, 1940), 39; Cynthia Pearl Maus, *Christ and the Fine Arts: An Anthology of Pictures, Poetry, Music, and Stories Centering in the Life of Christ* (New York: Harper, 1938), 253. For more on religious and church struggles during the Great Depression, see Ali-

son Collis Greene, "'No Depression in Heaven': Religion and Economic Crisis in Memphis and the Delta, 1929–1941" (Ph.D. diss., Yale University, 2010).

6 Murphy O'Hea, "Christ," *Railway Times*, November 1, 1895; Robin D. G. Kelley, *Hammer and Hoe: Alabama Communists during the Great Depression* (Chapel Hill: University of North Carolina Press, 1990), 135, 151, 196–97; Edward J. Blum, *W. E. B. Du Bois, American Prophet* (Philadelphia: University of Pennsylvania Press, 2007), chap. 5.

7 Jacob Lawrence, *The Great Migration: An American Story* (New York: Harper-Collins, 1993), 54; Edward L. Ayers, *Promise of the New South: Life after Reconstruction* (New York: Oxford University Press, 1992), 156–59; W. Fitzhugh Brundage, *Lynching in the New South: Georgia and Virginia, 1880–1930* (Urbana: University of Illinois Press, 1993).

8 Philip Dray, *At the Hands of Persons Unknown: The Lynching of Black America* (New York: Modern Library, 2003); Edward J. Blum, *Reforging the White Republic: Race, Religion, and American Nationalism, 1865–1898* (Baton Rouge: Louisiana State University Press, 2005), 199; Grace Elizabeth Hale, *Making Whiteness: The Culture of Segregation in the South, 1890–1940* (New York: Pantheon, 1998); Dora Apel and Shawn Michelle Smith, *Lynching Photographs* (Berkeley: University of California Press, 2007).

9 Kathy A. Perkins and Judith L. Stephens, eds., *Strange Fruit: Plays on Lynching by American Women* (Bloomington: Indiana University Press, 1999), 58, 61, 83; Mary Church Terrell, *A Colored Woman in a White World* (1940; New York: G. K. Hall, 1996), 106; James Baldwin, *Go Tell It on the Mountain* (1952; New York: Random House, 1985), 221; Richard Wright, *Native Son* (1940; New York: Perennial Classics, 1998), 340.

10 Quoted in Leon F. Litwack, *Trouble in Mind: Black Southerners in the Age of Jim Crow* (New York: Alfred A. Knopf, 1998), 17–18; quoted in John Morton Blum, *V Was for Victory: Politics and American Culture during World War II* (New York: Harcourt Brace Jovanovich, 1976), 184.

11 Arthur Huff Fauset, *Black Gods of the Metropolis: Negro Religious Cults of the Urban North* (1944; New York: Octagon Books, 1970), chap. 4.

12 *The Autobiography of Malcolm X* (1964; New York: Ballantine Books, 1999), 193–94; Louis A. DeCaro Jr., *Malcolm and the Cross: The Nation of Islam, Malcolm X, and Christianity* (New York: New York University Press, 1998), 66–67.

13 Richard Kluger, *Simple Justice: The History of* Brown v. the Board of Education *and Black Americans' Struggle for Equality* (New York: Knopf, 1975); James T. Patterson, Brown v. the Board of Education: *A Civil Rights Milestone and Its Troubled Legacy* (New York: Oxford University Press, 2002).

14 E. Franklin Frazier, *Negro Youth at the Crossways: Their Personality Development in the Middle States* (1940; New York: Schocken Books, 1967), 115–16.

15 Howard Thurman, *Jesus and the Disinherited* (1949; Boston: Beacon Press, 1996), 43.

16 Terry Lindvall, *Sanctuary Cinema: Origins of the Christian Film Industry* (New York: New York University Press, 2007); Richard Walsh, *Reading the Gospels in*

the Dark: Portrayals of Jesus in Film (Harrisburg: Trinity Press International, 2003); Gerald E. Forshey, *American Religious and Biblical Spectaculars* (Westport, Conn.: Praeger, 1992); Lloyd Baugh, *Imaging the Divine: Jesus and Christ-Figures in Film* (Kansas City: Sheed and Ward, 1997); Adele Reinhartz, *Jesus of Hollywood* (New York: Oxford University Press, 2007); W. Barnes Tatum, *Jesus at the Movies: A Guide to the First Hundred Years* (Santa Rose: Polebridge Press, 2004).

17 Lindvall, *Sanctuary Cinema*, 59; Allen J. Scott, *On Hollywood: The Place, the Industry* (Princeton: Princeton University Press, 2005).

18 Lindvall, *Sanctuary Cinema*, 41.

19 James Shapiro, *Oberammergau: The Troubling Story of the World's Most Famous Passion Play* (New York: Pantheon, 2000), 116, 130, 27, 153, 126; Montrose J. Moses, *The Passion Play of Oberammergau* (New York: Dodd, Mead, 1930); Ivan Butler, *Religion in the Cinema* (New York: A. S. Barnes, 1969), 33.

20 Sidney Olcott, director, *From the Manger to the Cross* (1913), UCLA Film and Television Archive; Terry Lindvall, ed., *The Silents of God: Selected Issues and Documents in Silent American Film and Religion, 1908–1925* (Lanham, Md.: Scarecrow Press, 2001), 90; Lindvall, *Sanctuary Cinema*, 182.

21 Lindvall, *Silents of God*, 49, 145–46.

22 George M. Marsden, *Fundamentalism and American Culture: The Shaping of Twentieth-Century Evangelicalism, 1870–1925* (New York: Oxford University Press, 1980); Edward J. Larson, *Summer for the Gods: The Scopes Trial and America's Continuing Debate over Science and Religion* (New York: Basic Books, 1997).

23 Lindvall, *Silents of God*, 28, 119, 276, 311; "The Modern Church," *King's Business* 12 (December 1920): 1113; Tona J. Hangen, *Redeeming the Dial: Radio, Religion, and Popular Culture in America* (Chapel Hill: University of North Carolina Press, 2002).

24 Lindvall, *Silents of God*, 129.

25 John Kenyon Kilbourn, ed., *Faiths of Famous Men in Their Own Words* (Philadelphia: Henry T. Coates, 1900), 191; Lindvall, *Silents of God*, 177; Lindvall, *Sanctuary Cinema*, 92.

26 Matthew Avery Sutton, *Aimee Semple McPherson and the Resurrection of Christian America* (Cambridge: Harvard University Press, 2007), 21–22, 67–68, 79, 157, 160.

27 Cecil B. DeMille, director, *King of Kings* (1927).

28 Hayne, *Autobiography of Cecil DeMille*, 276; Butler, *Religion in the Cinema*, 39–40. See Warner's film biography at "H. B. Warner," *The Internet Movie Database*, http://www.imdb.com/name/nm0912478/ (October 6, 2011).

29 Hayne, *Autobiography of Cecil DeMille*, 275; "Coming Attractions," *Washington Post*, December 11, 1927, F3; Charles Higham, *Cecil B. DeMille* (New York: Charles Scribner's, 1973), 168–69; "D. W. Griffith Visits C. B. DeMille on Set," promotional short film for *The King of Kings* (1927), in UCLA Film and Television Archive, Los Angeles, California.

30 Hayne, *Autobiography of Cecil DeMille*, 279–80, 276.

31 "Cecil de Mille and 'The King of Kings,'" *Film Spectator*, June 11, 1927, 3–6.

32 Gilbert Simons, "Christ in the Movies: New and Bold Efforts to Interpret His Life," *World's Work* (May 1928): 68–74; "The King of Kings," *Outlook: An Illustrated Weekly of Current Life* 146 (May 4–August 31, 1927): 72.

33 Lindvall, *Sanctuary Cinema*, 193; Hayne, *Autobiography of Cecil DeMille*, 281.

34 Francis LaFlesche, Bureau of American Ethnology, Ayer MS 907, Report of Board of Indian Missions, Newberry Library, Chicago. LaFlesche testified to a committee of the House of Representatives in 1918; his testimony, together with that of Fred Lookout (Osage), is reprinted in Frederick Hoxie, ed., *Talking Back to Civilization: Indian Voices from the Progressive Era* (Boston: Bedford/St. Martin's, 2001), 82. More extensive reprinting of the testimony may be found in Omer Stewart, *Peyote Religion: A History* (Norman: University of Oklahoma Press, 1987), 218–21.

35 Stewart, *Peyote Religion*, 89.

36 Ibid., 81, 120; Delaware quotation from Richard Smoley and Jay Kinney, *Hidden Wisdom: A Guide to the Western Inner Traditions* (Wheaton, Ill.: Quest Books, 2006), 170–71.

37 Charles Eastman, *From the Deep Woods to Civilization* (Boston: Little, Brown, 1916), 138, 142–43.

38 Clyde Ellis, "'There Is No Doubt . . . the Dances Should Be Curtailed': Indian Dances and Federal Policy on the Southern Plains, 1880–1930," *Pacific Historical Review* 70 (November 2001): 543–69.

39 John R. Wunder, *Retained by the People: A History of American Indians and the Bill of Rights* (New York: Oxford University Press, 1994), 65.

40 Sonnet H. Retman, *Real Folks: Race and Genre in the Great Depression* (Durham: Duke University Press, 2011); Tisa Wenger, *We Have a Religion: The 1920s Pueblo Indian Dance Controversy and American Religious Freedom* (Chapel Hill: University of North Carolina Press, 2009).

41 Black Elk, *Black Elk Speaks: Being the Life Story of a Holy Man of the Oglala Sioux*, ed. John Neihardt (1932; Lincoln: University of Nebraska Press, 1979), 188; Michael Steltenkamp, *Black Elk: Holy Man of the Oglala* (Norman: University of Oklahoma Press, 1993), 102. Another version of the vision, taken more directly from Neihardt's notes of conversations with Black Elk, is in *The Sixth Grandfather: Black Elk's Teachings Given to John G. Neihardt*, ed. Raymond J. DeMallie (Lincoln: University of Nebraska Press, 1984), 263. The most skeptical take on Black Elk may be found in William Powers, "When Black Elk Speaks, Everybody Listens," *Social Text* 24 (1990): 43–56.

42 Marie Therese Archambault, "Native Americans and Evangelization," in *Native and Christian: Indigenous Voices on Religious Identity in the United States*, ed. James Treat (New York: Routledge, 1996), 137, 142.

43 David Levering Lewis, *When Harlem Was in Vogue* (New York: Knopf, 1981); Paul Allen Anderson, *Deep River: Music and Memory in Harlem Renaissance Thought* (Durham: Duke University Press, 2001).

44 Blum, *W. E. B. Du Bois, American Prophet*, chap. 4; Phyllis R. Klotman, "'Tearing a Hole in History': Lynching as Theme and Motif," *Black American Litera-*

ture Forum 19 (Summer 1985): 55–63; Mary Beth Culp, "Religion in the Poetry of Langston Hughes," *Phylon* 48 (3rd quarter, 1987): 240–45; Trudier Harris, *Exorcising Blackness: Historical and Literary Lynching and Burning Rituals* (Bloomington: Indiana University Press, 1984); Claude McKay, "The Lynching," in *The Book of American Negro Poetry*, ed. James Weldon Johnson (New York: Harcourt, Brace, 1922); Qiana Whitted, "In My Flesh Shall I See God: Ritual Violence and Racial Redemption in 'The Black Christ,'" *African American Review* 38, no. 3 (Fall 2004): 379–93.

45 David Levering Lewis, *W. E. B. Du Bois: Biography of a Race, 1868–1919* (New York: Henry Holt, 1993); David Levering Lewis, *W. E. B. Du Bois: The Fight for Equality and the American Century, 1919–1963* (New York: Henry Holt, 2000).

46 Blum, *W. E. B. Du Bois, American Prophet*, chap. 4; Jonathon S. Kahn, *Divine Discontent: The Religious Imagination of W. E. B. Du Bois* (New York: Oxford University Press, 2009).

47 W. E. B. Du Bois, "The Son of God," *Crisis* 40, no. 12 (December 1933): 276–77.

48 Countee Cullen, *The Black Christ and Other Poems* (New York: Harper, 1929).

49 Langston Hughes, "Christ in Alabama," *Contempo* (December 1, 1931); another version can be found in Langston Hughes, *The Panther and the Lash: Poems of Our Times* (New York: Knopf, 1977), 37.

50 Perkins and Stephens, *Strange Fruit*, 134, 180.

51 Cullen, *Black Christ and Other Poems*, 67–110.

52 "Current Exhibitions," *Parnassus* 7, no. 3 (March 1935): 20–25; Helen Langa, "Two Antilynching Art Exhibitions: Politicized Viewpoints, Racial Perspectives, Gendered Constraints," *American Art* 13, no. 1 (Spring 1999): 10–39; Stacy I. Morgan, *Rethinking Social Realism: African American Art and Literature, 1930–1953* (Athens: University of Georgia Press, 2004), 147; Milly Heyd, *Mutual Reflections: Jews and Blacks in American Art* (New Brunswick, N.J.: Rutgers University Press, 1999), 100.

53 Morgan, *Rethinking Social Realism*, 146–47, 221–22.

54 Richard J. Powell, "In My Family of Primitiveness and Tradition: William H. Johnson's 'Jesus and the Three Marys,'" *American Art* 5 (Autumn 1991): 21–33.

55 Carol Crown, ed., *Coming Home: Self-Taught Artists, the Bible, and the American South* (Memphis: Museum of Art, 2002); Cheryl Rivers, "Clementine Hunter: Chronicler of African American Catholicism," in *Sacred and Profane: Voice and Vision in Southern Self-Taught Art*, ed. Carol Crown and Charles Russell (Jackson: University Press of Mississippi, 2007), 146–72; Joanna Braxton, "Exhibits: Anderson Johnson," *The Middle Passage Project*, http://web.wm .edu/middlepassage/exhibits/johnson/?svr=www (October 6, 2011). The arguments here about race and religious expression among these self-taught southern artists are much further developed in Paul Harvey, *Moses, Jesus, and the Trickster in the Evangelical South* (Athens: University of Georgia Press, 2011), esp. 120–50.

56 Josiah Ulysses Young, *No Difference in the Fare: Dietrich Bonhoeffer and the Problem of Racism* (Grand Rapids, Mich.: Eerdmans, 1998); Geffry B. Kelly and F. Burton Nelson, eds., *A Testament to Freedom: The Essential Writings of Diet-*

rich Bonhoeffer (New York: HarperCollins, 1995), 122, 353. We thank Phil Sinitiere for his points about Bonhoeffer.

57 Shirley Jackson Case, "The Life of Jesus during the Last Quarter-Century," *Journal of Religion* 5, no. 6 (November 1925): 561–75.

58 Frazier, *Negro Youth at the Crossways*, 116, 126, 131.

CHAPTER EIGHT

1 "Advice for Living" column, in *Threshold of a New Decade*, vol. 5 of *The Papers of Martin Luther King, Jr.*, ed. Clayborne Carson et al. (hereafter *King Papers*) (Berkeley: University of California Press, 2005), 279–80. There is no record of King's reply.

2 William Chafe, *Civilities and Civil Rights: Greensboro, North Carolina, and the Black Struggle for Freedom* (New York: Oxford University Press, 1980); Tom Sugrue, *Sweet Land of Liberty: The Forgotten Struggle for Civil Rights in the North* (New York: Random House, 2009); Clive Webb, *Massive Resistance: Southern Opposition to the Second Reconstruction* (New York: Oxford University Press, 2005); Jason Sokol, *There Goes My Everything: White Southerners in the Age of Civil Rights, 1945–1975* (New York: Alfred A. Knopf, 2006).

3 David Morgan, ed., *Icons of American Protestantism: The Art of Warner Sallman* (New Haven: Yale University Press, 1996); David Morgan, *Visual Piety: A History and Theory of Popular Religious Images* (Berkeley: University of California Press, 1998); Colleen McDannell, *Material Christianity: Religion and Popular Culture in America* (New Haven: Yale University Press, 1995), 28–32; Jack R. Lundbom, *Master Painter: Warner E. Sallman* (Macon, Ga.: Mercer University Press, 1999).

4 Morgan, *Icons of American Protestantism*, 26, 19, 44.

5 Ibid., 29; Morgan, *Visual Piety*, 34–35, 43; McDannell, *Material Christianity*, 28–32.

6 Morgan, *Visual Piety*, 118–19; John Lewis Gaddis, *The Cold War: A New History* (New York: Penguin, 2006); Kevin M. Kruse and Thomas J. Sugrue, eds., *The New Suburban History* (Chicago: University of Chicago Press, 2006); Stephen Prothero, *American Jesus: How the Son of God Became a National Icon* (New York: Farrar, Straus and Giroux, 2003), 117; Eric Avila, *Popular Culture in the Age of White Flight: Fear and Fantasy in Suburban Los Angeles* (Berkeley: University of California Press, 2004), 100–101.

7 Gaines S. Dobbins, "Can We Save Our Homes?" *Hearthstone* (December 1949): 6–7.

8 Patrick Allitt, *Religion in America since 1945: A History* (New York: Columbia University Press, 2003), 33; Martin Anderson, *Planning and Financing the New Church* (Minneapolis: Augsburg, 1946); William Ward Watkin, *Planning and Building the Modern Church* (New York: F. W. Dodge, 1951); Katharine Morrison McClinton, *The Changing Church: Its Architecture, Art, and Decoration* (New York: Morehouse-Gorham, 1957), 133; Paul Tillich, "Contemporary Protestant Architecture," in Albert Christ-Janer and Mary Mix Foley, *Modern Church Architecture: A Guide to the Form and Spirit of 20th Century Religious Buildings* (New York: McGraw-Hill, 1962), 122–24.

9 Lundbom, *Master Painter*, 68, 138.

10 Kevin M. Schultz, *Tri-Faith America: How Catholics and Jews Held Postwar America to Its Protestant Promise* (New York: Oxford University Press, 2011); Randall Balmer, *God in the White House: A History* (New York: HarperCollins, 2008), chap. 1.

11 Morgan, *Visual Piety*, 4, 56, 32, 159.

12 Michael Omi and Howard Winant, *Racial Formation in the United States: From the 1960s to the 1990s* (New York: Routledge, 1994), 14–18; Nell Irvin Painter, *The History of White People* (New York: W. W. Norton, 2010), chap. 24.

13 Martin Luther King Jr., *Stride towards Freedom: The Montgomery Story* (New York: Harper, 1958), 134–35; Martin Luther King Jr., *Strength to Love* (New York: Harper and Row, 1963), 106–7; David Garrow, "Martin Luther King, Jr., and the Spirit of Leadership," *Journal of American History* 74 (September 1987): 442; Lewis V. Baldwin, *There Is a Balm in Gilead: The Cultural Roots of Martin Luther King, Jr.* (Minneapolis: Fortress Press, 1991), 187–89; Stewart Burns, ed., *Daybreak of Freedom: The Montgomery Bus Boycott* (Chapel Hill: University of North Carolina Press, 1997), 17.

14 "Loving Your Enemies," sermon delivered at Dexter Avenue Baptist Church, November 17, 1957, in *Symbol of the Movement*, vol. 4 of *King Papers*, 323–24.

15 Palm Sunday sermon on Mohandas K. Gandhi, delivered at Dexter Avenue Baptist Church, March 22, 1959, in *Threshold of a New Decade*, vol. 5 of *King Papers*, 146; "Negro Gandhi" quotations from Joseph Kip Kosek, *Acts of Conscience: Christian Nonviolence and Modern American Democracy* (New York: Columbia University Press, 2009), 82; Lawson quotation from Juan Williams and Quinton Dixie, *This Far by Faith: Stories from the African-American Religious Experience* (New York: William Morrow, 2003), 226.

16 Garrow, "Martin Luther King," 444, 446; "Suffering and Faith," April 27, 1960, draft of material to be added into *Christian Century* article, in *Threshold of a New Decade*, vol. 5 of *King Papers*, 443–44; "Address to MIA Mass Meeting at Holt Street Baptist Church," March 22, 1956, in *Birth of a New Age,* vol. 3 of *King Papers*, 199.

17 Mrs. Pinkie Franklin to Martin Luther King Jr., January 31, 1956, in *Daybreak of Freedom: The Montgomery Bus Boycott*, ed. Stewart Burns (Chapel Hill: University of North Carolina Press, 1997), 136; Lewis interview in Howell Raines, *My Soul Is Rested: Movement Days in the Deep South Remembered* (New York: Penguin, 1983), 83.

18 Mays in Raines, *My Soul Is Rested*, 449; Lewis V. Baldwin, *The Voice of Conscience: The Church in the Mind of Martin Luther King, Jr.* (New York: Oxford University Press), 218; "What Martin Luther King Jr. Means to Me," *Ebony* (January 1986): 74; Niall Stokes, *U2: Into the Heart* (New York: Thunder's Mouth Press, 2005), 53.

19 Carey Daniel, "God the Original Segregationist," pamphlet found in John Owen Smith Papers, box 1, Special Collections Library, Emory University; *Charleston News and Courier*, December 8, 1955, clipping in folder "Petitions by Local Churches against Integration," General Board of Church and Soci-

ety, records in General Commission on Archives and History, United Methodist Church, Drew University, Patterson, N.J. For more on religion and the civil rights movements, see Paul Harvey, *Freedom's Coming: Religious Culture and the Shaping of the South from the Civil War through the Civil Rights Era* (Chapel Hill: University of North Carolina Press, 2007).

20 Jane Dailey, "Sex, Segregation, and the Sacred after Brown," *Journal of American History* 91, no. 1 (June 2004): 119–44; Fay Botham, *Almighty God Created the Races: Christianity, Interracial Marriage, and American Law* (Chapel Hill: University of North Carolina Press, 2009); T. B. Maston, *The Bible and Race* (Nashville: Broadman Press, 1959), 7, 29.

21 Charles Marsh, *God's Long Summer: Stories of Faith and Civil Rights* (Princeton: Princeton University Press, 1997), 55, 60–61, 82–90; Randy J. Sparks, *Religion in Mississippi* (Jackson: University Press of Mississippi, 2001), 228–31.

22 "The Meaning of the Birmingham Tragedy," conversation with Reinhold Niebuhr and James Baldwin, http://speakingoffaith.publicradio.org/programs/niebuhr/sermons.shtml (October 6, 2011).

23 Anne Moody, *Coming of Age in Mississippi* (New York: Dial Press, 1968), 60, 255.

24 Ibid., 271, 336.

25 Ibid., 285.

26 Muhammad Ali with Hana Yasmeen Ali, *The Soul of a Butterfly: Reflections on Life's Journey* (New York: Simon and Schuster, 2004), 65; Henry Hampton, Steve Fayer, and Sara Flynn, *Voices of Freedom: An Oral History of the Civil Rights Movement* (New York: Bantam, 1991), 325.

27 Cornel West with David Ritz, *Brother West: Living and Loving Out Loud, a Memoir* (Carlsbad, Calif.: SmileyBooks, 2009), 49–50; Cornel West, *Prophesy Deliverance! An Afro-American Revolutionary Christianity* (Louisville: Westminster John Knox Press, 2002).

28 Vincent Harding, "Black Power and the American Christ," reprinted in *Columbia Documentary History of Religion in America since 1945*, ed. Paul Harvey and Philip Goff (New York: Columbia University Press, 2005), 179–83.

29 Kelly Brown Douglas, *The Black Christ* (Maryknoll, N.Y.: Orbis Books, 1994), 53–77; Gayraud S. Wilmore, *Black Religion and Black Radicalism: An Interpretation of the Religious History of Afro-American People* (Maryknoll, N.Y.: Orbis Books, 1994), 192–242; C. Eric Lincoln, *The Black Church since Frazier* (New York: Schocken, 1974), 135–52; Laurie Maffly-Kipp, *Setting Down the Sacred Past: African-American Race Histories, 1780–1910* (Cambridge: Harvard University Press, 2010).

30 Vernon E. Jordan Jr. with Annette Gordon-Reed, *Vernon Can Read! A Memoir* (New York: Public Affairs, 2001), 91–92.

31 John Henrik Clarke, "The Boy Who Painted Christ Black," in *Brothers and Sisters: Modern Stories by Black Americans*, ed. Arnold Adoff (New York: Macmillan, 1970), 55–62.

32 "The Quest for a Black Christ," *Ebony* (March 1969): 170–78; "Artists Portray a Black Christ," *Ebony* (April 1971): 177–80; Angela D. Dillard, *Faith in the City:*

Preaching Radical Social Change in Detroit (Ann Arbor: University of Michigan Press, 2007); Douglas, *Black Christ*; Jennifer Lynn Strychasz, "'Jesus Is Black!' Race and Christianity in African American Church Art, 1968–1986" (Ph.D. diss., University of Maryland, 2003), chap. 3; Williams and Dixie, *This Far by Faith*, 267–78.

33 Albert B. Cleage Jr., *The Black Messiah* (1968; Trenton, N.J.: Africa World Press, 1991), 46–47; Albert B. Cleage Jr., *Black Christian Nationalism: New Directions for the Black Church* (New York: William Morrow, 1972); Dillard, *Faith in the City*, 238.

34 Quotes from James Cone, *A Black Theology of Liberation* (Philadelphia: J. B. Lippincott, 1970), 157, 215; James H. Cone, *Risks of Faith: The Emergence of a Black Theology of Liberation, 1968–1998* (Boston: Beacon Press, 1999), 126. Other works by Cone on liberation theology include James H. Cone, *Black Theology and Black Power* (New York: Seabury Press, 1969); James H. Cone, *My Soul Looks Back* (Nashville: Abingdon Press, 1982); and James H. Cone, *God of the Oppressed* (1975; Maryknoll, N.Y.: Orbis Books, 1997).

35 Cone, *A Black Theology of Liberation*, 114, 29.

36 Cone, *Risks of Faith*, xi, 122.

37 Ibid., 34.

38 Gayraud S. Wilmore and James H. Cone, eds., *Black Theology: A Documentary History, 1966–1979* (Maryknoll, N.Y.: Orbis Books, 1979), part 3; J. Deotis Roberts, *A Black Political Theology* (Philadelphia: Westminster Press, 1974).

39 Cone, *My Soul Looks Back*; Dwight N. Hopkins, *Introducing Black Theology of Liberation* (Maryknoll, N.Y.: Orbis Books, 1999); Douglas, *Black Christ*; Jacquelyn Grant, *White Women's Christ and Black Women's Jesus: Feminist Christology and Womanist Response* (New York: Oxford University Press, 2000); Cheryl Townsend Gilkes, *"If It Wasn't for the Women . . .": Black Women's Experience and Womanist Culture in Church and Community* (Maryknoll, N.Y.: Orbis Books, 2001).

40 Quoted in Wilmore and Cone, *Black Theology*, 46; Strychasz, "Jesus Is Black," 162.

41 Cone, *A Black Theology of Liberation*, 59; Wilmore, *Black Religion and Black Radicalism*; Cleage, *Black Christian Nationalism*, 10.

42 Wilmore and Cone, *Black Theology*, 19, 23–28; Cone, *Risks of Faith*, 3–12.

43 Terry M. Anderson, *The Movement and the Sixties: Protest in America from Greensboro to Wounded Knee* (New York: Oxford University Press, 1996); Todd Gitlin, *The Sixties: Years of Hope, Days of Rage* (New York: Bantam, 1993).

44 Morgan, *Visual Piety*, 118–20; Lundborn, *Master Painter*, 153–54.

45 Eileen Luhr, *Witnessing Suburbia: Conservatives and Christian Youth Culture* (Berkeley: University of California Press, 2009), 77–78; Ronald M. Enroth, Edward E. Erickson Jr., and C. Breckenridge Peters, *The Jesus People: Old-Time Religion in the Age of Aquarius* (Grand Rapids, Mich.: Eerdmans, 1972); Doobie Brothers, "Jesus Is Just Alright" (1969).

46 Luhr, *Witnessing Suburbia*, 77.

47 Lloyd Baugh, *Imaging the Divine: Jesus and Christ-Figures in Film* (Kansas City:

Sheed and Ward, 1997), 20–22; Gerald E. Forshey, *American Religious and Biblical Spectaculars* (Westport, Conn.: Praeger, 1992), 89; Ivan Butler, *Religion in the Cinema* (New York: A. S. Barnes, 1969), 46.

48 Vine Deloria, *For This Land: Writings on Religion in America* (New York: Routledge, 1999), 116, 259.

49 Vine Deloria, *God Is Red: A Native View of Religion* (Golden, Colo.: Fulcrum, 2003), chap. 13.

50 James Treat, *Around the Sacred Fire: Native Religious Activism in the Red Power Era* (New York: Palgrave Macmillan, 2003).

51 Leslie Marmon Silko, *Ceremony* (New York: Penguin, 1977), 68–69, 126–27.

52 Paul Schultz and George Tinker, "Rivers of Life: Native Spirituality for Native Churches," in *Native and Christian: Indigenous Voices on Religious Identity in the United States*, ed. James Treat (New York: Routledge, 1996), 56–67.

53 James L. West, "Indian Spirituality: Another Vision," in ibid., 36.

54 Marie Therese Archambault, "Native Americans and Evangelization," in ibid., 135; Luke Eric Lassiter, "'From Here On, I Will Be Praying to You': Indian Churches, Kiowa Hymns, and Native American Christianity in Southwestern Oklahoma," *Ethnomusicology* 45 (Spring–Summer 2001): 339, 350.

55 Will Herberg, *Protestant-Catholic-Jew: An Essay in American Religious Sociology* (Chicago: University of Chicago Press, 1983); Schultz, *Tri-Faith America*.

56 Karen Brodkin, *How Jews Became White Folks and What That Says about Race in America* (New Brunswick, N.J.: Rutgers University Press, 1998); Jonathan D. Sarna, *American Judaism: A History* (New Haven: Yale University Press, 2005); Painter, *History of White People*, 360.

57 Malcolm Marmostein, *Will the Real Jesus Christ Please Stand Up?* (New York: Dramatists Play Service, 1965).

58 Matthew Frye Jacobson, *Roots Too: White Ethnic Revival in Post–Civil Rights America* (Cambridge: Harvard University Press, 2008); Ruth Tucker, *Not Ashamed: The Story of Jews for Jesus* (New York: Multnomah Books, 2000).

59 James C. Hefley, *The New Jews* (Carol Stream, Ill.: Tyndale House, 1971), 40.

60 Ibid., 3, 8, 12.

61 Norman Jewison, director, *Jesus Christ Superstar* (1973).

62 Ibid., Special Edition (2004), DVD commentary.

63 Forshey, *American Religious and Biblical Spectaculars*, 104–7.

64 "Jewish Group Hits 'Superstar' Movie," *Los Angeles Times*, August 10, 1973, d14.

65 Botham, *Almighty God Created the Races*.

66 "Jewish Group Hits 'Superstar' Movie," *Los Angeles Times*, August 10, 1973, d14; Forshey, *American Religious and Biblical Spectaculars*, 113–14.

CHAPTER NINE

1 Clarence E. Walker and Gregory D. Smithers, *The Preacher and the Politician: Jeremiah Wright, Barack Obama, and Race in America* (Charlottesville: University of Virginia Press, 2009).

2 "Jeremiah Wright," *Bill Moyers Journal*, April 25, 2008, http://www.pbs.org/

moyers/journal/04252008/profile.html (October 6, 2011); "Black Liberation Theology, in Its Founders' Words," *NPR Books*, March 31, 2008, http://
www.npr.org/templates/story/story.php?storyID=89236116 (October 6,
2011); James Carney and Amy Sullivan, "The Origin of Obama's Pastor Problem," *Time*, March 20, 2008, http://www.time.com/time/politics/article/
0,8599,1723990,00.html (October 6, 2011); Amy Sullivan, "Jeremiah Wright
Goes to War," *Time*, April 28, 2008, http://www.time.com/time/politics/
article/0,8599,1735662,00.html (October 6, 2011).

3 "Jeremiah Wright: 'Hottest Brother in America,'" April 27, 2008, http://
michellemalkin.com (October 6, 2011); Allie Martin, "Black Pastor Calls
Jeremiah Wright's Comments Divisive, Unscriptural," *OneNewsNow*, March
24, 2008, http://www.onenewsnow.com/Church/Default.aspx?id=72553
(October 6, 2011); "Festival of Wrights," *Daily Show*, April 30, 2008, http://
www.thedailyshow.com/watch/wed-april-30–2008/festival-of-wrights
(October 6, 2011).

4 Barack Obama, *Dreams from My Father: A Story of Race and Inheritance*
(New York: Three Rivers Press, 2004), 280–86; a transcript of Obama's
"More Perfect Union" speech in response to the Wright controversy can be
found at "Transcript of Obama's Speech," CNNPolitics.com, March 18, 2008,
http://edition.cnn.com/2008/POLITICS/03/18/obama.transcript/ (October 6,
2011).

5 Joel Roberts, "Obama as Jesus Sculpture Causes Stir," CBSNews.com, April
3, 2007, http://www.cbsnews.com/stories/2007/04/03/politics/main2641741
.shtml (October 6, 2011); Drew Zahn, "100 Days in Office, Coronated Messiah," *WorldNetDaily*, April 25, 2009, http://www.wnd.com/?pageId=96138
(October 6, 2011); Drew Zahn, "Obama's Triumphal Entry: Gentle, Riding on
Donkey," *WorldNetDaily*, January 24, 2009, http://www.wnd.com/?pageId=
87040 (October 6, 2011); Matthew Avery Sutton, "Why the Anti-Christ Matters
in Politics," *New York Times*, September 26, 2011, A29.

6 "Population of the United States by Race and Hispanic/Latino Origin, Census
2000 and 2010," *Infoplease*, http://www.infoplease.com/ipa/A0762156.html
(October 6, 2011); "Table 1: United States—Race and Hispanic Origin, 1790 to
1990," http://www.census.gov/population/www/documentation/twps0056/
tab01.pdf (October 6, 2011).

7 Alfonso J. Damico, ed., *Liberals on Liberalism* (Totowa, N.J.: Rowman and
Littlefield, 1986).

8 Christopher Rowland, ed., *The Cambridge Companion to Liberation Theology*
(Cambridge: Cambridge University Press, 2007).

9 James B. Nickoloff, ed., *Gustavo Gutiérrez: Essential Writings* (Minneapolis:
Fortress Press, 1996), 27, 30.

10 "Jesus's Friendship," in *Cesar Chavez: An Organizer's Tale: Speeches*, ed. Ilan
Stavans (New York: Penguin, 2008).

11 Richard Edward Martínez, *Padres: The National Chicano Priest Movement*
(Austin: University of Texas Press, 2005); Virgil Elizondo, *Galilean Journey:
The Mexican-American Promise* (Maryknoll, N.Y.: Orbis Books, 1983); Jeffrey S.

Siker, "Historicizing a Racialized Jesus: Case Studies in the 'Black Christ,' the 'Mestizo Christ,' and White Christ," *Biblical Interpretation* 15 (2007): 26–53.

12 Andres G. Guerrero, *A Chicano Theology* (Maryknoll, N.Y.: Orbis Books, 1988); Abelardo Barrientos Delgado, *Reflexiones: 16 Reflections of Abelardo* (Salt Lake City: Barrio Publications, 1976), 33; Genaro González, *Rainbow's End* (Houston: Arte Publico Press, 1988), 101; "Hispanic Tattoo Designs," http://www .tattoojohnny.com/search/hispanic (October 6, 2011).

13 Edward E. Curtis IV, *Encyclopedia of Muslim-American History* (New York: Facts on File, 2010), 314–15; Stephen Prothero, *American Jesus: How the Son of God Became a National Icon* (New York: Farrar, Straus and Giroux, 2003), chap. 8; Ravi Ravindra, *Christ the Yogi: A Hindu Reflection on the Gospel of John* (Rochester, Vt.: Inner Traditions, 1998); "Yogi Christ Fridge Magnet," *A Little Peace and Karma*, http://www.alittlepeaceandkarma.com/yogi-christ-fridge-magnet-by-mystical-rose-studios-180-p.asp (October 6, 2011).

14 Peter C. Phan, *Christianity with an Asian Face: Asian American Theology in the Making* (Maryknoll, N.Y.: Orbis Books, 2003), 98–170; Neela Banerjee, "In Manga Bible, the Tough Guy Is Jesus," *New York Times*, February 10, 2008. These images and works built upon longer engagements of Asian artists and Asian Americans with Christ and his relationship to their cultures. See Prothero, *American Jesus*, chap. 8; and *The Life of Christ by Chinese Artists* (Westminster: Society for the Propagation of the Gospel, 1940).

15 Ivan Petrella, "Globalising Liberation Theology: The American Context, and Coda," in *The Cambridge Companion to Liberation Theology*, ed. Christopher Rowland (Cambridge: Cambridge University Press, 2007), 278–303.

16 *Orbis Books*, http://www.orbisbooks.com/ (October 6, 2011).

17 Kelly Brown Douglas, *The Black Christ* (Maryknoll, N.Y.: Orbis Books, 1994), chap. 5; Jacquelyn Grant, *White Women's Christ and Black Women's Jesus: Feminist Christology and Womanist Response* (New York: Oxford University Press, 2000).

18 Gustavo Gutiérrez, *The Truth Shall Make You Free: Confrontations*, trans. Matthew J. O'Connell (Maryknoll, N.Y.: Orbis Books, 1990), 19–20.

19 Petrella, "Globalising Liberation Theology," 302n74; Grant, *White Women's Christ and Black Women's Jesus*, 221; Jonathan L. Walton, *Watch This! The Ethics and Aesthetics of Black Televangelism* (New York: New York University Press, 2009), xiii.

20 "The Quest for a Black Christ," *Ebony*, March 1969, 170–78; "Artists Portray a Black Christ," *Ebony*, April 1971, 177–80; Jennifer Lynn Strychasz, "'Jesus Is Black!' Race and Christianity in African American Church Art, 1968–1986" (Ph.D. diss., University of Maryland, 2003), 128.

21 Strychasz, "Jesus Is Black."

22 Allen Dwight Callahan, *The Talking Book: African Americans and the Bible* (New Haven: Yale University Press, 2006), 234–35.

23 Jean-Claude La Marre, director, *Color of the Cross* (2006); Todd McCarthy, "Color of the Cross," *Variety*, October 26, 2006, http://www.variety.com/review/VE1117931977.html (October 6, 2011).

24 "Featurette" DVD, of La Marre, director, *Color of the Cross*; Jeannette Catsoulis, "Christ, with a Color Change," *New York Times*, November 9, 2006; Chris Kaltenbach, "Film with Black Jesus Raises Few Questions," *Baltimore Sun*, October 27, 2006; Stephen Hunter, "A Powerful Man of 'Color,'" *Washington Post*, October 27, 2006, WE33.

25 Kaltenbach, "Film with Black Jesus Raises Few Questions"; Hunter, "A Powerful Man of 'Color.'" We thank Allen Callahan for this astute observation about the representation of Mary Magdalene.

26 Allison Calhoun-Brown, "The Image of God: Black Theology and Racial Empowerment in the African American Community," *Review of Religious Research* 40, no. 3 (March 1999): 197–212.

27 Cover, *Rolling Stone*, February 8, 2006.

28 Janet McKenzie, "Jesus of the People," http://www.janetmckenzie.com/joppage1.html (October 6, 2011).

29 Joel Martin, *The Land Looks After Us: A History of Native American Religion* (New York: Oxford University Press, 1999), 63.

30 Ibid., 171; Alice Mitchell, "The Stained Glass Windows of 'Our Lady of Seven Sorrows' Church: A Cree Visualization of Biblical Themes," May 2002, http://www.portalcomunicacion.com/bcn2002/n_eng/programme/prog_ind/papers/m/pdf/d_m012_mitch.pdf (October 6, 2011).

31 Lister Sinclair and Jack Pollock, eds., *The Art of Norval Morrisseau* (Toronto: Methuen, 1979), 41–45.

32 From James Treat, ed., *Writing the Cross Culture: Native Fiction on the White Man's Religion* (Golden, Colo.: Fulcrum, 2006), preface. The reference originally comes from Paul Smith, "Jesus Christ in Native American Literary Cultures," paper for Christ in Contemporary Cultures Conference, Gordon College, September 29, 2006.

33 Treat, *Writing the Cross Culture*, 178, 216.

34 *The One Year Book of Josh McDowell's Youth Devotions 2: Volume 2*, entry for January 22 (Carol Stream, Ill.: Tyndale House, 2003), 22.

35 Michael O. Emerson and Christian Smith, *Divided by Faith: Evangelical Religion and the Problem of Race in America* (New York: Oxford University Press, 2000).

36 Darren Dochuk, *From Bible Belt to Sunbelt: Plain-Folk Religion, Grassroots Politics, and the Rise of Evangelical Conservatism* (New York: W. W. Norton, 2011); George Lipsitz, *The Possessive Investment in Whiteness: How White People Profit from Identity Politics* (Philadelphia: Temple University Press, 1998).

37 Billy Graham, *Just as I Am* (New York: HarperCollins, 1999), 340.

38 Philip Yancey, *The Jesus I Never Knew* (Grand Rapids, Mich.: Zondervan, 2002), 86–87.

39 Richard P. Cimino and Don Lattin, *Shopping for Faith: American Religion in the New Millennium* (San Francisco: Jossey-Bass, 1998); Walton, *Watch This*, 111; Shayne Lee and Phillip Sinitiere, *Holy Mavericks: Evangelical Innovators and the Spiritual Marketplace* (New York: New York University Press, 2009), chaps. 2, 3.

40 Tyler Wigg Stevenson, *Brand Jesus: Christianity in a Consumerist Age* (New York: Church Publishing Incorporated, 2007), 143; Eric Roundtree, "(Re)focus," August 7, 2010, http://www.newbreak.org/sermons/?id=109 (August 15, 2010).

41 Tanya Erzen, *Straight to Jesus: Sexual and Christian Conversions in the Ex-Gay Movement* (Berkeley: University of California Press, 2006), 104.

42 Jeffrey J. Kripal, *Esalen: America and the Religion of No Religion* (Chicago: University of Chicago Press, 2007), 225.

43 Anthony B. Pinn, *Embodiment and the New Shape of Black Theological Thought* (New York: New York University Press, 2010), 97.

44 *Let's Thank God for Freedom* (Cincinnati: Standard Publishing, 2004).

45 *The Book of Mormon: Another Testament of Jesus* (Salt Lake City: Church of Jesus Christ of Latter-day Saints, 1981), ill. 7.

46 Florance S. Jacobsen, "Christus Statue," *Light Planet*, http://www.lightplanet.com/mormons/art/christus.html (October 6, 2011).

47 Prothero, *American Jesus*, chap. 5; Ronan Head, "Picture Perfect," *New Era* 25 (May 1995): 14–15.

48 Phillip H. Wiebe, *Visions of Jesus: Direct Encounters from the New Testament to Today* (New York: Oxford University Press, 1997), 4, 48, 52, 60–61.

49 Gerald E. Forshey, *American Religious and Biblical Spectaculars* (Westport, Conn.: Praeger, 1992), 57, 165–70; Adele Reinhartz, *Jesus of Hollywood* (New York: Oxford University Press, 2007), 49.

50 Forshey, *American Religious and Biblical Spectaculars*, 57, 165–70; "Jesus of Nazareth," *The Internet Movie Database*, http://www.imdb.com/title/tt0075520/ (October 6, 2011).

51 *The Living Lord: The Drama of Jesus, the Christ, as Told in the Gospel of John* (filmstrip presented by the Board of Christian Education of the United Presbyterian Church in the U.S.A. [Philadelphia: Westminster Press, 1959]), in Special Collections, Presbyterian Historical Society, Philadelphia; John G. Turner, *Bill Bright and Campus Crusade for Christ: The Renewal of Evangelicalism in Postwar America* (Chapel Hill: University of North Carolina Press, 2008), 181–87; Terry Lindvall, *Sanctuary Cinema: Origins of the Christian Film Industry* (New York: New York University Press, 2007), 220–23.

52 "Languages Completed and Official Statistics," *The Jesus Film Project*, http://www.jesusfilm.org/film-and-media/statistics (October 6, 2011).

53 "Frequently Asked Questions and Answers," *The Jesus Film Project*, http://www.jesusfilm.org/questions-answers (October 6, 2011).

54 Robert Duvall, director, *The Apostle* (1997).

55 Prothero, *American Jesus*; Richard Wightman Fox, *Jesus in America: Personal Savior, Cultural Hero, National Obsession* (San Francisco: HarperSanFrancisco, 2004).

56 Dan Brown, *The Da Vinci Code* (New York: Doubleday, 2003).

57 Michael B. Oren, *Power, Faith, and Fantasy: America in the Middle East, 1776 to the Present* (New York: W. W. Norton, 2008).

58 Jeordan Legon, "From Science and Computers, a New Face of Jesus," Science & Space, CNN.com, December 26, 2002, http://edition.cnn.com/2002/TECH/science/12/25/face.jesus/ (October 6, 2011). From 2005 to 2009, when Edward J. Blum showed this image to classes of college students and senior citizens, they have routinely identified the individual as looking "like a terrorist."

59 Caroline Vander Stichele and Todd Penner, "Passion for (the) Real? *The Passion of the Christ* and Its Critics," *Biblical Interpretation* 14, nos. 1–2 (February 2006): 18–36.

60 Mel Gibson, director, *The Passion of the Christ* (2004), DVD commentary on special effects.

61 Ibid., DVD commentary with John Debney on music; Stichele and Penner, "Passion for (the) Real," 28–29.

62 Pamela Grace, "Sacred Savagery," *Cinetaste* 29, no. 3 (Summer 2004): 13–17; Richard Bryne, "Out of This World," *Chronicle of Higher Education* 50, no. 33 (2004): A22; Mel Gibson and Ken Duncan, *The Passion: Photography from the Movie "The Passion of the Christ"* (Carol Stream, Ill.: Tyndale House, 2004); *The Passion of the Christ Wall Calendar* (Time Factory, 2005).

63 "Pope, Graham Said to Like Gibson's Movie," *Christian Century* 121, no. 1 (2004): 13; Jerry B. Jenkins, "Mel Gibson: Passionate Art from the Gut," *Time*, April 26, 2004, 120–21.

64 "The Passion of the Christ," *Box Office Mojo*, http://boxofficemojo.com/movies/?id=passionofthechrist.htm (October 6, 2011).

65 "The Right Ear," *Human Events* 61, no. 3 (2005): 16; Grace, "Sacred Savagery"; Douglas P. Cunningham, letter to the editor, *Christian Century* 121, no. 8 (2004): 43; Irene Monroe, "A Bloodshed Theology," *AGW*, www.thewitness.org/agw/monroe040804.html (October 6, 2011); Richard E. Koenig, letter to the editor, *Christian Century* 121, no. 8 (2004): 40.

66 Charity Dell, "One African-American's View of *The Passion of the Christ*," *Enter Stage Right*, www.enterstageright.com/archive/articles/0304/0304aapassion.htm (October 6, 2011); James A. Noel and Matthew V. Johnson, eds., *The Passion of the Lord: African American Reflections* (Minneapolis: Fortress Press, 2005), 53–54.

67 Kwaku Person-Lynn, "'The Passion' and the Truth?" Blackvoicenews.com, http://blackvoicenews.com/inside-pages/religion/36740-qthe-passionq-and-the-truth.html (October 6, 2011); Viola Fehr, "What's So Shocking about the Passion?" *Indian Life* 24, no. 5 (March/April 2004): 4.

EPILOGUE

1 "Damien," *South Park*, season 1, episode 8 (original air date February 4, 1998). Our thinking on the meaning of comedy comes from Susan Purdie, *Comedy: The Mastery of Discourse* (Toronto: University of Toronto Press, 1993); Jan Walsh Hokenson, *The Idea of Comedy: History, Theory, Critique* (Madison, N.J.: Farleigh Dickinson University Press, 2006); and John Lowe, "Theories of Ethnic Humor: How to Enter, Laughing," *American Quarterly* 38, no. 3 (1986): 439–60.

2 On the rise of atheism, see "U.S. Religious Landscape Survey," *The Pew Forum on Religion and Public Life*, February 2008, http://religions.pewforum.org/pdf/report-religious-landscape-study-full.pdf (October 6, 2011). On religion and comedy, see Larry Charles, director, *Religulous* (2009).

3 Kelly Boyer Sagert, *The 1970s* (Santa Barbara, Calif.: Greenwood, 2007), 195; Charles L. Sanders, "Is Archie Bunker the Real White America?" *Ebony* (June 1972): 186.

4 "Black Jesus," *Good Times*, season 1, episode 2 (original air date February 15, 1974).

5 *The Colbert Report*, episode 2041 (original air date March 28, 2006).

6 Adam McKay, director, *Talladega Nights: The Ballad of Ricky Bobby* (2006).

7 "The Convict," *The Office*, season 3, episode 9 (original air date November 30, 2006).

8 Samantha Bee, *I Know I Am, but What Are You?* (New York: Gallery Books, 2010), 2, 23–32.

9 Howard Rambsy II, "Shine2.0: Aaron McGruder's Huey Freeman as Contemporary Folk Hero," in *The Funk Era and Beyond: New Perspectives on Black Popular Culture*, ed. Tony Bolden (New York: Palgrave Macmillan, 2008), 143–60; Aaron McGruder and Reginald Hudlin, *Birth of a Nation: A Comic Novel* (New York: Crown, 2004).

10 McGruder and Hudlin, *Birth of a Nation*, 65.

11 Ibid., 72.

12 Kevin Smith, *Dogma: A Screenplay* (New York: Grove, 1999), 55–56.

13 Jay Roach, director, *Meet the Parents* (2002).

14 "Fantastic Easter Special," *South Park*, season 11, episode 5 (original air date April 4, 2007); "I Dream of Jesus," *Family Guy*, season 7, episode 2 (original air date, October 5, 2008).

15 Bart Phillips, director, *Paul Mooney: Know Your History: Jesus Was Black . . . So Was Cleopatra* (2007); *Paul Mooney's Analyzing White America* (2006).

16 Rayna Green, "High Cotton," in *Writing the Cross Culture: Native Fiction on the White Man's Religion*, ed. James Treat (Golden, Colo.: Fulcrum, 2006), 64–66.

17 Jake Jacoby, *The Biggest Joke Book Ever* (Victoria, B.C.: Trafford, 2008), 260–61.

18 Roland Merullo, *American Savior: A Novel in Divine Politics* (Chapel Hill: Algonquin Books, 2008), 25.

19 Barack Obama, *The Audacity of Hope: Thoughts on Reclaiming the American Dream* (New York: Crown, 2006), 224–26.

Note: Page numbers in italics refer to illustrations.